Global Economy and World Order in the Post-COVID-19 Era

This volume is jointly written by twenty experts and scholars from China. It aims to reflect and answer at least two kinds of questions from historical experience and academic perspective. First, how to view the world in the post-pandemic era? Second, how to view China in the post-pandemic era?

From the perspective of macroeconomics and international relations, the book discusses in detail the trend of economic globalization, the risk of global economic recession, the industrial chain affected by the COVID-19 pandemic, the world order in the post-pandemic era, global governance, and relations between and among major world powers.

This book presents Chinese scholars' in-depth and timely reflections on the international pattern of the post-pandemic era. It will be a great read for students and scholars of international relations, East Asian studies, and those interested in the world economy in general.

Zhao Jianying is President of China Social Sciences Press. He is also Professor at the School of Philosophy, University of Chinese Academy of Social Sciences. Professor Zhao received his Master of Philosophy from Renmin University of China and his PhD degree from the Postgraduate School of Chinese Academy of Social Sciences.

Global Economy and World Order in the Post-COVID-19 Era

Edited by Zhao Jianying

This book is published with financial support from the Chinese Fund for the Humanities and Social Sciences.

First published 2024
by Routledge
4 Park Square, Milton Park, Abingdon, Oxon OX14 4RN

and by Routledge
605 Third Avenue, New York, NY 10158

Routledge is an imprint of the Taylor & Francis Group, an informa business

© 2024 selection and editorial matter, Zhao Jianying; individual chapters, the contributors

Translated by Li Guicang

The right of Zhao Jianying to be identified as the author of the editorial material, and of the authors for their individual chapters, has been asserted in accordance with sections 77 and 78 of the Copyright, Designs and Patents Act 1988.

All rights reserved. No part of this book may be reprinted or reproduced or utilised in any form or by any electronic, mechanical, or other means, now known or hereafter invented, including photocopying and recording, or in any information storage or retrieval system, without permission in writing from the publishers.

Trademark notice: Product or corporate names may be trademarks or registered trademarks, and are used only for identification and explanation without intent to infringe.

English Version by permission of China Social Sciences Press.

British Library Cataloguing-in-Publication Data
A catalogue record for this book is available from the British Library

Library of Congress Cataloging-in-Publication Data
Names: Zhao, Jianying, editor.
Title: Global economy and world order in the post-COVID-19 era / edited by Zhao Jianying.
Other titles: Hou yi qing shi dai de quan qiu jing ji yu shi jie zhi xu. English
Identifiers: LCCN 2023018127 (print) | LCCN 2023018128 (ebook) | ISBN 9781032561004 (hardback) | ISBN 9781032561011 (paperback) | ISBN 9781003433897 (ebook)
Subjects: LCSH: COVID-19 (Disease)--Economic aspects. | International economic relations.
Classification: LCC HF1359 .H681513 2024 (print) | LCC HF1359 (ebook) | DDC 330.9--dc23/eng/20230516
LC record available at https://lccn.loc.gov/2023018127
LC ebook record available at https://lccn.loc.gov/2023018128

ISBN: 978-1-032-56100-4 (hbk)
ISBN: 978-1-032-56101-1 (pbk)
ISBN: 978-1-003-43389-7 (ebk)

DOI: 10.4324/9781003433897

Typeset in Times New Roman
by SPi Technologies India Pvt Ltd (Straive)

Contents

Preface	*viii*
ZHAO JIANYING	
Note on Chinese names	*xi*
List of Contributors	*xii*
Translator's Acknowledgement	*xiv*

1 Sino-US Relations in the Context of the COVID-19
Pandemic: Risks, Options, and Routes   1
FU YING

2 De-Globalization: The Shadow Hovering Over the World
Economy in the Post-Covid-19 Era   19
CAI FANG

3 A Prospect of the Digital Economy in the
Post-COVID-19 Era   31
JIANG XIAOJUAN

4 Getting Prepared for a New Type of Long-Term Recession   44
LI YANG

5 The Logic and Warning of Providing Limitless Amount of
Funds by the Federal Reserve   58
YU YONGDING

6 Globalization, the Pandemic, and International Economic
Governance   73
ZHANG YUNLING

vi *Contents*

7 Responding to the Severe Impact of the Pandemic, and
Accelerating High-Level Opening Up   88
CHI FULIN

8 The Pandemic Impact on the Global Supply Chain and
China's Response   103
HUANG QUNHUI

9 Some Thoughts on the Current World Economy and
Globalization   115
LIU YUANCHUN

10 China and the World Under the Impact of the Pandemic   120
YAO YANG

11 Looking into the Financial Turmoil During the COVID-19
Pandemic: Causes, Characteristics, Impacts, and Responses   130
ZHANG MING

12 The COVID-19 Pandemic and the Changes in the
Past Century   142
YUAN PENG

13 Avoiding the "Free Fall" of Sino-US Relations   156
ZHENG YONGNIAN

14 Europe in the Post-COVID-19 Era and the Problems in
Sino-Europe Relations   165
ZHOU HONG

15 The US Internal Affairs, Diplomacy, and Sino-US relations
During the COVID-19 Pandemic   178
NI FENG

16 Impact of the COVID–19 Pandemic on the World and
Sino-Japan Relations   191
YANG BOJIANG

17 Africa and China–Africa Relations in the
Post-COVID-19 Era   207
LI XINFENG AND ZHANG CHUNYU

Contents vii

18 Material Interest and the Concept of Values:
International Conflicts and Cooperation
During the Pandemic   227
WANG ZHENGYI

19 COVID-19 and Global Governance Reform   242
SUN JISHENG

20 The Outbreak of the COVID-19 Virus: Nowhere to
Avoid it and an Interrogation of Misery   263
ZHAO TINGYANG

Index   *279*

Preface

In 2020, no one could believe that today, with the increasing advancement of science and technology, human society would undergo such a great change because of a global public health event. However, since the end of 2019, a previously unknown novel coronavirus (COVID-19) has raged across China, and later the whole world, causing tens of millions of infections and tens of thousands of deaths worldwide. Today, it is the time for the living to mourn for the dead, but it also reminds us that we are in an era that seems to be more uncertain than the past two decades. Surely, the COVID-19 virus will become a real black-swan event that might rewrite the process of human history.

In as short a period as just half a year, COVID-19 has greatly changed the world we are familiar with. On the one hand, it has changed our way of life, and made a huge impact on the world economy. For instance, it severely disrupted the industrial chain, and sank the global economy into a crisis that may lead to a long-term recession. This crisis is significantly spinning to the financial field, causing the stock markets of many countries to break a few times, international oil prices and gold prices to plunge, and relevant international economic and financial institutions to lower their outlooks for this year (2020). On the other hand, the continuous development of the pandemic has greatly changed the pattern of world politics, and intensified many contradictions in the pre-pandemic era. The consequences of increased populism, rising protectionism, and the lack of governance capacity are becoming increasingly obvious, the strategic rivalry between China and the United States is more intense, and the conflicts in hot spots are increasing instead of decreasing. The interweaving of traditional and non-traditional security issues has brought a far more severe test to all mankind than ever before. In a word, the international community's demand for global governance reform is more urgent than ever because of this pandemic. Improving the level of international governance capacity will be a major issue to be addressed in the post-pandemic era.

Against this backdrop, it is urgent for the Chinese academic community to reflect and answer at least two types of questions from historical experience and academic perspective.

The first is how to look at the world in the post-pandemic era. The post-pandemic world must be interrelated with many potential contradictions in the pre-pandemic era. What are the connections and differences between these contradictions? To what extent will it continue to change the world we know about? Whether the existing theories and historical models are sufficient to predict the world trend in the post-pandemic era, and how to deal with traditional and non-traditional security issues in the context of globalization and informatization? How to make up for the "deficit" in national and global governance capacity exposed by the COVID-19 pandemic? At the same time, how will these questions be answered is closely related to the development of the pandemic. It must be recognized that although the trend of thought and movement against globalization brought about by the deficit in the governance capacity has become an inevitable phenomenon in the future for a long time, the efforts to deal with the common crises of mankind will only be global cooperation beyond a single national territory. Finally, how to deal with the tension between globalization and anti-globalization is a difficult issue that human society must jointly address in the post-pandemic era.

The second is how to look at China in the post-pandemic era. Everyone is anticipating answers to the following questions: what role will China play in the world in the post-pandemic era, and what attitudes and strategies will it adopt to cope with this era of uncertainty? There is no doubt that in the post-pandemic era, China will face unprecedented opportunities and challenges. On the one hand, with the attitude and sense of responsibility of jointly building a community with a shared future for mankind, China has actively cooperated with the WHO in its anti-pandemic work, timely informed the world of the development of the pandemic, and achieved for the time being almost a decisive victory in the fight against the pandemic. On this basis, China announced that it would provide public health goods for the global fight against the pandemic, and fulfill its due responsibilities, which undoubtedly enhanced China's international image and status as a responsible major country. On the other hand, China is faced with more severe challenges in terms of its bilateral and multilateral relations with developed countries, especially with the United States. The US has significantly changed its strategic understanding of China, which has worsened Sino-US relations, which had gone awry since 2018. At the same time, the disruption of economic and trade exchanges caused by the pandemic will inevitably give rise to changes and shifts in the global economic and trade pattern, which will pose more challenges for China's future opening-up. At the meeting of the Standing Committee of the Political Bureau of the CPC Central Committee on April 8, 2020, General Secretary Xi Jinping stressed that we should stick to the bottom-line thinking and be prepared to deal with the changes in the external environment for a long time. In particular, China's attitude and way to deal with the challenges and conflicts initiated by the United States and other Western countries, and how to seek cooperation in building a community with a shared future for mankind in the inevitable conflicts in the future, will certainly shape the international pattern in the post-pandemic era.

To this end, in April 2020, when the number of people infected with COVID-19 was increasing exponentially, China Social Sciences Press invited

x *Preface*

twenty top domestic experts and scholars to contribute to *Global Economy and World Order in the Post-COVID 19 Era*. They articulate, from the perspective of macroeconomics and international relations, on a range of widely controversial and key topics such as the trend of economic globalization, the risk of world economic recession, the industrial chain disruption by the pandemic, the world order in the post-pandemic era, global governance, and relations between and among the great world powers.

This book is intended to show the awareness of the questions and crises Chinese academic circles have in the face of the COVID-19 pandemic. In this special period, it is hoped that the publication of the book can present Chinese scholars' in-depth and timely thinking on the international pattern in the post-pandemic era for domestic readers. At the same time, it is also expected that this book will become a platform for Chinese academic circle to communicate with foreign scholars and do its part for mankind to jointly cope with the potential challenges in the post-pandemic era.

On the occasion of the publication of this book, I would like to express my deep gratitude to the experts who accepted my invitation and contributed to this book, and sincerely thank all the leaders and experts for their strong support for the work of China Social Sciences Publishing House.

Zhao Jianying, Ph.D.
President of China Social Sciences Press
August 20, 2020

Note on Chinese names

All the Chinese names in this book, including the contributors' names, follow the order of family names and given names. For instance, Zhang Bojiang, Zhang is the family name, and Bojiang is his given name.

Contributors

Yang Bojiang, Research Fellow, the Institute of Japanese Studies, Chinese Academy of Social Sciences; Chapter 16.

Zhang Chunyu, Assistant Researcher, the China–Africa Institute, Chinese Academy of Social Sciences; Chapter 17.

Cai Fang, Professor, Chinese Academy of Social Sciences; Chapter 2

Ni Feng, Research Fellow, Institute of American Studies, Chinese Academy of Social Sciences; Chapter 15.

Chi Fulin, Research Fellow, China Institute of Reform and Development (Hainan); Chapter 7.

Zhou Hong, Research Fellow, Institute for International Social Sciences, Chinese Academy of Social Sciences; Chapter 14.

Zhao Jianying, Professor, China Social Sciences Press, Chinese Academy of Social Sciences; Preface.

Sun Jisheng, Professor, China Foreign Affairs University; Chapter 19.

Zhang Ming, Research Fellow, Institute of World Economics and Politics, Chinese Academy of Social Sciences; Chapter 11.

Yuan Peng, Research Fellow, China Institute of Contemporary International Relations; Chapter 12.

Huang Qunhui, Research Fellow, the Institute of Economics, Chinese Academy of Social Sciences; Chapter 8.

Zhao Tingyang, Research Fellow, the Institute of Philosophy, Chinese Academy of Social Sciences; Chapter 20.

Jiang Xiaojuan, Professor, the School of Public Policy and Management, Tsinghua University; Chapter 3.

Li Xinfeng, Research Fellow, the China–Africa Institute, Chinese Academy of Social Sciences; Chapter 17.

Li Yang, Research Fellow, National Institution of Finance and Development, Chinese Academy of Social Sciences; Chapter 4.

Yao Yang, Professor, the National School of Development, Peking University; Chapter 10.

Fu Ying, Founding Director, the Center for Strategic and Security Studies, Tsinghua University; Chapter 1.

Yu Yongding, Research Fellow, Chinese Academy of Social Sciences; Chapter 5.

Zheng Yongnian, Professor, Institute of Public Policy, South China University of Technology; Chapter 13.

Liu Yuanchun, Professor, Shanghai University of Finance and Economics; Chapter 9.

Zhang Yunling, Professor, the Institute of International Studies, Shandong University; Chapter 6.

Wang Zhengyi, Professor, the School of International Relations, Peking University; Chapter 18.

Li Guicang, Ph.D (Translator) from Indiana University of Pennsylvania, is currently a professor of English, and Director of the Research Institute for Foreign Languages and Culture, at Zhejiang Yuexiu University of Foreign Languages. He focuses his research on Chinese North American Literature, Comparative Literature, Literary Theory, and Ecological Criticism.

Translator's Acknowledgement

Professor Wu Yong of Zhejiang Conservatory of Music, Wang Min, Associate Professor, of Zhejiang Yuexiu University of Foreign Languages, Nie Yonghua of Zhejiang Normal University, and Professor Patrick D. Murphy of The University of Central Florida have made invaluable contribution to the current translation.

1 Sino-US Relations in the Context of the COVID-19 Pandemic

Risks, Options, and Routes

*Fu Ying**

In February 2020, I attended the 56th Munich Security Conference (MSC) in Germany with several Chinese scholars. The theme of the conference was "West-lessness," reflecting a European perspective on the decline of the West as the most important geopolitical center after the First World War.[1] This is a theoretical issue with historical significance, which aroused a lively discussion among the participants, but is inevitably diluted by real contradictions between China and the United States. It was at the most difficult time of the outbreak of the COVID-19 pandemic in China, but the US delegates present at the conference, indifferent to any discussions or information-sharing about the pandemic, raised their tone of criticism of China, and forcefully demanded that the Europeans take sides in an attempt to form a unified Western position on strategic competition against China. The American delegation for the conference included more than 20 members of the House and Senate, such as House Speaker Nancy Pelosi, Secretary of State Mike Pompeo, Secretary of Defense James Esper, Ambassador to the United Nations Mark Kraft, former Secretary of State John Kerry and other dignitaries, senior officials and think-tank scholars. They apparently coordinated the Republican and Democratic position, and singled out the "threat of China's rise" for the main conference topic, proclaiming that Huawei products were "a Trojan horse placed inside the West by the Chinese intelligence system." They accused China of pursuing a "coercive marine policy" and using military and diplomatic power to provoke other countries. They also declared that "the West is not in decline," and that the "Western values will prevail over Russian and Chinese aspirations for becoming 'empires'," urging Europe and the United States to work together against "the growing aggressiveness of the Communist Party of China (CPC)."[2]

These strong statements echo the adjustment of Trump's policy towards China since he took office, viewing China as primarily a "strategic competitor." In recent years, the United States has launched a trade war, a sci-tech war, and a war of public opinion. It has also reinforced its military deployment against China, openly attacked the CPC, and questioned China's political

---

* The author is an adjunct professor and director of the Center for Strategic and Security Studies at Tsinghua University, and former Vice Minister of the Chinese Foreign Ministry.

DOI: 10.4324/9781003433897-1

system. This series of provocations has forced China to react and take counter-measures, causing Sino-US relations to decline rapidly.

The changes in US policy signify that China and the United States have evolved in two different directions since the end of the Cold War. China envisioned a global prospect of peaceful development, timely grasped the theme of peaceful development, and followed the trend by adopting policies to reform and to open up, and concentrating on economic development. In the second decade of the 21st century, China has grown into the world's second-largest economy, established a global cooperation network, and begun to participate in and influence international affairs. The United States, however, has indulged in the fantasy of the "end of history" and the unipolar order, trying to transform other countries by its own will and model, launching a number of wars and falling into a self-destruction of its hegemony. In addition, the lack of effective supervision of capital expansion in the environment of economic globalization led to the financial crisis in 2008. At the same time, the poor handling of domestic conflicts, and the unequal distribution of income in the US, have lowered the quality of life of the middle and lower classes. The contradictions of identity have widened social disagreement and expanded political polarization in the US. Of course, the American people have begun to reflect, and most of them believe that their country's policies and directions are unsuccessful. The Trump administration has simply abandoned liberal international policies, getting trapped in conservatism and upholding the slogan of "America First." As a result, the US hegemony shows the signs of a strategic retrenchment, dimming its "lighthouse effect."

China's "stepping-up" and America's "retrenchment" show a reverse trajectory within the same international system, which inevitably causes tensions in the adjustment of international power. On the one hand, the United States needs to "heal its wounds" and solve the problems caused by domestic and foreign policy failures over the years, while, on the other hand, the United States is increasingly wary of China, and trying to suppress it. This change in US policy and attitude creates a new international uncertainty. The United States fears that China is competing for dominance in the world, and regards its competition with China as a battle to defend its fundamental national interests that it cannot afford to lose. Hawkish forces in the United States intent on pushing relations with China towards full-scale confrontation, believing that it is the only way to halt China's chasing. What is worse, the mobilization and influence of the US hawkish forces are expanding. The US military is focusing on the West Pacific and East Indian oceans, upgrading its military deployment, strengthening its alliance network, promoting the "Indo-Pacific Strategy," doubling effort to contain China. There is widespread concern that China and the US will close their eyes and jump into the so-called "Thucydides Trap," because the rivalry between the ruling power and the rising power will inevitably lead to a military conflict. Will the framework of multilateral global cooperation thus split or even collapse?

What happened in Munich at the beginning of 2020 now seems to foreshadow an accelerated decline in Sino-US relations over the course of the rest of the year.

Shortly after the MSC, the COVID-19 pandemic began to spread globally, and in early April 2020, the United States became the new "epicenter" of a "global pandemic" announced by the World Health Organization. This pandemic is the third major event that has changed the world agenda since the 21st century. The previous two were the events of the 9/11 attack in 2001 and the international financial crisis in 2008, especially the latter, which plunged the United States into serious difficulties. At those times, almost the whole world united and worked with the US to overcome the adversities. However, this time, the US showed no signal of solidarity and cooperation, and completely failed to extend any willingness and ability to play a leading role. The US didn't tap its resources to organize the prevention of the pandemic; instead, it tried to hinder cooperation and create confrontation. Not a small surprise to the world.

The international community initially had high expectations for the Sino-US cooperation in fighting the pandemic. On the one hand, after 13 rounds of difficult negotiations, the first phase of the Sino-US economic and trade agreement was signed in early 2020, finally easing the economic and trade frictions that lasted for more than a year, and putting the brakes on the declining bilateral relations. Prior to the formal signing of the agreement, the Chinese and US heads of state spoke on the phone on December 20, 2019, and President Xi Jinping noted that

China and the United States reached the first phase of the economic and trade agreement on the basis of equality and mutual respect. Against the backdrop of the current extremely complex international environment, such an agreement is beneficial to China, to the United States, and to the peace and prosperity of the entire world.[3]

Under such circumstances, people's judgments on the prospects for Sino-US relations and the expectations of the bilateral cooperation have picked up. On the other hand, in the face of the sudden epidemic, people habitually believe, based on the experience of China and the United States in working together to fight terrorism in 2001, cooperating against SARS in 2003, coping with the international financial crisis in 2008, and fighting Ebola together in 2014, that this time the two countries may still turn the common challenges brought by COVID-19 into an opportunity to improve relations and resume cooperation.

However, things didn't go as expected. Instead of showing any concern and desire to cooperate, the US unilaterally evacuated its nationals and cut off flights from China after the COVID-19 outbreak. The Secretary of Commerce Wilbur Ross even referred to the outbreak in China as "an opportunity to accelerate the return of jobs," showing not a tidbit of sympathy. Some US enterprises, individuals, and overseas Chinese sent material assistance to China, but, according to the Chinese government, no substantial assistance was organized by the US government. To make it worse, *The Wall Street Journal* published an editorial with the title of "China is the Real Sick Man of Asia," jabbing the Chinese for painful memories, which in turn inflamed angry opinions on both sides.[4] As the US refused to apologize, China revoked the licenses of three US journalists in China, and the US reduced the number of Chinese reporters in Washington.[5] The momentum of détente in Sino-US relations brought by the first-phase economic and trade agreement was quickly lost.

But before long, the pandemic broke out and spiraled out of control in the United States, causing a severe economic recession, which surely affected the 2020 presidential election. In order to shift the blame for the lack of preparedness for the pandemic, and to improve his election chances, the Trump administration adopted a strategy of "China-blaming," stirring up a wave of public criticism of China. The opinion of the White House was used as a guideline for an official wording.[6]

China has not shown any weakness either, firmly countering the untrue claims of the US side, by presenting the responsible measures taken by the CPC and government with a wealth of data and facts. On June 7, 2020, the State Council Information Office released a white paper titled *Fighting COVID-19: China in Action*, which offers a more comprehensive and systematic account of the Chinese people's experience and practices in fighting the pandemic.

The Trump administration has not eased its crackdown on China during the pandemic, as it promulgated new trade and export regulations against Huawei, restricting and then blocking Huawei's access to US software and hardware supplies. Moreover, the US government put more Chinese companies and institutions on the "entity list," and blocked Chinese companies from the US stock market. It can be seen that the United States is stepping up its efforts to promote the sci-tech "decoupling" from China.

At the same time, the US Congress continued to stir up dissension by way of passing *Taipei Act of 2019* and other new legislation to openly interfere with China's internal affairs. It is said that a number of China-related bills await approval. Contrary to the "One-China" policy, the US government increased official contacts and substantive engagement with Tsai Ing-wen administration in her second term. These, coupled with the suspension of the Sino-US air travel and personnel exchanges due to the pandemic, surely accelerated the pace of "humanistic decoupling" between the two countries.

The serious deterioration in the Sino-US relations has a negative effect on public opinion on both sides, as a rapid expansion of mutual resentment and hostility arose. According to the survey of 1,000 Americans conducted by Pew Research Center from March 3 to 29, 2020, 66% of the respondents had a negative view of China, which was the highest since the survey began in 2005, while in 2017, the rating was 47%. In this survey, another 62% of people believed that China's strength and influence was a major threat to the United States.[7] In a nationwide survey conducted by Harris Poll in April, 90% of Republicans and 67% of Democrats believed that China was responsible for the spread of the pandemic. Moreover, 66% of Republicans and 38% of

Democrats entertained the idea that the Trump administration should adopt a tougher policy towards China.[8] Although there was no such survey conducted by Chinese pollsters, the number of comments in the media and the internet indicated that the Chinese people were extremely disgusted with the suspicious and anti-China remarks and actions of the US government and the public. In China, the negative sentiment and distrust of the US have reached the highest point since the establishment of the Sino-US diplomatic relations.

On May 20, the White House released a report on its website with the title "United States Strategic Approach to the People's Republic of China" (hereinafter referred to as "Strategic Approach").[9] The report, not as a new strategy towards China, was submitted to Congress in accordance with the requirements of the *National Defense Authorization Act for Fiscal Year 2019*, but it contains updated policy thinking in light of the changing situation, a clearer rejection of the engagement policy with China adopted by previous US administrations, and a more impassioned exaggeration of the "threats" and "challenges" posed to the United States by a rising China. The report concretely depicts the route of competition with China in the tone of a stronger ideological antagonism. It is almost certain that the new US competitive strategy towards China has taken another step to be finalized.

The reason is that the hardline forces in the US wanted to tighten the strategic competition with China, and did not want to distract or even disrupt their "strategic deployment" by allowing the two sides to alleviate their rivalry in fighting the pandemic; instead, they tried to take the opportunity to intensify the competition. The concept of "principled realism" is proposed in the "Strategic Approach,"[10] which becomes a premise to explain the strategy towards China. Reviewing the tradition of realism in US foreign strategies, the most influential one was the Reagan-era realism of "peace through strength" ("Reagan Doctrine"). The Reagan administration lured the Soviet Union into the trap of an arms race by vigorously exaggerating the expansion of armaments and nuclear deterrence during the Cold War, which was not very favorable to the United States. In recent years, in the face of challenges such as the revival of Russia and the rise of China, some US scholars propose "offensive realism",[11] the basic judgment of which is that the anarchy of the international system predestines the tragic fate of the competition between great powers, and suggest that the US should use offensive thinking and take actions to warn opponents, maintain its dominance, and defend its hegemonic position. The "principled realism" is more like the combination of "the Reagan Doctrine," "peace through strength" and "offensive realism." It cannot be ruled out that based on this, the White House could attempt to develop a new theory of competition with China, which could give shape to the China policies by the future US government.

The Sino-US relationship is in a downward spiral, entering a very difficult phase since the normalization of diplomatic ties between the two countries. If the process of adjusting the US strategy towards China resembles drawing a 360-degree "circle," the first semi-circle was almost completed by the end of 2018, when the US government, the leading parties, the public, and academia had essentially formed a consensus that an adjustment of the US strategy towards China was imminent. However, there lacked a consensus on how to draw the second semi-circle, namely, there was no agreement on what strategy towards China could be the most effective. Some called for a "smart competition," meaning that the US must engage and cooperate with China while strengthening containment. Others incited all-out efforts to suppress China at all costs. The trend of political mobilization in the US since 2019 is to build a clearer "society-wide" consensus about competing with China. The disputes between the two countries during the pandemic clearly accelerated the consensus-reaching process. The nadir of the Sino-US relations is yet to come.

Dwarfing other international disputes, the current Sino-US contradiction, largely created by the US, has unfolded into four great disputes between the two countries in different areas.

The first dispute is over political systems and values. Before the outbreak of COVID-19, Western intellectuals were already worried that China's success as a non-Western democratic country would have the effect of diluting the appeal of Western values, further proving the failure of the United States and the West to dominate the world in terms of political systems and values after the Cold War. From the perspective of American strategic circles, China's rise is not only a challenge to the real interests and international status of the United States, but also a threat to the stability and value transference of the United States. This is a challenge of deeper significance. From the perspective of China, the United States has never given up its attempt to subvert the socialist system led by the CPC. Recently, the US authorities have tried to alienate the CPC and the Chinese people, openly provoking the legitimacy of the CPC, and China's political system. Therefore, China must resolutely fight against it.

The "Strategic Approach" targets China's governance and the ruling party, and lists the "value challenge" as one of China's three major challenges to the United States.[12] It highlights the ideological roots of China's domestic and foreign policies, and seems to deliberately treat China as the Soviet Union in the Cold War era. It intends to prioritize political and security issues in Sino-US relations, and to provide the rationale for coercing enterprises and the economic community to accept the policy of "decoupling." If things don't get better, the two countries will inevitably fall into a zero-sum confrontation over ideological issues.

The second is the war of public opinion. Since 2020, although the focus of the US rivalry with China has shifted from a trade war to a public opinion war, it doesn't mean that the US gives up competitions in other areas. It is true that the agreement of the Phase-one Sino-US Trade Deal eased the trade friction, but it will take some time to resolve the technological dispute. In the security area, the current mainstream US military position is to maintain adequate deterrence, rather than provocation. In terms of winning public opinion, the US has rich experience, discursive power, and traditional influence in the field of international public opinion. As China and the US, even the whole Western world, have separate information banks and public opinion fields, the first-hand information about China has not been sufficiently accessible to the United States and the international community.

The US knows well that the key to win a public opinion war is to find a simple and clear keyword that directly touches the hearts of the people, and then to make it a trendy topic through multi-angle discussion and multi-narrative articulations so as to form an overwhelming wave of public opinion. The speeches and actions of the American hardline figures over a period of time have drawn a trajectory of their strategic approach to China in the public opinion war. Their topic is "China is not credible." Their purpose is to smear the image of a successful and responsible country China has established since its reform. In other words, their purpose is to change China's "public persona" and label China as a "dishonest" and "unreliable" country, thereby damaging the environment for favorable external opinion on China. Similarly, during the Cold War, the United States never ceased putting all kinds of labels on the Soviet Union so as to demoralize its opponents to be unacceptable to the public.

The third is the dispute over economic and financial security. The pandemic has had a major impact on the US economy. According to the US Department of Labor, the US unemployment rate reached 14.7% in April 2020. It declined slightly in May, but it was still as high as 13.3%.[13] The economic downturn has led to a rapid deterioration in the US fiscal health. In the first eight months of fiscal year 2020, US fiscal expenditure is expected to exceed $3,925 billion, an increase of $912 billion over the same period in 2019, equating to a growth rate of more than 30%; among them, in April and May, when the pandemic was in full swing, the federal government's revenue fell by 45.8%, while expenditures increased by 93.6%, and the deficit was as high as $1,162 billion.[14] It is estimated that the fiscal deficit of the US federal government will reach $3.7 trillion and $2.1 trillion in fiscal years 2020 and 2021, respectively.[15] The fiscal deterioration has led to a rapid increase in the federal debt. As of June 10, 2020, its total amount has been close to $26 trillion.[16] This means that the federal debt has increased in the first 8 months of this fiscal year, by more than $3 trillion.[17] The Federal Reserve predicted that the US economy would shrink by 6.5% in 2020.[18] Therefore, it was expected that by the end of fiscal year 2020, the fiscal deficit and federal debt would account for 18% and 140% of GDP, respectively. This could be an extremely heavy burden for the US government.

In response to the economic recession caused by the COVID-19 pandemic, the US government has launched a rescue plan of about $3 trillion. The Federal Reserve plans to keep the federal funds rate unchanged at 0–0.25% until the goal of full employment and price stability is achieved.[19] These unlimited economic stimulus measures and irresponsible money-giving measures not only raise the debt ratio and deficit rate, but also stimulate a high-leverage speculation and proliferation of liquidity, burying hidden market risks. With the continuous expansion of debt, the US federal deficit as a proportion of GDP may remain above 10% in the next few years or even for a long time.

Surely, such an economic situation worsened the US sense of anxiety. The COVID-19 pandemic forced many countries to reflect on their supply chain security. The US saw it as an opportunity to exaggerate the risk of China's strategy of using its industrial strength as powerful "weaponry," and to persuade other countries to speed up their "de-Sinicization" process as they restructure their industry and supply chains. The ideal goal of the US strategic consideration is to achieve this "de-Sinicization" by way of "de-globalization." Specifically, the US is to revise rules, make new standards, re-establish regional trading groups, reform international mechanisms, and suspend the export of core technologies and parts so as to paralyze China's key industries. There are other voices that call for the use of the US's financial dominance to suppress China. Although the abuse of financial instruments will harm the credibility of the United States and the credit of the US dollar, this option cannot be completely ruled out.

The formation and adjustment of the global supply chain is the result of the continuous deepening of the international division of labor. Many foreign-funded enterprises in China regard the local market as their most important one. Without greater political and security pressure, it is unlikely that they will leave China on a large scale in a short period of time.

The fourth is the dispute over strategic security and maritime security. In the field of military security, the United States has become more doubtful about China at the strategic, tactical, and operational levels, trying to increase pressure to contain China. On issues involving China's sovereignty and security, China must respond to the US pressure and provocation by taking appropriate countermeasures and necessary proactive actions. The present trend signals more uncertainty in Sino-US military relations in the near future and beyond, and it is hard to restore the strategic trust between the two countries. It will not be an uncommon experience for the ships and aircraft of the two countries to meet at close range at sea and in the air, and the probability of friction between the two sides will increase. Although the COVID-19 pandemic forced the US military to reduce its global operations, as its troops deployed overseas were faced with the threat of the virus, it increased the frequency of patrol, reconnaissance and provocations against China in the South China Sea, the Taiwan Strait, and the East China Sea. These unusual military actions by the US were taken to prevent China from taking the opportunity to fill the strategic void.

The strategic deterrence relationship between China and the United States is also marked with some new changes. For instance, the United States has not only adjusted its nuclear strategy, updated its nuclear arsenal, lowered the nuclear threshold, committed to developing missile defense systems and hypersonic aircraft, but also prepares to deploy intermediate missiles around China. It may widen the disparity in nuclear power between China and the United States. It remains to be seen whether this will force China to consider appropriate adjustments. In addition, both China and the United States are major explorers of new weapon platforms and military technologies driven by artificial intelligence technology. The fast development of the militarization in cyberspace, outer space, and the North Pole makes it urgent to find ways to keep related competitions within bounds.

Many scholars regard the COVID-19 pandemic as a watershed in the history of the post-Cold War world, and believe that its impact on mankind is not only psychological, but also material. But looking at the impact now, I would say it was not as catastrophic, but somehow served as something like a catalyst that would speed up the trend of what had already taken place. For example, the COVID-19 pandemic quickened the pace of adjusting economic globalization and regionalization, further divided the international power, made clearer the strategic competition among major powers, etc. The internal governance conflicts have become more severe in some countries. The deterioration of Sino-US relations does not occur in isolation. It needs to be examined from many angles and respects.

The COVID-19 pandemic further challenges the concept of globalization from the perspective of economic globalization. Major economies have reflected and re- examined the risk of external dependence of the industrial chain under the current globalization protocol. Some analysts believe that under the framework of economic globalization, it is possible to form three subsystems centering around China (East Asia), the United States and the European Union. If true, offshore outsourcing will be increasingly replaced by inshore outsourcing. The production base will be built close enough to the end consumer market, and the supply chain process will be shorter and more diversified, so as to flexibly deal with sudden fluctuations. The formation of the three centers will also prompt the corresponding adjustment of the flow of international capital, and objectively quicken the "decoupling" of China and the United States. Judging from the current policy discussions and proposed measures in various countries, the trends are as follows: first, the production of goods that are crucial to the US national security, such as biomedicine, personal hygiene protection equipment (PPE), and some cutting-edge manufacturing companies, may be moved out of China. It cannot be ruled out that the US will pass legislation to force companies to relocate to the US; second, due to the changes in the cost of production factors, the pace of labor-intensive industries moving out of China may accelerate, and the US dependence on China for consumer durables will decline; third, those giant corporations that have well met the needs of the Chinese market will stay operating in China, and continue to benefit from the recovery of the Chinese market when global sales are declining; fourth, there is the possibility of forming two systems and two set of standards as the consequence of excluding Chinese 5G and hi-tech products from the markets of the United States and its allies.

From the perspective of global governance, China and the United States still have extensive common interests in addressing global challenges. In fact, the professional communities of the two countries have not ceased functional cooperation in such important areas as infectious disease prevention and climate change. However, the current US government does not have any policies to support cooperation between the two countries in the global field, nor does it distribute any resources for that purpose. On the contrary, it tries all means to prevent China from exerting influence on international affairs, as one of its important diplomatic goals is to exclude China from multilateral institutions. The Trump administration made the World Trade Organization defunct, terminated cooperation with the World Health Organization, and prevented

10   *Fu Ying*

Chinese candidates from holding key leadership positions in the World Intellectual Property Organization, the International Monetary Fund, the World Bank and other international institutions. At the same time, it signed new bilateral free trade agreements with many countries. The core content of those trade deals is not only characterized by "zero tariffs, zero barriers, and zero subsidies," but also with the implantation of "poison clauses" that exclude China. This slew of actions by the United States has greatly disrupted and interfered with the international governance and cooperation system under the United Nations, thus inevitably affecting the will and ability to solve the common global challenges.

China judged and described the post-Cold-War world as the one led by "one superpower and a few powerful countries." This judgment is less accurate now as the United States and China have changed in their relative strength. At the beginning of 2020, the Tsinghua University Strategy and Security Research Center held its annual symposium on the state of international affairs. The Chinese and international strategic scholars present at the symposium assessed the strength and influence of the major powers in today's world. A more important view then was that the United States could no longer hold its hegemonic position, but as a superpower, it would still surpass others in strength and influence. Also, the scholars reached their conclusion that although the gap between China and the US was considerably wide in terms of strength and soft power, China widened the gap with those countries behind it. Combined, China and the United States account for about 40% of the world's total economy, and 44% of world military expenditures. In the future, how these two relatively powerful countries will develop their bilateral relationship, and whether they can bring stability or instability to the world, are the biggest topics in international politics today.

Chinese scholars believe that there is a relatively large gap between China and the United States in terms of strength. Although the international community also has a distressing historical memory of the "polarized world," the two leading powers inevitably have greater influence on world development, and therefore must assume more responsibilities, including accurately judging each other's intentions, and avoiding developing the strategies that are based on misjudgments. This was originally a slow process of complex interactions. However, the outbreak of the pandemic in 2020, the constant changes in the general election, and the intensification of domestic political, economic, and social conflicts were so intertwined that they made the United States less confident but more fearful and doubtful about China. This will inevitably affect the way and pace of the two countries searching for interactions. Whichever direction they go, they will significantly pick up speed. It has become all the more urgent for China and the United States to define each other and to find ways to get along.

In the process of Sino-US rivalry, the third-party perspective cannot be ignored. Sino-US relations have become the main factor that influences the reshuffling of the world. Will the world remain on the track of peace and development in the future? Or will there be a strategic competition, and even confrontation, among the major powers? To a large extent, the answers to these questions depend on how China and the United States define each other and their relationship. To be "enemy" or "non-enemy" will determine a very different outcome. In search for a proper developmental direction, both China and the United States will be influenced by the policy orientations of other countries. Other major international players, whether they are such allies of the United States as Europe, Japan, and Australia, or developing countries such as India, are currently adopting a certain "wait-and-see" attitude. These other players constitute a kind of "third party."

China has a huge influence on the world economy as the largest trading partner of 70% of the countries and regions in the world. As the United States leads the world in finance and technology, has a traditionally strong influence on international affairs, and can easily rally support from its allies, it still plays a leading role in the world. Generally, the third party doesn't want Sino-US rivalry so escalated that the world might be divided. Also, the third-party countries have no wish to choose sides as they have formed all kinds of connections with both China and the United States. That said, if China and the United States move headlong into an irreversible conflict, many countries will find it difficult to choose to support China, without a huge amount of interest and security guarantee from China, even if they do not actively side with the United States. When I participated in some online academic conferences at home and abroad during the pandemic, I noticed that the international academic community was discussing "the rise of the others." The implication is that if there is a void of real-world leadership, it is time to consider how to build a new leadership of appeal.[20] In 2019, France and Germany proposed the formation of a "Multilateralism Alliance" so as to unite other countries to meet the challenges of unilateralism, and safeguard their own interests and the global governance system.[21]

The factors that have constituted the global background of the Sino-US contest are complex, multilayered, floating and changing. Although the rivalry between China and the US is inevitable in one sense, the nature of this competition is no analogy to the confrontations between the big powers for dominance in recent history. What comes to mind are the three typical contests between the big powers, namely, the one between Great Britain and Germany prior to the First World War, the one between the United States and Japan in the 1930s and 1940s, and the most recent one, the well-known Cold War, between the Soviet Union and the United States in the second half of the 20th century. These rivalries had something in common: there was a global economic crisis, the rising challenger was itching to show its muscles, and the "boss" tried to secure its supremacy by adopting policies to contain the challenger as the boss was afraid of being surpassed. However, the current Sino-US competition differs from the above three in that this one has been manipulated to emerge from different geopolitical conditions: there has been no economic crisis but quite a long period of peace and economic globalization, when China and the US have established deeply interdependent relations. In addition,

12 *Fu Ying*

both countries have established similar relations with many countries throughout the world. Moreover, China has increased its overall influences.[22] The new characteristics and conditions, absent from the previous competitions, will determine the nature of the Sino-US competition to be more complicated and harder to straighten up. Although this competition can be comprehensive and intense, sometimes there is still space for both sides to maneuver. Given that, China and the United States must decide or choose how to settle their disputes. They can settle them within the existing global system so as to keep the system intact or, they can split the global system into two, which are independent and connected. The choice of the latter means the termination of globalism and the division of the existing international system.

The curtain is raised for an epoch contest, wherein China, willingly or unwillingly, will have to take part, because China has no choice. Meanwhile, it needs to be seen that the United States no longer occupies the supreme position of influencing international affairs and international relations as it did at the end of the Cold War, nor does it have sufficient reasons and appeal to incite a new round of comprehensive strategic containment and ideological criticism against China. Sino-US relations have entered a new phase, as the two sides not only have differences in concepts, objectives, and paths, but also have a common responsibility to maintain the existing system and the overall trend of peaceful cooperation. The two peoples have broad common interests on major issues such as world stability and sustainable development.

The future direction of Sino-US relations needs to be seriously considered and rationally discussed by both sides for the foreseeable future. The trajectory of the US attitude towards China clearly indicates that two driving forces are present in the US in brewing and implementing new strategic approaches to contain China. Specifically, the one led by the right wing in Washington advocates confrontation and "all-round suppression" of China by constantly bringing up controversial issues on "national security concerns" and "political differences." They work ever harder to reduce bilateral exchanges in various fields, and continuously promote the strategy of "decoupling." Another relatively rational force also exists. It does not push for giving up the policy of "limited contact," but hopes to maintain pragmatic relations, urge China to change and rectify its "illegal" and "unfair" practices.

The major challenges for China in the course of the 21st century are as follows: how to deal with the US provocation for more competition, how to accurately judge and follow the world trend, how to internally ensure that the process of realizing the goals of the "two centenaries" is not disrupted, and how to externally win and protect world peace and the cooperative environment needed for national development? How can we get more countries to know and understand our policies so as to safeguard the general trend of world peace and development from serious interference? How can we effectively strive for and carry out international cooperation on the road of building a community with a shared future for mankind? How China chooses to develop bilateral Sino-US relations will largely determine its answers to the above challenges.

To be honest, the US adjustment of its policy and strategy towards China poses a real challenge to us. If the US takes the hardline approach, it means that an open confrontation with China will drag the bilateral relations into the track of vicious competition and mutual damage. If so, it is unimaginable that China will not be severely impacted for its development. Once China and the United States slide towards a partial or even an all-round "decoupling," the United States will be less concerned about taking extreme actions towards China. And it will be more difficult for China to further deepen its reform. If the United States takes the sensible approach, which seems not as hard as the other one, it cannot be ruled out that the United States will continue to make more demands over the course of time. Then, the demand for China to follow the international "rules" in economy and trade will be expanded to political and security areas, so as to regulate China to be part of the new global system under the leadership of the United States.

It should be recognized that the success of historical figures depends on whether their thoughts and actions conform to the objective law of historical development. Reviewing the current US policy adjustment towards China, we should not underestimate the damage to Sino-US relations inflicted by the deliberate misperception and misjudgment of China by some politicians out of various interests. Their actions could even make the bilateral relations derail for a while, though we don't need to overestimate their ability to change the historical trend. As President Xi Jinping proclaims, it is natural for countries to gradually form a community of interest, a community of responsibility, and a community of shared fate.[23] He also mentioned that we should grasp the trend of the times, objectively understand the development and changes of the world, and respond to new situations and challenges in a responsible and customary way.

It follows that we need to seriously think and design a developmental route for Sino-US relations in the future, and put forward our own choice and plan, which should not only effectively protect our fundamental interests, but also address the reasonable concerns of the United States. Our initiatives should be in alignment with the spirit of world peace and development. After all, China's development has been closely related to the world. It is widely acknowledged that China and the United States, as the two most powerful countries, will both benefit if they cooperate, but will both lose, if they confront. Therefore, the consensus reached by the leaders of the two countries on building a "stable, cooperative and coordinated Sino-US relation" should be the fundamental guideline for thinking about and designing the specific route of the bilateral relations.

A better prospect for future Sino-US relations is to forge a kind of "competitive cooperation" as the result of struggles, rapprochement, and weighing the balance of state interests. Such a relationship signifies that there will be limited and controllable competition, an effective coordination mechanism that maintains a relatively stable development of bilateral relations on specific issues, and cooperation in various fields and global affairs. Of course, much effort by both sides is needed to realize such a new relationship of healthy competition.

As the current US administration shows little interest in pushing for cooperation, but stepping up its efforts in the opposite direction, it is therefore very difficult for China to work otherwise. In the months before the next US election, there is little hope that the United States will show a more positive attitude towards China. In the months to come, China's choice and action will have more shaping power on the right direction for the development of the Sino-US relations.

We should learn to handle the relations with the US on a more equal footing, objectively and calmly evaluate the world situations we are in, and make good use of the recently acquired shaping influence. We need to have sufficient confidence, composure, and good strategy in our dealings with the US, a sophisticated world power. The renewal and adjustment of the Sino-US relations must go through a difficult process of rivalry for a long time. A desirable outcome cannot be begged; it can only be won through hard struggle, courageous rivalry, and effective coordination.[24]

In the current Sino-US competition, China needs to take the lead in more positively developing Sino-US relations, and to be more rational and pragmatic. We can push for open dialogues in key areas, truly listen to each other, and effectively resolve the reasonable concerns of both sides. We are encouraged to accumulate experience and create favorable conditions. The first phase of the Sino-US trade agreement is a successful case of efforts in this direction. Although neither side has realized all its demands, the results benefit both, and are conducive to the long-term development of Sino-US bilateral relations. The implementation of this agreement will inevitably encounter greater difficulties, resistance, and pressure, as the diplomatic atmosphere is becoming increasingly hostile. Despite that, giving up the agreement is riskier. In fact, it is up to an effective implementation of the agreement that can avoid a faster deterioration in the bilateral relations. Honestly, many of the problems involved in the agreement are the ones that have to be solved if China continues to deepen its reform.

China is determined to safeguard its political system and the road it chooses for development, and opposes any attempt to interfere in its internal affairs. At the same time, China never aims to eliminate other systems, nor will it follow the scheme of the US and the West to promote its values to the world. To achieve a stable Sino-US relationship in the new era, the two sides need to deepen their understanding of each other's core interests, and respect their political systems and values through dialogues and negotiations. In addition, both sides should sort out and prioritize their own and mutual concerns, and try to reach a consensus and mutual understanding on the bounds of behavior. It takes time for both sides to develop the habit and ability to respect each other's concerns and to exchange appropriate interests. Both sides should be able to keep within bounds their irreconcilable security interests and differences.

The United States and other traditional sea powers are naturally concerned with the intention and purpose behind China's effort to grow its marine force.

A strong Chinese marine force poses a new problem for them to deal with. However, we need to maintain our presence and establish an effective deterrence in the Western Pacific, so as to safeguard our national security, and maintain regional peace through necessary rights protection actions, active communication and consultation, pragmatic maritime cooperation and professional and effective risk control. To this end, it is necessary for China to be more transparent about its defense policy and objectives, and let all parties really understand its military security proposition and bottom line. As a matter of fact, the international strategic circle is also concerned about whether China and the United States can build a strategic balance of power for the peaceful coexistence of their military forces through negotiations. Although the atmosphere for their negotiation at present is absent, China and the United States, as the two important military forces in the Asia-Pacific region, should know that it is particularly important for them to establish channels of dialogue in the field of strategic security. They should establish effective and multi-layered communication channels, and a crisis-control mechanism to avoid any misjudgment. Although it didn't participate in the nuclear disarmament treaty negotiation between the United States and Russia,[25] China, as an important member of the international arms control system, was an active member in almost all important agencies, and has a good reputation in the world in that regard. Of course, China can take such initiatives as urging nuclear weapon states to commit to China's policy of "no-first-use nuclear weapons."

What the Chinese people are concerned with and good at is mainly to do their own things well in all circumstances. Nowadays, as the field of science and technology becomes the forefront for competition, we have to turn the great pressure enforced by the United States into a driving force for self-improvement. We should strengthen our innovation capabilities by utilizing the open source sci-tech knowledge in today's world so as to enhance our self-sufficiency in technology, parts, and components. We need to greatly improve in areas where we fall behind, and, more importantly, exploit to the utmost what we take the lead in to support the world for scientific and technological progress. Only by better maintaining China's influence in the global economic system, and the field of science and technology, and by maintaining the healthy operation of the global system can we really destroy the attempt of Sino-US "decoupling," which could mean splitting the world. This is a wise approach and it is time that we adopted an "anti-decoupling" strategy by resolutely maintaining and promoting exchanges in all fields. All departments should do more to connect the two countries, and avoid doing anything that might lead to a faster "decoupling."

Guided by Xi Jinping's diplomatic thinking, we need to make known that China not only supports the current international order and systems, but also, at the same time, supports efforts to reform them to meet the requirements of the time. We must uphold the banner of global governance and multilateralism, "step up" when and where the US "steps back," set off the US destructive actions with Chinese initiatives to safeguard peace, and promote global economic growth so as to maintain the momentum of economic globalization. Faced with increasing problems and contradictions in the world in the post-COVID-19 era, we should be committed to more consultations, and to helping other countries solve problems. In other words, we should "help" and "aid" more to strengthen international relations, and take the responsibility entrusted onto a cooperative powerful country. Whilst developing relations with any other country, that is, a third party to both the US and China, we should aim to develop mutually beneficial cooperation in the spirit of promoting world peace. Creating a zero-sum competition between China and the United States is the least we need.

China and the United States share more concerns than contradictions on many global issues. And many countries expect China to step up in areas where the Trump administration steps back. The area of climate change is one such area where China has established an effective cooperation mechanism and policy reserve between the government and think-tanks. China has maintained good official and non-official interactions with the international community. At present, the spirit of cooperation is palpable. This can be used as a blueprint to cultivate good cooperation between governments and think-tanks, expand channels for international dialogue, and constantly enhance our capabilities to provide effective resources to the world so as to solve such practical problems of global concern as counter-terrorism, non-proliferation, drug control, transnational infectious disease prevention and control, as well as artificial intelligence governance and combating transnational crimes.

We need to increase our international communication ability by way of encouraging and mobilizing diversified communication means and channels, actively training professionals, and improving China's international image. We need to provide more first-hand information and materials about China to the international information bank, so that the world could get China-related information from the Chinese sources rather than from indirect channels. In the current US election, both the Republican and Democratic parties are campaigning on China issues and soliciting votes by such media hypes as "China threat" and "China challenge," which turns out to be a real challenge to us. At the same time, the external focus on China by the logic of communication also facilitates China to actively provide knowledge and information about the country. If we treat it as an opportunity and use it effectively and reasonably, it can be a blessing in disguise. That is, more Americans, and even the international public, will know what is real about China, and how the Chinese people think about the fabricated hypes.

In short, as it has accumulated some strength to have become a country with some power and certain international influence, China has entered an era when it needs to handle internal affairs and diplomacy on the basis of strength and a broader platform of interests. The way we handle the relations with the US needs to reflect and adapt to this change. Harvard University professor Graham Allison, known for his continuous research on whether there is the "Thucydides trap" between China and the US, refocuses his studies on how to avoid Sino-US conflict, and calls for "Searching for a Grand Strategy to Meet in the China Challenge."[26] Certainly, he is not alone in being engaged in such research in the United States. Does China's strategic community also need to proactively search for a "grand strategy to meet the US challenge?" I think it is necessary.

Notes

1 Munich Security Conference. *Munich Security Report 2020*. p. 6. https://security conference.org/en/publications/munich-security-report-2020/.
2 Ying, Fu. "Feeling the Complicated Western Attitude towards China at the Munich Security Conference." *Guancha Syndicate*. https://m.guancha.cn/fuying/2020_02_21_537581. shtml?s=wapzwyzzwzbt.
3 "Xi Jinping Invited to Speak over Phone with US President Donald Trump." *Xinhuanet*, December 21, 2019. http://www.xinhuanet.com/2019-12/21/c_1125371565.htm.
4 Mead, Walter Russell. "China is the Real Sick Man of Asia." February 3, 2020, https://www.wsj.com/articles/china-is-the-real-sick-man-of-asia-11580773677.
5 On February 3, 2020, *The Wall Street Journal* published a commentary titled "China is the Real Sick Man of Asia" by Walter Russell Mead, a professor at Bard College of the United States. On February 19, Chinese Foreign Ministry spokesman Geng Shuang announced at a regular press conference that the Chinese people did not welcome those media that made racist remarks, maliciously smeared and attacked China. In view of this, China decided to revoke the press accreditation cards of three Beijing-based reporters of *The Wall Street Journal* with immediate effect. On March 2, the US State Department announced that the number of Chinese employees of Xinhua News Agency, China International Television (CGTN), *China Daily*, China Radio International, and *People's Daily* in the United States would be reduced from 160 to 100. On March 18, the official website of Chinese Ministry of Foreign Affairs declared that China had introduced reciprocal measures, including requiring the Voice of America, *The New York Times*, *The Wall Street Journal*, *The Washington Post*, and *The Times* to submit application materials, and that US journalists whose press credentials would expire by the end of the year should return their press cards within a time limit and would not be allowed to work as journalists in Chinese territory, including Hong Kong and Macau. In early June, Reuters reported that the US planned to classify four Chinese media outlets, including CCTV and China News Service, as "diplomatic missions," and require them to register their personnel and property in the US with the State Department.
6 Isenstadt, Alex. "GOP Memo Urges Anti-China Assault over Coronavirus." April 24, 2020. https://www.politico.com/news/2020/04/24/gop-memo-anti-china-coronavirus-207244.
7 Devlin, Kat, Laura Silver and Christine Huang. "US Views of China Increasingly Negative Amid Coronavirus Outbreak." April 21, 2020. https://www.pewresearch. org/global/2020/04/21/u-s-views-of-china-increasingly-negative-amid-coronavirus-outbreak/.
8 Zachary, Evans. "Poll: Americans Report Bipartisan Distrust of Chinese Gov't, Support for Tariffs." April 8, 2020. https://www.nationalreview.com/news/poll-americans-report-bipartisan--distrust-of-chinese-govt-support-for-tariffs/.
9 "United States Strategic Approach to the People's Republic of China." May 20, 2020. https://www.whitehouse.gov/wp-content/uploads/2020/05/US-Strategic-Approach-to-The-Peoples-Republic-of-China-Report-5.20.20.pdf.
10 "United States Strategic Approach to the People's Republic of China." May 20, 2020. https://www.whitehouse.gov/wp-content/uploads/2020/05/US-Strategic-Approach-to-The-Peoples-Republic-of-China-Report-5.20.20.pdf.

11 See Mearsheimer, John J. *The Tragedy of Great Power Politics*. New York: W. W. Norton, 2001. Mearsheimer, a professor of political science at the University of Chicago, is widely recognized as a representative figure of "offensive realism."

12 "United States Strategic Approach to the People's Republic of China." May 20, 2020. https://www.whitehouse.gov/wp-content/uploads/2020/05/US-Strategic-Approach-to-The-Peoples-Republic-of-China-Report-5.20.20.pdf.

13 "US Unemployment Rate: Seasonally Adjusted May 2020." June 5, 2020. http://www.statista.com/statistics/273909/seasonally-adjusted-monthly-unemployment-rate-in-the-us/.

14 "Monthly Budget Review for May 2020." June 8, 2020. http://www.cbo.gov/system/files/2020-06/56390-CBO-MBR.pdf.

15 "Monthly Budget Review for April 2020." May 8, 2020. http://www.cbo.gov/publication/56350.

16 According to the US Treasury, the US public debt had amounted to $2.598 Trillion by June 10, 2020. https://treasurydirect.gov/govt/reports/pd/pd_debttothepenny.htm.

17 According to the US Treasury, the US public debt had reached $2.27 trillion by the end of fiscal year 2019. https://treasurydirect.gov/govt/reports/pd/pd_debttothepenny.htm.

18 "Federal Reserve Board and Federal Open Market Committee Release Economic Projections from the June 9–10 FOMC Meeting." June 10, 2020. http://www.federalreserve.gov/newsevents/pressreleases/monetary20200610b.htm.

19 "Federal Reserve Issues FOMC Statement." June 10, 2020. http://www.federalreserve.gov/newsevents/pressreleases/monetary20200610a.htm.

20 Rubinovitz, Ziv. "The Rise of the Others: Can the US Stay on Top?" *Great Powers and Geopolitics* 4 (2015). pp. 31–64. https://link.springer.com/chapter/10.1007/978-3-319-16289-8_3#citeas.

21 "Germany, France to Launch Multilateralism Alliance." April 3, 2019. http://www.dw.com/en/germany-france-to-launch-multilateralism-alliance/a-48172961.

22 See Lixin, Wang. "The Sino-US Relations in the Era of Competition: A Historical and Comparative Perspective." June 9, 2019. http://www.thepaper.cn/newsDetail_forward_3611847.

23 "Xi Delivers Keynote Speech at APEC CEO Dialogues." http://www.xinhuanet.com/politics/leaders/2018-11/17/c_1123728801.

24 Referring to the New STart.

25 Allison, Graham. "Contest: Do You Have a Grand Strategy to Meet the China Challenge?" March, 2019. http://belfercenter.org/publication/contest-do-you-have-grand-strategy-meet-china-challenge.

2 De-Globalization

The Shadow Hovering Over the World Economy in the Post-Covid-19 Era

Cai Fang

Introduction

The global numbers show that the COVID-19 virus is developing in waves in many countries. And more and more medical experts predict that the pandemic will peak a second or more times. There is also a great possibility that mankind will have to coexist with COVID-19 for a long time to come. Therefore, the shape of the global epidemiological curve clearly indicates that a W-shaped trajectory is forming.[1]

The epidemiological curve will determine the time and course of global economic recession and recovery. The pandemic trend prevents even the most optimistic economists from expecting a V-shaped global economic recovery. It is even hard to predict a U-shaped global recovery. The International Monetary Fund (IMF) predicts that the world's major economies and the world economy will experience serious negative growth in 2020, with the world economic growth rate of –3.0% and the global trade growth rate of –11.0%.[2] Soon after, the World Bank made a less optimistic prediction that the world economy will shrink by 5.2% in the whole year, and all major economies will have negative growth, with the exception of China, which will grow by 1%.[3] Meanwhile, the World Trade Organization's forecast for global trade in goods is to shrink by between 13% (optimistic) and 32% (pessimistic).[4]

If it is not a temporary pandemic, as more and more medical experts believe, COVID-19 will not be a single event, and will not disappear after one round of attack. On the contrary, it may co-exist with humans for a long period or even forever. There is no doubt that COVID-19 has not only caused a serious global public health crisis, but also exerted unprecedented impact on the economy, society and even politics of all countries. What is worse, it is still in full steam at the time of writing. Therefore, COVID-19 will have a long, far-reaching and disruptive impact on the world economy and the global governance system.

Anyway, this once-in-a-century pandemic will eventually complete this cycle, as such prevention and control measures as lockdowns and social distancing implemented by various countries have achieved certain results. Moreover, some countries may have achieved sort of herd immunity as the consequence of a huge loss of life. Many teams from different countries can also achieve a certain degree of success in developing specific drugs and vaccines. Although the COVID-19 virus is ruthless and cunning, human beings are becoming smarter as well, as we have accumulated enough experience and drawn some lessons. We are willing and good at using the precious information, and we know how to take history and the present as a mirror to predict the future. However, how to deal with the crisis can form very different policy preferences, which will have very different consequences.

A more popular judgment about the world in the post-COVID-19 era is that the outbreak of the pandemic will terminate the current round of globalization. Less radical views hold that the pandemic will at least alter the globalization process in terms of its direction and operation mode. Past experience and lessons show that even if globalization is a historical necessity, the economic globalization not only produces obvious positive effects, but also produces many adverse by-products. Therefore, globalization governance requires the formation of a series of rules and mechanisms to give full play to the positive externalities of globalization and eliminate its negative externalities at the same time.

Since the reform and opening up period, China has not only benefited from economic globalization, but also made its unyielding efforts to safeguard globalization and its related multilateral mechanism. In the face of the new situation and trend brought about by the pandemic, it is necessary for us to accurately judge the trend of globalization after the pandemic, and recognize the possible options and challenges brought to us, in order to establish effective response strategies and means.

Populism and the COVID-19 Politics

In the West, how a government responds to emergencies such as this pandemic always has an impact on how people might vote, which might change the election result. Therefore, such events will inevitably become politicized. Generally speaking, what is behind the implementation of endless populist policies in many Western countries is that the politicians never dare to fix the political system that is the root cause for numerous ever-existing insolvable domestic problems. Since the domestic problems amount to a Gordian Knot which the politicians are unable to cut, they, therefore, have only three populist paths to take: finding an external scapegoat to deflect people's attention; making substantial promises to better people's life; or adopting stimulus policy to boost economy, an act of drinking poison to quench thirst.

The history of the West shows that the intentional concealment of the causes of disasters or the severity of such disasters as large-scale warfare, and pandemics is not uncommon. In addition, this concealment is usually followed by stigmatizing competitive countries or ethnic groups as traditional scapegoats (such as the Jews), and attacking political opponents for the disasters. Western countries are good at making anything and everything in social life ideological, thereby germinating all kinds of nationalist and populist thoughts, all kinds of desperate government policies, and all kinds of absurd social behaviors to think of.

De-Globalization 21

Take the infamous influenza pandemic of 1918, for example. This occurred nearly a century ago and killed between 50 and 100 million people across the world.[5] According to most accounts, it first appeared in Haskell County, Texas, and Camp Funston, Kansas, rapidly spread to the rest of the United States through military mobilization, then traveled to Europe through troopships, and finally snowballed into a deadly pandemic. However, the federal and local governments of the United States, under the pretext of participating in the First World War, ignored the repeated warnings of scientists and doctors, deliberately downplayed the serious threat of the influenza, blocked and suppressed facts about its lethal nature, and failed to make necessary responses to help stop the spread of the disease, which eventually caused great losses not only to the lives and health of the American people, but also to people across the world.

At that time, the US government tried all means to divert public attention, shirk its responsibilities, control public opinions with high hands, ignore people's concerns, sabotage domestic non-mainstream political groups, and rampantly stigmatize ethnic groups and other countries. The most ironic and landmark scenario of the 1918 Influenza Pandemic was that Spain was identified as the origin of the virus, a neutral country that had nothing to do with the spread of the virus. Spain was the scapegoat because it was one of the first countries to report on infected cases. All those countries that were involved in the war blocked any report of the pandemic because of wartime restrictions. Ever since that time, the 1918 Influenza Pandemic has been known as the Spanish Influenza. And the name sticks.

It is a long tradition for many countries to have been inclined to adopt various populist policies, including drastic economic ones, an act similar to drinking poison to quench thirst, when they are challenged with extreme difficulties that cannot be solved for the time being or eventually. For example, Dornbusch and other economists first put forward the concept of macroeconomic populism and conducted empirical research on Latin America. Their conclusion is that the economic failure of some Latin American countries lies nowhere but in the application of populist policies.[6]

In fact, the United States, the most developed economy in the world, also has a deep tradition of macroeconomic populism. For example, Raghuram Rajan once pointed out that the US government had tried to stimulate consumption by expanding credit in order to alleviate the deep-seated anxiety of the middle class and low-income groups caused by widening income gaps.[7] The consequence of such policies is the excessive development of finance, which leads to the mismatch of material capital and human capital. One case in point is the US subprime mortgage crisis in 2007, which caused the 2007–2008 global financial crisis. However, although many important changes have taken place since the crisis, there has been no change in either the widening income gap or the problems of the shrinking middle class in the United States, and the polarization between the rich and the poor and the social division and political opposition caused by it have become more and more intense.

22   *Cai Fang*

The devastating impact of COVID-19 on the United States exposed the ineffectiveness of the Trump administration in dealing with the pandemic. On January 23, 2020, when Wuhan, China, was locked down, there was only one case of infection in the United States. The Novel Coronavirus Pneumonia was declared a "public health emergencies of international concern" by the WHO on January 30, when only 82 cases were reported outside China, and no deaths had been reported. However, many countries, including the United States, did not cherish this time window and failed to decisively implement the necessary isolation measures. The United States did not declare a state of emergency until March 13, when the confirmed cases had reached more than 1,600. Despite sufficient information, the United States repeatedly misjudged the situation, resulting in huge losses of life, and caused a deep economic depression with a soaring unemployment rate. Eventually, the American people vented their boiling resentment when they cast their ballot for a new leader.

As can be expected, President Trump and his team urgently needed to find scapegoats again in order to win the 2020 re-election. They spared no effort to transfer domestic contradictions abroad by all means. To this end, they did not hesitate to exhaust various disgraceful means, including stigmatizing China's domestic anti-pandemic strategy and its global assistance to combat the disease, urging American enterprises to decouple from China's supply chain, and restricting the WHO's ability to play its coordinating role in international cooperation in battling the pandemic, concocting various conspiracy theories about China and China's cooperation with the WHO and other countries, and implementing a monetary policy (deficit monetization) that may have a huge negative spillover effect. It can be seen that populism in US domestic policy and nationalism in international relations have the same motivation as politicizing the pandemic. Moreover, this consciousness and behavior will also produce the result of de-globalization.

De-globalization in the Post-COVID-19 Age

In fact, many countries began to turn inward for measures to deal with the global financial crisis more than ten years ago, an act working as fanning the flames for de-globalization. This trend can be clearly seen from the fact that the growth of global trade has slowed down significantly during this period (see Figure 2.1). From the late 1980s to 2007, the growth rate of global total exports was significantly higher than that of the world economy. Under the impact of the financial crisis, global exports fell to negative growth by a much larger margin in 2009 (–11.8% and a GDP growth rate of –1.7% in the same period). After rebounding to positive value by a much larger margin in 2010 (11.8% and GDP growth rate of 4.3% in the same period), so far, the export growth rate has been generally stable in the sense that it has remained lower than the GDP growth rate.

Evidently, the decline of economic globalization, or the retreat from globalization after the financial crisis was doomed to happen with or without the outbreak of the COVID-19 pandemic. The implementation of a series of

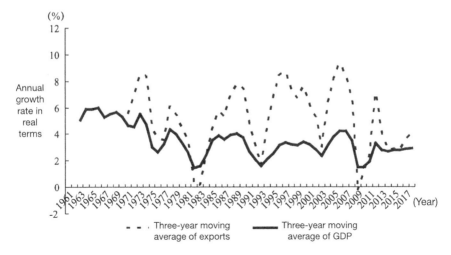

Figure 2.1 The two curves in the figure are the three-year moving average of global trade and world economic growth rate respectively.

Source: http://data.worldbank.org/

unilateralist policies by the Trump administration, in particular, not only seriously threatened the multilateral institutions and mechanisms established after the Second World War, but also accelerated the retreat from them. The outbreak of the pandemic provided opportunities for some countries to adopt policies that posed serious challenges of the previously accepted concepts, mechanisms and practices of globalization.

Many scholars have made their own judgments and prospects for the world after the pandemic. *Foreign Policy* invited 12 leading thinkers in the world to share their view on "How the world will look after the coronavirus pandemic." Generally, most of the experts regarded the pandemic as a world-shattering event with far-reaching consequences. Some believe that after the pandemic, there will be more anti-globalization phenomena as many countries will reinforce a movement toward nationalism, a movement that will further divide the world, disrupt supply chains, and cause more decoupling. A more optimistic reading of their points of view shows that many experts may not think that this means the end of globalization. They still call on all countries to fully understand the situation, respond with right policies, and work together to save globalization.[8]

Many other international mainstream media have also published a large number of articles with different points of view on the impact of the pandemic on the world and the development trend of globalization. If we put aside the differences in the views of different authors, a common understanding is that the world will undergo profound changes after the pandemic. Thomas Friedman, an opinion columnist of the *New York Times*, implied that the outbreak of COVID-19 resembles the birth of Jesus Christ in its transformative power when he writes, "There is the world BC – before Corona, and the world AC – after Corona."[9] Certainly, a rhetorical play, though, the analogy indicates how the pandemic is and will change the world.

Whether considering historical experience or the various current phenomena outlined so far, we believe that the world economy after the pandemic will be inevitably shrouded in a deeper shadow of de-globalization. The constituent elements of this de-globalization smog are certainly diverse, and likely too many to list all here. The manifestations of this de-globalization trend are dazzling. However, if we just focus on the trend for its potential destructiveness to the most important pillars of economic globalization in the past 30 years, we need to concentrate on the following aspects: the challenge trade protectionism poses to free trade in the concept of development; the substitution of multilateralism with unilateralism in global governance; and the passive disruption of global supply chains as the consequence of nationalist decoupling policies.

Based on the impact of the COVID-19 virus in the early days, many people believe that the virus would shatter the economic order, and social systems as much as public health and medicine. The media of various countries have also disclosed many examples to confirm this judgment. All the pandemic-related examples could be viewed as new challenges to globalization

In fact, many countries initially overlooked the threat of the virus in their responses, but adopted all kinds of desperate measures because of panic when they got a real hold of the threat of the pandemic. They changed overnight. And selfish acts of benefiting oneself at the cost of others were not uncommon. For example, at the darkest moment, when Italy was hit hard by the pandemic, none of the European Union (EU) countries offered a helping hand. What's worse, the "pirate" acts of intercepting such life-saving items as masks, respirators, drugs, and PPE also occurred from time to time.

Similarly, under the pretext of national security, policies and means of protectionism are commonly adopted to manage the disease. A survey shows that between 2020 and May 1, 2021, 22 countries and regions around the world implemented a total of 31 restrictive measures on the export of agricultural products and food, and 82 countries and regions implemented a total of 132 control measures on the export of medical supplies and drugs.[10]

The rapid rise of domestic COVID-19 mortality forced many countries to adopt some desperate responses out of panic. The measures seem to be temporary, but the real problem lies in the lack of coordination and synergy of macroeconomic policies, an inherent defect of many globalization systems and mechanisms. In fact, the defect was there from the very beginning. Take the Eurozone as an example. In the past, there was doubt about the role of the Euro mechanism, and the continuity of its existence, because of the structural defects in the financial system under the unified currency. The obvious flaw is that the Euro as the primary currency and sole legal tender for the 19 member states implies that the member states have to sacrifice their right to make their own flexible macroeconomic policies when needed. The COVID-19 pandemic disclosed the imperfection and ineffective operation of the coordinating mechanism in the Eurozone. When many countries realize that neither allies nor global and regional mechanisms are reliable in times of crisis, the rise of nationalism, protectionism and unilateralism is easier to gain the upper hand in policy formulation and implementation.

After the outbreak of the COVID-19 virus, especially when the situation got worse, many countries found the loopholes in their social security systems, and realized that the rich and the poor had very different capabilities in terms of resisting the virus. The pandemic also brought to light that the financial impact by the pandemic on different social classes is different. The perpetual problems like the gap between the poor and the rich, although always there and insolvable, could be used by politician to promote populism. Anyway, populism is always popular with the mass of people. These are age-old insolvable problems. Politicians have to turn to populist policies to handle them, vainly though. The policies are no less than a placebo for the mass of common people. The pandemic itself and the strict prevention and control measures not only hindered the normal operation of the domestic economy from both the supply side and the demand side, but also inevitably inhibited international trade and foreign investment activities. This forced more and more countries to turn inward and rely on protectionism to boost their economy. Countries such as the United States, which has long dominated the global governance and has vigorously pursued unilateralism in recent years, will inevitably open fire at the existing free trade concept and multilateral system.

The huge impact on the global economy caused by the rapid spread of the pandemic around the world prompted a strong awareness in many countries of protecting their strategic industries. Some countries actually implemented protective measures. Whether out of concern that their important domestic enterprises would be acquired by foreign capital during the crisis or just as an excuse to combat the competitiveness of other countries, many countries issued stricter regulations to curb transnational investment activities.

For example, Australia, India, Italy, Canada, Germany, Spain, and France strengthened their restrictions on foreign enterprises' investment and acquisition in specific industries through passing or revising relevant existing laws and regulations. Most of these policies and regulations have a strong discriminatory nature against China as China was conceived as nothing but an enemy. The most typical was the United States as it increased its supervising power and expanded the reviewing scope of exports, investment and acquisitions in key technology fields. Those measures are directly aimed at China.

Along with the pandemic, an ostensible phenomenon is the damage of global supply chain. There are both objective and subjective reasons for the disruption. Whether it was due to the passive termination of various economic activities during the lockdowns, or to the insufficient demand when the economic activities were resumed, the damage to supply chains was palpable. Whether it was for the sake of strengthening their own supply chain security, or for the intention to curb competitors, or for the existence of both factors at the same time, or out of sheer frustration, many countries took the initiative to

26 *Cai Fang*

implement decoupling strategies. The global supply chain, as the most important accomplishment of this round of economic globalization since the 1990s, might yet suffer from long-term damage. The disruptions alone as an obvious factor might make people wonder if the current economic globalization will continue to develop, halt, or terminate when the pandemic is over.

Chinese Responses to De-globalization

It is undeniable that China has benefited so much from the current round of economic globalization and from its own reform, that it has become the world's second-largest economy and the largest exporter of goods. At the same time, this round of economic globalization has also promoted the unprecedented interconnectedness of the world economy and poverty reduction in developing countries. The proportion of the world's population living below $1.9 per day (purchasing power parity in 2011) decreased significantly from 36% in 1990 to 10% in 2015. For this reason, China should continue to unswervingly promote opening up, and, at the same time, make use of its international economic status and governance voice to resolutely safeguard the concept of free trade and the multilateral system on the international stage.

After achieving enviable progress in preventing and controlling the spread of COVID-19, China started resuming and promoting the normalization of economic and social life. For China, one of the most urgent tasks facing economic recovery was to fix the production chain damaged by such factors as the pandemic itself, the virus prevention measures, and the lagged responses by other countries to the disease. It is imperative for China to ensure the long-term security of the supply chain in response to the new phase of globalization.

When devastated by the COVID-19 virus, China implemented a series of strict prevention and control measures, which resulted in a massive stoppage of consumer and production activities. Economic activities were not resumed long after the Spring Festival of 2020. While the tertiary industry experienced a serious contraction, the manufacturing sector also experienced an unprecedented decline. The National Bureau of Statistics data shows that both the non-manufacturing business activity index and the Manufacturing Purchasing Manager Index (PMI) fell to the lowest point in history in February 2020, at only 29.6% and 35.7% respectively. The monthly decline of PMI even exceeded the largest decline in history, that is, 38.8% in November 2008 (see Figure 2.2).

Subsequently, from the extremely low base in February 2020, the manufacturing PMI rebounded to 52.0% in March and remained above the boom and bust line (50.8%) in April. However, the new export order index in the PMI component fell sharply again, that is, after falling to the extremely low point of 28.7% in February. It rebounded to 46.4% in March, then fell again to 33.5% in April, 35.3% in May and 42.6% in June. To a certain extent, this was predicted by many economists and business people. Even if China accelerated the resumption of work and production when the disease was under control, the pandemic

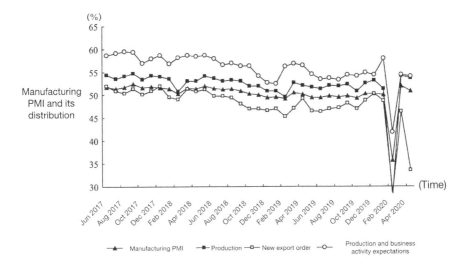

Figure 2.2 Purchasing manager index and sub-index of manufacturing industry.
Source: National Bureau of Statistics. http://data.stats.gov.cn/easyquery.htm?cn=A01

spread rapidly in the rest of the world, and many important economies and China's trading partners were forced to lock down. Export orders were also expected to be cancelled.

The new export order index reflected the reality of the pandemic outside China after March 2020. The sharp rise of confirmed cases in major economies led to a substantial suspension of economic activities, resulting in a significant contraction in import demand other than PPE (personal protective equipment), and some related drugs. However, the reality of the global pandemic also made many countries reassess the security of medical and health supplies, so as to promote the diversification of supply sources, and to match production activities with consumption activities. In addition, countries such as the United States smeared China amidst the pandemic, and initiated malicious decoupling measures, which would certainly destroy the existing supply chains, and harm the development of China's manufacturing industry.[11] The global pandemic indeed added fuel to the reverse movement of globalization that had started prior to the outbreak of the pandemic.

At the present, China is obliged and pressed to fix the supply chain of manufacturing industry, maintain and promote the status of Chinese industry in the division of the global value chain, and ensure the safety of the industrial chain and the supply chain. Only by focusing on the above tasks can China adhere to its reform, and safeguard economic globalization. To this end, we need to have an accurate grasp in the concept of the law of industrial development, and have a clear understanding of our short-term, medium-term and long-term goals.

First of all, there is no contradiction between enhancing high-level opening to the outside world by maintaining the supply chain of manufacturing industry, and tapping the advantages of the super large-scale market and the potential of domestic demand. Economic globalization has not yet ended, and China is still and increasingly the largest open economy. In our understanding, the value chain of globalization itself is the source of productivity. This global division of labor cannot be changed against the will of some countries. Meanwhile, China should not give up easily. Even the products and industries that mainly meet domestic demand must face competition from external producers. There is no and should not be a haven free from competitive pressure.

China is transiting from an upper-middle-income state to a high-income state, and facing the arduous task of accelerating the transformation from the high-speed growth mode to the high-quality development mode. In this transitory period, China's goal is to establish a modern economic system. Only under the condition of continuing to actively participate in the global division of labor system can China have sufficient internal power to innovate ways to develop its economy, and marshal the potential for the improvement of labor productivity and total-factor productivity, two crucial means to gradually increase China's overall competitiveness.

Secondly, there is no contradiction between maintaining the manufacturing industry chain to enhance high-level opening to the outside world, and ensuring the security of the supply chain and solving the key technological "bottleneck" problems. China's manufacturing industry has strong supporting capacity and the most complete industrial categories in the United Nations classification standards. The total added value and export scale of manufacturing industry rank first in the world. However, as a whole, China's manufacturing industry still at the middle and low end of the value chain, strongly depends on developed countries in key technology, and is hence subject to more and more severe restrictions.

China used to be highly dependent on the high-income countries in the trade in goods. Throughout the 1990s, about 84% of China's total import of goods came from the high-income countries, and about 87% of China's total export of goods went to the high-income countries. As China passed the Lewis turning point around 2004 (referring to a situation in economic development where surplus rural labor is fully absorbed into the manufacturing sector), the phenomenon of labor shortage became more and more common, and the labor cost increased, resulting in the accelerated loss of the traditional comparative advantage of manufacturing industry. As a result, the trade proportion of goods to high-income countries decreased significantly. However, as the result of vigorously upgrading and optimizing its manufacturing industry, China has made much progress in industrial innovation, and slowed down the downward trend of the proportion of exports to high-income countries in recent years. At the same time, the proportion of imports has rebounded.

Generally speaking, to break the technological blockage does not mean that we should take the initiative to decouple, and nor should we try to make the best out of a bad bargain. Instead, it is necessary for us not only to stabilize the traditional trade partnership, but also develop a new trade partnership. At the same time, we should precisely select areas and items, and optimize all the resources for independent research so as to develop key technologies. That is the right way to make breakthroughs. As we are engaged in promoting a higher level of opening to the outside world, we have to be firmly nested in the global value chain so as to break the constraints, and ensure the safety of industrial and supply chain.

Finally, we have to deepen the reallocation of resources, improve the total-factor productivity of the manufacturing industry, continue and tap the dynamic comparative advantage, and improve the international competitive advantage of the industry. For a long time, the competitiveness of China's manufacturing industry is mainly based on giving full play to the comparative advantage of resources. Under the condition of having a sufficient labor force, by promoting the transfer of labor force from the primary industry to the secondary industry and the tertiary industry, the reallocation of resources has been realized, and the overall total-factor productivity of China's economy has been improved. In the past ten years or so, with the rapid disappearance of demographic dividend and the increase of labor cost, the traditional comparative advantage tends to weaken. Accordingly, the proportion of the added value of the manufacturing industry in GDP has been in a downward trend since 2006. In theory and by transnational comparative data, it is inevitable that the proportion of manufacturing industry will decline with the increase of per capita income. At present, the decline of the proportion of China's manufacturing industry is premature and occurs when the development potential has not been fully tapped.

In the final analysis, the competitiveness of the manufacturing industry lies in the continuous improvement of total-factor productivity. According to the law of economic and industrial development, under the condition that the space for labor transfer from agriculture to non-agricultural industries is reduced, and the contribution rate of resource reallocation among the three industries to productivity improvement is reduced, there is still a huge space for resource reallocation between the smaller classified departments within the secondary industry and manufacturing industry, and even between the enterprises in these classified departments. The process of rational allocation of production factors into smaller classified departments and into the enterprises is not only a process of deepening resource reallocation, but also an important source of total-factor productivity in the future. The process is what we should focus on to make any breakthroughs to improve the quality of supply chain.

Notes

1 See https://www.ecdc.europa.eu/en/geographical-distribution-2019-ncov-cases.
2 "Chapter One: The Great Lockdown." *World Economic Outlook*. Washington, DC: International Monetary Fund, April 2020. p. ix.
3 See *Global Economic Prospects*. June 2020. Washington, DC: World Bank Group, 2020. p. 4.
4 World Trade Organization. *Annual Report 2020*. 2020. https://www.wto.org/english/res_e/booksp_e/anrep_e/anrep20_e.pdf.

30   *Cai Fang*

5 Barry, John M. *The Great Influenza: The Story of the Deadliest Pandemic in History*. Trans. Zhong Yang, Zhao Jiayuan, and Liu Nian. Shanghai: Shanghai Scientific & Technological Education Publishing House, 2008.
6 Dornbusch, Rudiger W., Edwards, and Sebastian. "Macroeconomic Populism in Latin America." *NBER Working Paper*. No. 2986. May 1989.
7 Rajan, Raghuram G. *Fault Lines: How Hidden Fractures Still Threaten the World Economy*. Trans. Liu Nian. Beijing: CITIC Press Group, 2011.
8 John Allen, Nicholas Burns, Laurie Garrett, et al. "How the World Will Look After the Coronavirus Pandemic?" *Foreign Affairs* March 20, 2020. https://foreignpolicy. com/2020/03/20/world-order-after-coroanvirus-pandemic/.
9 See Thomas Friedman. "Our New Historical Divide: B. C. and A. C.: The World Before Corona and the World After." *The New York Times*, March 17, 2020. https:// www.nytimes.com/2020/03/17/opinion/coronavirus-trends.html.
10 The Global Trade Alert. "The GTA Reports." May 2020. https://www.globaltradealert. org/reports.
11 Stephen Roach summarized the three purposes of the United States and other countries to promote the decoupling of supply chains: to blame and punish China for COVID-19, eliminate their potential vulnerability in key equipment production lines, and relocate overseas production capacity to solve the problem of domestic hollowing out. See Stephen Roach's "Don't Blame Supply Chains." *Yale Global Online*, May 7, 2020. https://yaleglobal.yale.edu/content/dont-blame-supply-chains.

3 A Prospect of the Digital Economy in the Post-COVID-19 Era

Jiang Xiaojuan[*]

China's Economic Growth in the Digital Age: Relatively Optimistic Expectations

Since the reform and opening-up periods, China's economy has maintained rapid growth, with an average growth rate of 9.7% over the past 40 years. However, since 2009, China's economy has entered a slow downward track, and the growth rate has continued to decline. The downward point dated from the global impact of the US financial crisis, but the length of the downward time and the stability of the trend exceeded the impact point. Fundamentally speaking, the decline is due to the fact that we have entered a development stage dominated by the service industry, and the proportion of the service industry in GDP continues to rise. Economic theory and international experience show that economic structures dominated by service industries tend to lower the rate of economic growth. The same pattern has been observed in many other countries. When the proportion of the service industry within an economy exceeds 50%, economic growth begins to decline while the proportion of the service industry in the economy increases. This is a common phenomenon in the history of world economic development.

The reason for this is that the service industry is a relatively inefficient industry. With the increase in the proportion of the service industry, the efficiency of economic activities will decline. In other words, the same amount of investment in service sector will have less output. That is how the growth rate of the whole economy will be dragged down. Why is the service industry an inefficient one? This stems from the fact that many service processes require both production and consumption at the same time, e.g., "person to person" and "point-to-point," such as in education, health, live performance, security, etc. In this process, human capital is the main supply factor, so it is difficult to use efficient machinery and equipment for mass production. While manufacturing can improve labor productivity with efficient equipment and mass production, the

[*] The author is a member of the Standing Committee of the National People's Congress, Deputy Director of the Social Construction Committee of the National People's Congress, Professor and Dean of the School of Public Policy and Management of Tsinghua University.

DOI: 10.4324/9781003433897-3

service industry has remained at a constant level for a long time in terms of labor productivity. At the same time, workers in different industries require similar levels of remuneration. The service sector is low in efficiency, but the salary level cannot be low. In fact, service is becoming increasingly expensive in comparison with producing commodities. Now, as China's economy has entered an era dominated by the service industry, the continuous downward economic growth is expected to repeat what has happened to many economies before.

But is China certain to follow in others' tracks and enter the period of medium and low growth? Is there any way to maintain the growth rate at a relatively high level? On the whole, it is difficult to avoid a slower growth, but we hope to perform relatively better than other countries. Our hope is not an irrational desire, but has a real basis, that is, we have entered a period dominated by the service industry in the digital age.

The digital economy has three remarkable characteristics, which can increase the traditional low efficiency, can create new business models for services, and create new areas for growth.

First, digital technology has greatly improved the labor productivity of the service industry. The main problem of the service industry is that the labor productivity is not high, which drags down the whole economy. If the labor productivity is improved, this problem will not exist. For example, banks are a very labor-intensive industry. Why are banks unwilling to provide services to small and medium-sized enterprises? Because the labor cost of a large loan is similar to that of a small loan. Now, Internet banks have introduced digital technology to provide lending services, basically an intelligent lending transaction without manual intervention. About three or four hundred people can now provide loans of trillions to tens of millions of small and medium-sized enterprises. Its efficiency was unimaginable in the past. Another example is education. In more than a century, the teacher–student ratio of primary and secondary schools has remained roughly the same. In other words, the labor productivity of teachers has not improved. However, there has been a huge change since the introduction of massive online open classes (MOOCs). The number of students one teacher could reach can be hundreds of times more in MOOCs. For instance, nearly one million students have registered in the most popular MOOCs at Tsinghua University, a number unimaginable for ordinary in-class teaching, which normally has only a few dozens of students at the maximum. From the economic perspective, the high efficiency of digital services comes from the following: the high initial cost and the low marginal cost of many network services, typical of the economy of scale. This is especially true of the replicable cultural and information services. Whether an online video has one or 100 million viewers, the production cost is the same, and the marginal cost of increasing the viewers is very low.

Relatedly, the economy of scope is extremely significant. The establishment of a huge platform means firms can offer a variety of products and services, and continuously produce new products and new services with brand advantages. For consumers, logging into such a platform will meet most of their needs. For enterprises, it can maximize the use of platform assets, reduce costs and improve efficiency. Another advantage is the long tail effect. The so-called long tail effect refers to the fact that when the cost of product and service is low enough because of diversification, selling low volumes of hard-to-find items, namely, providing personalized services, can realize significant profits. In fact, products in low demand or with low sales volumes can collectively make up market share that can rival or exceeds the few hot selling products. Internet enterprises have no inventory, and the website maintenance cost is much lower than that of traditional stores. The platform can reach out to countless sellers and buyers, greatly expanding the varieties of goods, and effectively forming the "long tail effect." For example, a large bookstore can usually shelf 100,000 books, so it is impossible to shelf those books that are very low in demand or in volumes. However, online bookstores are completely free from this restriction. In fact, the low-demand sales of books, namely the total sales of those books each generate less than $100,000 in revenue, make up one-fourth of Amazon's revenue. If the online sales are nothing but services, the distribution cost is zero. Such a business model can give full play to the long tail theory. This is the case with online video and music paid-downloads. Because the "tail" is very long, sales of those items in low volumes can add up to huge sales. This shows that in the network era, the increase of diversity and complexity does not mean the increase of average cost.

Second, digital technology can quickly create new products, services and business models. In traditional industries and in the past, it is extremely time-consuming to put new products and services onto the market. You have to design the products first, and let consumers know about them through advertisements, on-site demonstration, and preferential sales, so as to reach a limited number of consumers. In the digital age, the innovation of products and services are much faster. More than three million products and services are added on the few major online sales platforms every day, which attracts consumers to constantly try new products and services, and accelerates the speed of consumption substitution. Now, more than 70% of consumers are willing to try new goods and services instead of only consuming the known brands. Digitalization can also quickly create new types of goods and services, and stimulate consumption growth. Online games, for example, are at the front of my mind, new and popular these days when everyone stayed home during the pandemic.

Third, digital technology has become a force in the allocation of resources. One, it allocates stock resources, and matches scattered resources and time with demand at low cost, so as to contribute to economic growth and social services. Two, it can allocate incremental resources, such as financial institutions, and decide who can get funds and other resources by intelligent data analysis and compliance with risk control indicators. In addition, digital technology can also allocate preference/interest resources. In the past, enterprises had to do market research, develop products, try them out, get feedback, promote, trial sale, etc., before they had an idea what the consumers wanted, and how to finally reach the consumers. Now, we can directly use big data to discover individual and personalized needs, and offer items consumers might want. In the past, advertising, and sampling promotion are the primary channels for consumers to know about products, but now, sellers can accurately find what consumers are interested in with help of digital technology. What consumers search and want to know more about will be offered to them on their digital devices. Digital platforms are where there are most advertising, the result of a new way of resource allocation.

Our particular national conditions and industrial characteristics are conducive to the development of the digital economy. First of all, we are the most populous country with nearly 1.4 billion consumers, a natural condition for developing digital platforms. The economy of scale is there, but the marginal cost is basically zero. There is basically no additional expenditure to increase customers. A large number of customers could keep a few big digital platforms to operate. Huge numbers are the conditions for an economy of scale, and more platforms mean more intense competition. The economy of scale and competition among the platforms surely quickens the development of better products and services for consumers. As we are a populous country with a large number of consumers, the less popular items for a small number of consumers will collectively make up an economy of scale. If only 1% of people are interested in an item, this means 14 million people are the prospective consumers, a number that could ensure the success of a new business model.

It follows then that China's large domestic market can support the growth of digital enterprises in China before they have had their global competitiveness on the international market. If an enterprise in a smaller country initiates a digital platform, it must be a global platform from the beginning. The domestic consumers can support the growth and development of several platforms, create a business atmosphere for competition, and force enterprises to continuously strive to improve their competitiveness. For example, Tencent and Alibaba, two big digital platforms (companies) in China, worked hard to offer online home office apps and upgraded their apps more than ten times in a few dozen days during the early phase of this pandemic. The social responsibility of the enterprises and the high morale of the employees are the internal cause, and the fierce market competition is the external cause. Only by matching the two could they achieve a series of such rapid upgrading. The fierce competitive domestic market propels enterprises to become globally competitive ones even if they operate on the domestic Chinese market. Huawei, Lenovo, Alibaba, Xiaomi, and ByteDance, the top five of China's 50 internationally well-known corporations, all started in China at the beginning, and became very competitive enterprises in China before they expanded their business globally. Their global operation has enhanced their capabilities to compete around the world.

In a word, digital technology has fundamentally changed the nature of the service industry. In China, these two happened at roughly the same time. What great luck for Chinese economy! A service-dominating economy has many

A Prospect of the Digital Economy in the Post-COVID-19 Era 35

advantages to further develop the digital industry. Therefore, at this stage, we may break the past law of "a low-growth service-dominating economy," and may maintain a relatively rapid growth rate and show a better growth trend than the countries before us.

Long-Term Favorable Conditions for China's Development of the Digital Economy

With regard to the long-term favorable conditions, we talk about the following four points: both the Party and the state attach great importance to the development of digital economy; the demand of digitalization to develop and support new technology; the development of the industrial Internet will boost digital technology; and the strong demand for digitalization to secure the integrated development of manufacturing and service industries.

The party and the state attach great importance to the development of the digital economy. In recent years, China's Central Government has stressed the importance of innovation of digital technology and the development of the digital economy. So far, the 19th Politburo of the CPC Central Committee has conducted 19 collective studies, four of which were directly related to digital technology and the digital economy. One was about the implementation of the national big data strategy, one was about the development status and trend of artificial intelligence, one was about the all media era, and the development of media integration, and the most recent was the development status and trend of blockchain technology. The Central Economic Work Conference in December, 2018, included in the economic development tasks for 2019 the speeding up the commercial use of 5G networks, and the construction of new infrastructure for the development of artificial intelligence (AI), and the Industrial Internet and Internet of Things. This was a signal that the Central Government would focus on the development of digital economy, digital technology, and the new-generation communication technology, a clear development strategy after careful deliberation.

There is a strong demand of digitalization to develop and support new technology. Over the past two years, the development of digital economy has actually lost some steam. Although it is still growing, the growth rate and growth potential have slowed down, as shown in the following. Regarding the scope of the market, the number of mobile Internet users and the average browsing time remain steady. Both numbers reflected a lower growth rate for some time, and nearly stopped growing before the pandemic. For the online market, the total size of the market is the number of Internet users multiplied by the average length of time they spent browsing the Internet. The main restriction on the real market expansion is purchasing power. Consumers with sufficient financial resources can buy a large number of products, but they have little time to enjoy what they have bought. It seems to them that possession is enjoyment. For example, the rich can own dozens of luxury vehicles and many villas around the world at the same time. However, the consumption of digital services is experiential, and consumers must take time to participate in it personally. Consumers cannot watch two movies, listen to two songs or listen to two classroom lectures simultaneously. Therefore, digital services are strongly constrained by the total time of Internet browsing of the whole nation. A higher digitalization level requires that new products and services of higher value per unit of time be created and offered. As for the supply side, the performance of new Internet products is generally poor. An important reason is that with the support of 4G technology, the demand for applications that the Internet can support has been relatively saturated. A new round of development needs new technology to support. In the future, with the development of 5G and other new-generation Internet technologies, we can start more digital consumption. For example, if the new technology supports the dual-wheel drive of the mobile Internet and the Internet of Things, prospective consumption of 10 billion, and even 100 billion CNY is expected to be commercialized.

The second stage, of "Internet plus," will be the development of industrial Internet. Nowadays, people think that the digital platform for consumers is the first stage of "Internet plus," and the second stage of "Internet plus" should be for the producers. Under the new generation of communication technology, the prospect of the industrial Internet is very broad. The amount of communication and computing required by the industrial Internet is completely different from our consumption of the Internet. No matter Taobao, Tmall or Jingdong, it has a digital platform that is available to all enterprises, all consumers and C-end. But in the case of the industrial Internet, every platform is personalized. If online consumption can be considered stable and calm, the provision of goods and service for online consumption is ruthlessly competitive. Moreover, the Internet consumption is mainly about information, while the industrial Internet is about things, the transport of goods, and different communication capacity. The development of new technology supports the Internet with better admission conditions so as to accommodate more users and participants.

The industrial Internet enhances the integrated development of service industry and manufacturing industry. We are now painfully hesitating about how to prioritize the two. Sometimes we are inclined to the development of the service industry and, sometimes, the manufacturing industry (the so-called real economy). In fact, the modern economy is a highly integrated economy. Now we often talk about service-oriented manufacturers and manufacturing service providers, both of which are integrated enterprises. The development of digital technology can provide more and more efficient services for production and realize the integrated development of service industry and manufacturing industry

Here are a few examples. The first is a comprehensive platform, named www.zbj.com, which provides enterprises with professional services throughout the life cycle of their production. If you want to start a business, you are required to write a business plan, register your business, search for a name, design your product prototypes, develop your product, prepare paperwork, set loans, apply for appropriate trademarks, patents or copyrights, license and permits. After you manufacture your product, you pay taxes. A smooth operation of different enterprises requires different IT systems and the like. If you want to offer the best product, you have to design it and make it from the onset. You need translation for international conferences. It is almost impossible for small and medium-sized enterprises to satisfactorily meet all these requirements unless they feel comfortable with inefficiency and making mediocre products. In reality, small and medium-sized enterprises cannot afford hiring professionals to do all these. But, they could turn to such Internet platforms as www.zbj. com for all kinds of professional services throughout the life cycle of their production. This company is based in Chongqing. How large is it? The total investment is 22 million CNY. The number of its shared talents is more than 10 million people working in millions of enterprises, who could provide professional services. More than 1.2 million of its clients are shop owners, and about 10% of them now have their own companies. This Chongqing-based company has provided services to more than 10 million clients, offered more than 1,000 types of productive services, designed brands for more than 3 million enterprises, designed logos for more than 1 million enterprises, and provided more than 1.8 million services related to marketing. It has also maintained Internet systems for enterprises more than 800,000 times, and provided intellectual property services more than 1.2 million times.

There is also another kind of enterprise, which provides special services because they are highly specialized in producing parts and components. Although the single-unit value of their product is low, they make profits on large orders. For example, there is an enterprise in Hangzhou which makes printed circuit boards (PCB). They make sample PCBs after many trials. Such enterprises do not have orders on a regular basis, and the unit price is not high. Their orders, though irregular, are large in quantity, and urgent in time. The Hangzhou enterprise only makes PCBs, and is so specialized in every process that it can complete a sample PCB in 24 hours, instead of the five days previously required. It is thus a highly specialized enterprise.

Shengyibang (mutual business help) is a very different enterprise in Ningbo, more like a social organization. Its website is www.easylink.com.cn. Taking advantage of the characteristics of the dense industrial clusters made up of small and medium-sized enterprises in the Ningbo and Jiangsu regions, the enterprise tries to link other enterprises. Usually, the small and medium-sized enterprises have some idle equipment between orders, and most of them are not always in full operation. Shengyibang knew this and came up with the idea of a new manufacturing model, although it has no factory or equipment. Shengyibang will turn to the enterprises in the region for access to particular idle equipment after it receives an order. It then sets up a "cloud factory" with particular equipment from other enterprises, and starts to produce a particular item. The factory is then closed (dismissed) if there are no more orders. And a new cloud factory will be set up when there is a different order.

This case is of particular economic significance. Professor Ronald Coase, an American economist, questions the validity of the existence of firms. To him, it is better to produce goods through social organizations. There will be idle equipment when a firm doesn't have enough orders. Also, a firm can only make certain goods, and is inflexible in its production in the sense that it cannot take the orders of goods that it cannot make. In a word, it cannot adjust its production capacity in time to make different items.[1] If so, how do firms emerge? Coase argues that firms emerge because they are better equipped to deal with the transaction cost in production and exchange than individuals are. The costs include search and information costs about the credibility and reputation of a particular firm, about the quality of its product, about the way it treats orders, etc. To have all those types of equipment together, and the necessary oversight, the production procedures can potentially add to cost of procuring something through the market. He believes that firms arise to produce something internally to avoid these costs. However, in the digital era, the cost of searching for proper firms, equipment, and information about those firms will be greatly reduced. Under the new conditions, firms might organize their production in fundamentally different way. The new organization might be common in the future.

The Pandemic Enhances Digital Economy

In addition to the above long-term factors conducive to the development of digital economy, the current pandemic can actually boost the digital economy as it opens up new areas for digital technology.

First, digital technology has been outstanding in preventing and fighting the COVID-19 pandemic. It is widely used in patient diagnosis and treatment, drawing the pandemic map, crowd tracking, and classified management. Briefly, in terms of patient diagnosis and treatment, several new applications have been rapidly developed. A kind of assistive robot is used to transport medical material, which not only reduces the physical burden of medical staff, but also reduces the possibility of cross infection among medical staff. Second, intelligent medical image analysis technology has improved the efficiency and accuracy of diagnosis. Large technology platform enterprises, such as Alibaba, Tencent, and Huawei, have done well in this regard. Third, telemedicine makes it possible for patients to virtually "visit" specialists in other places, a technology that "levels" out medical resources in a much safer way during the pandemic. Real-time pandemic maps visually display the pandemic situation, pinpoints the location where an infected case occurs, and helps to track where the patient has been. In case investigation, we can have the patient recall when, where, how, and with whom he/she travelled in the timeframe. Anyone can check if he/she has had close contacts in public space and on public transportation by logging in an app. In terms of classified management, the typical one is the health code.

Digital technology has also played a very important role in such social operations as online education, food delivery, conference meetings, and e-commerce. Take online education, for example. In the spring semester, 2020, all the classroom teaching from primary schools to colleges was carried out online. One platform, DingTalk, offered free video-conference apps for primary and secondary education users, which allows users to try all kinds of innovative online teaching models. Food delivery and retail e-commerce sales are two other areas that are closely related to people's life. With digital technology, non-contact purchase and delivery are possible, unimaginably convenient for consumers. Working from home is made possible with digital technology. A few IT companies provide tech tools for people to work remotely after the resumption of economic activity. The video conference tools allow people meet virtually, significantly reducing the possibilities of cross-infections. The users of Tencent's DingTalk was multiplied more than ten times.

Digital enterprises are still in the process of continuous innovation. Meituan, a leading delivery platform, and the China Association of Scenic Spots jointly issued the pandemic prevention standards for the Pure Brightness holiday (tomb-sweeping), and the May Day of 2021. Scenic spots that met the standards would be marked as safe to open to the public. During the Pure Brightness long weekend, the scenic spots marked as safe received tourists 2.1 times as many as those spots without the green mark. The China Association of Scenic Spots, and China Association of Hotels issued the pandemic prevention standards and recommended the hotels that met the standards. The occupancy of the "peace of mind" hotels was 1.6 times more than the hotels that were not recommended. Thanks to digital tech companies that kept innovating their tools and services that would meet the requirements of the consumers for re-starting work after the lockdown. In addition to ensuring the normal life and work of Chinese people, these digital enterprises also showed the world their competence and responsibility. For example, the Alibaba's excellent DingTalk was recommended by the United Nations to students and teachers around the world for distance learning, and Tencent's VooV Meeting was used by the United Nations for video conferencing.

The pandemic has opened up a broader market for digital consumption. Due to its excellent performance in pandemic prevention and control, and in providing service to people's everyday life, digital enterprises are favorably recognized and accepted for their service, an important social foundation for their future development. No matter what kind of services the Internet provides, consumers must be online, which is a basic condition. China's number of active Internet users reached the peak of 1.138 billion in 2020, although the number decreased slightly thereafter. The average browsing time remained unchanged before the outbreak of the pandemic. However, during the pandemic, digital consumption and digital life became increasingly popular as the original online consumers spent more time exploring possibilities, and communities wo had been previously offline began browsing more on the Internet, and gradually got used to online shopping. Both the number of people and the length of time spent online have increased, opening up a broader online consumption space, and a larger market for digital enterprises.

The pandemic has accelerated the application of a new generation of digital technology. If we liken online consumption to the first half of a game, the industrial Internet is the second half. The big players have entered or are itching to enter the second half. If we don't see the magnificent and splendid spectacle with the industrial Internet as we did with online consumption, I believe it is because the current technical support is limited. During the pandemic, the concept of "new infrastructure" attracted extensive attention, which would serve the development of 5G, AI, the industrial Internet, the Internet of Things, and data centers. According to the China Academy of Information and Communications Technology (CAICT), the commercialization of 5G technology will directly increase China's total economic output of 10.6 trillion CNY, and create 3 million jobs from 2020 to 2025. I believe we have several advantages. The most obvious is that we have a strong ability to use the 5G technology, a large number of consumers, and a large-scale industrial foundation. The huge number of consumers can support the existence of multiple giant platforms. Our product upgrade is very fast, which is a very obvious advantage. At present, the 5G communication capability with ultra-high reliability and ultra-low delay can meet the application of higher standards in the digital service industry. For example, in teaching, 5G technology enables multiple students to communicate one-on-one with their teacher directly, so timely interactive and hands-on education can be done on the Internet. Another area that relies on 5G technology to develop is telemedicine. Using this technology, medical examination and surgery can be conducted remotely because of the 5G's great communication capability. Yet another area for potential development is fitness, which may be benefit greatly from the use of smart technology. There are actually some new forms of smart fitness, which will grow fast in the future. Cycling at home on smart bikes in the United States has had a significant impact on fitness clubs. A smart bike with a digital simulation system brings you the real immersive experience of going up and down the slope on real roads. If you think it's boring to ride alone, you can ask friends to ride in social groups. You can race on a virtual track. If you ride fast, you feel your speed in the VR scene, which requires high traffic communication capability. In this sense, 5G has great potential for application in home fitness center.

The "new infrastructure" will accelerate the development of the industrial Internet, a platform that should be able to have many enterprises and equipment connected. Only when the 5G network accelerates its development can large-scale industrial Internet develop. In the future, it can also support intelligent data systems, machine learning, etc. What is crucial for machine learning to develop? It needs a huge amount of data to be inputted continuously. China is large with a large-scale industry. The data that can be inputted for machine learning should be the largest in the world. With the support of 5G and other new-generation communication technologies, our advantages can be brought into full play. In addition, we have a number of companies that are not only capable of continuous innovation, but also hard-working and socially responsible. During the pandemic, due to the rapid expansion and upgrading of digital applications, many teams in these companies are updating their apps on an almost daily basis, working overtime every day, providing better services, and expanding their market. During the pandemic, the Jack Ma Foundation and others have jointly established an international doctor exchange center, where, with the assistance of machine translation (11 languages), medical workers from 104 countries and regions could exchange their latest clinical experience of preventing and controlling the COVID-19 virus. The international medical workers could either choose to talk with their Chinese counterparts one-on-one or to participate in live classes in different hospitals. The center was internationally recognized and praised.

The pandemic intrigued a sudden demand of digital service in the areas that were otherwise difficult to enter. Although the technology for e-learning, e-conference, e-medicine and e-office was there prior to the pandemic, the technology and related platforms were not widely known and used for various reasons. Everyone is used to digital technology by now, and willing to accept new applications. The prospect for digital services in the future looks great. Some of the services will continue thriving when the pandemic is over. For example, video-conferencing will be a new normal. Is it still necessary in the future to invite foreigners to speak for ten minutes at a 20-minute conference? A video conference will do if the guest has the access. The pandemic facilitated digital technology to enter many areas so expectedly, in such speed and magnitude that were only dreamed about before. It was a dream because it was unimaginable to conduct such a wide range of testing and application in real life. The pandemic helped lifting some of the restrictions on the development of digital economy. For example, prior to the pandemic, telemedicine was not allowed for initial examination, and the National Basic Health Insurance was not allowed to cover the cost. However, in April, 2020, the National Development and Reform Commission, the National Health Commission, and the National Healthcare Security Administration jointly issued a new policy that allows the National Basic Health Insurance to cover the online diagnosis. Although a pilot work, it is a huge breakthrough and of great significance. We can use our insurance to see a doctor on the Internet in the future. Although this has been a constant and continuous appeal by the telemedicine field, it was the pandemic that made initial medical examination and diagnosis a reality.

The Government and Enterprises to Resume Work to Quicken Development after the Pandemic

In the new round of the digital economy, the market mechanism and the market itself should play a leading role, which is our basic view. The field of the digital economy is innovative and changing every day. It is hardly possible to plan the development of the digital economy in advance, because the field is so innovative that it is different everyday with eye-opening new tools and products. It is only the market that can boost the development of the digital economy. Due to the uncertainty of competition and the high failure rate, the new market, anxious and frustrated, often turns to the government for support. People from all walks of life have made all kinds of suggestions for the government to help develop the digital economy. However, the government can't do these things, let alone do them well. That is the reality. Now, it is different from the early and middle period of the reform and opening-up periods, when we were certain about some sectors, and knew what products should be developed and what technologies should be adopted. We also knew the advantages of our state-owned enterprises at that time. But, even under those favorable conditions, it had no effect when the government had supportive policies and plans of what to produce, how much to produce, how to produce, and who to produce, except for interfering with the normal function of the market. In this era of innovation and rapid change, enterprises must be the main body of innovation. The digital service sector offers a large number and a wide range of service, tools, and business models. How can the government plan for all these? Even if it can, the moment a planned product is on the market, a new one is ready to replace it for better quality. In a word, the digital economy must be in the hands of the enterprises for development based on their independent decisions.

The government should have a better role to play. In the past, the "reasonable" relationship between the government and enterprises was roughly as follows: It was up to the enterprises to design and produce products, and it was also up to the enterprises to explore the market. It was the government's duty to support those basic R & D projects with large investments, since they are time-consuming, and fraught with uncertainty and risk. It was the consensus that the government should financially support internal R & D projects, and those projects undertaken by external professional institutions and enterprises. Nowadays, the government's commitment to those supports are still of paramount importance, although there are signs of changes. The big corporations, such as Alibaba, Tencent, the telecommunication giants, PetroChina, Sinopec, China National Offshore Oil Corp, etc., have the financial power to invest in R & D. In addition, these enterprises have their strong research teams which are as capable as those in professional institutions. The enterprises have improved their independent R & D ability, so the overall R & D of the industry sector is improving. However, they can't do all the market exploration and localization as they did before. Why? Because many market entry permits are in the hands of the government. For example, some enterprises have the necessary networking and digital technology and skills to offer remote medial services such as examination, diagnosis, and even surgery, but they cannot enter the field without a government permit. The whole medical system is supported by the state-owned hospitals, and the basic healthcare insurance is managed by the government. As long as these two aspects are in the hands of the government, no enterprise can enter the market no matter how advanced their technology, or how innovative their business model. Without implementation, no innovation or new areas of service can develop into new business models.

Building smart cities is another example. Certainly, it is the responsibility of the municipal governments to develop their cities into smart ones. Although traffic, community development, environmental protection, security, etc., rely on digital technology for better management, the application of digital management in separate departments is unrelated, and fragmented. It is up to the municipal governments to integrate all the digital resources. In this sense, the government has a crucial role to play in offering digital services. Education is another sector that needs the permission of the government to go smart. Public education is a national system. Without the government permission, no school could do much about smart education.

Generally speaking, in the era of digital technology, the concepts of "market efficiency" and "market failure" are still useful and important, though their connotation has undergone important changes. In the past years, people believe where "market failure" occurs is where the government should intervene. The typical areas where market often fails are education, medicine, and social management, etc. Now, with the onset of advanced digital technology, sophisticated networking, and social interconnectedness, service efficiency in the above-mentioned areas has been greatly improved, indicating that they can be partially commercialized. In fact, the cost of commercializing these services might be the same or even lower than that provided by the government. This means that the boundary between the government and the market has changed, and that the market can provide more effective and more efficient services.

In short, we believe that the digital economy will not only be the most promising area with important growth prospects for the future, but that it can also be seen as so important that it will be able to break the bottleneck of lower economic growth at this stage of our economy. Surely, it will enable our economy to maintain relatively rapid growth for a longer period of time. We are confident in this. The outstanding advantages we have in developing the digital economy will increase our global competitiveness in this new economic field, a competitiveness similar to that of our traditional manufacturing industry. In the near future, the digital industry will play an important role in economic recovery after the pandemic, in terms of enhancing employment, increasing consumption, continuing economic upgrading, and raising international competitiveness. In the development of the digital economy, we need to keep in mind that the market is the fundamental force, but government control is also of paramount importance. So long as both the free market and government control can fully ramp up their advantages as the new economic situation requires, a long-term and sustainable development of the digital economy can be expected.

Note

1 See "The Nature of the Firms" by Ronald Coase.

4 Getting Prepared for a New Type of Long-Term Recession[*]

Li Yang[**]

Before the outbreak of the COVID-19 pandemic, the global economy was showing sign of downturn. The impact of the pandemic will affect the momentum of global economic growth and development potential in both the medium and the long run. Therefore, the prospect of global economic growth is hardly optimistic at all, but a new type of long-term recession is highly probable. At present, the most important task is to control the public health crisis. On this premise, economic policies should be focused on preventing economic crisis from becoming a serious recession. In response to the challenge of the pandemic, we should use the fiscal tool, and manage government debt responsibly. With regard to monetary policy, we should quickly lower interest rates, and increase the supply of credit. In response to the severe challenges brought about by the pandemic, we should take the spirit of the Third Plenary Session of the 18th CPC Central Committee as the guideline to further deepen domestic reform, to hold the banner of building a community of common destiny of mankind, and to actively engage in the implementation of the Belt and Road initiative.

Introduction

The author of this chapter prefers to use the term "new long-term recession" to describe the current global economic situation and its development trend, by which two layers of meaning are implied: one is that we will face a long-term recession; the other is that this recession is very special in the sense that nothing similar occurred in the past, so we have no experience to deal with it. Before the outbreak, the global economy and China's economy showed a downward trend in 2019. As people say, misfortunes never come singly. The raging COVID-19 virus further sank the global economy, sending it off a normal track.

---

[*] This is the revised version of my speech at the online forum on "The Release of Global Economic Confidence Index under the Pandemic" held by the *Caijing Magazine* on April 10, 2020.

[**] The author is the former Vice President, and Member of the Chinese Academy of Social Sciences; Director of National Institution of Finance and Development, the Chinese Academy of Social Sciences.

DOI: 10.4324/9781003433897-4

It should be clear that the impact of the pandemic on the global economy is both comprehensive and huge. Specifically, the impacts are seen on demand, supply, finance, loss of life, employment, the bankruptcy of small enterprises, and disruptions to the global supply chain. Any one of the above seven is hard to deal with. When they are all combined, the impact is catastrophic. These impacts will affect and erode the growth momentum and development potential of the global economy in the long term, deviate the global economy from the normal track, and send it onto a lower growth track. On April 9, 2020, Kristalina Georgieva, President of the International Monetary Fund (IMF), said in her opening speech for the IMF World Bank Spring Meeting, that the coronavirus pandemic will turn global economic growth "sharply negative" this year, and warned that the world would face the worst economic crisis since the Great Depression of the 1930s.[1] I basically agree with her.

Economic Situation under the Pandemic: The Selection of Research Methods

Nothing is more important in understanding the economic situation than choosing a proper method. All conclusions for policy-making are none other than the analytical result of the economic facts with the assistance of certain methods. Different methods may lead to completely different judgments and conclusions about the economic situation. So, in the face of the new situation of the COVID-19 pandemic impact, what analytic framework is the most suitable? The author believes that pandemic economics may be the most suitable. More precisely, among various analytic methods, pandemic economics may be the most direct and straightforward. Based on this framework, there are three important aspects that cannot be ignored when we analyze the economic operation during the COVID-19 pandemic.

First, under the spread of the virus, the premise for all policies to take effect is that the pandemic can be controlled. This is a prerequisite. In other words, first and foremost, if we cannot respond properly to the public health crisis caused by this virus, and if we cannot effectively manage the spread of the virus by cutting off its transmission route, all policies, including monetary policy and fiscal policy, will be proven ineffective.

Second, it follows from the above argument that self-isolation at home is a public health measure to slow the spread of this virus. However, all the measures we have taken have hindered the flow and combination of the production factors, thereby exacerbating the decline of the supply side. They have also reduced incomes and hindered consumption, thereby exacerbating the recession on the demand side. This means that during the pandemic, economic recession is sure to occur as it is the result of government policy. In other words, recession is inevitable. In this way, the three key factors of economic operation during the pandemic, namely, medical assistance, prevention of the loss of life, and economic growth, are integrated under the same analytical framework.

46   *Li Yang*

Third, some industrial chain disruptions caused by the pandemic may be fixed or resumed afterwards, while others may never be fixed. If the pandemic continues for a long time, and the unrecoverable breakpoints increase because of "ideology," the economic operation in the wake of the pandemic will be dragged to a lower growth track than before.

Based on the above three points, the main policy focus should be on controlling the spread of COVID-19, which must be the overriding objective. Here, unlike in other fields and at normal times, there is basically no trade-off between policy objectives, and there is no "substitutes" with other economic policy objectives. Therefore, on the premise of ensuring the realization of the goal of pandemic control, economic policy can only be temporary and limited. To a certain extent, the time for COVID-19 virus prevention could be prolonged or shortened, subject to the scientific judgment on the development of the pandemic. Therefore, the use of economic policies should focus on preventing excessive economic recession. In this sense, the "stimulus plans" adopted by various countries are essentially "protection plans." Such plans should be designed to protect and support all employees, enterprises, banks, and production networks, to inspire people's confidence that the economy will eventually be recovered, and provide financial support for the people in trouble to meet their basic living needs.

Recently, people in many parts of China begin to return to work, but the production is not satisfactory. Some held the opinion that it is better not to have people return to work without the resumption of production. The author believes that under the current pandemic condition and routine prevention measures, even if production is not resumed, having the workers back is also a necessary gesture to fight the pandemic. When the lights are on in the firms, this means that the firms are still there, and people are there in the firms. It is surely a strong signal of hope. This tells us that during the spread of the virus, the policy is not mainly intended to stimulate the economy, but to maintain the survival of enterprises, and employment. Where there are people healthy and alive, there is hope. Therefore, we are really obliged to maintain the operation of enterprises as much as possible, to restore people's confidence and to provide assistance to the underprivileged. This is our analytical method for studying the current situation

Careful analysis of the policy statement released by the Federal Reserve on April 9, 2020 will help us understand this analytical method based on the control of the pandemic, and the sequential policy position. According to Federal Reserve Board Chair Jerome H. Powell, "Our country's highest priority must be to address this public health crisis, providing care for the ill and limiting the further spread of the virus… The Fed's role is to provide as much relief and stability as we can during this period of constrained economic activity, and our actions today will help ensure that the eventual recovery is as vigorous as possible."[2] The measures taken by the Feds were strong, proactive, and even aggressive to ensure a strong economic recovery after the pandemic. What is behind the actions is to maintain stability and confidence. We can see that since the unprecedented integrated rescue measures were launched in early March 2020, the fiscal and financial support of the United States covered every corner of the economy, and assisted households, businesses of all size, local and state governments. Careful analysis of the orientation of the Federal measures makes it clear that maintaining survival is the highest priority. This is true of all countries in the world. This kind of policy logic sets an example, worthy of our careful analysis.

Policy Orientations: Promoting Maximum Employment, Fighting for Survival, and Prioritizing People's Life

By the logic of the above analysis, the overall policy should focus on the following three aspects during the pandemic: promoting employment; fighting for survival; and prioritizing people's life. We have seen that countless financial and monetary policies have been launched around these three, such as tax deduction, all kinds of subsidies, cash support, rent deductions, increasing loans, lowering interest rates, so on and so forth. I believe that all these policies are very important, and the next task is to speed up their implementation. In my opinion, among all these rescue measures, the most crucial is to support small and medium-sized businesses, and to launch large-scale public projects.

Effectively Support Micro-Small-and-Medium-Sized Businesses

Such businesses are directly related to employment, and indirectly related to social stability. Their importance cannot be overemphasized. Therefore, since the outbreak of the pandemic, local and central governments have issued countless measures to support such businesses on a daily basis. However, objectively speaking, the majority of these businesses have benefited relatively little from the support. It has not been uncommon in recent years that "good policies cannot be ideally implemented." The reasons must be carefully uncovered. We believe that there are three types of prominent reasons. The first type relates to the system. Anyone, scholars and officials alike, who has carefully studied the problems China's small businesses knows that in China, most micro-small-and-medium-sized businesses are privately owned. The governments at all levels do support them, but far from enough. There are systematic and institutional obstacles for private economy, known as "high thresholds," and "glass doors" (invisible restrictions and obstacles). As these obstacles are systematic, they are hard to overcome. As a matter of fact, the situation for private economy is getting worse. The second relates to technological support. The small and medium-sized businesses, when they grow, are usually in dire need of support of information, technology, credit, management, human resources, and markets. Providing support in these areas to businesses may be more important than providing funds. The third is about the form of financial support. Most such businesses have a greater demand for investment, instead of having loans. Therefore, at a time when the majority of businesses are struggling for survival, our policy focuses mainly on providing loans to them. Isn't it both irrelevant and wrong to let them shoulder additional debt burden? Therefore, the author

48 *Li Yang*

believes that it is time for China to seriously reform the system that is supposed to support small and medium-sized businesses in their development. The outbreak of the COVID-19 virus made the reform more urgent.

Promoting Maximum Employment

When discussing the strategy of revitalizing the economy during the pandemic, people are interested in discussing both the "old infrastructure" (railroads, bridges, airports, etc.) and the "new infrastructure" (infrastructure for new technology). The author believes that infrastructure is surely the key. In the foreseeable future, on the demand side of economic growth, exports, and domestic consumption will see negative growth, which may possibly be a long-term phenomenon. Therefore, increasing investment is bound to become the only way to stimulate economic growth.

Whatever opinion we have about our investment-driven economy, the fact that we have to invest to stimulate economic growth is hard to change in the short term. Moreover, there is no contradiction between an investment-driven economy and an innovation-driven economy. No matter how different the technological process of any innovation is, there will be no economic process from the technological stage without investment. However, before implementing the investment strategy, we must solve two major problems: what to invest, and how to get the investment?

The core principle of "what should we invest in?" should be in alignment to prioritize growth or employment. For a long time, our economic development and development plan has tilted toward growth. Therefore, the main areas of investment are known as the "tiegongji" (railroad, highway, and other basic infrastructure). We repeated the investment pattern during the 2008–2009 global financial crisis. For a long time, the dominant official view is that there is employment whenever there is economic growth. Therefore, the employment target can be covered by the growth target. It should be said that, in the process of high-speed industrialization, the relationship between the two is understandable and reasonable. However, after the industrialization process has essentially been completed, and the proportion of the service industry in the national economy is increasing, the relationship between growth and employment cannot cover each other. Usually, if there is employment, there must be growth. Now, the growth is there, but the level of employment remains the same. Gradually, people have come to acknowledge this difference, and finally put "promotion of employment" in the Central Government Document, becoming the major goal of our economic development and macro-control.

The author believes that during the pandemic, we should fully uphold the principle of prioritizing employment, focus on solving the survival problems of most enterprises, and make sure most people have enough food on their table. The pandemic has opened our eyes to the sober fact that there are so many people out there who spend every penny they make for survival. To our surprise, the vast majority of people in China basically have no other income, no income from their property, for instance, than from their job. Without employment, they will have no income, and might go hungry. Of course, these people also include the urban cohort who live paycheck to paycheck, and the working-class people. In the face of this cold fact, it is imperative to launch large public construction projects to mitigate people's financial burden, a roundabout way to provide relief for people when we make our investment strategies.

Focus on Public Construction Projects

Before discussing this question, it will be refreshing to review what President Xi said a few years ago about excess capacity, land governance, and basic urban infrastructure. The gist of his talks is that if we are committed, as many European countries have done, to redesigning and planning our land, and if we are determined to upgrade our urban infrastructure, there will be still decades for us to make such investment. Land redesigning and planning, or urban infrastructure upgrading, need a huge amount of steel and cement, the so-called overcapacity materials. If we are engaged in launching the full-scale projects in land planning, and urban infrastructure upgrading, China will not have the pain of excess capacity. Our problem is the incompatibility of investment and the financing system. It is our narrow logic of fund-raising, transference, allocation and operation, which blocks the objective formation of a healthy relation between supply and demand in the real economy, making them difficult to match in reality, resulting in massive overcapacity. In addition, the logic hinders us from doing anything meaningful in regard to our huge urban infrastructure and land development. The problem remains with us for a long time. After decades of intense industrialization, it is high time now for us to seriously solve the problems in investment and financial systems, while we are committed in the process of the large-scale urban–rural integration.

Under the general direction of public construction projects, four areas deserve special attention. First, infrastructure, especially the "new infrastructure," should become the focus of investment. This is about China's future development, and about the scientific and technological proportion of China's development. We must not relax at all in this regard. Second, vigorously carry out land improvement, and urban-rural infrastructure construction under the strategy of urban-rural integration and rural revitalization. The core here is to change the traditional concept of urbanization, take urban-rural integration as the development goal, establish a unified land market in urban and rural areas, and promote the equalization of urban and rural public services. Third, in cities, especially the megacities, we should take public health and disease prevention as a breakthrough to comprehensively improve urban infrastructure. This pandemic has opened our eyes to the truth that there are countless deficiencies and loopholes in our urban development. Singapore has a population of less than 6 million, but has set up 889 fever clinics. This helped Singapore respond to the pandemic effectively and calmly. In contrast, Shanghai, with a population of more than 20 million, had only 117 fever clinics before the pandemic. After the outbreak of the COVID-19 virus, 182 temporary fever clinics were urgently set up in communities, only one-third as many as in Singapore. Beijing, also with a population of more than 20 million, has fewer fever clinics than Shanghai. It must be noted that megacities, with a population of over ten million, and the density above a certain threshold, may naturally have many public health and public safety problems that we do not understand. The outbreak of the COVID-19 virus is one of the hidden risks. In order to deal with these completely unfamiliar modern risks, we must comprehensively improve the quantity and quality of urban infrastructure in accordance with the requirements of modern urban development. Fourth, we must comprehensively raise the level of urban and rural education. According to the "World Development Report 2019: The Changing Nature of Work" by the World Bank,[3] technological advances constantly reshape work, and introduce new ways of production, hence the change of firms and employment. The change makes it necessary for workers to normally do odd jobs. The report strongly suggests that in order to keep up with this change, countries should ramp up their economic resources to reform the existing education system, and establish lifelong learning mechanisms. The report also urges developing countries to invest in their people with a strong sense of urgency, especially in such cornerstones of human capital as health and education. To be honest, China has just started investing in these two fields.[4]

Fiscal and Monetary Policies

Only by adopting more active fiscal and monetary policies, and making the two policy systems more coordinated can we effectively deal with the spread of the COVID-19 virus and its adverse impact on the national economy.

First Things First: Proper Fiscal Policy

There is no doubt that fiscal policy should play a greater and leading role in battling the pandemic. The Political Bureau of the CPC Central Committee on April 17, 2020 made some basic arrangements for the fiscal policy in the coming period, and urged the Department of Treasury to adopt a proactive fiscal policy, increase the deficit ratio, issue special anti-pandemic treasury bonds, increase special bonds of local governments, improve the efficiency of the use of funds, and truly play a key role in stabilizing the economy. It is noted that the government's fiscal revenue has decreased relatively, when social and economic development most needs the government to increase expenditure. The national financial statistics of 2019 showed that as many as 28 provinces, autonomous regions, and municipalities directly under the Central Government, saw lower revenue. At the time of writing, the figures for February of 2020 have just been released: among the 28 provinces, autonomous regions, and municipalities directly under the Central Government, only Zhejiang and Yunnan provinces reported positive growth, and all the others reported

Getting Prepared for a New Type of Long-Term Recession   51

negative growth. In the long run, we have to face another problem, that is, the widening gap between revenue and expenditure in the future.

The solution to narrow or eliminate the long-term gap between revenue and expenditure is also very clear, that is, issuing bonds on an increasingly large scale. The meeting of the Political Bureau of the CPC Central Committee on April 17 listed three categories of bond: deficit debt, anti-pandemic debt, and local debt. This poses a serious and unprecedented problem of how to manage the debt from the Central to local governments. As a researcher on finance, the author has never opposed government borrowing. Moreover, for a long time, the author's views were in the minority in China. Today, the development of practice makes the conclusion fall from the sky. As a researcher, the author's interest has turned to the problem of debt management. It should be noted that there is still a lot of basic work to be done in China. For example, the problem of local government borrowing needs to be solved systematically. By the Constitution and relevant laws, China's local governments cannot have a deficit budget. Even if they can, they cannot bear the debt expansion through increasing spending at such a scale and speed as is currently required. Besides, some local governments' financial management ability is even more worrying. It should be noted that the government, as the main body of financing, has a variety of financing techniques. Needless to say, there is a lot of room for deficit financing, just as there is much room for non-deficit financing. Most of the current special debts of local governments in China belong to the latter. Generally speaking, deficit financing is used to make up for the government's public consumption expenditure, while non-deficit financing is widely used for various public investment projects, which may generate cash flow, and accumulate assets. However, since it is public facility investment, its commercial sustainability is far from ideal. Therefore, the management of such government financing activities poses a severe challenge to China's fiscal policy and even the overall macro-control policy. It should be noted that it is the current policy that empowers the government both to borrow by issuing bonds and to invest in public projects, but the financial activity must follow the market principle in essence against the background of a socialist market economy. The author believes that because of this, all the investment and financing activities around these projects can be classified as policy financing. This means that in the process of anti-pandemic, with the government's investment and financing activities playing an increasingly important role, and with the rapid expansion of government debt into the largest security in the financial market, the coordination of fiscal policy and monetary policy has undoubtedly become a key link related to the construction of the macro-control mechanism and the efficiency of macro-control.

Monetary Policy: Creating a Favorable Monetary and Financial Environment

Of course, the role of finance is indispensable, and there are many things that can be done. To sum up, as far as the total amount is concerned, the author wants to see that the interest rate level is reduced relatively and quickly.

52   *Li Yang*

In this process, we should reduce the types of interest rates and strengthen the "one price" mechanism. In terms of quantity, of course, the supply of liquidity and credit should be increased. At the same time, the long-term split of "price" and "quantity" in China's financial system also needs to be fixed. In short, there is absolutely no need for us to deliberately maintain a different status in the context of low global interest rates and all kinds of quantitative easing. This is neither necessary nor, in fact, possible. Struggling to maintain the status cannot achieve the overall effect.

It should be clearly recognized that the effectiveness of monetary policy has gradually weakened over the years. The testimony of Alan Greenspan, former Chairman of the US Federal Reserve, before the US House committee on Financial Services, was a landmark event that reflected his idea on monetary policy.[5] This famous testimony not only declares that the traditional monetary policy paradigm with "single rule" as the main content has passed, but also declares the beginning of a new era in which monetary policy is more concerned with regulating interest rates. Many scholars focus in their research on the change from direct regulation to indirect regulation, from quantity regulation to price regulation, and stress the change of its regulation mechanism. Although it is fine with what they are committed to doing, they have been distracted from the fact that the regulation efficiency of monetary policy is decreasing. The current monetary policy, in term of quantity or price, makes it very difficult to achieve an "accurate regulation" effect. The goal of a monetary policy is to create a suitable monetary and financial condition for the operation of the real economy macroscopically. In the past two months, the Federal Reserve issued many policies, kept the benchmark interest rate close to zero, and provided limitless credit. What was its purpose and function? The author believes that its main purpose was to announce to the whole society that in order to overcome the pandemic, and facilitate the structural adjustment of the real economy, the monetary authorities had provided a relaxed environment that would not cause any obstacles to the operation of the real economy. This highest priority of the policy was to create a healthy environment for economic growth. The macro-control philosophy behind the policy is worth our careful consideration.

In the structure of financial policy, the author emphasizes three points. First, while providing credit support to small and medium-sized enterprises, we should effectively increase the investment that might become equity. As discussed earlier, when survival is a huge challenge, the majority of small and medium-sized enterprises are unwilling to just accept loans. Therefore, we should seriously consider creating a mechanism to provide capital and raise equity capital for small and medium-sized enterprises through reform. In this regard, Germany, Japan, and the United States all offer experiences to learn from. Second, we should develop all kinds of policy-based financial business. Since the financial crisis in 2007 and 2008, policy-based financial business has regained the favor of monetary authorities of various countries, and even some policy-based financial institutions have reappeared on the economic stage. Therefore, it can be expected that policy-based finance will play a more important role, at least during the period of pandemic control and economic recovery. In fact, most of the social infrastructure investment discussed above can only be supported through the policy-based financing mechanisms. Third, we should transform the existing small and medium-sized financial institutions in cities below the third tier to become institutions that will meet the needs of local economic development, the needs of small, medium-sized, and micro-firms for investment and debt funds, and the needs of financial development. Of course, this transformation implies that in the future development of these institutions, their policy-based business will occupy a considerable proportion. In this regard, the Community Reinvestment Act of the United States is a useful framework. Other developed countries also have mature experience in encouraging financial institutions to meet the credit needs of small businesses in small cities.

Coordination Is the Most Important

After discussing the fiscal policy and monetary policy respectively, the problem of coordination and cooperation between the two policy systems is imminent. We note that, in recent years, there have been frequent discussions on this issue in China, but the overall trend is to separate the two systems. Moreover, due to the position of the researchers, comprehensive explorations of the relationship between the two from the perspective of system and mechanism are to be seen. The advent of the crisis alerts people to the urgency to ensure coordination and cooperation between fiscal policy and monetary policy. As we all know, social scientists pay special attention to the study of crisis. Unlike the natural sciences, social sciences cannot take controlled experiments as its main means of study. We social scientists focus on crises because it is only through crises that the deepest and essential factors and relevance of social and economic operation are revealed in the most extreme, tragic, and destructive way. Therefore, serious analysis of social crises has become an indispensable scientific effort. We can see that in the case of the United States, the research on the great crisis of the 1930s has formed a huge economic discipline, which is even regarded as the "Holy Grail" in economic research systems. It is precisely because of the continuous and in-depth study of the historical crises that the Fed and the US Treasury Department were able to take the comprehensive, rapid and decisive countermeasures in response to the 2007–2008 financial crisis, and the current health crisis. It is precisely due to the thorough research that the corresponding policies to deal with the crisis are more realistic and on target. By contrast, our research on previous economic fluctuations is so scarce that we often stumble twice against the same stone.

This chapter does not intend to discuss this grand topic in a more comprehensive and in-depth way. The author just wants to explain that crises often show us that finance and financing business are intrinsically linked. Generally speaking, it is the needs of the state finance (representing the will of the state)

54 *Li Yang*

that determines the trends inf financing business. In this sense, looking back at the "modern monetary theory" (MMT), which has been widely discussed in the international community in recent years, is by no means an assumption. It goes to the essence of the problem. In the crisis, people gradually realize its practical significance and theoretical value. Here, the author has no intention to make any conclusion on such a topic involving the most basic theory of finance, but hopes to point out that in order to effectively respond to the pandemic, we must carefully study the coordination and cooperation between the two major policy systems of fiscal planning and financing. Among them, the mechanism of debt monetization and the risk management in the whole process should be put on the agenda.

The Deepening Debt Crisis

Needless to say, the comprehensive result of various fiscal responses to the pandemic is to raise the world's debt to a new level. High debt is a prominent phenomenon in global finance, and even global economy since the 21st century, a phenomenon that is related to the global response to the 2008 debt crisis. Some different characteristics emerged from the 2008 debt crisis, and the global response mechanism, the most important of which is the process of the crisis. On the one hand, there was no typical economic depression observed in the real economy. On the other hand, at the financial level, it was not accompanied by financial "downsizing" and "shrinking." On the contrary, the debt level was so substantially raised and financing continued to flourish so much that the whole world sank into the bubble of debt expansion. This is definitely a phenomenon worthy of serious analysis. We have also seen that since the 2008 financial crisis, with the joint global efforts, the downward trend of the global economy was slowed down with a mild volatility. This is the result of the increasingly proficient macro-control skills of various countries in recent decades, and the result of the joint measures taken by various countries to overcome difficulties after the crisis. However, it is also obvious that a range of regulations can only either eliminate or curb the crisis, but fail to eliminate the causes of the crisis. Gains are accompanied with losses. Although economic volatility is no longer seen as a sign of recession, it leaves huge debts to haunt us from time to time.

In this sense, it can be said that debt accumulation is the cost of rescuing the market. The 2008 financial crisis was obviously a debt crisis. The necessary condition for overcoming the crisis was debt reduction and leverage reduction. However, by the end of 2019, the total debt of the world had reached $355 trillion, that is $31,500 per capita in the whole world of 7 billion people. The brutal COVID-19 outbreak forced all countries to respond to the crisis as they did in 2008, fast and decisively. In just two months, excessive liquidity at interest rates close to zero flooded the market, causing a liquidity trap.

As so many countries rushed to supply excessive liquidity, unintended and far-reaching counterproductive consequences might be caused. I have three points to make here. First, the relationship between financing and the economy will be more and more alienated, and the effectiveness of monetary policy will be further reduced. Because a large amount of money does not pump into the real economy, but goes to the financial institutes in a manner of self-entertainment, monetary and financial policies can only be adopted to create a suitable macro environment for the operation of the real economy Second, the cycle of economic operation has increasingly become a pure financial cycle. As the full development of financial innovations makes such an impact on the real economy that the economic operation significantly keeps pace with the "prosperity-depression" cycle of finance. As a huge amount of money and credit is continuously injected into the financial system, the deviation of the financial system from the real economy worsens, making the financial distortion often occur before that of the real economy. This means that under the modern financial system, the crisis can occur directly through the path of asset price rather than from the traditional path of price and interest rates. Certainly, this poses a severe challenge to monetary policy, financial supervision, and even financial theory. Third, if the debt is a long-term phenomenon, then the negative interest rate may also be a long-term phenomenon. We might as well consider this question: in the case of long-term debt, what are the necessary conditions to make debt sustainable? Research shows that the necessary condition is to keep the debt interest-to-GDP ratio lower than the debt-to-GDP ratio. To achieve this goal, keeping negative interest rates is naturally necessary. In this analysis, we not only found an internal consistency between high debt and quantitative easing and negative interest rate in the field of monetary and fiscal policies, but also found a series of new problems that merit further explorations.

Guarding Against Financial "de-Sinicization"

In the course of the onslaught of the pandemic, we are worried to see the new trend of "de-Sinicization." If the process of "de-Sinicization" since the Sino-US trade friction in 2018 was carried out under the leadership of a major country, sometimes covertly, the outbreak of the COVID-19 virus gave rise to an overt, and coordinated effort to accelerate the process. "De-globalization" came along with the spread of the pandemic by way of stigmatizing and isolating China, which was "de-Sinicization" in public opinion. However, the lockdowns in many countries, regardless of their subjective intention, objectively cut off the supply chain, industrial chain, and worsened the process of de-Sinicization in the way of de-globalization. If such development continues, the world may return to the era of "fortress economics" after a country is closed for about three months. The international community has also strongly expressed its concern about de-globalization. In the latest issue of the *World Economic Outlook*, the International Monetary Fund calls what many countries were experiencing during the pandemic the "Great Lockdown."[6] Some scholars hope to dim the color of "conspiracy theory" as the term "Great Lockdown" implies. They prefer using "great closure" instead. Even so, the concept of lockdown

56 *Li Yang*

implies that even if policymakers did not have the motivation to lock the whole country down, the objective requirements and collective action of pandemic prevention resulted in the closure of national borders, and the disruption of industrial chains. The global economy might collapse, and some supply chains may never be repaired in the wake of the lockdown. Subsequently, a slow rate of growth in the world economy might be expected as the de-globalization process accelerates.

"De-Sinicization" in the Financial Field

It is noteworthy that while the clomping of "de-Sinicization" and de-globalization are palpable in the real economy, the monetary and financial field seems to be moving in the opposite direction, that is, the pace of new global monetary and financial integration (excluding China and CNY) seems to have never stopped, or even accelerated. There are two representative phenomena.

First, in the context of the raging COVID-19, the Federal Reserve established a temporary US dollar liquidity swap arrangement of $450 billion on March 19, 2020, with the nine central banks of Australia, Brazil, Korea, Mexico, Singapore, Sweden, Denmark, Norway, and New Zealand. The Federal Reserve, on March 31, less than two weeks later, announced the establishments of overseas central bank repurchase tools to further provide dollar liquidity to the world over the swap arrangement. It is safe to ascertain that a new international monetary and financial network with the US dollar as the core has taken shape. The network with the support by major world economies, and the exclusion of China and Chinese currency (CNY), further consolidated the US dollar, and augmented its international status as the dominant world reserve currency when the worry of the "US dollar shortage" worsened.

Historically, the currency swap agreement between central banks began in December 2007. At that time, the impact of the subprime mortgage crisis led to a rapid rise of the risk premium in the global financial market. In response to the impact of liquidity shock, the Federal Reserve reached currency swap agreements with the central banks of Australia, Brazil, Canada, Denmark, the United Kingdom, Japan, South Korea, Mexico, New Zealand, Norway, Singapore, Sweden, Switzerland, and the European Central Bank (14 members). It was agreed that, when necessary, the central banks could conduct spot exchange in their own local currencies, and agree to exchange back their own local currencies at a fixed exchange rate in the future. Obviously, the currency swap mechanism established by these central banks in March, 2020, was the continuation and extension of the 2007 swap arrangement under a similar condition and for the same purpose. However, the 2020 central bank currency swap arrangement further consolidated the position of the US dollar. An in-depth analysis clearly shows that the comprehensive result of the impact of the pandemic in the international financial field is a new period of "dollar shortage" in the world, which secures the position of the United States as the world's Savior.

There is no doubt that the United States is still the country that benefits from this global health crisis, at least financially.

Second, although the pandemic situation in most countries outside China showed an upward trend, and China took the lead in controlling the pandemic, the external value of the CNY decreased slightly. At the same time, the US dollar was relatively strong and stable. This shows that during the times of "risk off," the value of the safe haven currency is strengthened. As we know, the so-called safe haven currency refers to a currency whose external value will appreciate when investors' risk appetite decreases or the economic outlook is unclear. It is generally believed that low interest rates, high overseas net assets, and highly developed financial markets are the necessary conditions for a country's currency to become a safe haven currency. Judged by these three requirements, the US dollar is obviously the number one choice, followed by the Japanese yen, and the Swiss franc. Other currencies, including the euro, do not really qualify. Similarly, judged by the same requirements, the CNY falls short of performing the function of a safe haven currency.

The author believes that China, as the largest developing country in the world, and as the second largest economy, cannot afford to ignore the following fact: a new international monetary system is being formed, which excludes the CNY. The launch of the crypto-currency Libra by Facebook in 2019 clearly excluded the CNY, another evidence to exclude China.

In short, the pandemic has posed a series of severe challenges to us. How to respond to these challenges is our main task in the future. We should earnestly take as our guideline the spirit of the meeting of the Political Bureau of the CPC Central Committee on April 8, and April 17, 2020: In the face of the severe and complex international pandemic and economic situation, we should adhere to bottom line thinking, and become prepared in mind and work to deal with the external changes for a long time. We must push for domestic reform under the guidance of the spirit of the Third Plenary Session of the 18th CPC Central Committee by helping to implement the Belt and Road initiative, and building the community of shared human destiny. These should become our two major strategic systems to respond to the new challenges.

Notes

1 https://www.bbc.com/news/business-52236936.
2 https://www.federalreserve.gov/newsevents/pressreleases/monetary20200409a.htm.
3 https://www.worldbank.org/en/publication/wdr2019.
4 https://openknowledge.worldbank.org/handle/10986/30435.
5 https://fraser.stlouisfed.org/title/monetary-policy-oversight-671/federal-reserve-s-first-monetary-policy-report-1991-22328.
6 https://www.imf.org/en/Publications/WEO/Issues/2020/09/30/world-economic-outlook-october-2020.

5 The Logic and Warning of Providing Limitless Amount of Funds by the Federal Reserve[*]

Yu Yongding[**]

On March 23, 2020, the Federal Reserve announced that it would continue to purchase not only government bonds and mortgage-backed bonds without restrictions, but also high-risk corporate bonds. These excessive measures broke all the taboos. Metaphorically, the United States began to use "B-52 bombers to scatter money" after using "helicopters" to do it for ten years. The Fed is flooding the world with dollars. Whether the stock market crash triggered by the impact of the COVID-19 virus and the oil price plunging will develop into another global financial crisis remains to be seen. When the Fed starts printing money without limit, as the largest overseas creditor of US Treasury bonds, China must pay close attention to the evolution of the US financial storm, and figure out how to protect its own interests

A Review of the Evolution of American Subprime Mortgage Crisis

In order to better understand the US stock market crash and the Fed's policies, and to predict the future trend of US finance and economy, we need to review the evolution of the 2007–2008 US subprime mortgage crisis, and a series of policies adopted by the US government in response to the crisis.

The subprime mortgage crisis in the United States can be divided into six development stages. At the first stage, a large number of lower-quality subprime mortgages were given to borrowers who were poor, jobless, and short of assets. The sharp rise of mortgage delinquencies and foreclosure for various reasons started the second stage. At the third stage, the price of subprime mortgage-based assets (such as Mortgage-Backed Securities (MBS) and Collateralized Debt Obligations (CDO)) fell sharply due to the sharp rise in the default rate. At the same time, there was a shortage of liquidity in the money market, and the interest rate of short-term bonds such as asset-backed

---

[*] This chapter is based on the keynote speech by the author at the Tenth Session of "Pushan Forum" on April 7, 2020: "The US Stock Market Crash and the Rescue of the Federal Reserve: Reasons and Implications." The main content was posted in the WeChat Official Account of "China Finance 40" on April 9, 2020. Revised here.

[**] Yu Yongding, Research Fellow, and Member of the Chinese Academy of Social Sciences.

DOI: 10.4324/9781003433897-5

commercial paper (ABCP) rose sharply. During the fourth stage, financial institutions had to shrink their balance sheets to meet the requirements of the capital adequacy ratio, so a credit crunch appeared. During the fifth stage, financial institutions, especially some systemically important ones, went bankrupt, and the whole financial system fell into a serious crisis. The bankruptcy of Lehman Brothers was a landmark event of the outbreak of the subprime mortgage crisis in the United States. The US economic recession marked the sixth stage.

The third stage (money market liquidity shortage) and the fourth stage (credit crunch) of the subprime mortgage crisis shared many similarities with the current stock market crash in the United States. Comparing the similarities and differences between them is very helpful for us to understand the American stock market crash. Let's start with the discussion of the third stage: the stage of insufficient liquidity.

Why did the sharp drop in the prices of MBS and CDO assets during the subprime mortgage crisis cause insufficient liquidity? Because MBS, CDO and other assets are long-term ones, with 10-, 20- or 30-year terms. The purchase of these financial assets is a long-term investment. However, financial institutions that want to hold these long-term assets need to borrow money from the money market. For example, many financial institutions need to issue short-term financing tools such as ABCP for three months or a little longer. For instance, if a financial institution intends to buy $10 billion MBS, it needs to raise that amount of money from the money market for a period of three or six months. However, the term of MBS assets may be 10 years, 20 years or even longer. Therefore, the financial institution must continue raising funds from the money market, namely, borrowing new to repay the old, so as to hold MBS and CDO for a long time. It is through the strategy of short-term borrowing and long-term investment that the financial institutions make their gains (investment return minus financing cost). However, once the price of MBS and CDO bonds falls, the short-term lenders who provide funds for long-term investors in the money market, such as buyers of ABCP, are no longer willing to buy ABCP, because they are worried that long-term investors may default. As a result, the money market is suddenly short of liquidity.

If asset prices fall, money market investors are unwilling to buy ABCP and other short-term financing bonds. In that case, financial institutions holding long-term assets have to do everything possible to raise funds to solve the problem of insufficient liquidity. If they can't borrow enough, they have to sell their long-term assets. That is how the fourth stage (the credit crunch stage) begins.

If a financial institution wants to buy assets and make profits, it must rely on leverage, not just on capital. In other words, financial investors must borrow other people's money for long-term investment and increase profits by increasing assets. At this time, there will be the problem of leverage. The so-called leverage ratio commonly refers to the debt–equity ratio. In the period of rising asset prices, the leverage ratio of financial institutions is usually very high. In normal times, the leverage ratio is 10 times or 20 times, and it may be as high as 50 times or more when the asset prices rise. Before the subprime mortgage crisis broke out, the leverage ratio of major financial institutions in the United States was very high. Once the asset price decreases, the fair value is used for valuation according to the accounting principles, and the price of the balance sheet must be revalued. For example, the original book assets were $10 billion, but only $5 billion after revaluation, so the assets were reduced by half. Suppose a financial institution has 1,000 units of assets and 50 units of capital, the leverage ratio of this institution is 20 times. When asset prices fall, the numerator and denominator should be reduced by the same number when calculating the leverage ratio. This means that if 30 units are also deducted, the price of assets will be reduced from 1000 units to 970 units, and the capital will be changed from 50 units to 20 units, so the leverage ratio will become 48.5 times.

A high leverage ratio is extremely risky during a financial crisis, when financial institutions should reduce rather than increase the leverage ratio, otherwise no investors dare to hold the assets of these institutions. If no investor buys the short-term bonds issued by the financial institutions with high leverage ratio, the financial institutions must take measures to reduce the leverage ratio to a level acceptable to investors.

There are two ways to reduce the leverage ratio. One is to increase one's own capital. For example, a financial institution now has only 970 units of assets and 20 units of capital. If it increases 28.5 units of capital, the leverage ratio will fall back to 20. Another way to decrease the leverage ratio is to reduce the balance sheet by reducing assets. This approach is commonly used in reality. Suppose the asset price dips, leaving only 970 units. At this time, if 570 units more are reduced, the institution only has 400 units. The leverage ratio will return to 20 times. Therefore, reducing assets is the main way to keep the leverage ratio of financial institutions at a level that reassures public investors. Reducing assets means the reduction of liabilities. The money accumulated from selling assets is used to pay off debts, which means that assets and debts are reduced at the same time. In other words, a financial institution can stabilize its leverage by reducing assets and shrinking its balance sheet.

For a single financial institution, it is a reasonable decision to sell assets to repay debts and deleveraging. The error of the so-called synthetic reasoning will occur if all the financial institutions deleverage at the same time. The prices of assets will plunge, and the financial institutions are forced to sell off more to decrease the leverage ratio that becomes higher because of the lower price of assets. In this way, there is a vicious circle: the more asset prices fall, the more assets are sold, and the prices plunge further. My assets are the liabilities of others. For example, the bank's assets are loans to enterprises (liabilities of enterprises), and reducing assets means reducing loans to enterprises. Enterprises can't get loans (no liabilities). On the one hand, the financial crisis will lead to the collapse of financial institutions; on the other hand, it will also cause an economy crisis. Without bank loans, enterprises will find it difficult to maintain their production. Without production, enterprises will go bankrupt.

In short, the general process of the evolution of the subprime mortgage crisis is: (1) Subprime mortgage default; (2) The price of securitized assets (MBS, CDO) drops; (3) There is a liquidity shortage in the money market; (4) Banks, investment banks, hedge funds, and other financial institutions deleverage and shrink their balance sheets; (5) Due to the shortage of liquidity, credit crunch, and the disruption of the capital chain, financial institutions close down; (6) Lending activities stop, enterprises are unable to invest and produce, and economic growth slows down. At the same time, the sharp decline in asset prices affects the consumers, who will reduce their spending and investment. As a result, the economic growth rate will be negative, sending the economy into recession.

Stabilizing Finance and Stimulating Economy: Two Steps the Federal Reserve Took to Respond to the Subprime Mortgage Crisis

In order to deal with the subprime mortgage crisis, the Federal Reserve took measures in two steps: the first was to stabilize the financial systems; the second was to stimulate the economy. Similarly, severely challenged by the pandemic now, we should take two steps to restore the macro-economy. The first step is to stabilize the whole supply chain, and restore the production system; the second is to stimulate economic growth.

At that time, the Federal Reserve and the Treasury Department used three weapons to stabilize the financial system: the asset side, the liability side, and the capital.

The root cause of the subprime mortgage crisis was the decline of asset prices, such as the decline of MBS, CDO and others. At that time, the highest priority of the Fed was to prevent the further decline of the price of these assets. If investors refused to buy them, the government would buy. Therefore, an important portion of QE1 was to buy toxic assets. Similarly, the Hong Kong Monetary Authority entered the market to buy stocks when investors sold off in panic in 1998. The Hong Kong (China) government saved the stock market by buying stocks, which prevented the market from sliding further.

In short, the first step taken by the Federal Reserve in response to the financial crisis was to buy assets. Of course, it was also possible to take several measures at the same time, so it can also be said that buying assets was just one of the Fed's measures.

Another approach was to inject liquidity through open market operations. Short-term investors were unwilling to buy ABCP again, and refused to buy them again after maturity. Large institutions cannot hold long-term assets by integrating short-term funds. At this time, the Fed injected liquidity into the money market, making short-term investors willing to continue to buy short-term bonds such as ABCP. At the same time, it provided financial support for financial institutions that would sell short-term asset bonds such as ABCP, so that they were no longer forced to sell such assets at a low price

Capital replenishment is another way. For example, the UK nationalized Northern Rock when it faced bankruptcy. Or the government may inject capital into financial institutions by means of a debt-to-equity swap.

As shown in Figure 5.1, suppose that the assets are 5,000 units, the liabilities are 4,900 units and the capital is 100 units. Once the financial crisis occurs, without the help of the government, the reasonable response of financial

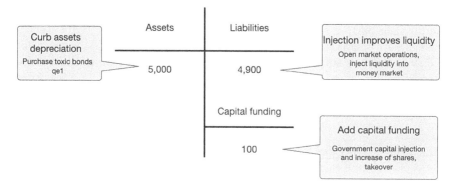

Figure 5.1 Three ways to rescue the market.

institutions will cause the numbers become smaller and smaller through the error of synthetic reasoning, leading to a vicious circle.

Stabilizing these figures means to stop the decline of asset prices on the asset side, and preventing financial institutions from being forced to reduce their liabilities on the liability side. In terms of capital, the government replenishes capital for financial institutions by increasing their stock shares, and others. The bailout of the Federal National Mortgage Association (Fannie Mae) and the Federal Home Loan Mortgage Corporation (Freddie Mac) in the United States, and the nationalization of Northern Rock Bank in the United Kingdom, are concrete examples of curbing the further deterioration of the financial crisis by way of providing capital.

After the occurrence of the subprime mortgage crisis, the Federal Reserve stabilized the whole financial system through the above three ways. When we analyze the US stock market crash and try to understand the US government's policies, we can learn how the US government stabilizes the financial market from the above three aspects.

The focus of the second stage of controlling the financial crisis was to stimulate the economy after stabilizing the financial market. The main policy of the United States was QE plus a reduction in the level of interest rates. There were four QE operations, namely the QE1, QE2, QE3, and QE4, with different objectives. Overall, the purpose of the Fed's QE was mainly to raise asset prices.

The Fed bought both toxic assets (mainly MBS) and a large number of long-term Treasury bonds. The former stabilized the prices of assets such as MBS, while the latter led to the rise of Treasury bond prices. The price hike of the Treasury bonds means the decrease of the yield of Treasury bonds. Usually, Treasury bonds are the safest asset. Once there is an external risk, investors will rush to the Treasury bond market, a scene the Federal Reserve does not want to see. The Federal Reserve slashes the interest rate of Treasury bonds in order to push investors and public investors to other asset markets. However, funds will not flow to the infamous MBS and CDO, but to the stock market. As a result, the rise of stock prices has a strong wealth effect: If the stocks people have increase in value, people's assets increase in value as well. The increases will boost consumption. In addition, the rise in stock prices makes it easier for enterprises to get loans.

QE led to a surge in stock prices, which stimulated consumption and investment through the wealth effect and Tobin's Q effect. The increase of effective demand quickly brought the United States out of the economic crisis, and maintained an economic growth for nearly 10 years. In this sense, QE played an effective role in promoting economic growth. QE has two other important purposes, one is to push inflation higher, and the other is to induce the depreciation of the US dollar. Both are conducive to boosting US economic growth and decreasing the debt burden. However, the objectives of the two policies were not ideally achieved.

As a form of unconventional monetary policy with which a central bank purchases longer-term securities from the open market, is QE a form of money printing? When the QE policy was launched more than a decade ago, academic circles in the United States and China debated: is QE a form of ordinary open market operation or money printing? Certainly, QE is different from the ordinary open market operation: first, the scale of QE was huge; second, QE not only purchased US Treasury bills, but also toxic assets such as MBS and CDO; third, QE not only purchased ordinary US Treasury bonds, but also long-term treasury ones. These operations were very unconventional.

There are three main arguments that QE was not a form of money printing. Whether or not it can be considered money printing depends on the purpose. If the purpose was deficit financing, it was money printing. On the other hand, if the purpose was to stimulate economic growth, it was not money printing. QE was a temporary policy. When the economy returns to normal growth, the Federal Reserve will withdraw from QE and sell the excess Treasury bonds. The toxic assets now can be sold when their prices rise, which can not only recover the extra money released, but also make profits for the Treasury. The main problem facing the United States is the economic recession, and there is no need to worry about inflation for the time being. In fact, the United States began to talk about withdrawing from QE in mid-2013, but how about the actual implementation?

As shown in Figure 5.2, the Fed's assets didn't increase after 2014. Before the outbreak of the current pandemic, the Federal Reserve had more than $800 billion worth of assets, which later rose to more than $4,000 billion. The Fed decreased its asset from 2016, and the decrease was more prominent in 2018. But now, because of the COVID-19 virus, and the stock market crash, the Fed's assets soar to $5 trillion. The withdrawal of QE is out of sight.

The author believes that QE is money printing. From the perspective of the United States, QE was reasonable, and there was no better choice at that time. But any policy has a price to pay, and QE is no exception. The Fed's QE and other policies, including the US fiscal policy, have had a substantial impact on the size and structure of the US capital market. After the subprime mortgage crisis, the changes of American capital market, especially the structural changes, are inseparable from today's stock market crash.

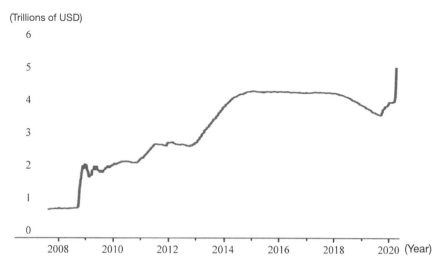

Figure 5.2 Federal reserve assets (2008–2020).

Can QE Cause the Stock Market Bubble? Can a New Round of Financial Crisis Be Avoided?

What changes have taken place in the asset structure of the United States? First, the total amount of various types of Treasury bonds is close to $20 trillion. Before the subprime mortgage crisis, the balance of US Treasury bonds was not high. Now it has become very high, more than 100% of GDP. This is the most important change in the US capital market. Second, the stock market has always occupied the most important position in the US capital market. Before the subprime mortgage crisis, the stock market became all the more important. By the end of 2019, the market value of the stock market was about $30 trillion, and its changes had a great impact on the US finance and economy. Third, the current corporate bonds are worth about $10 trillion, a significant increase over the past. Fourth, in the past, the importance of housing mortgage loans ranked second in the US capital market. At present, its importance has declined. This is the change in the US capital market after the Federal Reserve implemented a series of QE policies during the subprime mortgage crisis.

Therefore, the overall situation is: the more the national debt increases, the more important the stock market appears, the more significantly the long-term corporate bonds increase, and the less important the housing mortgage loans become

Before the stock market crash, most people thought that the surge in share prices was a result of the good performance of the US real economy, rather than being a sign of a stock market bubble. The stock market crash clearly proves that there was a super large bubble in the US stock market. What causes the bubble? There is no doubt that the bubble was the result of the QE. In other words, QE was intended to create a stock market bubble so as to stimulate economic growth.

What are the specific ways for the Fed to "push" funds into the stock market? There seem to be two main ways. First, because of the long-term low interest rate caused by QE, long-term investors such as insurance funds and pensions began to invest in the stock market. They are very concerned with the safety of their investment. The risk of national debt is low but the yield of national debt is way too low now. The financial institutions that manage the long-term investment funds need to ensure a certain rate of return, otherwise they can't explain to their clients. However, the risk of stocks is higher than that of government bonds, but its return might be very high. Moreover, the risk of stock market does not seem to be particularly high now, so the financial institutions take a stronger interest in the stock market. Their demand will push the stock market up.

Second, the repurchase of their own shares by large companies is another way to inject fund into the market. The rise of the US stock market is related to the buybacks of large companies. It is reported that the S&P 500 companies repurchased their shares worth $4.37 trillion during the period 2012–2015. The top 10 companies in the United States bought back a large number of shares. Buybacks push up the stock price, reduce the P/E ratio, and increase dividends, but the actual profit may not increase at all. There is research that the compound annual growth rate of US public companies' profit reached 11%, while the compound profit growth rate of the companies was only 8%. The 3% difference was because of the repurchase, which means that about 27% of the profits of the US public companies was made through buybacks. The specific percentage could be discussed, but the bubble in the stock market is indeed inextricably linked to the stock price caused by the repurchase.

In short, the hot US stock market was due to the extremely expansionary monetary policy adopted by the Federal Reserve (such as zero interest rate, QE, etc.); From the specific operational level, it was caused by long-term investors turning to the stock market, and the buybacks of the big companies. A serious problem will surely occur sooner or later, when stock prices are out of line with the growth of the real economy. The COVID-19 pandemic, and a free fall in oil prices, were just the straw that broke the camel's back.

In many investment banks' research reports, the reasons for the US stock market bubble, and the stock market crash were the natural consequences of its monetary policies, and the investment strategies of asset market participants and financial institutions. After the subprime mortgage crisis, the roles of some financial market participants have changed. The chief culprit of the subprime mortgage crisis was the investment bank. After the financial crisis, investment banks have become financial holding companies, and their business areas and investment methods have also changed. From the perspective of investment strategy, the subprime mortgage crisis was largely caused by the excessive securitization of subprime mortgages. In the US stock market crash, hedge funds and asset management institutions were the most active in the capital market. The risk parity strategy was the most discussed as an investment strategy for the cause of the current stock disaster, a strategy that determined the asset allocation according to the risk and return of different assets.

The fund managers have specific volatility targets. Once the targets are exceeded, they will automatically reduce their holdings.

At the early stage of the US stock market selloff, those funds that followed the risk parity strategy such as Bridgewater (the risk parity strategy was invented by Ray Dario, the founder of Bridgewater Associates LP many years ago) sold a large number of stocks and other assets. Some market participants accused the risk parity strategy fund of being the culprit of the stock market crash. Other market participants pointed out that the risk parity strategy was to reduce the impact of external shocks on asset prices, implying that those who took the risk parity strategy were actually the victims rather than the perpetrators. Victim or perpetrator, it is a matter of never-ending debate. However, the US stock market crash proved that, no matter what technical measures were taken, even if the asset category was very different and the correlation was very low, once such disasters as the COVID-19 pandemic, and the oil crisis struck, no strategy of risk diversification could prevail.

Some traders complained that the "Volcker Rule" prevented them from getting the necessary liquidity in times of crisis. After the subprime mortgage crisis, the purpose of the Volcker Rule was to prohibit banks from using their own accounts for short-term proprietary trading of securities, derivatives, and commodity futures, as well as options on any of these instruments. The Rule has improved the security of financial markets, but it restricts banks from providing liquidity to the financial institutions with insufficient liquidity. Therefore, when the stock market bubble pops frequently, the Volcker Rule really aggravates the liquidity shortage in the capital market, which is not conducive to the stabilization of the stock market. But is there a better choice?

The pandemic was the most fundamental and important factor for US stock market selloff since the mid-February 2020, although the free fall in oil price was really significant. All the major indexes on the US market plunged from their peak between February 12 and March 20. Over this period, the Dow Jones fell 35.1%, reminding us of the sharp decline in the prices of MBS, CDO and other financial assets during the subprime mortgage crisis.

Once there is a problem in the asset market, it will soon cause a shortage of liquidity, and the interest rate spread in the money market will begin to rise. The interest margin to measure the degree of liquidity shortage includes the difference between various short-term asset interest rates, and the overnight index swap interest rate (OIS), as well as the three-month AA financial CP–OIS interest margin. When the 2007–2008 subprime mortgage crisis broke out, the interest rate in the money market rose sharply. After the recent stock market crash, the interest rates of various hot assets and risk-free assets were suddenly raised. They are the signs of liquidity shortage. It can also be seen that although the interest rate spread between LIBOR and OIS has also increased significantly, it is still some distance from the increase in 2008, which may be related to various measures taken by the United States after the 2007–2008 financial crisis. After the outbreak of the stock market disaster, the decline in the gold price was also a manifestation of liquidity shortage. When people are in urgent need of dollars, they will choose to sell gold.

The Logic and Warning of Providing Limitless Amount of Funds   67

After the outbreak of the financial crisis, the rise of the US dollar index was also predictable. Since the 1980s, once the economic and financial crisis broke out in developed countries, their currencies, instead of depreciating as they did in developing countries, often appreciated. This is because when domestic problems arise, financial institutions and large companies begin to transfer back their overseas funds to alleviate domestic liquidity shortage, a way to solve the problem of capital shortage.

The US Treasury bonds are regarded as a safe haven. Generally, when something goes wrong with an asset, funds will flee the corresponding market and enter the Treasury bond market. As the demand for Treasury bonds increases, the price will rise and the yield will fall. But in this stock market crash, the price of US Treasury bonds fell instead of rising, and the yield rose instead of falling. What's going on? The rise in the yield of US Treasury bonds showed that there was an extreme shortage of cash in the money market, and even Treasury bonds were sold for cash. Therefore, compared with the subprime mortgage crisis in 2008, the liquidity shortage after the US stock market crash may be more serious.

Now people are talking about the stock market disaster, but the greater threat to financial stability may come from corporate bonds. Milton Friedman once said that no matter what happens to the stock market, as long as there is no major problem with monetary policy, nothing serious will happen. But in the case of corporate bonds, it might be a different story.

As mentioned earlier, due to the Fed's QE and zero interest rate policy, corporate bonds in the US capital market sharply increased in volume. Moreover, the proportion of high-yield bonds in the US bond market was very high. High-yield bonds generally refer to junk bonds with high risk. The proportion of energy sector in high-yield bonds is dangerously high. If Saudi Arabia and Russia have problems, energy prices will fall, and risks will rise. That is the time when high-yield bonds soar in price.

Taking the interest rate of US Treasury bonds as the benchmark, the interest rate spread of different grades of US corporate bonds has risen sharply. As a rule, when corporate bond spreads rise significantly, it is a sign that the market is not optimistic about US corporate bonds. Although the debt interest margin of American companies has not reached the level observed during the subprime mortgage crisis, it has obviously increased. Corporate bonds are different from the stock shares. There is a strong consistency in the stock market, whether bullish or bearish. Due to different length of maturities, and varieties, corporate bonds are less consistent in terms of price. This may be the reason why we must pay close attention to corporate bonds.

Due to the rapid increase in the leverage ratio, American corporate bonds had been under great pressure before the outbreak of COVID-19, which only made the situation worse. It all depends on how and how long the pandemic will develop. If the epidemic continues for a long time, a large number of highly leveraged companies will inevitably go bankrupt. The default of a large number of corporates will make the financial crisis difficult to avoid. In this case, the US, and even the world, will be caught in both financial and economic crises.

68 *Yu Yongding*

In the US stock market turmoil, the decline rate of risky assets was even higher than that during the subprime mortgage crisis, but nothing similar to the bankruptcy of Lehman Brothers and other big financial institutions during the subprime mortgage crisis had occurred to date. Therefore, according to the conventional definition, it cannot be said that there is currently a financial crisis in the United States.

The US Macroeconomic Responses to COVID-19 and their Impact on Global Finance

It is safe to ascertain that the measures taken by the Federal Reserve to deal with the stock turmoil are appropriate and timely. A good understanding of the anti-crisis measures taken by the US monetary authority since 2008 not only enables us to better understand all the measures taken by the Federal Reserve since March, 2020, but also helps us better assess the outcomes of these measures, and their possible impact on China.

After the stock market crash, the Fed mainly took the following measures. On March 15, the discount rate was reduced by 1.5 percentage points to 0.25%, and the statutory deposit reserve ratio was reduced to 0. On March 16, the Fed announced a reduction in the overnight interest rate to 0, and resumed quantitative easing (QE) of $700 billion. On March 17, the Fed established the commercial paper financing facility (CPFF) and primary dealer credit facility (PDCF) to support the flow of credit. On March 18, the Fed established the money market mutual fund liquidity facility (MMLF) to broaden its program to support the flow of credit to households and businesses. On March 19, the Fed announced that it would provide up to $60 billion of liquidity to the Reserve Bank of Australia, the Central Bank of Brazil, the Central Bank of Korea, the Central Bank of Mexico, the Monetary Authority of Singapore, and the Central Bank of Sweden, and $30 billion of liquidity to the Central Bank of Denmark, the Central Bank of Norway and the Reserve Bank of New Zealand. On March 20, the Federal Reserve Bank of New York announced a daily repurchase operation of $1 trillion for a week. On March 23, the Federal Reserve announced an unprecedented "no bottom line" rescue plan.

Specifically, the plan included the following measures: (1) The launch of Term Asset-backed Securities Loan Facility (TALF) was mainly to provide financing to the issuers of ABS, who would provide funds to private or small enterprises. This policy was used in 2008. (2) The launch of the Primary Market Corporate Credit Facility (PMCCF), the setting up of Special Purpose Vehicles (SPVs), and the purchasing of investment-grade corporate bonds with a term of less than 4 years from the primary market. (3) The launching of the Secondary Market Corporate Credit Facility (SMCCF), which set up SPVs and purchased investment grade corporate bonds with a remaining maturity of less than 5 years from the secondary market, as well as Exchange-Traded Fund (ETF) for investment grade corporate bonds.

In addition, the Trump administration launched a stimulus plan of providing $1.2 trillion in fiscal stimulus, which included providing $1,000 to each American, a total of $250 billion, $300 billion in small business loans, and a $200 billion stabilization fund and tax deferrals.

The experience of the 2027–2008 financial crisis enables us to understand that the Fed's rescue policy would focus on increasing liquidity, stabilizing asset prices, and injecting capital. In terms of the general direction, the current rescue protocol resembles the last one.

First, on the debtor side of financial institutions, the Federal Reserve injected a lot of liquidity to ease the liquidity shortage in the money market. The Fed had a great number of tools to deal with liquidity shortages. Some tools are original and others are newly created. These tools include: a Commercial Paper Fund Facility, a Term Auction Facility, a Discount Window, and an Asset-backed Commercial Paper Money Market Mutual Fund Liquidity Facility. All these policy instruments are there to solve the problem of insufficient liquidity during a crisis.

We already know that if the financing channels are blocked in the money market, financial institutions will have to further reduce the scale of assets, a move to result in the further decline in asset prices. In order to avoid this vicious cycle, a large amount of liquidity must be injected into the money market immediately.

Secondly, on the asset side the financial institutions side try to stabilize asset prices. This is done by buying long-term assets such as MBS and CDO. The Federal Reserve launched some new policy tools to help investors hold their long-term financial assets, such as corporate bonds, stocks and so on. The Federal Reserve said it was also entirely possible to buy a large number of corporate bonds when necessary. On March 18, Ben Shalom Bernanke and others published an article suggesting that the Federal Reserve could request Congress to authorize the purchase of a limited number of investment-grade corporate bonds.

Finally, in terms of shareholders' equity (capital), the nationalization of financial institutions is an important direction to maintain financial stability. Although there was no big move in this regard, Stephen Mnuchin said that the US government would take stakes in airline carriers in exchange for direct grants.

In addition to monetary policies, fiscal policies were also introduced one after another. Before taking office, Trump emphasized that the United States should upgrade its infrastructure. Taking advantage of the current situation, Trump proposed $2.5 trillion in stimulus package.

The above-mentioned measures worked to improve the financial situation, helped the US stock market rebound, kept the volatility index low, weakened the US dollar, and helped gold rise. These seemed to be the signs of the stabilization of the US financial market.

Unfortunately, the deterioration of the pandemic in the United States rendered everything unpredictable. The Federal Reserve established a repurchase agreement facility for foreign and international monetary authorities (the FIMA Repo Facility), which allows FIMA account holders, meaning central banks and other international monetary authorities with accounts at the Federal Reserve Bank of New York, to enter into repurchase agreements with the Federal Reserve. In these transactions, approved FIMA account holders temporarily exchange their US Treasury securities held with the Federal Reserve for US dollars (dollar liquidity).

Overall, it is difficult to judge whether the stock market crash in the United States will develop into a financial crisis, but there is no suspense that the US economy will fall into recession, and the possibility of entering depression is very large. In the future, the development direction of the US economy will be determined by the virus. All countries are now facing unprecedented challenges, and there are many uncertainties that need our attention, and demand our careful study.

The asset bubbles and liquidity shortage show that the recent stock market crash was not fundamentally different from the 2008 financial crisis. Therefore, reviewing the 2008 financial crisis not only helps us in our analysis of the present situation, but also enables us to predict the future. The US adopted similar policies to stabilize the financial market as it had done before, e.g., increasing liquidity, stabilizing asset prices, and replenishing capital. If there is any difference, it is in the details.

What the Fed did in response to the recent stock market crash repeated its measures to deal with the 2008 subprime mortgage crisis. All in all, the ready-made panacea remains the same: money printing. On March 23, the Federal Reserve announced a bottomless rescue plan, to desperately prevent asset prices from falling further. The plan broke all taboos. It is understandable that whenever the United States is confronted with serious problems, it will do anything to maintain the stability of financial markets. The Federal Reserve could save the US financial market, but not the US economy. It all depends on whether medical science can defeat the COVID-19 virus. The United States is flooding the world with dollars as it "throws cash by helicopters." The future policy direction of the United States is very clear: significantly increasing the government budget deficit and printing money without a bottom line. The US seems to tell the world: If I am saved, who cares about the deluge tomorrow? When the Fed starts printing money without a bottom line, as the largest overseas creditor of US Treasury bonds, China must pay close attention to the germination of the US financial storm, and figure out how to protect its own interests.

Focus on Economic Recovery, but no Rush to Dismantle the Financial Barrier

First, there is no doubt that the Fed's policy will have a strong spillover effect. The author's view on how the US economic depression will impact China's economy is consistent, that is, China should determine the pace and degree of opening up. A good grasp and control of the cross-border capital flow will not only benefit us, but also help us avoid disadvantages, hence eschewing many external impacts.

Second, the author still emphasizes the importance of the exchange rate. The exchange rate surely needs flexibility, because it is also an important tool to alleviate the external impact. At the same time, the capital market, especially the Treasury bond market, should be further opened, and the supply of derivative financial products should be further developed so as to provide Chinese enterprises with a variety of risk aversion tools, and to enable them to manage future risks. A certain degree of capital control, flexible exchange rate, and capital market reform will certainly guarantee us to avoid external financial impact while adhering to financial openness.

Third, although the US's limitless money printing has stabilized the US financial system in the short term, it has diluted the value of the dollar. The money printing may not cause inflation in the short term, but there is no guarantee for the long-term stability of the dollar. Besides, the US government is also wild about slamming financial sanctions. The practice of using the US dollar as a political tool has damaged its status as an international reserve currency. In view of this situation, China should seize the opportunity to promote the internationalization of the CNY, and promote the construction of an international settlement system so as to elude the hegemony of the US dollar.

Fourth, the possibility of the United States taking some action against China's US dollar assets cannot be ruled out due to its serious mistakes in handling the pandemic, and long-term geopolitical considerations. Even if we overlook the issue of resource allocation, we have to take caution that the security of US Treasury bills is not unproblematic. Who can guarantee that the United States will not default? In 1971, the Nixon administration unilaterally announced that it would stop the solemn commitment of converting $35 into an ounce of gold. Was this not a serious breach of contract? Lawrence Summers, a former US Treasury Secretary, coined the term "balance of financial terror" in 2002. Summers' argument goes like this: neither the United States nor China and the other East Asian countries which hold a huge amount of US dollar reserves, dare to attack each other, because the United States needs the latter's money and the latter needs the former's market, hence the balance of financial terror. But, the balance is never absolute and proportional. Just as Martin Wolf, a British economic and political commentator, wrote in *Financial Times*, on December 4, 2013,

> If open conflict arrived, the US could cut off the world's trade with China. It could also sequester a good part of China's liquid foreign assets. The economic consequences would be devastating for the world, but they would, almost certainly, be worse for China than for the US and its allies.[1]

In fact, shortly after the outbreak of the US subprime mortgage crisis in 2008, the "Fannie and Freddie" bonds were on the verge of default. If Henry M. Paulson, Jr., the then Treasury Secretary, had not pushed aside all opinions and insisted on rescue, China's $400 billion of "Fannie and Freddie" bonds would have been washed away. Were someone else as the then US Secretary of

Treasury, would the US government have rescued Fannie and Freddie Mac? No one knows.

Fifth, China should continue to strive to achieve a trade balance between China and the United States. There is no need for China to continue to maintain a trade surplus with the United States, and to continue to exchange real gold and silver for "IOUs of US dollars." To this end, we should implement the China–US trade agreement with the utmost sincerity (unless the United States is unable to supply and export). A large number of imports of US grain (genetically modified product issues should be solved by scientists), oil and other products are conducive not only to China's economic security, but also to China's financial security.

At present, China has entered the stage of full recovery of production from the stage of pandemic prevention and relief. Although we will still face a series of difficulties and challenges, as long as we act sensibly and composedly, China's economic growth prospects are still very bright.

Note

1 Wolf, Martin. "China Must Not Copy Kaiser's Errors." *Financial Times*, December 4, 2013. https://www.ft.com/content/672d7028-5b83-11e3-a2ba-00144feabdc0.

6 Globalization, the Pandemic, and International Economic Governance

Zhang Yunling[*]

The COVID-19 virus continues to transmit all over the world, and few countries could be spared from its wrath. Millions of people have been infected and the economic losses are too big to calculate. Faced with the worldwide rampage of COVID-19, people from various walks of life are looking for reasons. Besides tracing the source of the virus itself, people are also exploring its economic and social impacts. Interestingly, globalization has become the target of public criticism, because this system has the world connected, making it easier for the virus to transmit all over the world. The global supply chain collaterally formed by globalization has been damaged by the pandemic, resulting in supply chain disruptions, which have worsened global economic decline. Some people, therefore, assert that the COVID-19 virus is the harbinger of the end of globalization. In other words, globalization is dead. This begs a number of questions: How do we understand globalization now? How can we enhance globalization after the pandemic? How can we promote international economic governance? These are the issues of paramount importance, worthy of in-depth analysis and research.

Great Development of Globalization after WWII

To judge how globalization will progress after the pandemic, we need to first understand what globalization is, how it has developed, and what role it has played. As far as economic globalization is concerned, it is a process of interactions, and the integration of the world market. The economic globalization after the Second World War has accelerated due to a mechanism set up through institutionalization, a mechanism that is mainly based on the original General Agreement on Tariffs and Trade (GATT), a mechanism that promotes market opening all over the world.

After the Second World War, there was an imminent need of a new world economic order, the most important of which was to build an open world market. This consensus was based on the lessons drawn from the economic crisis

---

[*] Member of the Chinese Academy of Social Sciences, Chair Professor of Shandong University, and Dean of the Institute of International Studies, Shandong University.

DOI: 10.4324/9781003433897-6

in the 1930s before the Second World War. The economic crisis in the 1930s forced many countries to adopt protection policies with the aim of benefiting oneself at the cost of others. As a result, economic exchanges were blocked, and the crisis deepened. After the Second World War, the United States and European countries created an international mechanism to promote free market by way of setting up the General Agreement on Tariffs and Trade (GATT). In order to open the European market, the United States actively promoted the market-opening negotiations under GATT. Later, more and more countries joined the organization, including Japan as a developed country, and a large number of developing countries. With the success of several rounds of negotiations, the world market became increasingly open. With the termination of the Cold War, GATT was upgraded to be the World Trade Organization (WTO), which China and a large number of countries joined successively, transforming it into an international trade governance mechanism. As a multilateral international organization, the WTO has played a central role in formulating rules guiding international trade, investment, and service, and settling trade disputes on the basis of law.

Of course, the developmental and opening policies by many countries have enhanced the opening of the world market, as those policies have been the fundamental condition for the development of international trade and international investment. The opening policies implemented by many countries, and international governance systems such as the WTO, which has almost all countries and regions as its members, laid the base for economic globalization. The progress in globalization has made it freer and more convenient for international trade, and the flow of services, funds, and personnel, accelerating the growth of the world economy.

From the perspective of economic development, under the condition of open markets, resources are better allocated and utilized. At the same time, since most countries have joined the global multilateral system, the market space is expanded, thus obtaining the scale effect of economic development. In this way, companies can engage in investment and other operations in a more open regional and global market, which helps many companies develop into multinational ones. Even small companies could participate in the international division of labor, thereby promoting the further development of the international division of labor. In particular, emerging developing countries gain access to the world market by joining the multilateral trading system, and solve the bottleneck of development – the shortage of capital, technology and management – by accepting industrial transfer and participating in international division of labor, so as to achieve rapid economic development.

Globalization has two sides. While promoting world development and benefiting many people, it also has a negative impact, which leads to the rise of the anti-globalization movement.

First, industrial transfer will lead to the "hollowing out," making some traditional industrial areas a declining "rust zone." Enterprises transfer a large number of manufacturing capacity to developing countries with lower production costs. As a result, production costs have been reduced and consumers can

Globalization, Pandemic, and International Economic Governance   75

buy cheaper goods. However, if there are no other emerging industries to make up in time after the transfer, the local economy will decline, and employment will be reduced. Take the United States as an example. Outsourcing much of the manufacturing capacity, some formerly prosperous areas in the United States have become bleak, and both blue-collar and white-collar workers are poorer. The United States is not unusual in this respect; many other developed countries are facing the same structural difficulties.

Second, in the open market space, the difference of competitiveness leads to the uneven benefits of growth. On the one hand, the unattractive countries are marginalized, resulting in a large outflow of capital and personnel. Therefore, despite the rapid growth of the world economy and the substantial increase in the total amount of wealth, a considerable number of countries and regions have been "marginalized" and excluded from the development process, making the gap between the rich and the poor in the world even larger. In the 1970s, the former German Chancellor Brandt raised this question in *The Limits of Growth*, a report he presided over, but the problem has not been well solved.

Third, there is a polarization in wealth accumulation. The open world market space provides expansion space for companies and individuals with capital, technology and management advantages. Therefore, the world's wealth is increasingly concentrated in a small number of companies and individuals. More and more companies are rich, and increasing numbers of individuals have a stunning amount of wealth. There is the problem of 1% and 99% of wealth distribution, meaning that the richest 1% has as much wealth as the rest of the world combined.[1]

Anti-globalization began modestly, with the participation of a small number of people, but gradually grew into a social movement. In some countries, this shows the trend of protectionism, populism and extremism. Anti-globalization politicians collect wider support. In the US general election, Trump's victory represented a change. Many of his supporters were the so-called blue-collar voters, living in the traditional manufacturing states. Most of the traditional industries in these states has been transferred, causing the dissatisfaction of blue-collar workers and the middle class. Therefore, they supported Trump, who held the banner of protectionism and populism. In fact, this development has been witnessed not only in the United States; anti-globalization in Europe has also been on the rise. Support rate for extreme right-wing political parties in France, Italy, and Austria has increased significantly.[2]

Reflections on Globalization

Opening up is an effective way for economic development, but there should also be effective social policies to solve the problems brought about by opening up. At a time when globalization was on the rise, everyone was keen on promoting opening up. Now, the so-called de-globalization is coming to the fore. This doesn't mean we should turn to protectionism, and develop behind closed doors, but rather that we should reflect honestly on the implications of the

76　*Zhang Yunling*

rapid development of globalization, and try to fix the problems, when we identify them.

This so-called reflection is not simply to say that globalization is bad, but to trace the root of the problem, and strike a balance between openness and protection. If there is an imbalance, there will be problems, and contradictions will accumulate. Certainly, opening up promotes competition, and competition improves efficiency and thereby industrial upgrading. However, from the perspective of the society as a whole, we should take balance into consideration, because some sectors cannot afford a full and complete opening up. A slow, but steady opening is suitable for them. Some start-up enterprises need more protection, and the traditional industries need assistance. Certain groups of people need help. The excessive concentration of wealth requires effective social policies, including tax adjustment policies. With regard to the whole world, the new development cooperation to support marginalized countries is needed.

Globalization has progressed so fast that it has reached a phase that needs both reflection and adjustment. As far as the world is concerned, the issue of development has always been a major one. The imbalance of development under open conditions endangers world development and security. The Doha Round, namely a round of multilateral trade negotiations known as the "development round," addressed the concerns of the developing countries for improving the economic development environment and the conditions in developing countries. For example, one of the most important requirements in improving development conditions for developing countries was to call for the developed countries to terminate their agricultural subsidies. High subsidies enabled developed countries to export cheap agricultural products, and it was cost-effective for developing countries to import agricultural products rather than growing them, causing the underdevelopment of agriculture in developing countries. However, the developed countries refused to remove their agricultural subsidies because the protection of agriculture was their core interest. In addition, during the negotiations, the developing countries also called for the gradual opening up of their markets, and refused to adopt zero tariffs overnight. Otherwise, the impact on domestic industries would have been so hard that national industries would never develop. Meanwhile, the developed countries called for the developing countries to completely open their markets. The difference was so big that the Doha Round ended without resolutions.

Before President Trump took office, the US policy was basically dominated by the liberal creed in the sense that the US wanted to accelerate and deepen market opening to gain competitive advantage, eliminate differential treatment for developing economies, and reduce their low-cost competitiveness. For example, the United States complained that multilateral negotiations were too slow, so it formed its own circle of friends to engage in the general agreement on trade led by the United States, which later became the Trans-Pacific Partnership Relationship Agreement (TPP). President Trump opposed the creed of liberalism and was very dissatisfied with the terms of the TPP. After taking office, Trump terminated the TPP, renegotiated the North American Free Trade Agreement (NAFTA), and other bilateral trade agreements. Through bilateral negotiations, the Trump administration forced the partners to concede, and implement reciprocal arrangements. We know that countries have different levels of economic development, and the standards or tolerance of openness cannot be the same. The market opening under the free trade agreement should be gradual and differentiated in order to enhance trade cooperation. Only in this way can developing countries have the space to continuously improve the conditions and environment for development, and only in this way can all countries benefit in a balanced way in the process of globalization. Balanced development is key to the development of sustainable globalization.

In realizing economic development, market opening is one of the factors, but not all. Comprehensive development conditions need to be improved, such as infrastructure construction, capacity-building, capacity cooperation and other issues, which should be included in this new comprehensive arrangement for market opening. If only developing countries are required to open their markets without improving their comprehensive development environment, many of them will have difficulty to develop, and some may become more marginalized, resulting in no capital being willing to flow there. Therefore, there should be good basic development conditions for opening up. When China and the Association of South East Nations (ASEAN) negotiated to set the free trade zones, we noticed this problem and adopted a gradual and piecemeal approach to opening up. In the negotiations, we first discussed goods, then services, and, finally, investment. All parties agreed to set a longer transition period for less developed countries, and to establish special contents for economic cooperation.

The Regional Comprehensive Economic Partnership Agreement (RCEP),[3] negotiated by 16 East Asian countries, should work out a new comprehensive regional arrangement model suitable for the development of all the 16 countries, and conducive to creating a new driving force for the development of the East Asian economy. For example, all the parties should focus on the interconnection as the key content of cooperation under the framework of RCEP, and on drawing the implementing guidelines and detailed plans.[4]

The Trump administration pursued a protectionist strategy of benefiting the US at the cost of others, which absolutely created a lot of trouble for the development of globalization. The strategy can be viewed as a turning point that prompted all countries to reflect and adjust their policies on the openness-driven globalization. East Asia should uphold openness and promote cooperation through innovative models. China should become the backbone in maintaining the opening up of the world market, and should also play an important role in promoting cooperation.

To sum up, rapid economic development is a good thing; if it is too fast, however, it is not ideal. Similarly, foreign trade is nice, but an overdependence on exports is never good. We need stable and sustainable development and to build an internal sustainable driving force for development. From the

78   *Zhang Yunling*

perspective of world economic development, the emerging economies are committed to their catch-up model by pursuing a fast economic growth rate, but rapid growth often causes all kinds of problems. In addition to causing the development of gaps between regions, and between sectors, another biggest problem is to "swallow" the pollution transfer caused by industrial transfer. In fact, the environmental problems are gradually emerging. A country must achieve a comprehensive balance in its development. In the past, the developed countries followed the pattern of development with pollution. Environment protection can involve considerable expenditure. Now the whole world is competing for economic growth, and aiming to produce more. If we repeat the pattern of the development countries as they had developed their economies, an environmental disaster will surely result.[5] The increase in the overall amount of human activities has led to the overall imbalance and an increased frequency of extreme weather. Only a comprehensive adjustment can make a change for the better. After the Second World War, through decades of development, the world has not only achieved unprecedented growth in total wealth, but also been caught up with many serious problems. Among them, the deterioration of the ecological environment and the related climate change are the most serious, endangering the earth's ecology and human survival. To solve these problems, we need not only to renew our conceptions, but also to take practical action immediately.

Impact of the Pandemic on Globalization

The outbreak of the COVID-19 virus threatens the whole world. The pandemic controlling and prevention measures have affected the world in an unusual and comprehensive way. The most important measures are isolation and lockdown. China imposed a lockdown on Wuhan, as it was the first city to report affected cases. Soon afterward, China implemented unprecedented strict isolation controls throughout the country, resulting in a precipitous decline in economic and social activities, and bringing almost all activities to a halt. As China is the supply chain center of East Asia and the world, China's supply disruption immediately led to the rupture of many regional and global supply chains. At the same time, in order to prevent the spread of the virus, many countries took significant measures to reduce or even block personnel and business exchanges with China. In this case, those enterprises that rely on the supply chain have to close their factories, and service industries such as tourism that rely on interpersonal communication were forced to close.

The spread of the virus in the world forced many countries to take various isolation and closure measures, a combined global effort in further cutting off contact with each other. Originally, after the curve flattened, China stepped up its resumption of work and production, hoping to swiftly recover the supply chain. However, the second wave of supply chain disruption caused by the deterioration of the pandemic in other countries also affected China in turn. In particular, the unsynchronized spread of the pandemic in countries around the world not only lengthens the time of supply chain disruption, but also forces more industries to stop production as the disruption impact spreads. Even financial markets are affected. At present, it is impossible to predict when the pandemic will end worldwide, and it is possible for another wave to come around. Therefore, even if the curve is flattened, many of the prevention and control measures should be retained. As a result, it is difficult for the world economy to recover in the short term. Pessimistic forecasts believe that the world will fall into a serious economic crisis.

It is no small shock that the pandemic could have such an impact and destruction that the interdependent world has become so fragile and globalization is so vulnerable. In this case, people who had been critical of globalization seemed to have found a valid reason. Not surprisingly, the voices of anti-globalization are becoming louder, a phenomenon that prompted the government, enterprises, and individuals to further think about globalization. Generally speaking, the reflection on globalization focuses on how to guarantee the security of countries, enterprises and individuals.

As mentioned earlier, the adjustment of globalization accelerated after the 2008 financial crisis. The adjustment triggered by this pandemic is more profound and has transformative characteristics in some aspects. First of all, governments, enterprises and individuals place greater emphasis on economic and social security. At the policy level, the government will pay more attention to the ability to ensure the safe supply of basic necessities, reduce the external dependence on some imports, increase the support for industrial return, and take even legal and regulatory measures to limit the outflow of core industries, such as core science and technology, key industrial links of national economy and people's livelihood. At the same time, the inflow of foreign capital, especially for the purchase of domestic industries related to core competitiveness and public security, will be subject to greater scrutiny. For example, the United States and Japan have begun to formulate stricter laws and regulations on the examination and approval of foreign investment, restrict foreign investment from entering the core technology field, and strictly prevent foreign investment from purchasing domestic companies at low prices in times of domestic economic difficulties. It seems that "national conservatism" on the basis of economic security, social security and political security will have greater influence.[6]

At the level of business strategy, enterprises will pay more attention to the safety of the supply chain. Therefore, they may reduce the links of the supply chain, and strive to have the core links under control. In order to reduce operating costs, they may use robots and functional technologies on a large scale. At the same time, it is possible to modify the original "zero inventory" and "real-time supply chain" system (mainly parts), moderately increase inventory, establish a double-insurance supply system, and establish a standby supply chain partner mechanism.

At the social level, the pressure of citizens' demands on the government has increased, and the voices of restricting the inflow of foreign capital and immigrants, ensuring employment opportunities, and improving social security have

80 *Zhang Yunling*

become stronger. Social support for protectionism and populism will increase and form more influential political groups.

Thus, the creed of liberalism will come to an end, and globalization theory and public opinion will turn to the articulation of "managed globalization" or "limited globalization," or "balanced globalization," as it is sometimes called. Obviously, as the original concept of globalization cannot be reinstated, it has entered a new period of readjustment and reconstruction.[7]

However, we should realize that globalization has become an important part of the global economic and social operation system, and cannot be simply abandoned. As a process of development, globalization is adjustable, controllable, and changeable, but it cannot be abandoned. It is impossible for countries, enterprises, and social groups to retreat into "tribalism," closed off from each other. Certainly, a government can support its companies to shift their production back to their home countries, but it is impossible to force them to relocate. In reality, a large number of enterprises cannot shift their production back home, especially those relying on local markets and resources. Going back is a dead end. Larry Kudlow, Trump's economic adviser, once said publicly that it would be difficult for the government to bear all the moving costs when enterprises shifted their production back to the US. First, the government cannot afford the relocation costs, and second, even if it could, what about the operation cost? In fact, not many enterprises really responded to shifting their production back. Fundamentally speaking, whether or not to relocate is a question for enterprises to adjust their operations as needed. A government can supervise, and even intervene in, the international operation of enterprises, but it is impossible for the enterprises to completely "decouple" from China.

For enterprises, relying on the world market can obtain huge space for development. Large companies expand their operation network. Small and medium-sized businesses participate in the network. Shifting production capacity back home will lose expansion space, and nobody can ensure operational safety, because domestic problems will also occur. In the face of emergencies, it is difficult to ensure safety at home. For instance, the Nagoya Earthquake, and the Fukushima nuclear leak in Japan, also disrupted the supply chain. It is impossible to predict the occurrence of such emergencies as the COVID-19 pandemic. Therefore, there is no way to get prepared for the supply disruption because you cannot treat it as a new normal. It follows that the adjustment of any business operation should be the result of a series of factors, aiming for better development and profitability. The enterprises dependent on the local market may pay more attention to the overall condition of security for operations rather than move away.

From a social perspective, the people's increasing sense of security and safe livelihood will have a stronger influence on the political collaboration and government policies of those countries that have general elections. Populism in different forms will be on the rise as the impact caused by the pandemic is aggravated. However, populism does not seem to become the mainstream consciousness, because it will spawn more problems, exacerbating social contradictions. It is true that the pandemic occasioned people to reflect, but hardly in

Globalization, Pandemic, and International Economic Governance 81

extreme consciousness. In fact, more rational thinking seems to be the mainstream. People begin to think about modernization, modern life, the role of the government, the relation between individuals and the society, so on and so forth. Such reflections show a more rational understanding of the development of the future world, the development of the country, and the individuals. The COVID-19 pandemic awakens people to the realization that frequent disasters are the result of global system imbalance, and that we humans must strike a better balance. Otherwise, more disasters will occur.[8]

As is the case with the reflection and transformation of "post-liberalism," the reflection along with the discussion, debate, and adjustment on post-pandemic policies, business strategies and civic awareness will continue for a long time. Indeed, in the face of the global threat of COVID-19, sad, pessimistic and extreme emotions tend to prevail. After the virus subsides, people will gradually return to normal in the sense that balanced action, rationality, and wisdom will gradually become the mainstream. The historical experience proves that the lessons humans draw from every catastrophe help to make them more rational and intelligent. Disasters can become driving forces for progress rather than a regression. The COVID-19 pandemic is no exception.

It is worth noting that the impact on globalization is not only from the pandemic, but also from the political forces fueled by the pandemic. The United States, in particular, adopted a rather comprehensive containment strategy against China by blocking China's normal contacts and cooperation with the United States, and some other countries in science and technology, information and network, academic and cultural exchanges. As the United States is very advanced in these areas, other countries have to follow the United States in decoupling with China, because they cannot do without the US's technology, information and networking. Also, as the most important link of the international supply chain, China has close ties with the outside world. The political transformation of the United States has had a considerable impact on the development of globalization. In some aspects, the original supply chain based on the principle of universal openness will be broken.[9]

However, it should also be noted that in terms of the development of globalization, a new wave is developing. This wave can be called the network globalization, that is, with the development of information and intelligent technology as the driving force, the Internet of Things, a special network that integrates various economic and social activities, and changes the global supply chain from chain structure to network structure. It is worth noting that the network economy, such as online teaching and learning, video-conferencing, and online shipping has been rapidly developed during the pandemic. People's basic living needs are met in cyberspace during the pandemic. These cyber activities will not disappear after the COVID-19 virus. The network economy will experience a greater development, and become the powerhouse for the new economy. The prominent feature of network globalization is global in range. It is big data, big framework, supranational and regional construction and operation. The currency that facilitates network globalization – digital currency

82 *Zhang Yunling*

– has also appeared. This is not a retreat from globalization, but a new development and transformation of globalization.

International Economic Governance under Adjustment

After the Second World War, tremendous progress has been made in international governance, especially in international political security, and international economy. The goal of international governance was to create an orderly environment for the international community and solve problems that cannot be solved by a single country through the establishment of organizations, the formulation of statutes and cooperation. International governance has become an indispensable and important mechanism in the world. Although the state is still the foundation of governance, international governance plays an increasingly important role in involving national interests and the common interests of mankind.

The United Nations is the most important component of international governance. The objective of the United Nations is to formulate the basic rules of inter-state relations, and, simultaneously, to build a globally-based international management mechanism by integrating all countries into an international system. The international organizations under the framework of the United Nations are the basic components of international governance. Those involved in the field of world economy are mainly the International Monetary Fund (IMF), the World Trade Organization (WTO), the World Bank, regional development banks, etc., as well as international organizations that are involved in specific fields, such as the United Nations Industrial Development Organization (UNIDO), the Food and Agriculture Organization (FAO) and the United Nations Development Programme (UNDP). All the organizations undertake different functions. So far, the majority of nations in the world have been incorporated into these organizational frameworks, and their rules have become widely recognized as international rules and codes of conduct

The international dialogue and cooperation mechanism is an important form of international governance. More importantly, the group of seven (G7), as a dialogue mechanism for the developed countries, focuses mainly on the economic field. First, the G7 aims to coordinate economic policies among developed countries. Second, it plays a guiding role in the development of the world economy. However, with the great changes in the global economic structure, the proportion of developed countries in the world economy has decreased. When the main driving force of world economic growth comes from developing countries, the role of G7 in guiding world economic development has weakened. After 2008, the group of twenty (G20) has developed as an intergovernmental forum composed of both developed countries and developing countries with large economies. It was originally founded to deal with the financial crisis. It has become a consultation mechanism for discussing major issues of world economic development. International governance is constantly developing both in terms of the scope of governance and in the way of governance. This general trend is compatible with the international development of international politics, international relations, international economy and social life. No country is in an independent isolation space. It can be said that on the basis of continuous development of international governance, the world has built an international order of somewhat effective governance.[10]

However, these international governance organizations and mechanisms established after the Second World War were initially led and constructed by the US and other developed countries. Therefore, they play a leading role in both organizational compositio, and management. With the improvement of the comprehensive strength and participation of developing countries, there is a strong voice for reforming the governance structure of international organizations so as to better reflect the interests and demands of developing countries. It must be admitted that some adjustments have been made, though far from meeting the needs of reform. In promoting the construction of the post-war international governance system, the United States, as the most powerful country, once played a key role in providing ideas, plans, talents, and funds. Of course, the United States has also benefited the most. As a hegemonic country, it has maximized its interests owing to its dominance in almost all international governance. Nowadays, faced with the development of globalization, the transformation of power pattern, and many domestic problems, the United States seems no longer willing to assume the obligations and responsibilities of international governance. The United States either "withdrawal from the organizations" or strongly imposes self-interest policies. The United States has a sort of metamorphosis, a sign of an inevitable end of its hegemonic power. Strengthening international governance is a general trend, and the international governance system should also develop to respond to the future adjustments and changes. Perhaps the international community no longer needs a powerful country to set the agenda. According to the development of the times, it is not only necessary but also feasible to reach group consensus through consultation and dialogue, and promote the construction of an effective, fair, and inclusive new system. The adjustment and reform of international governance doesn't call for a breaking-and-remaking strategy, but an improvement of the current system.[11]

In the transformation of world economic development, especially when the pandemic led to the disruption of supply chains, and the sharp decline of economic growth, the world should strengthen international economic cooperation and enhance international economic governance, so as to stabilize the market and boost the confidence of the financial market participants, and the public. However, unilateral actions such as the "withdrawals from international organizations," and imposing sanctions based on the strategy of "America First" made international coordination and cooperation extremely difficult. Now the world urgently needs to reach consensus on the many challenges it faces through consultation, give full play to the function of international organizations, and promote peace and development. At present, there are many platforms for dialogue and cooperation. Leaders of all countries meet many times a year to discuss key regional and global issues. The pandemic will surely be gone, and the world needs to rely on openness and

84 *Zhang Yunling*

cooperation to support economic growth. Taken as a whole, development is still the top priority. More problems will arise, if there is no development. If the economy continues to decline rapidly, and trade slides significantly, everyone will suffer. If that is the case, even the United States cannot be spared.

Globalization and China

China's reform and opening up has opened the door to the country's participation in globalization, and enhanced China's rapid economic development. Therefore, China, as a beneficiary of globalization, is naturally an active promoter and defender of globalization. China's participation in globalization can be roughly divided into two stages. The first stage was mainly participation. By participating in the international division of production and using foreign capital to develop an export-processing industry, China has achieved rapid economic development, become the world's largest trade exporter, and the central link of the world supply chain. Now China has entered the second stage, as it is transforming from an economy based on export into an economy of import and outward expansion, striking a balance between export and import. In the future, China will become the largest global investor and importer. This transformation means that China will participate in reforming international governance rules, not merely accepting the current ones.[12]

However, as a developing country, China obviously cannot assume the leadership role. Whether in terms of its own development needs or its responsibility to promote the sustainable development of the world economy, China can play an important role in promoting the opening of the world market and safeguarding the general trend of globalization. With the rise of protectionism, China should continue to promote the opening of the world market. First of all, China should not engage in trade protectionism, and refuse to participate in a trade war. At the same time, at the multilateral level, China should make full use of its international influence to promote the formation of a consensus on positive reform in the world.

It is impossible for China to avoid the political confrontation with the United States, but China should not and will not launch a comprehensive confrontation with the United States. First, taking the path of peaceful development is China's national policy, and China will not follow the old path of rivalry for hegemony by way of confrontation. Although China will take necessary measures in response to the political pressure of the United States, China will use a positive strategy to promote the improvement of the international environment, gather consensus on peaceful development, and promote openness and cooperation. The strategy is in the interests of China, and those of the vast majority of countries in the world. Second, China should promote the international agenda and action based on openness and cooperation. Previously, China has promoted the Belt and Road initiative construction, and the establishment of the Asian Infrastructure Investment Bank. These are meant to essentially promote new types of development and cooperation, and to improve the comprehensive economic development environment and conditions through joint efforts with the participating countries.[13]

China has surely benefited a lot from the economic globalization. It is not even an overstatement to say that China is the biggest beneficiary of globalization. The assessment holds when we look at China's achievements after the implementation of reform and opening up. Therefore, although participation in globalization has also led to many problems, such as environmental problems, excessive dependence on external markets, regional development imbalance, etc., these problems cannot be solved by anti-globalization and need to be solved through active adjustment and reform.

China's strict and drastic responses to the COVID-19 virus led to the shutdown of many factories, and a precipitous decline in economic and social activities. As China was the regional, and even global, supply center, the shutdown shock was immediately transmitted to the outside world, resulting in the disruption of supply chain with China. No longer than the pandemic was under control, China immediately took measures to resume supply and production, and tried its best to restore the disrupted industrial chain. However, due to the spread of the virus in other regions, and to the measures taken by various countries, the economic and social activities slowed down and the external demand sharply decreased. Except for the PPE and other products for the virus prevention and control, the external orders for Chinese products were greatly reduced or even cancelled, which frustrated China's efforts to resume production and supply, a phenomenon that made Chinese people deeply realize that the reverse impact of globalization could be so serious, and the enterprises that relied on the supply chain to survive were very fragile.

With the serious spread of the pandemic, many people increasingly blamed China, and expressed serious doubts about China's role as the central link in the global supply chain. The public opinion was channeled to a biased criticism of China. It was fashionable in many countries to "blame China" for their own fault. Oftentimes, China was picked the scapegoat. Some politicians and political forces made up some loud slogans, not only blaming China for the spread of the virus, but also identifying China as the root cause of almost all problems. They called for separation from China, required enterprises to withdraw from China, and prevented China from investing in their own countries. Especially for a time in the United States, "decoupling" from China seemed to be the key solution to its own problems.

Since foreign capital, trade, and foreign investment occupy a very important position in China's economic and social development, we need to calmly analyze and make a correct judgment about the shift of some production capacity from China. As for the withdrawal of capital, due to the increase of operating costs in China, some foreign capital withdrew from China long before the outbreak of the virus. Indeed, many Chinese enterprises also transferred some of their production capacity elsewhere, a normal business action. East Asia is the center of the world supply chain. The supply chain in the region is a dynamic development structure. The development differences between different

86 *Zhang Yunling*

countries enable enterprises to adjust in the regional space. However, foreign capital will not be completely or mostly withdrawn from China. As the largest regional market, China is irreplaceable in many aspects.

In fact, the withdrawal and transfer of some foreign capital will force Chinese enterprises to upgrade. At the same time, the withdrawal objectively provides opportunities for the enterprises to expand their survival space. Chinese enterprises can fill up the market gaps by producing many intermediate parts after the transfer of foreign capital and production capacity. In addition, with the expansion of China's own demand market, many enterprises that mainly rely on foreign demand can begin to explore the domestic market. Of course, it should also be noted that the "supply disruption" and "decoupling" caused by the political pressure of the United States will inflict considerable impact on the relatively high tech field. China needs to find ways to get by.

Globalization is undergoing and will continue to undergo important changes. For this change, not only China, but all countries in the world need to respond to the changes. After the reform and opening up, China's participation in globalization resembles making a "sea voyage by another's boat." In the new development of globalization, China has built its own boat. In the development of network globalization, China is ahead in many fields. It should be said that China has more and better development opportunities than most other countries. In many aspects, China will become a navigator in the development of new globalization.

Notes

1 See Mike Collins. "Pros and Cons of Globalization." https://www.forbes.com/sites/mikecollins/2015/05/06/the-pros-and-cons-of-globalization/#6d9b3174ccce, and Murray Weidenbaum's. "Weighing the Pros and Cons of Globalization." https://www.wilsoncenter.org/event/weighing-the-pros-and-cons-globalization.
2 See Zhang Yunling's "We Should Listen to the Anti-globalization Voices." February 14, 2017. 2017. http://people.chinareform.org.cn/Z/zhangyunling/Article/201702/t20170214_261364.htm.
3 There are 15 member states as India was not ready to join. The RCEP was drafted in 2019.
4 See Hong Guoyan's "The Differences between RCEP, CPTPP, and USMCA." http://www.china-cer.com.cn/hongguanjingji/202001161927.html
5 After paying the price of environmental deterioration, China recognized the importance of green sustainable development, and put forward a corresponding strategy based on the scientific outlook on development and new development concepts.
6 This change may not only occur in developed countries. Developing countries are giving more consideration to the security of technological introduction. For developing countries, there has always been the problem of foreign capital monopolizing the market. Under the current situation, they will be more concerned with such security.
7 Huang Renwei discussed a concept of a "selective globalization." Countries differ from each other, and would only participate in areas that could benefit them the most as globalization progresses. See Huang Renwei. "From Globalization, and Anti-globalization to Selective Globalization." In *Where is Globalization Heading?* Eds. by Wang Huiyao and Miao Lu. Beijing: China Social Sciences Press, 2019. pp. 91–95.

Globalization, Pandemic, and International Economic Governance 87

8 Due to the increasingly serious ecological and environmental problems, people began to reflect on the paradigm of traditional industrialization since the middle and late 20th century, and presented their ideas at such conferences as the United Nations Conference on Human Environment, the United Nations Conference on Environment and Development, the 2020 World Summit on Sustainable Development, etc. For an overview of the speeches, see Pan Jiahua's. *China's Environmental Governance and Ecological Construction.* Beijing: China Social Sciences Press, 2015. pp. 39–41.

9 The Trump administration has not only increasingly strengthened various measures to block China, but also pressed its allies and relevant countries to do the same by expanding the so-called "entity list." The measures had a serious impact on the supply chain worldwide. See Peter E. Harrell's "US-China Economic Relations under the Trump Administration at the 2-Year Mark." *Joint US-Korean Academic Studies.* Vol. 30 (2019): 216–217.

10 Global governance is considered to be closely related to the development of globalization and is the inevitable result of the expansion of globalization, the spread of global problems and global in-depth cooperation. See Cai Tuo's. *An Introduction to Global Governance.* Beijing: Beijing UP, 2016. p. 1.

11 Pang Zhongying argues that globalization needs to be rebalanced, but how to adjust and change is uncertain. See Pang Zhongying's "How Will the Globalization Flag Be Wielded?" In *Where is Globalization Heading?* Eds. by Wang Huiyao and Miao Lu. Beijing: China Social Sciences Press, 2019. p. 100.

12 Some scholars have suggested that China can put forward non-Western global governance concepts based on its own practice, so as to provide China's contribution to improving and enriching global governance concepts. See Cai Tuo's *An Introduction to Global Governance.* Beijing: Beijing UP, 2016. p. 424.

13 See Zhang Yunling's. "The Belt and Road: A Strategy or an Initiative?" In *Chinese and World Scholars on the Belt and Road.* Eds. Xue Li, Beijing: China Social Sciences Press, 2017. p. 23.

7 Responding to the Severe Impact of the Pandemic, and Accelerating High-Level Opening Up

Chi Fulin[*]

The global pandemic had a terrible impact on global economic growth, damaged economic globalization, and delivered a hard blow to existing international economic and trade patterns. Facing this severe and complex international situation, China pushes for institutional opening up by focusing on setting up rules, and accelerates the establishment of a new high-level open economic system. These are a major choice for comprehensively deepening reform and opening up, a practical action to enhance economic globalization, and a major task to accelerate the modernization of the national governance system and capability.

Severe Challenges for Economic Globalization

The pandemic has not only seriously affected the trend of economic globalization, but will also affect the existing pattern of economic globalization. In this context, the characteristics of "challenging globalization" are becoming increasingly prominent. Moreover, the challenges are unprecedented. For example, the disruption of industrial chain and supply chain leads to some reflections on economic globalization. The call for de-globalization is louder, and economic globalization is facing the challenges of retrogression and structural reorganization.

Prominent Characteristics of "Challenging Globalization" under the Impact of the Pandemic

First, the spread of the COVID-19 virus has boosted the trend of anti-globalization and threatened the process of global free trade. In recent years, trade protectionism and unilateralism have risen and threatened the process of global free trade. In the specific context of the spread of the virus, isolationism, unilateralism, nationalism, and trade protectionism are more prevalent, which may reverse the process of economic globalization. Between January and April 2020, 310 new measures against free trade were added in the world, exceeding the entire total for 2018, and making up 80% of the 2019 number.[1]

---

[*] Director, and research fellow of China Institute of Reform and Development (Hainan).

DOI: 10.4324/9781003433897-7

Second, the spread of the COVID-19 virus has seriously impacted the global supply chain and industrial chain. At present, the international division of labor is marked with a phenomenon that production is broken into activities and tasks carried out in different countries, a large-scale extension of the division of labor in the global value chain. The participation of the global value chain has increased from 47.6% in the 1990s to 56.5% in 2018.[2] The spread of the virus has a systematic impact on the global supply chain and industrial chain, which may cause large-scale disruption of the global supply chain. On the one hand, when the United States and Germany, the two supply chain centers, were locked down, the upstream and high-tech industries of global supply chains, such as in aerospace, optical medical treatment, and information equipment, were seriously affected. On the other hand, the pandemic is likely to last for a long time, and its impact will gradually spread to the midstream and downstream of the supply chain, bringing severe challenges to global food security.

Finally, the spread of the virus has seriously hindered the process of bilateral and regional trade and investment liberalism and economic integration. On the whole, the pandemic has seriously impacted economic globalization, which, in turn, has seriously affected bilateral and multilateral free trade arrangements, and the process of regional economic integration. In this context, there may be new variables in content and schedule in completing the negotiation of China–EU Investment Agreement, launching the feasibility study of China–EU Free Trade Agreement, accelerating the negotiation process of China–Japan–ROK Free Trade Agreement, and jointly promoting the signing of the Regional Comprehensive Economic Partnership Agreement (RCEP).

Slow Global Economic Growth by the Pandemic Might Cause a Global Recession

First, the pandemic caused a global recession in 2020. On the one hand, the pandemic slammed international trade. According to the *WTO World Trade Statistics Review*, the global commodity trade will decline by between 13% and 32% in 2020.[3] On the other hand, the pandemic also hit global investment hard. According to the latest data of the United Nations Conference on Trade and Development, global transnational direct investment will contract by between 30% and 40% from 2020 to 2021.[4] The decline in trade and investment will directly lead to the global economic recession in 2020.

Second, the spread of the virus increases the possibility of a global economic crisis. Since the 2008 financial crisis, most countries in the world have generally adopted stimulating fiscal policy, and quantitative easing monetary policy to replace structural reform, which has led to the continuous rise of the global economic debt ratio. According to the data from the World Bank regarding settlements, the non-financial sector debt ratio of all reporting countries in the third quarter of 2019 has risen to 221.4%, that is, 36.7% points higher than that during the financial crisis in 2008.[5] Judging from the recent situation,

90   *Chi Fulin*

the pandemic has exerted serious impact on the confidence of the global capital market. In addition, the sharp decline in international oil prices dragged the global stock market almost to a crash. The worldwide economic recession in the short term has begun to become a reality. In order to effectively alleviate the impact of the pandemic on their own economies, governments and central banks have taken greater rescue and stimulus policies, further increasing global debt risk and world financial vulnerability. If the pandemic continues for a long time, if the fiscal responses by the major powers are ineffective, and if the global coordinated action is slow, the debt risk may have evolved into a global economic crisis. It should be said that this danger is increasing. In this regard, we need to make objective judgments and maintain high vigilance.

Third, the low-speed growth of the world economy will become a long-term trend in the post-pandemic era. On the one hand, the pandemic has seriously impacted a number of industries. On the other hand, the pandemic has seriously impeded the promotion of major international projects. More importantly, the pandemic has broken some global industrial chain and supply chains, which may lead to the long-term decline of global economic total-factor productivity.

The Pandemic Will Change the Existing Pattern of Economic Globalization and a New Paradigm is Forming

First, the pandemic has complicated the economic and trade relations of major countries. In recent years, against the background of the insufficient momentum of world economic growth and relative changes in economic strength, especially under the influence of the "America First" strategy pursued by the US government, many countries have adjusted their policies towards the United States. The relations between the United States and China, the United States and Europe, the United States and Japan, the United States and Russia and other major powers are undergoing major adjustments. Under the background of the spread of the virus, the economic and trade relations between major countries will become more complicated and strained.

Second, in the post-COVID-19 era, "zero tariff, zero barrier, and zero subsidy" may become the goals of economic and trade reform for developed economies, such as the United States, Europe, and Japan. At present, the United States, Europe, and Japan have carried out negotiations on zero-tariff trade, Europe and Japan have reached a consensus in that regard, zero-tariff negotiations between the United States and Europe, and between the United States and Japan are accelerating. For example, Japan has signed the Economic Partnership Agreement (EPA) with the European Union (EU), which would take effect on February 1, 2019. Japan will gradually implement zero tariffs on about 94% of products imported from the EU, and the EU will gradually implement zero tariffs on about 99% of products imported from Japan.[6] The member countries under the Comprehensive and Progressive Trans-Pacific Partnership Agreement (CPTPP) will also phase out 98% of tariffs on agricultural and industrial products.[7] Given the severe impact of the pandemic on the global production

Responding to the Severe Impact of the Pandemic   91

network, developed countries, such as those in Europe and the United States, are likely to accelerate this trend from the perspective of economic security. The developed countries will take the lead in the new round of forming global economic and trade rules to maintain their international competitiveness. Unfortunately, many developing countries will be excluded in the negotiations.

Third, the pandemic will help form a new paradigm of globalization. The pandemic will change the previous global industrial chain model based on low-cost and zero-inventory orientation, and the issues of supply chain security and controllability will become prominent. On the one hand, the macro-policy will place greater emphasis on inward and independent development, and the technical control of key technologies and core links will be further strengthened. On the other hand, the trend of localization, regionalization and decentralization of global supply chain will be more obvious.

Important Measures to Respond to the Serious Impact of the Pandemic on Economic Globalization

The spread of the COVID-19 virus has brought about more complicated changes in international economic and trade relations. First, the Sino-US economic and trade relations are challenged with the "second big test," and the result might further complicate the relations. Second, the pandemic has increased the variables and uncertainties of Sino-EU economic and trade relations. Third, the economic and trade relations between the United States and Europe are not optimistic. In this context, we should strive to promote the new process of economic globalization with practical measures.

Make New Breakthroughs in China–Japan–ROK Economic and Trade Cooperation

First, we should promote the formation of a new mechanism for division of labor and cooperation in the manufacturing industry between China, Japan, and South Korea. Taken as a whole, the three countries have strong industrial complementarity, and close division of labor and cooperation in the manufacturing industry. In the context of the serious impact of the global pandemic on the manufacturing supply chain, the three countries should focus on jointly maintaining the security and stability of the manufacturing supply chain, and promote the formation of a new mechanism of division of labor and cooperation in the manufacturing industry of the three countries. (1). A new mechanism of division of labor and cooperation should be formed in the pharmaceutical sector, the medical equipment industry, and other anti-pandemic materials directly related to the COVID-19 virus. The three countries should work together to ensure the supply of anti-pandemic products and materials, and jointly maintain the security and stability of the supply chain of regional medical products, and other anti-pandemic materials. (2). A new mechanism of the division of labor and cooperation should be formed in such fields as automobile, electronic communication, mechanical equipment, and industrial robots so as to raise the level of trade and investment liberalization and facilitation of the three countries, to maintain the security and stability of the manufacturing supply chains, and steer the three countries' manufacturing industries for the upstream of the global value chain. (3). A new mechanism of division of labor and cooperation should be formed in cross-border e-commerce, online retail and other fields. We should support enterprises of the three countries to jointly build cross-border online sales platforms, and cross-border online service platforms for manufacturing industry, strengthen the construction of network security supervision and coordination mechanism for supply and sales in the three countries, and promote the circulation and consumption of manufacturing products in each other's market. (4) The three countries should strengthen cooperation in the fields of cross-border transportation, logistics, customs clearance, inspection and quarantine, entry and exit of business personnel and technicians to ensure the smooth supply chain of manufacturing industry. We also need to dock standards and strengthen regulatory coordination, so as to improve the convenience of trade, and personnel exchange in the manufacturing industries.

Second, there is a need to establish a tripartite coordination, joint assessment, and early-warning mechanisms for the security and stability of the manufacturing supply chain. In response to the serious impact of the pandemic, China, Japan, and South Korea should aim at maintaining the security and stability of regional industrial supply chains, and strengthening the construction of tripartite industrial supply chain security information communication and coordination, joint assessment, risk early warning and other mechanisms (1). We should establish a tripartite information communication and coordination mechanism to guarantee the security of the manufacturing supply chain. The three countries' relevant government departments or industry associations should push for the establishment of a tripartite information communication, and a coordination mechanism to prevent the disruption of the manufacturing supply chain, promote the timely sharing of resumption information and data between upstream and downstream enterprises in the manufacturing supply chain of the three countries, and between relevant enterprises and government departments, and establish a coordination mechanism to support enterprises of the three countries to take reasonable pandemic prevention measures to speed up resumption of work and production. (2). It is necessary to establish a tripartite joint assessment mechanism, and a risk-warning mechanism for the security of the manufacturing supply chain. It is suggested that relevant government departments or relevant industry associations of the three countries take the lead to conduct regular joint assessments on the security and stability of the manufacturing supply chain, form a supply chain security report, send timely early warnings of supply chain disruption to the government and enterprises, and also put forward suggestions and reports to the government to prevent supply chain security crisis, so as to advise the government on assistance for small and medium-sized enterprises in the manufacturing supply chain of the three countries.

Responding to the Severe Impact of the Pandemic 93

(3). In line with the progress of the pandemic prevention and control, the three countries should adjust the flow of people, logistics, and other control measures to promote the smooth operation of the manufacturing supply chain. They should make full use of the existing public health and security cooperation mechanism, gradually and steadily make a smooth flow of information, logistics and people to enable economic and trade cooperation on the premise of joint anti-pandemic measures, and promote the liberalization and facilitation of investment and trade. The most important is to establish a coordination mechanism involving public health, commerce, industrial management departments, and customs of the three countries. We should ensure the smooth access of anti-pandemic medicine, and other anti-pandemic materials between the three countries. At the same time, we need to reduce or even lift the tariffs on anti-pandemic medical products, medical treatment equipment and related materials, and relax the border restrictions for the flow of these products. On the premise of having the pandemic under control, we should promote the interconnection of the pandemic prevention and control guidelines of the three countries. There is a need to cancel the temporary restrictions on the flow of people, and logistics. The three should jointly safeguard and promote the liberalization and facilitation of trade and services among the three countries. We should vigorously develop contactless transportation, storage and logistics distribution so as to promote the smooth operation of the manufacturing supply chain between the three countries.

(4). Responding to the new changes in economic globalization and practically promoting the process of the China–Japan–ROK Free Trade Agreement are the major strategic choices in the process of the regional economic integration in East Asia. First, the three countries should speed up negotiations in the fields of trade in services and investment, intellectual property rights, and sustainable development. At the same time, we must work together to promote the signing of the Regional Comprehensive Economic Partnership Agreement (RCEP), as scheduled in 2020. First, the three countries should establish the institutional mechanism for maintaining the safety and smoothness of the manufacturing supply chain by the power of trilateral and multilateral free trade agreements. Second, we should practically promote industrial cooperation between China, Japan, and South Korea in public health, medical treatment, health, elderly care, environmental protection, scientific and technological research and development. The three countries should vigorously develop digital trade, accelerate the implementation of the early harvest list of "China–Japan–ROK + X" early projects, and the projects listed in the "Trilateral Cooperation Vision for the Next Decade" released at the Eighth China–Japan–ROK Summit at the end of 2019. Third, the top priority for the three countries is to finalize the list of "early harvest" projects before reaching the comprehensive and high-level trade and investment agreement. The list should include the free trade policies in key modern service industries such as health care, culture and entertainment, digital economy, finance and insurance in the list of "early harvest" projects at the Hainan round of talks. Hainan, as a Free Trade Port, should help make a breakthrough in finalizing the list of "early harvest" projects

94 *Chi Fulin*

(5). We should quicken the process of economic and trade cooperation between Northeast Asia and the Northeast regional economic integration. As the forefront of China's opening to the north, the economic and trade ties between Northeast China and Northeast Asia are very close. Northeast China should make use of the closer geographical and economic and trade ties with Northeast Asia to connect the economic integration of Northeast Asia with the economic integration of the three Northeast provinces. First, we should accelerate the process of regional economic integration in Northeast China. For example, in the industrial field, we should promote the cross-regional optimization and reorganization of Northeast manufacturing industry, form the vertical division of labor among the three provinces, reconstruct the industrial chain by focusing on equipment manufacturing industry, and enhance the core competitiveness of Northeast manufacturing. In the field of agriculture, we should promote agricultural cross-regional cooperation, lengthen the agricultural industrial chain in Northeast China, and promote the integrated development of agriculture, industry, and service in Northeast China. At the same time, we should promote the formation of a new pattern of regional infrastructure integration. Second, we should make effort to integrate the supply chain and industrial chain between Northeast China and Northeast Asia. We should make use of the regional advantages and industrial conditions of the economic integration development of the three Northeastern provinces, strengthen the cooperation with the industrial chain and supply chain of the countries around Northeast Asia, and promote the transformation and upgrading of the industrial structure of Northeast China. Third, we should take various forms to promote the process of market opening in Northeast Asia. Based on the principle of "starting with the easier and gradually moving on to the more difficult," we need to adopt various forms of cooperation, including the "Early Harvest Plan," framework agreement, and multilateral investment agreement, to jointly discuss and build a flexible and diverse bilateral, multilateral and regional free trade zone.

With the Goal of China–EU Integrated Market, Form a New Pattern of China–EU Economic and Trade Cooperation

(1) We should firmly uphold multilateral principles as it is a strategic choice for China–EU economic and trade cooperation. The pandemic is profoundly changing the internal and external environment and conditions of China–EU economic and trade cooperation. If the pandemic causes the Euro zone debt crisis again, EU integration may fall into crisis. The pandemic has brought severe challenges to China's opening-up process and has an impact on China's economic transformation and reform process. Here, at this historic juncture, China and the EU should firmly uphold the principle of multilateralism, and cooperate to deal with the adverse tide of economic globalization exacerbated by the pandemic, which is a major strategic option for China–EU economic and trade cooperation.

Responding to the Severe Impact of the Pandemic 95

(2) Taking the integrated market as the goal is a pragmatic strategic choice between China and the EU. The EU as a whole has entered the post-industrialization period, and China is entering the late stage of industrialization. In 2018, the EU's per capita GDP was close to four times that of China. The proportion of EU's overall service industry (78.8%) is much higher than that of China's service industry (52.2%). The complementarity of the China–EU economic structure is far greater than competitiveness. The potential of trade and investment demand between China and the EU, especially the potential of service trade, is far from being explored. In the next 10–15 years, China's urbanization, industrial transformation and upgrading will generate a huge market space for China–EU economic and trade cooperation. Since 2010, China has been the fastest-growing market for EU service exports. With the rapid release in China's service consumption demand, promoting the formation of a new pattern of China–EU economic and trade cooperation with the goal of integrating a large market will greatly release the potential of China–EU trade and investment. This can not only stimulate the economic recovery of the EU, so as to provide assistance for the stable development of the EU, but also release China's huge consumption potential.

(3) Accelerating the negotiation process from investment agreement to free trade agreement is a strategic option for China and the EU to deepen economic and trade cooperation. The release of the market demand potential of China–EU integration depends on the institutional arrangement of free trade between the two sides. Frankly, the release of China–EU trade and investment potential is increasingly limited by the lack of institutional arrangements for free trade between the two sides. It is a realistic strategic option for China and the EU to promote the negotiation of China–EU investment agreement to China–EU free trade agreement so as to achieve the China–EU integration market. China and the EU should strive to complete the negotiation of investment agreement in 2020, and launch the joint feasibility study of the China–EU free trade zone. This will send a strong signal to the world that the world's two major economies will promote the process of free trade, and will inject new confidence and energy into a world economy seriously impacted by the pandemic.

Promoting the Process of Asia-Pacific Economic Integration Based on RCEP

(1) Promoting Asia-Pacific economic integration is highly significant for economic globalization. The proposed Asia-Pacific Free Trade Area is one of the most populous and promising regions in the world. If completed, it will become a multilateral free trade bloc with the widest coverage, the largest number of member states, the most inclusive, and the largest trade volume in the world. It will have an important impact on maintaining the multilateral trading system with the WTO as the core, promoting balanced global economic growth, and exploring the more inclusive economic and

trade rules that would benefit everyone. For example, if the Asia-Pacific Free Trade Area is established, it will bring $2 trillion in economic benefits to APEC members in 2025, more than any currently existing regional free trade arrangement.[8]

(2) We should promote the process of establishing the Asia-Pacific Free Trade Area on the basis of RCEP. Due to the large differences in the level of openness between developed and developing countries, the Asia-Pacific Free Trade Area should consider establishing a multi-level free trade agreement, with different levels corresponding to different opening standards, so that economies at different levels of development in the Asia-Pacific region can choose their own level to join. There should be a set transition period in order to speed up the negotiation process.

High standards: in addition to resolving the traditional issues in trade, services, investment, and intellectual property rights, we should make institutional arrangements to achieve roughly the same standards as the high-level free trade agreement in terms of emerging issues such as customs supervision, trade facilitation, government procurement, transparency, and anti-corruption.

Intermediate standard: we should further resolve the traditional issues in trade, services, and intellectual property protection, improve the coverage of zero-tariff goods in trade in goods, and focus on the connection of regional rules to improve the level of liberalization and facilitation of trade in services.

Basic standard: on the basis of the negotiation of the Regional Comprehensive Economic Partnership Agreement, we should implement the free trade policy on manufacture, service, energy, infrastructure, tourism, environmental protection, etc., and make a critical breakthrough of free trade and investment in key areas on the basis of not requiring comprehensive tariff reduction and comprehensive market opening.

(3) We should push for the integration of RCEP and CPTPP, because the Asia-Pacific economic integration is currently caught between the two. RCEP and CPTPP are similar in terms of participating members, member states preferences, and coverage. There is an obvious relationship of competition and coercion between the two.[9] It is suggested that there should be an active adoption of some of the CPTPP provisions in the fields of tariff reduction, service trade standards, government procurement, e-commerce, financial services, regulatory application, and dispute settlement mechanism, and also a striving to explore the possibilities of some changes in the terms of WTO +.

Establish a New High-Level Open Economic System

To seize the new opportunity presented in terms of restructuring the global economic and trade pattern, and adapting to the new trend of reforming global economic and trade rules, China should focus on institutional opening up, building a new high-level open economic system, and promoting the state-owned

Responding to the Severe Impact of the Pandemic   97

enterprise reform, and that we should then readjust our policies and regulations about intellectual property protection, industrial policies, government subsidies, and environmental protection standards. The changes should be made in accordance with the principles of open market and fair competition. Thus, such a structure can further integrate into the world economy, and make a louder voice. How shall we build a new high-level open economic system by prioritizing institutional opening up?

(1) We should promote the transformation from commodity and factor flow opening to institutional opening, and strive for the initiative to expand opening up. In accordance with the principles of open market and fair competition, we will promote the reform of state-owned enterprises, and try to adopt the world economic and trade rules on intellectual property protection, industrial policies, government subsidies and environmental protection standards, in order to further integrate our market economic system with the world.

(2) How to respond to the challenges of the "three-zero" international economic and trade rules. At present, the global trade in goods is moving towards the direction of zero tariffs, service trade has focused on readjusting global free trade rules, and the establishment of digital trade rules has become urgent. In order to adapt to this trend, as a new open country, China should take the initiative to grasp the new trend of changes in international economic and trade rules such as the "three zeros," i.e. adopting high-standard trade rules in terms of market access, technical standards and competition neutrality, and creating a business environment of fair competition with market-oriented reform, so as to make China's voice heard in the formulation of a new round of global trade rules.

(3) We should push for institutional opening up and deepen market-oriented reform. The important connotation of institutional opening is to use more market-oriented and legal means to promote opening up in the process of adopting rules, and participating in rule-making. Over the period of the 14th Five-Year Plan, China will vigorously quicken institutional opening up, and deepen market-oriented reform to raise the overall opening up to a higher level so as to provide a sustained driving force for expanding the huge domestic demand market.

Focusing on the Service Industry and Expanding the Market Opening

(1) We should fully open the service market to both domestic and foreign investment. On the one hand, we should push for the full opening of the service market to social capital. In accordance with the connotation that what is not legally prohibited is permitted, all service industries that are not explicitly prohibited by laws and regulations shall be open to social capital, and all the discriminatory obstacles to social capital should be removed. In addition, we should drastically reduce the pre-approval and qualification

98 *Chi Fulin*

recognition procedures. We need to follow the principle of "operation upon approval." On the other hand, we should accelerate the process of opening up the service industry to the outside world, and significantly reduce the restrictive items on the negative list of foreign capital access.

(2) We should expand the opening up of the financial industry to domestic and foreign investors. On the one hand, we should remove all the access obstacles to the market to increase the asset proportions of foreign-funded financial institutions in order to create a new pattern of market competition in China's financial industry. On the other hand, we should speed up the process of CNY internationalization and expand the scope of CNY settlement in cross-border trade, so as to adapt the process of CNY internationalization to China's status as a new open country.

(3) We should open the service market to stimulate service-oriented consumption. Great potential could be unleashed in the upgrading process of China's service-oriented consumption. From the perspective of reality, to break the shortage of service-oriented consumption supply, we should focus on accelerating the opening up process of the service industry market, and speeding up the relevant policy adjustment about the development of the service industry.

(4) We should increase the proportion of service trade. Trade in services has become an important driver of global trade. In 2018, China's service trade accounted for only 14.7% of its total trade volume, far below the global average of 23.1%.[10] China should therefore promote the development of service trade by fully opening the service market, optimizing the structure of service trade, and making the proportion of service trade in the 14th Five-Year plan reach the global average while improving the international competitiveness of service trade. The goal is to increase the proportion of service trade in total foreign trade to more than 20% by 2025.

Create a Convenient Business Environment

(1) We should strengthen the basic position of competition policy, and make a "high-level opening of the market, and efficient operation of the government" as an important goal of governance reform, and promote the reconstruction of the government responsibility system based on the principle of competition neutrality. We should establish an open economic system marked by openness and standardization, and adapt to the basic international economic and trade rules. In addition, we should strengthen the foundation of competition policy, improve the fair competition system, and enforce the supervision and review of fair competition policy by market regulators. In addition, as the rise of a new scientific and technological revolution led by digital technology gradually reduces the positive effects of some industrial policies and subsidies, we should comprehensively clean up industrial policies that hinder fair competition, and treat all kinds of

ownership enterprises equally in terms of factor acquisition, access permit, operation, and government procurement.

(2) We should comprehensively underpin intellectual property protection, and property protection. *The Decision of the CPC Central Committee on Some Major Issues of Comprehensively Promoting the Rule of Law*, adopted at the Fourth Plenary Session of the 18th CPC Central Committee, proposed to "strengthen the construction of market legal system, and compile the *Civil Code of the People's Republic of China*." By the spirit, we should establish a long-term mechanism for equal protection of property rights, entrepreneurs' property rights and innovation benefits according to the law. Specifically, we should soon promulgate laws on the promotion of private economy, and the protection of intellectual property. We need to make sure that our intellectual property law is in line with the international intellectual property treaties.

(3) We should significantly reduce institutional transaction costs. The first is for the government to set up a pandemic relief fund to provide special assistance to small and medium-sized private enterprises with development prospects and in line with the direction of industrial transformation. Second, we should further reduce the direct tax rate, especially the enterprise income tax rate. At the same time, further reduce or cancel various fees such as the land transfer fees, and social security fees in the broad tax burden, and effectively reduce the tax burden of enterprises. Third, we need to accelerate the transformation from indirect tax to direct tax, and reform the tax system dominated by enterprise tax, turnover tax and value-added tax. We should fully implement the business registration, and simple cancellation system, and remove the filling system of the general business investment project.

(4) We should build an efficient government. We should make a "high-level opening of the market, and efficient operation of the government" as an important goal of governance reform. For example, we can comprehensively promote the Service Zhejiang experience of "One Stop, One Trip, and One Paper" as the goal and principle of all the provincial public services. We should push for the government efficiency reform by holding the principle of "one window, one network, one simple step, and immediate response," expand the scope of the notification and commitment system, and greatly improve the efficiency of the government.

Deepening Comprehensive Reform by Way of Institutional Opening Up

Reform is the key to "turning crisis into opportunity." At present, the new system of a high-level open economy relies on a high-standard market economy, and institutional opening has a significant impact on the development of a high-quality market economy. Thus, a new pattern of mutual promotion between opening up and reform has been formed.

(1) We should promote market-oriented land reform. We should accelerate the market-oriented reform of land factors by breaking the dual-track system of urban and rural land, and the government monopoly of the land market at the urban level, establishing a system of "the same land, the same price, and the same rights" under the two types of ownership, and forming an open, fair, and unified trading platform and rules. While realizing the unified construction land market in urban and rural areas in 2020, we will further grant farmers complete right of their residential lot, including the use, lease, transfer, disposal, mortgage, etc., explore the direct entry of rural residential lot into the market, and further expand farmers' land property rights. In essence, this will basically complete the market-oriented reform of interest rates. We should accelerate the process of integrating the market interest rate and the benchmark interest rate, and make it true that the loan interest rate of the banking system is determined by the market. At the same time, we should dredge the channels for the transmission of interest rates from the money market and bond market to the credit market, and create an interest rate corridor by strengthening open market operations.

(2) We should accelerate the process of urban–rural integration. First, under the impact of the pandemic, the urgency for pushing urban–rural integration is all the more apparent. The pandemic forced many countries to significantly cut their imports, which has had a serious impact on China's labor-intensive industries, that part of the economy in the migrant workers made up the main workforce. Therefore, the overall income of migrant workers and farmers in China has been seriously affected. Second, from the perspective of China's actual situation, urban agglomeration, metropolitan area development, and urban–rural integration are all important factors supporting China's economic growth, as well as major measures for stable growth under the impact of the pandemic. In particular, the development of urban agglomerations plays an important role in releasing consumption potential. Third, the development of urban agglomerations is conducive to providing important space for the development of service industry, and an important driving force in promoting the upgrading of residents' consumption structure. Therefore, it is time to take the opportunity of developing the urban agglomerations to use the residence permit system to replace the separate residence registration systems for urban and rural residents, and bridge up the inter-provincial residence permit system, so as to fully release the huge potential of urban and rural integration.

(3) We will make greater efforts to support the development of the private economy and small and medium-sized enterprises. An important prerequisite for expanding domestic demand is to maintain good employment. At present, the private economy and small and medium-sized enterprises generate more than 80% of jobs. To cope with the impact of the pandemic and alleviate the pressure on employment, the panacea is the stable development of the private economy and small and medium-sized enterprises.

Responding to the Severe Impact of the Pandemic 101

Recently, governments at all levels have introduced measures such as tax reduction, fee reduction and interest-discount loans. However, considering that the pandemic will not be over any time soon, these policies are insufficient, and relevant institutional arrangements are needed. Therefore, we should create a better development environment for private enterprises under the guidance of open market and fair competition, ensure the equal use of resource elements by private enterprises by law, and enhance open and fair competition for all enterprises, whether private or not. These are realistic and urgent tasks we have to complete as the economy increasingly moves downward. In addition, in order to prevent the large-scale bankruptcy of private economy, and small and medium-sized enterprises, we still need to adopt stronger policies to support both the private economy and small and medium-sized enterprises. We should give more prominence to help the private economy and small, medium and micro-enterprises solve their problems, forming a liaison system for the Party and government leaders to be in contact with enterprises so as to provide timely door-to-door services. Considering the irresistible factors of the pandemic, we should allow the enterprises to pay salaries according to the minimum wage standard or minimum living security standard according to the actual situation, so as to tide over the difficulties with employees. In addition, the government should set a relief fund to support private economy, and the enterprises with development prospects, and in line with the direction of industrial transformation.

(4) We should comprehensively promote the reform of state-owned enterprises by focusing on mixed ownership. First, we should move from "managing enterprises" to "managing capital" as soon as possible, and form a state-owned capital management pattern dominated by "managing capital." To achieve this, we have to make sure that the main function of the state-owned capital preservation and appreciation supervision institutions is to optimize the layout of state-owned capital. In addition, we need to make the list of rights and responsibilities of "capital management" subjects, and form a national unified list of rights and responsibilities of state-owned capital investment and operation companies. Also, we need to straighten out the relationship between the Ministry of Finance, State-owned Assets Supervision and Administration Commission (SASAC), and the state-owned capital investment and operating companies. Second, we should focus on the development of mixed ownership and encourage the participation of social capital. We should support the investment of social capital in such general competitive sectors as energy, transportation, civil aviation, and telecommunications, and encourage private entrepreneurs to tax their talents to the utmost to maintain and increase the value of state-owned capital. At the same time, we will simultaneously reform the corporate governance structure, and the internal operation mechanism, to further enhance the confidence of social capital. Third, we should accelerate the strategic adjustment of state-owned capital, get ready to

form the catalogue and standards of "important industries and key fields related to national security, and the lifeline of the national economy," and speed up the formation of a supporting investment list. The new state-owned capital investment should focus on the fields of people's livelihood and infrastructure such as education, medical care, elderly care, and environmental protection. Generally, it should avoid entering the fields of complete competition, and the fields with sufficient market competition in the form of sole proprietorship. We will accelerate the process of allocating state-owned capital to social security, and broaden space for further reducing cooperate taxes.

Notes

1 See www.globaltradealert.org.
2 See "Trade and Development Report 2020: From Global Pandemic to Prosperity for All: Avoiding Another Lost Decade." https://unctad.org/system/files/official-document/tdr2020_en.pdf
3 See "World Economic Outlook, April 2020: The Great Lockdown by the WTO." https://www.imf.org/en/Publications/WEO/Issues/2020/04/14/weo-april-2020.
4 See https://sdg.iisd.org/news/trade-and-development-report-2020-outlines-path-to-avoid-lost-decade/.
5 See https://www.bis.org/.
6 See "Japan-EU Economic Partnership Agreement to Take Effect on February 1, 2019." https://www.chinanews.com.cn/gj/2019/01-02/8718015.shtml.
7 Vietnam to Implement CPTPP. http://www.mofcom.gov.cn/article/i/jyjl/j/201901/20190102827490.shtml.
8 See Tan Jina's "Asia Pacific Free Trade Area: Dreams Come True." November 10, 2016. https://www.gmw.cn/.
9 See Cao Guangwei's "The formation mechanism and subsequent influence of CPTPP from the perspective of Asia Pacific Economic Integration." *Commercial Research* 12 (2018).
10 See Chi Fulin's "Promote the Formation of a New Pattern of Reform and Development with a High-Level Opening-Up." *Economic Daily*, October 31, 2019.

8 The Pandemic Impact on the Global Supply Chain and China's Response

Huang Qunhui[*]

In today's international production pattern which involves the global value chain division of labor, the distribution of the global supply chain is dominated by efficiency logic, and has the basic characteristics of high efficiency. In the global supply chain layout dominated by this logic, China's manufacturing supply chain occupies an important position. However, as the COVID-19 virus is rampantly spreading across the world, its impact on the global supply chain is characterized by massive delivery delay and order shrinkage. This is increasing the risk of global supply chain disruption. The efficiency logic will be replaced by industrial safety logic, albeit temporarily. Under the superposition of multiple factors such as the impact of the pandemic, Sino-US trade friction, and the new industrial revolution, increasing numbers of European and American enterprises are trying to change their dependence on China's supply chain by way of "diversifying supply channels," and "localizing production." China urgently needs to transform its industry to climb up on the value chain. Against this backdrop, China will be multiply challenged for its critical position in the global supply chain. Improving the security and competitiveness of China's supply chain, accelerating targeted strategic adjustment, and issuing relevant policies are not only the responses to the pandemic. China must also change its strategic requirements to comply with the "great changes not seen in a century."

The Distribution of the Supply Chain in Today's World is the Result of Globalization Dominated by Efficiency Logic

The supply chain and industrial chain in today's world are formed in accordance with the division of labor in the global value chain. They are the product of capital globalization supported by modern transportation technology and information technology. From the perspective of economics, economic globalization is the result of capital's global pursuit of profits. Because modern transportation technology has substantially reduced transportation costs, and the development of information technology has greatly reduced the cost of knowledge

[*] Research Fellow, and Director of the Institute of Economics, The Chinese Academy of Social Sciences.

DOI: 10.4324/9781003433897-8

dissemination and exchange, enterprises can now realize their specific value creation activities through global resource allocation at a low cost, thereby forming a global value chain division across countries. According to the research data published by the Organization for Economic Cooperation and Development (OECD), the international shipping cost and passenger international air transportation cost in 2005 were only about 20% and 10% of those in 1930, while the international telephone cost was only about 1% of that in 1930.

Specifically, multinational corporations in developed countries conduct in-depth analysis of their business functions in the value chain, judge where and how to realize each function (outsourcing or internally producing) in order to maximize their business value, so as to efficiently allocate their resources globally to realize these business functions, which forms the division of labor in the global value chain. Under this division of labor, a global supply chain and an industrial chain are formed among the logistics supply and trading enterprises that realize enterprise value in the world. Therefore, the current global value chain division of labor, and the resulting supply chain and industrial chain layout, are efficient modes of production determined by this long-term market competition. Although multinational corporations in developed countries dominate this global division of labor, and developed countries are generally at the middle and high ends of the value chain, while late developing countries are generally at the middle and low ends of the value chain, all countries and enterprises participating in this global value chain division of labor have benefited and achieved. It is seen as a win–win situation. The former gets profit and growth, while the latter enjoys employment and development. Therefore, all parties actively accept this global value chain division of labor. This is also an important reason why economic globalization based on the division of labor in the global value chain (Globalization 3.0) is irresistible.

Of course, in terms of market competition, the supply chain, industrial chain and value chain will gradually undergo benign changes as a result of technological progress. For example, relying on technological innovation, the enterprises of late developing countries will gradually climb from the low end to the high end along the value chain. However, from the perspective of global economic growth, this change must be based on technological innovation and the gradual improvement of economic efficiency; otherwise, it cannot be realized. However, when a government, for various reasons such as national security, imposes tariffs, directly restricts the transnational operation of enterprises, and interferes in international production activities with domestic laws, it will inevitably increase the transaction costs of enterprises, and force the enterprises to redesign their value chain, which will inevitably force enterprises to break the existing global supply chain and industrial chain, thereby disrupting the global economic order and destroying the market competition system, and distorting the allocation of global resources. All these will eventually lead to great losses to the efficiency of the global economy. In fact, the division of labor in the global value chain formed after the Second World War, and under the global economic governance structure represented by the World Trade Organization, the International Monetary Fund, and the World Bank, are globally public

Pandemic Impact on Global Supply Chain and China's Response 105

organizations, conducive to the whole world. In today's economic globalization of the global value chain division of labor, disrupting the global supply chain and industrial chain will certainly damage the efficiency of the global economy.

The Increasing Risk of the Pandemic Impact on Global Supply Chain Disruption

The outbreak of the COVID-19 virus has become a pandemic, according to the pronouncements of the World Health Organization (WHO). In today's globalization, although countries take social isolation and other prevention and control measures, there will be a time difference as the pandemic hits different places. Similar measures will have an impact on the supply chain as people are prevented from socializing and gathering. Today, with the division of labor in the global value chain, the pandemic will soon destroy the global industrial chain and the supply chain, resulting in a disruption of the global supply. What we should worry about now is whether or not the disruption will lead to a new wave of anti-globalization.[1] The spread of the pandemic and the policies the world has adopted will make an impact on industrial chain and supply chain in three waves. The first was the massive supply chain disruption to China's economy after the outbreak of the COVID-19 virus, as China's domestic industrial chain and supply chain were halted, which not only slowed down or even blocked the domestic supply chain system, but also had a quick impact on the global supply network, resulting in a large number of delayed deliveries and a shrinking of orders. According to the analysis of the transaction volume payment data of Tradeshift, the world's largest business cooperation platform, minus the impact before and after the Chinese Spring Festival from January to February, 2020, and intercepting the data of the week beginning on February 16, it can be seen that China's overall trade activities decreased by 56%, orders between Chinese enterprises shrank by 60%, and the transaction volume between Chinese enterprises and international companies decreased by 50%.[2] Overall, the impact of the pandemic on the global supply chain at this stage was seen in the blocking of China's domestic supply chain, and China's one-way disruption to the global supply chain. This one-way negative impact was mainly reflected in delayed deliveries and shrinking orders. The second wave was marked by the supply shock on China's economy, due to the obstruction of the supply chain and the decline of demand in some countries as the result of the rapid spread of the virus. After March 2020, the pandemic was rampant in Japan, South Korea, Italy, Germany, France, other European countries, and North America. As a result, by mid-March, several automobile companies had closed their factories in Europe and North America. Although the resumption rate of work in China steadily picked up, the supply chain had not fully recovered. At this time, the global pandemic began to seriously affect China's supply chain, and the supply shocks in China and other countries began to have negative effects, which reinforced one another. The third wave was the supply shock on the global economy caused by the overall disruption of the global supply chain and industrial chain.

106   *Huang Qunhui*

In general, the world manufacturing industry can be divided into three networks: the North American Free Trade Area with the United States, Canada, and Mexico as the core; the EU area with Germany, France, Netherlands, and Italy as the core; and the East Asia area, with China, Japan, and South Korea as the core. From mid-March onward, the pandemic had a severe impact on each one of the three major manufacturing networks. Under the division of labor in the global value chain, supply and demand could have an impact on each other. The nature and direction of the impact of the pandemic on the global supply chain are undergoing fundamental changes, which will not only lead to more serious delay in delivery of goods and shrinking orders, but also lead to a large-scale disruption of the global supply chain, likely resulting in a global supply shocks.

Great Challenges to China's Supply Chain Security and Global Status

Among the three major global manufacturing networks, Asian manufacturing output accounted for more than 50% of the world. In 2019, the added value of Asian manufacturing exceeded $7 trillion, of which China accounted for nearly 60% in Asia. A basic fact is that although the United States dominates the global innovation system, the center of the global manufacturing system is in China – China's industrial added value accounts for nearly one-fourth of the global industrial added value, and China's share in the global intermediate market is as high as one-third. China is the largest trading partner of more than 120 countries, and the largest source of imports of 65 countries. Therefore, China plays a very important role in the global manufacturing supply chain. The impact of the pandemic on China's manufacturing industry will have a huge impact on the global supply chain.

The pandemic impact on the three manufacturing networks forced all countries to adjust their supply chain for the sake of supply chain security. Adjusting the supply chain from the perspective of security and emphasizing the security and controllability of the whole supply chain will inevitably aggravate the trend of de-globalization. Due to the influence of trade protectionism and a new round of scientific, technological and industrial revolution in recent years, the global supply chain has shown a trend of localization, regionalization and decentralization. The huge impact of the pandemic on the global production network will aggravate this trend. Consequentially, the global supply chain will face a substantial possibility of adjustment, and China's security and position in the global supply chain will be greatly challenged.

Although the pandemic has not changed the cost structure or the technical capacity of various countries, China's own factor cost and the trend of Sino-US trade friction mainly impact the division of labor in China's supply chain. However, the huge impact of the pandemic is not only that the increasing risk of global supply chain disruption threatens China's supply chain security, but also that the pandemic has greatly strengthened the proposition and determination of European and American entrepreneurs, researchers and policy-makers to adjust the so-called "China-centered global supply chain system," which will have a greater impact on the dominant position of China's supply chain at the level of "supply chain relationship." These are the most important issues China has to address for its strategic adjustment and policy deployment in the future. Due to the extensive and in-depth participation of Chinese enterprises in the three production systems of Asia, Europe, and North America, the safety of manufacturing systems in various countries and even public health safety (such as pharmaceuticals and PPE) are highly dependent on China's supply chain. Generally speaking, the current US and European countries battle China's dominant position in the global supply chain system on two fronts: first, increasing the diversity and flexibility of their supply chains through increasing the outsourcing outside the Chinese mainland or through multinational investment; second, improving the responsiveness of local supply by strengthening the production of local and surrounding countries. Therefore, it can be said that the spread of the pandemic has strengthened the expectation and sense of urgency of some countries to adjust the current "China-centered global supply chain system," and "catalyzed" the decentralization and localization of the global supply chain system.

Turning Crisis into Opportunity: Further Improving the Security and Global Status of China's Supply Chain

China is striving to modernize its industrial chain, and to climb to the high end of the value chain. The devastating impact of the pandemic on the global supply chain is not only a challenge, but also a great opportunity for China to modernize its industrial chain, an opportunity for China to climb to the high end of value chain. China looks likely to be the first country to have the virus under control, and to get prepared for economic recovery. During the first stage of the pandemic, the pressure of the large-scale relocation of China's industrial chain was lessened. In other words, the relocation anxiety is no longer an immediate concern. As long as China effectively controls the global pandemic, China will usher in a strategic opportunity window for supply chain repair and adjustment. On the one hand, we should comprehensively accelerate the orderly resumption of work and production, and repair the supply chain. On the other hand, we should focus on the high-quality development of the manufacturing industry, improve the modernization level of China's industrial chain, and climb to the high end of the value chain, so as to occupy a more favorable competitive position in the global supply chain. Perhaps we will recreate the miracle of our global status of the supply chain after the devastating blow of the SARS, a miracle of a higher status.

First, based on the impact of the pandemic on the industrial chain and the characteristics of the industry, we should carry out classified management of China's supply chain, specifically and quickly restore the supply chain, and promote the global strategic adjustment of the supply chain.

For typical process production industries such as the oil refinery, the upstream refining experienced little impact by the pandemic. The companies continued their production during the 2020 Spring Festival, although the level of output fell. However, the oil refinery is a capital-intensive industry, with large development inertia, and resilient industrial chain. Once the chain is disrupted, it is difficult to recover. We must ensure that such enterprises will not have major capital risks. Now, due to the plunge in oil prices, there appeared a major opportunity for the upstream refining and chemical industry. The downstream fine chemicals in this industry are in the hands of small and medium-sized enterprises that usually produce by order. The pandemic boosted the demand for prevention chemicals, creating a rare market opportunity. However, China is highly dependent on Japan, South Korea, the United States, Italy, and Germany for some raw chemical materials such as rubber and plastics. As the pandemic is still raging, China's industrial chain in this regard will be affected. It should be noted that due to the strong specificity of fine chemical terminal products, the impact of the pandemic will make the demand fluctuate greatly. In order to avoid the shock of the industrial chain, the proportion of intermediate chemical products should be appropriately increased. At the same time, we should build a more diversified global supply chain to deal flexibly with the risks caused by the change of orders of fine chemical terminal products. On the whole, the opportunity provided by the pandemic to the large chemical industry is greater than the impact. The key is to resume production in a timely and comprehensive manner, and seize the opportunity to promote the high-quality development of the chemical industry.

The pandemic hit the most such discrete manufacturing industries such as automobiles, electronics, machinery, household appliances, and clothing. In the first stage, judging from the perspective of industrial concentration in Hubei, and Wuhan, automobile, new-generation electronic information technology and biomedicine were greatly affected. For example, Hubei's automobile supply chain was the most badly disrupted. Hubei, as one of China's four major automobile production bases, also has the largest number of auto parts factories. Specifically, there are 1,482 automobile-related enterprises. In 2018, Hubei made 2.2 million vehicles, accounting for 9% of China's total output, and also 13% of all automobile parts in China. The outbreak of the first wave of the pandemic in China exerted a huge impact on the global automobile supply chain. On February 10, all the five major vehicle factories in South Korea suspended their overseas production because China stopped delivering parts. On February 14, both of the production lines of the Nissan Motor Company in Kyushu, Japan, were shut down. With the spread of the pandemic to the three major production networks in the second stage, many enterprises in Europe and the United States were forced to halt production. The overseas outbreak of the virus had an impact on China's imports of automobile parts, which so severely damaged the global auto supply chain that the global supply chain during the third wave of the pandemic was disrupted. Generally speaking, in the first stage, the hardest-hit sectors in the world were textile and clothing, furniture, electronics, machinery and equipment due to the supply chain disruption in China.

In the context of the pandemic impact on China's supply chain in the first stage, China as a supplier, due to the shrinking of foreign demand, saw a downturn in clothing, semiconductors and integrated circuits, optics and precision instruments, chemicals, air conditioning, toys, and household appliances. China as the demand side was highly dependent on Japan, South Korea, the United States, Italy, Germany, and other countries for its electromechanical devices, chemical products, optical instruments, transportation equipment, rubber, and plastics, more vulnerable to the pandemic impact. In particular, our imports of such high value-added products as optical imaging, medical devices, vehicles and parts, integrated circuits and semiconductors from other countries might be disrupted by the spread of the virus. However, this could also be an opportunity for China to produce them within its borders by way of innovation and self-upgrading. In addition, at present, the import of resource products (ore and energy) is less impacted by the pandemic, and the downward price lowered the cost of downstream industries in the domestic import chain.

Second, as a major task of the industrial foundation reconstruction project, while taking the comprehensive relief measures, we should urgently integrate the resources of the government, research institutions, enterprises, and professional associations, and establish a supply chain security assessment and risk warning system in key industries and regions.

Under the guidance of classified guidance and regional policy implementation, in addition to focusing on the pandemic prevention and control in heavily infected areas, we should also implement differentiated prevention and control strategies in other areas, and strive to orderly resume work and production, a key to coordinating pandemic prevention and control, and economic development. A series of measures were issued to help enterprises resume work and production, and support enterprises to stave off times of difficulty from the central to the local governments. On the one hand, from an overall and systematic perspective, we should coordinate and strengthen all the local government policies and measures for manufacturing enterprises, such as tax reduction, interest reduction, loan extension, operating cost subsidies, smooth logistics, and convenient customs clearance. On the other hand, we should focus on the crucial enterprises, solve the most important problems, and serve the enterprises to ensure the normal operation of the whole supply chain. Specifically, this includes helping enterprises coordinate and solve the difficulties and problems related to recruitment, delivery, and transportation of materials and products, and supply chain docking, push for the collaborative resumption of work of all upstream and downstream enterprises, strengthen the inter-regional industrial collaborative mechanism, and ensure smooth and efficient logistics. We should strengthen support for small and medium-sized enterprises, in particular to protect the stable operation of "little giant" enterprises that have core technology in key industrial chains. First of all, in terms of health and pandemic prevention, we should strengthen public welfare support for small and medium-sized enterprises, improve their health and epidemic prevention capacity, and allow them to return to work and production as soon as possible on the premise of ensuring their safety. Secondly, we should encourage these industries and enterprises to innovate their business models and expand their online and personalized service models as much as possible; finally, we should give full play to the service support role of public platforms and large platform enterprises for small and medium-sized enterprises, reduce the operating costs of small and medium-sized enterprises and improve their business convenience.

It is necessary and urgent to take comprehensive measures to temporarily rescue enterprises and repair the supply chain, but we must also consider establishing a supply chain security assessment and risk warning system in the long run, which can be viewed as part of the industrial foundation reconstruction project proposed by the Central Government in 2019. Through supply chain assessment and risk warning, we should scientifically evaluate the spillover effect of the pandemic on the supply chain impact, and analyze the impact resistance of the whole supply chain and key links so as to provide a scientific basis for coping with the pandemic disruption. On the one hand, it is necessary to establish the corresponding supply chain security assessment and early risk warning system according to the classification of industrial characteristics, such as process manufacturing and discrete manufacturing. At present, we should quickly establish the supply chain security assessment mechanism key such discrete manufacturing sectors as machinery, electronics, automobile and household appliances. They usually have a long industrial chain and significantly affects exports. On the one hand, we need to establish corresponding regional supply chain security assessment and early risk warning systems for key industrial agglomeration areas. For example, many industrial agglomeration areas, such as the Yangtze River Delta, and the Pearl River Delta, call for special attention. Through this system, the monitored data and information can be immediately fed back to supply chain participants and other stakeholders, so that all participants can take corresponding measures in time to prevent possible risks, so as to help the industry avoid risks caused by supply chain disruption.

Third, we should raise the digital level of the core enterprises of the supply chain and the supply chain platform, increase the elasticity of China's industrial supply chain, and promote the rapid recovery and adjustment of the supply chain by increasing the supply chain financing.

Supply chain elasticity is mainly reflected in two aspects: one is the ability to resist disruption, which can ensure that the chain will not be disrupted, but rather smoothly continued with minimal loss in case of major disasters; second, the ability to quickly respond to a disruption and return to a stable state when a disruption occurs. To promote supply chain elasticity, the government should increase the supply chain financing and the digital level of core enterprises.

Capital shortage is always the key constraint of China's small and medium-sized enterprises. In case of major disasters, it becomes all the more critical. The government should help enterprises resume supply chain operation by providing credit, which is an important part of the construction of industrial supply chain elasticity. We should establish a key monitoring mechanism for industries that are greatly disrupted by the pandemic, such as wholesale, retail, accommodation and catering, logistics, transportation, tourism, automobile, electronics, information, textile and clothing, etc. It is not suggested to withdraw, cut off, or delay loans for the enterprises and projects that look promising but are temporarily struggling. Instead, we should extend their loans, reduce fees and interest rates. Moreover, we should exempt the loans of the debtors severely hit by the pandemic through an out-of-court settlement, and exempt the guarantor's compensatory obligation so as to avoid the damage to its credit caused by breach of contract. In addition, the government should coordinate the relationship between core enterprises, supply chain enterprises, and financial institutions, promote core enterprises to confirm their rights in transactions, reduce the cost of operation of the financial institutions, and slash interest rates on loans to small and medium-sized enterprises.

The government should promote the industrial supply chain platform through all the means available, coordinate all the upstream and downstream partner enterprises, gather various production factors, foster a more efficient allocation of resources, more accurately match supply and demand, and push for the digitizing and networking of the whole process of the supply chain. These are the areas that the government can better serve the enterprises in the supply chain network. At the same time, it is also the starting point for the government to enhance the elasticity of the supply chain. The core enterprises in the supply chain often play the role of the supply chain platforms, and are able to coordinate the related enterprises. The government should pay attention to growing such enterprises in the industrial chain. On the one hand, by pushing for cultivating the innovation ability of these core enterprises, we can create an industrial chain with higher innovation and more added value. On the other hand, we need to push for digitization in the core enterprises to enhance their management and systematization. The government should aim at digital construction, push for a new round of infrastructure construction, support enterprises to strengthen the capacity-building of digital management of supply chain processes, use digital technology to offset the uncertainty of supply chain, and promote the efficiency reform of supply chain management.

Fourth, we should actively participate in international cooperation and governance of the global value chain, support our enterprises to speed up the pace of going global, ensure the safety of global supply chain, and promote the construction of the "digital silk road." 1. Thanks to the recovery of the huge Chinese manufacturing capacity, we must increase the global supply of the pandemic prevention materials, and support the world in its pandemic prevention effort. 2. We need to push for international cooperation in the field of supply chain security, issue a joint statement on supply chain security with major trading partners, establish a multi-channel and multi-level supply chain security system, explore such cooperation forms as "Supply Chain Counter-terrorism Partnership Plan," and "Supply Chain Natural Disaster Response Plan," and cooperate to deal with potential supply chain disruption risks. 3. We need to cooperate with international organizations such as the International Customs Organization, the International Maritime Organization and the Universal Postal Union to form a long-term cooperation mechanism in maritime, shipping, postal, and other fields, and build a cross-regional and even global flexible supply chain. 4. We have to encourage Chinese enterprises to accelerate the pace of "going global," increase the ability of Chinese enterprises to enter overseas markets and supply chains, reduce the "zero-sum game" and vicious competition with enterprises in other countries and regions, and form a highly collaborative and friendly supply chain strategic partnership. 5. We need to support our enterprises to control core technologies, important raw materials, and key resources, accelerate the construction of marketing networks in the global consumer market, and enhance the initiative to participate in and build the global supply chain. 6. We should integrate the Belt and Road infrastructure construction and with the construction of a digital supply chain system, and build a "digital silk road" to promote effective cooperation between the countries along the prospective "digital silk road" on the core elements of production, regional superior resources, and the upstream and downstream links of the industrial chain.

Efficiency-Oriented Economic Globalization Still Irreversible in the Long Run

To sum up, the current pandemic situation will have a long and significant impact on the global economic and political order. To a large extent, the pandemic may accelerate profound changes unseen in a century. In fact, before the pandemic, there appeared some significant signs in economic globalization. On the one hand, the new industrial revolution weakened the role of the traditional comparative advantage with labor cost as the core in promoting globalization, and profound changes were observed in the direction and dynamic mechanism of globalization. On the other hand, there has been a major structural adjustment trend in the global value chain. While China's manufacturing value chain has risen, the expansion trend of the global value chain is gradually stagnating. The rules of global governance based on multilateralism, cooperation, reciprocity, and consultation are being infringed. The multilateral trade system is being seriously challenged, and the efficiency and authority of WTO are greatly affected.[3] However, the trend of the now industrial revolution, or the US trade war on China, or the impact of the COVID-19 virus is able to reverse the trend of economic globalization in the long run. And it is a mission impossible to suppress China's position in the global supply chain, and constrain China's development in the process of economic globalization.

First of all, let's look at this from the perspective of the industrial revolution. At present, human society has ushered in a new round of industrial revolution characterized by digitization, AI, and networking, which promotes the vigorous development of new technologies, new business models, new industries, and constitutes the main engine of global economic growth in the future. However, the new industrial revolution will also bring a series of challenges to human society. For instance, the development of artificial intelligence will have an impact on career transformation and unemployment, possibly for moral reasons. In this context, countries all over the world are required to deepen cooperation, expand opening up, innovate together, and jointly meet the opportunities and challenges brought to mankind by the new industrial revolution. Facing the new industrial revolution, the innovation ecology of opening and cooperation is undoubtedly of great significance. Since the reform and opening up, China has made great progress by means of "technology for market." Unlike during the previous industrial revolutions when China was poor and weak, this time China has the foundation to work with the world to welcome the advent of the new industrial revolution. Especially in the fields of high-speed railway, 5G, artificial intelligence, mobile payment, and nuclear energy, China has a huge market scale and strong prospect for using these technologies. The space for cooperation with the developed countries in technological innovation is wide. For China and the United States, there is even more room for future technical cooperation in aerospace, climate change, medical treatment, energy, artificial intelligence, and other fields. The new world to be created by artificial intelligence is not far away, and the world will become more and more complex because of all the rapid changes. Therefore, in the context of the new industrial revolution, we should strengthen cooperation in order to help human society jointly meet the arrival of the new industrial revolution, and drive world economic growth.

Secondly, let's look at this from the perspective of the US trade war against China. Since the existing global value division of labor is gradually formed under the leadership of the multinational corporations in developed countries, and is the product of the globalization of transnational capital in developed countries, this division of labor pattern is, as a matter of fact, the most profitable for developed countries and their transnational capital. The trade war launched by the United States against China will not only have a negative impact on Chinese enterprises and economy, but also inevitably cause huge losses to the interests of American companies. As the American companies are forced to adjust their global layout of the supply chain, they will see a prominent rise in cost in logistics, infrastructure, choice of business partners, the maturity of supporting industries, so on and so forth.

Considering these factors, it is unrealistic for multinational corporations in China to withdraw their production and investment on a large scale in the short term. In fact, China is the only country that can make all the products on the United Nations Industrial Catalogue, implying that China has a complete modern industrial system, and a complete industrial supporting system. All these secure China in its position of its deep integration with the global value chain. In a word, China is difficult to be replaced by any other country in this regard in the short term. For American enterprises, getting rid of their dependence on China's supply chain will be costly and will lead to huge loss. A recent Goldman Sachs report pointed out that if Apple Company shifts the production of iPhones from

China to the United States, the cost will skyrocket by 37%. If it tries to maintain its profit level, Apple will spend five years to absorb some of the new costs on the condition that it increases productivity by adopting automation.

Finally, let's look at this from the perspective of the spread of the virus. The spread of the pandemic and the short-term disruption of the global supply chain may force many countries to think about how to strike a balance between the security orientation of self-reliance, and the efficiency orientation of global division of labor in the long run. Whether we think that the pandemic will become the final straw to the economic globalization, or another nail in the coffin of the economic globalization, or that the economic globalization led by the United States will turn to that by China, we still cannot give a positive answer. However, it is certain that the impact of the pandemic might be short-lived. The efficiency principle of economic activities will be resiliently dominant in the long run. Although the security-oriented principle of anti-globalization may interfere with the efficiency-oriented principle for some time, and although the order of economic globalization as an institutional supply may face some challenges in the rules of global governance, in the long run, the principle of efficiency will hold its basic dominant position.[4]

Notes

1 See He Fan and others' "The Four Impacts of the COVID-19 Virus: Will Globali-zation Retrogress?" *Caijing Magazine*, 18 March, 2020.
2 See Liu Qiudi's "Restructuring the Global Supply Chain under the Pandemic Impact." *China Newsweek*, 16 March, 2020.
3 See Huang Qunhui's "The Industrialization Process of New China from the Per-spective of the Centennial Goal." *Economic Research Journal* 10 (2019).
4 See Huang Qunhui's "Responses to the Impact of the COVID-19 Virus on Supply Side: Both Short and Long Terms." *Economic Review* 5 (2020).

9 Some Thoughts on the Current World Economy and Globalization

Liu Yuanchun[*]

With its high infectivity and lethality unseen in about a century, the COVID-19 pandemic has had a dramatic impact on the world economy and globalization in the modern communication system.

First, the global economy has experienced a sharp decline in synchronicity. Under the impact of the pandemic, there has been an economic and social shutdown which differs strongly from the endogenous collapse of the traditional economic crisis. Major economies in the world have suspended their economic activities successively as the pandemic was spreading, which sank the world economy more strongly than even during the 2008–2009 financial crisis. The predictions of many teams and experts show that if the pandemic continues to spread or a second outbreak occurs, the magnitude and duration of the world economic downturn will exceed the great crisis of 1929–1933.

Second, the world's financial and commodity prices have experienced unprecedented super-fluctuations in the following aspects. (A). In mid-March 2020, the US stock market experienced four circuit breakers in less than two weeks. (B). The yields of national bonds of various countries declined significantly, and some dropped to negative yields. (C). The sharp contraction of global liquidity led to the US dollar index breaking 103. (D). There was a plunge in oil prices, with West Texas Intermediate (WTI) oil futures of $-34/barrel in May. These changes were historically unprecedented, indicating that the panic and financial vulnerability caused by the pandemic reached a height unseen in history. Therefore, we need to break the traditional cognitive framework in order to grasp a real understanding of future economic changes.

Third, in response to the economic impact of the pandemic, a substantial number of countries have adopted extremely loose monetary policies. At present, more than 100 countries have adopted very loose monetary and fiscal policies, of which the global fiscal stimulus plan has exceeded $7 trillion, and the monetary capital injection has exceeded $20 trillion. In particular, the developed European countries, America, and Japan have adopted the super-policy combination of "zero interest rate," "unrestricted QE," "super fiscal stimulus," and "direct credit

---

[*] Professor, and Vice President of Renmin University of China.

DOI: 10.4324/9781003433897-9

injection." These policies are not only stronger than Roosevelt's New Deal, but also stronger than the 2008–2009 financial crisis, creating a new policy history.

The above three major changes will bring about an in-depth adjustment of the world economic order. First, the anti-globalization process may accelerate. Second, the power game between China and the United States will intensify to such an extent that the nature of the game might be changed. Third, the world economy might enter a period of super stagnation after the pandemic, which will lead to a further reconstruction of the world economic order.

But the first thing worth noting is that although the pandemic has brought a series of unprecedented changes, the impact of these changes on the world economic order is not a revolutionary turning point. The pandemic is just an accelerator. It has greatly widened the cracks in the world economic order, and compressed the process of the fracture zone of the world economic order. The changes in the world order, such as anti-globalization, populism, nationalism, protectionism and geo-economic and political conflicts, do not occur because of the pandemic; rather, COVID-19 has brought them to the forefront.

From the perspective of anti-globalization, the ratio of global trade to global GDP reached a historical height of 26.5% in 2008. After the US financial crisis in 2008, the parameter continued to decline. By 2019, the ratio had fallen by 5.5 percentage points, at only 21%. In other words, the turning point of anti-globalization appeared in 2008, and the landmark event was the outbreak of the US subprime mortgage crisis. From the perspective of the polarization of global income distribution, the ratio of the top 1% of global income to total income was 16.3% in 1980 and reached a historical height of 22% in 2008. Since then, it has continued to decline, and it dropped to 20.4% in 2019. Therefore, many times we think that 2008 and 2009 were the time when turning points appeared, ushering in an important period of a new historical situation.

From the perspective of populism, the populist index of developed countries was very low in the 1980s and 1990s, and it was also relatively low in 2007, at only 7%, but this parameter began to rise in 2013 and 2014, and reached a peak of 34% in 2018. This is similar to the levels observed in 1931 and 1932, the populist index in 1933 was 40%. Therefore, we can see that populism in various countries picked up steam after 2008.

There is also isolationism. With regard to this approach, the United States began its "retreats" in 2017. Between 2017 and 2019, the United States retreated, either fully or partially, from 13 international organizations. Now some people predict that the next scenario we will see might be that regionalism is replacing globalization. But when did regionalism begin to rise? There were 498 signed regional trade agreements in 2019, twice as many as the number signed in 2005. Indeed, 2018 and 2019 were the two years in which we saw the most signed regional trade agreements.

It was in 2008 that we saw a historical turning point with regard to anti-globalization, populism, nationalism, regionalization, and conflicts among major powers. As stated earlier, the pandemic itself served as essentially an accelerator, rather than a revolutionary force, because the division of labor pattern of the world economy, the interest pattern of the world economy, and the system of rules and organizations did not break overnight.

Some Thoughts on the Current World Economy and Globalization 117

It is worth noting that although the pandemic is an accelerator, it will cause many serious problems which are worthy of our attention.

The world economy began a long-term stagnation in 2008. Under the impact of the pandemic, this stagnation will not only continue, but also deepen. The growth rate of the world economy and that of many countries may further decline. At present, everyone is discussing whether or not the world economy is in a V-shaped reversal, a W-shaped adjustment or a L-shaped adjustment. The mainstream consensus is that a simple V-shaped rebound is very difficult to achieve, because various traditional structural and trend problems in relation to the world economy remain unsolved. The pandemic has not only reopened the old wounds, but also added a lot of new ones.

There are seven reasons for the long-term stagnation of the global economy after 2008. They are: the challenges an of aging population; technological advance in promoting the economy has declined; the polarization of global income, which leads to a decline in global demand; the high-debt problem caused by the fiscal responses by various countries to the pandemic; as a consequence of the polarization of income distribution in various countries, populism began to spread, and protectionism began to rise; the aggravation of geopolitical conflicts as a result of protectionism and isolationism; under the dual effects of the decline of benefits and the continuous rise of costs in maintain globalization, anti-globalization is becoming increasingly popular, and some industrial chains and value chains are being affected.

Have these problems been effectively solved in recent years? The answer is no. In fact, they are getting worse! First, population aging will continue to accelerate in the next two years. There was only 6% of the global population over the age of 65 in 1990, but 8% in 2017, reaching 10% in 2025, and 12% in 2032. In other words, the aging of the world population will accelerate from 2020 to 2025, especially in particular countries such as China, the United States, and some European countries.

Second, under the impact of the pandemic, the debt ratio of various countries will soar. In 2019, for example, the global debt ratio was 320%. In order to respond to the pandemic, many governments have borrowed huge sums. It is estimated that the US fiscal deficit may exceed 10% in 2020, and the global fiscal deficit ratio may rise by 6–7 points. Coupled with the debts of enterprises and individuals, the global debt ratio may exceed 330% in 2020.

Third, the globalization index will shrink rapidly. In 2020, the global GDP growth rate is expected to decline by 3%, while the trade growth rate will decline by 12% in the normal forecast. Our ratio of global trade to GDP will decline by 7–8 points in 2020. In other words, anti-globalization will accelerate, and populism and protectionism will elevate to a new high due to the pandemic and the shrinkage in the globalization index. As can be expected, all kinds of conflicts will intensify as a result.

Therefore, after the pandemic, there will a long-term global economic downturn, which may prove more serious than the previous round. This problem will soon lead to a second problem. In the global economic operation, when the revenue declines with the space for benefit distribution further shrining, the conflicts caused by distribution are certain to intensify. The basic logic tells us that the decline of growth actually indicates that the dividend due to international division of labor is greatly reduced, while the cost of global division of labor coordination continues to rise. Therefore, some significant changes will happen in the division of labor system as the result of shrinking profits. The changes have been actually embodied in the discussion of "decoupling," "de-globalization" and "de-Sinicization."

Of course, the scene we see here may be more complex and cannot be expressed by a single trend.

1. The global value chain and industrial chain have undergone some reconstruction. The first manifestation of reconstruction is that the length of the value chain will be shortened, because each country needs to reposition its economic benefits for the sake of economic security. They need to rehome some production capacity, which demands the reconstruction of the value chain and industrial chain. Another manifestation is that many countries have launched the "China +" strategic model and industrial chain strategy, which is not simply an effort in "de-Sinicization," but also serves as a spare tire to diversify the global value chain, independent from the single global supply chain. For example, Japan diversifies its supply chains in China, South Asia, Latin America and Africa. The third important thing is to establish a corresponding parallel system in the case of "hard decoupling." Of course, many people are very pessimistic about the current situation, but we think it exhibits strong uncertainty at present. What is the source of this uncertainty? It comes from the balance between market power, capital power, political power and national power. Many people think that the power of capital will prevail, but this is not always the case, as history tells us. Many times, some political forces may prevail as triggered by accidental factors. There will be many highly uncertain situations in the future

2. There will be an accelerated adjustment in the economic comparison between major countries. Under the influence of the change in the total amount, the relationship between different countries, regions and prices will also change. We will see that the Asian countries will rise rapidly over the next few years. In 2005, the Asian economy accounted for 25.9% of the world economy; it had reached 36.4% by 2018. During the same period, Europe decreased from 33.9% to 25.2%, down 8.7 percentage points, and North America decreased from 29.9% to 26.7%, down 3.2 percentage points. Asia filled up the gap. During the pandemic, the governance model of East Asia showed a comprehensive advantage, and the whole of East Asia took the lead in getting rid of the suspension effect brought by the pandemic, as the result of the advantageous governance. In 2020, the growth rate of developed economies was expected to be −6.1%, that of emerging economies, to be 1.0%, those of China and India, to be 1.2% and 1.9% respectively, while those of the United States and the Eurozone, were to be −5.9% and −7.5%, respectively. What are the implications of these projections?

Some Thoughts on the Current World Economy and Globalization   119

First, the portion of the Asian economy in the world will be further increased, likely from the current 36% to 40% over the next two years. Second, China's GDP will quickly exceed 70% of US GDP. In 2016, China's GDP accounted for 60% of that of the United States, meaning that it took only four years to climb 10 percentage points. In the past, it would have taken more than a decade to achieve such a change. The pandemic has quickened the narrowing of the gap between China and the United States. At present, the GDP growth rate for the United States is predicted to be −5.9%, and for China, to be 3%–4%, with a difference of about 8 percentage points between the two economies. If this pattern continues into the future, the Sino-US rivalry may change in nature in as short a period of time as 3–5 years. Therefore, the possible changes in the wake of the pandemic will be very critical. How to quickly get out of the pandemic and how to restore quick economic growth in the next few years have become extremely important. The next three years will actually be a critical period in terms of the economic rivalry between China and the United States. If China does not continue to recover its economy and surpass the United States in terms of growth rate, even though we try to augment our soft power, smart power, and effective power, it will still be difficult to hedge against this change in hard power. According to the predictions of our team, the United States will continue its economic growth rate at about 2%, whereas China will continue its economic growth rate about 6%. By 2025, China will be able to usher in a new period of breaking through the bottleneck in the Sino-US rivalry. Therefore, what impact the pandemic will have on the economic operation mode and economic operation efficiency of the two countries is the two question for current research. The answer to this might call for a diplomatic response.

3. There will be a surge in the ideological struggle at some point in the future. The general debate over whether the world will uphold liberalism or nationalism in the future is of little significance. Nationalism and authoritarianism cannot be used to do justice to China's political and economic systems, nor is it accurate to use liberalism to describe the current political form, and the future economic management and control model, of the United States. The two traditional modes of differentiation are likely to move closer to the middle under the impact of the pandemic. For example, it is still uncertain whether the WTO should be reconstructed on the principle of more freedom and openness or, alternatively, on interventionism and collectivism.

4. During the process of a sharp contraction of the room for profit, and the adjustment of the division of labor system, some key changes will take place in the model of the power play between major countries. We believe that the next few years will actually be the most critical window period of the rivalry between major countries on the economic front. Therefore, China must grasp some relevant trends, patterns, and the adjustment of rules in this window period. Only in this way can we develop effective strategic responses.

10 China and the World Under the Impact of the Pandemic*

*Yao Yang***

The global transmission of the COVID-19 virus is leading to profound changes in the international economic and financial situation. It is no exaggeration that the panic and decline rate of the international financial market exceeded those during the "subprime mortgage crisis" in 2008. However, the pandemic will not and should not reverse the trend of globalization. The adjustment of the global industrial chain in the future will not lead to the "decoupling" or "de-Sinicization." On the contrary, China's position in the global industrial chain may be further strengthened. The impact of the pandemic sank the US economy into recession. Although the duration of this recession may not be as long as the great depression in the 1930s, the depth of the recession is far greater than the depression. Moreover, the various market rescue measures introduced by the United States can boost the economy in the short term, but they will only increase the probability of a new and greater financial crisis in the long run. We must be prepared for the possible crisis. Under the pandemic, the biggest challenge facing China is that the West will launch a fundamental attack on China's political system and values. An ideological "new Cold War" is likely to start. In order to meet this major challenge, China must make a full and effective explanation of the advantages, disadvantages and operation logic of China's system in line with the requirements of the current times and tradition. In fact, China needs to rebuild its political discourse.

Most Countries Caught in "Dilemma" as COVID Spreads

Since March 2020, the COVID-19 virus had spread all over the world and become a pandemic. Some countries learned from China's experience and took measures to "lock down" cities. Italy was an example. Other countries halted large-scale activities, such as the suspension of the games of NBA, football, and other sports in the United States. Disneyland, entertainment venues such

---

* Part of the chapter was published in *Caijing Magazine*, 30 March, 2020, and *Beijing Cultural Review*, 24 April, 2020. Revised here.
** Dean of the National School of Development at Beijing University, Beijing University Boya Chair Professor, and a distinguished professor of Changjiang Scholars of the Ministry of Education since 2015.

DOI: 10.4324/9781003433897-10

as cinemas, and casinos in Las Vegas in the United States were closed. Affected by the spread of the virus, the US stock market experienced four circuit breakers in eight business days in mid-March, and the main stock indexes nosedived by about 30% since the beginning of 2020. At the same time, European stock markets sank by about 35%, Japanese and Korean stock markets fell by about 25%, and the stock markets of emerging market countries such as India, Vietnam, and Brazil also lost about 30%. Commodity prices represented by oil also plunged. The Global Purchasing Managers' Index (PMI) and other indexes hit record lows in March. These occurrences made the international situation all the more complex and fragile.

In the past two months, most countries were caught in a "dilemma." If they let the virus take care of itself, the stock market and economy would be very volatile as there was so much uncertainty. If they took strong measures to control the virus, the economy would be shut down. The reason why the stock market had so many circuit breakers, and the oil price plunged to even negative, was uncertainty about the pandemic, an uncertainty that would create many more uncertainties. At first, US President Trump tried to downplay the threat of the pandemic, claiming it was merely flu. Of course, his underplay was proven wrong. On the contrary, Italy locked down the whole country, and its economy was shut down. No matter what measures are taken, the global economy might fall into recession. Why can the continuous circuit breakers trigger an economic crisis? Because the US stock market is closely linked with economic entities, both directly and indirectly, the market crash will spill over to the real economy. At the same time, the decline in stock prices will affect the market's expectations for the future. If that is the case, investment will be low and consumption will drop. This "domino effect" may lead to a chain reaction in the financial sector, and eventually cause an international financial crisis, similar to that in 2008. Although the Fed's unlimited QE temporarily stabilized the US stock market, the policy would be unsustainable, because it increased the long-term risks to the US financial system.

At present, as the pandemic has stabilized, US President Trump has called for the resumption of normal work, and some other countries would do the same against the suggestions of the pandemic experts. The difference in opinions reflected the difficulty in making a choice.

Will China's Industrial Chain Suffer another Impact Because of the Pandemic?

After the outbreak of the COVID-19 virus in China, the manufacturing enterprises were shut down, resulting in the disruption of the industrial supply chain and the internal supply chain. Later, the pandemic situation in foreign countries continued to deteriorate, global consumption decreased, and China's import and export both dropped. Since we imported a lot from the US, Korea, and many European countries, the deterioration of the pandemic situation in these countries may have another impact on China's industrial chain.

In view of the above problems, on the one hand, we should speed up the overall resumption of work and production of the domestic industrial chain. On the other hand, we need to assess the impact on our industrial chain by other pandemic-hit countries, further strengthen the idea of the overall resumption of work of the industrial chain, explore the advantages of the improvement of the supporting facilities of the industrial chain, and increase the support for the resumption of work and production of key industrial links.

China's domestic economy was hit hard in February and March 2020. Affected by the spread of the virus, the economic downturn pressure, and the tax and fee reduction, the total national public revenue and the tax revenue were recorded negative from January to February in 2020. In February, the manufacturing PMI was only 35.7%, the lowest I have ever seen as a researcher. This PMI number was a fall of 14.3 percentage points compared with January, also a serious plunge. Generally speaking, if it exceeds 50%, this indicates that the economy is healthy and might be booming; otherwise, it is a concern or a sign of recession. Due to the community transmission of the virus, the service sector was hit hard. The business activity index of the service sector was only 30% in February, down 23% from the figure in January, and worse than that of the manufacturing industry.

The sharp decrease in the level of economic activities also led to the decline of manufacturing prices and other price indexes. For instance, the manufacturing price index in February was 7.5% lower than that in January, with a very large decline. The price index of the service sector fell by as much as 15%. Both data show that the domestic economy was slammed hard in February. The March data was no better. All indicated that the domestic economic situation was everything but optimistic. Perhaps it was because of the powerful Internet and social media that people were far more concerned with the current pandemic than with SARS. I remember that we went to work as usual when SARS was spreading. Nobody is at work this time; everybody us worrying away at home. The impact on China's supply and demand is a "double-kill." China's economy was slowing down, and the pandemic worsened the situation.

Of course, we should also see that the pandemic has catalyzed a number of emerging industries to promote future economic growth. For example, the development of new apps such as distance education, remote diagnosis, and work from home has been accelerated. Although the pandemic has prevented employees from returning to work, it has pushed the enterprises for automation. The construction of new infrastructure has got more attention. Now increasing numbers of people are used to video-conferencing, and webcast. I have recently participated in several video-conferences. The organizers did not have to pay dues. People didn't spend time on trips, and there was less traffic pollution. The conferences were held with very enthusiastic discussions. The webcast sector is bound to soar.

With regard to the nation's trade, both imports and exports fell in the first two months of 2020. Specifically, our exports denominated in CNY decreased by 15%, exports denominated in US dollars decreased by 17%, and imports decreased by 11%. Exports rebounded slightly in March, but they still shed 11%

in CNY in the first quarter. Before having the pandemic under control, overseas demand will be slashed, which is bound to lead to the contraction of China's exports. This year's exports will look unsatisfactory. Not much we can do about it. This year, I estimate that negative export growth is a high probability. Recently, the export orders of the domestic textile enterprises fell significantly, in addition to cancellations and postponed delivery. Meanwhile, our export enterprises are faced with the challenge of the CNY appreciation, mainly because China's current account has not deteriorated, and may be even better in the future. It is all because exports are declining and the value of imports is also declining. Especially, the decline of oil price will reduce the cost of imports even more. The decline in imports in January and February was less than the decline in exports, but it is estimated that the decline in imports will rise in the coming months.

In addition, if there is no big problem in China's stock market, foreign capital will flow into China. The interest rate spread between China and the United States has also expanded, increasing the global allocation value and attractiveness of the CNY assets. In this case, the CNY may appreciate, so foreign trade enterprises will face the pressure of the appreciation of the CNY.

The Trend of China's Economy and the World Economy in the Post-Pandemic Era

The phenomenon within China is a little perplexing. Although the COVID-19 virus is under control, and all the cities are basically open, the life of the ordinary people has hardly returned to normal in the sense that people keep a tight hold on their purse. Once a behavior pattern is formed, it will take a long time to change it. In the first quarter of 2020, our total retail sales dropped by 19%, the largest decline of various indicators, a signal that China's economy was not experiencing a V-shaped reversal pattern. The best to hope for might be a U-shaped reversal one, and the worse nightmare would be the L-shaped pattern. I hope this will never happen.

As it seems impossible to completely eliminate the virus in the short term, the author believes that the government must make a decision that the pandemic prevention and control should enter a stage of routine management. The author suggests that the pandemic management can now be assigned to the health department, and let other departments return to their normal work. In a word, each takes its own responsibility, rather than all being engaged in controlling the pandemic as if it were in the time of war.

It is hard to predict if people in other countries also hold onto their money tightly in the post-pandemic era. It is likely that foreign people are more willing to take risks than the Chinese. It is possible that once the restrictive measures are lifted, everyone will be excited that life has returned to normal.

However, an open eye should be kept on the US economy. In fact, there were signs of a financial crisis in the US economy before the outbreak of the pandemic. In recent years, the United States has entered a dead end of maintaining economic growth by printing money. In fact, people are very concerned with the

124   *Yao Yang*

deceleration in US technological innovation. Even if this were the case, the United States still wants a faster economic growth rate. The only way to achieve that is to print money. Liquidity is overflowing, but inflation is still low. Where did the money go? So much went to the financial sector that financial risks were accumulating. People often wrongly compare China's M2 with that of the United States. We should compare the complete monetary aggregates (such as M3 and M4). The M3 and M4 of the United States are far greater than those of China. The total financial assets of the United States are more than $5 billion, and its GDP is only $20 trillion. Therefore, the risks to the American economy are also higher than those to China. The outbreak of the pandemic forced the Federal Reserve to introduce unrestricted quantitative easing measures, which surely saved the stock market, but hardly helped the economy. The Fed's actions are only good at increasing the probability of another US financial crisis.

Therefore, the author believes that after the pandemic, the US economy may recover in the short term. However, in the long run, the probability of a financial crisis has increased rather than decreased. Of course, it is unknown when it will happen. We only know that the risk is accumulating. After that, the United States may suffer a vicious cycle: once the stock market falls to a certain extent (below 20.000 points, for example), the Federal Reserve will intervene to hold it. The markets can sustain for a period of time; in the long run, however, it is like taking care of immediate interests at the expense of the future, an attempt of drinking poison to quench thirst.

Therefore, when it comes to the long-term economic competition between China and the United States, the author is very confident in the prospects for China's economy, because we have accumulated some advantages and strength. Also, the Chinese government actively promotes innovation and manufacturing sector. What is more? We will not have the problem of industrial hollowing-out that frustrates other countries, which is where China's competitive advantage lies.

It is unlikely that the world will fall into a great depression as the result of the pandemic. The 1929 Great Depression lasted a very long time, much longer than four years generally claimed. Without the Second World War, the capitalist world would not have been able to get out of the great depression. Although the monthly data doesn't indicate that the current recession in the United States will last that long, the depth of the recession has exceeded that of the Great Depression. Moreover, as mentioned above, the author believes that the continuous rescue measures of the United States will lead to a greater crash than the 2008 financial crisis.

According to the International Monetary Fund (IMF), world economic growth would decline by 3.0% in 2020. I think the IMF's prediction is too optimistic. China's economy fell by 6.8% in the first quarter. I'm afraid it will be still negative in the second quarter. Whether it can turn positive in the third and fourth quarters depends on whether or not our consumption can go up, and whether our new infrastructure really takes effect. All the factors considered, I am sure that it is not a small achievement for China's economy to turn positive in the whole year.

Economic Nationalism to Hurt China Badly

Affected by the pandemic, China's industrial supply chain was definitely damaged in the short term. In the long run, the impact will not be great, because the global industrial division of labor has been firmly established, and it is too costly to change it. Furthermore, the pandemic is a global threat, and it is risky to shift all manufacturing capacity to any single country. Therefore, the author believes that there will be no major changes about the supply chain, although small changes and adjustments are sure to occur. The adjustment process may not cause much damage to China's economy, because China is the first country to get out of the pandemic. China's manufacturing industry is the first to recover, with a resumption rate of nearly 100%. Meanwhile, many countries have not resumed work, and the global supply chain is still in a broken state. Therefore, this situation will force China to make up for the previous industrial vacancies. Some people say that the industrial chain will be moved away on a large scale, as part of the effort to "de-Sinicize." The claim is groundless. On the contrary, the author believes that after this pandemic, China's position in the world industrial chain will be strengthened.

At present, two views on how to respond to the pandemic-related crisis are popular in China. One is that the pandemic serves as a warning that China should build a closed internal circular industrial chain and take a path of self-reliance in the future. To some extent, this reflects the so-called conception of the "economic nationalism." The other view is that globalization is irreversible, and it is impossible to "de-Sinicize" and reverse the globalization trend, so we should continue to promote globalization. My response to the first view is that we not only can't accomplish what is suggested, but it is also unnecessary. In the medium- and low-end fields, we have formed a closed loop. We can produce anything we want in China. But in the high-end field, we can't do much. For example, in terms of chip design, China's Cambrian and Huawei's Kirin are world-class, but we can't manufacture them. In chip manufacturing, China faces two problems. One is that we don't have lithography machines, and the other is that we do not have the yield rate of developed countries. High yield rate is the result of a long-term technological accumulation. Although the United States has some supply restrictions on us, it has not completely banned it. Even the restrictions on chips have been postponed. This shows that it is also difficult for the United States to cut off supply to China, because China is a huge chip market. In fact, the United States will suffer considerable damage if it gives up the Chinese market. Therefore, it is not really necessary for us to make everything on our own.

In addition, if we take the road of economic nationalism, we will just give other countries a pretext to do the same. Currently, the West is increasingly worried about China's technological advances. Besides the United States, some European countries are also taking actions to restrict China's access to advanced technology. It is a matter of time before the United States and Europe coordinate their policies. If China vigorously engages in self-reliance by establishing closed loops, they might be united out of worry. Therefore, in the long run, it is extremely disadvantageous for us to pursue a policy of economic nationalism.

Taking Measures to Boost Consumption and Restore Economy

At present, the academic circles are relatively consistent on how to restore China's economy, that is, to introduce more active fiscal and monetary policies to stimulate economic growth. However, there are still some different views with regard to the specific approaches. Most people still insist on focusing on supply-side structural reform, while giving some consideration to the demand side. At the same time, we should vigorously promote the upgrading of industrial structure, including the new infrastructure of emerging technologies and industries.

The first academic consensus aims to solve the long-term problem, but now the most urgent is to find a way to quickly get out of the immediate dilemma, because the economic recession is deep enough. Keynes has long told us that we will all die in the end. Immediate rescues should precede anything else. The biggest problem is that so many people lost their jobs, and so many small and medium-sized enterprises shut down. The highest priority is to save the economy before discussing other issues.

There are no more than three rescue measures. The first is to increase liquidity to stimulate demand. Although we support the enterprises with capital, they have no incentive to take bank loans, because they have lost many orders as the result of a sharp decrease of demand. Although the current monetary policy could keep our confidence, especially our confidence in the stock market, it is actually limited in its functions.

The second rescue measure goes with the infrastructure construction, our usual way of boosting economy, because infrastructure increases demand. However, this time is special, as the severe impact inflicted by the pandemic are on the small and medium-sized enterprises, and ordinary people. The new infrastructure could hardly help the people or the ordinary enterprises, because it is not labor-intensive, unable to employ a large number of workers. We cannot help the ordinary people and small and medium-sized enterprises by way of launching the new infrastructure, until the large and powerful construction corporations have their hands full. That is the time when the small and medium-sized enterprises could get the so-called trickle-down effect one or two years later. In short, the new infrastructure plays a certain role in boosting the economy, but it cannot directly help those, businesses and ordinary people alike, who really need assistance.

Therefore, the author now strongly advocates the third measure: to boost consumption. But how? To send checks to people or to send them consumption vouchers? Both are needed. We should pay cash to the unemployed low-income people as a relief effort. Meanwhile, we need to send consumption vouchers to the middle class to increase their spending. Higher consumption will improve the economic situation of small and medium-sized enterprises. The vouchers may have a magic effect. A one-Yuan voucher might lead, ultimately, to five Yuan of spending. That is how to quickly push consumption.

In addition, in terms of industrial structure adjustment and upgrading, the pandemic has made the adjustment for us as the inefficient enterprises "have already died." In the past, whenever the economy slid, there would be a new round of discussion of the structural adjustment. In my opinion, you don't have to bother for that, because the economy will adjust automatically. When the economy goes down, prices go down as well. Unable to survive in lower prices, the inefficient enterprises are forced to shut down. Economic operation has its own law. It is like a person coming down with a cold, which will renew the person, as the traditional Chinese medicine tells us. The same is true for the economic downturn, which will reshuffle the whole economy by eliminating those that should be eliminated. The pandemic will do the same, that is, forcing the inefficient enterprises out, and keeping the more efficient in.

A New Type of "Cold War" in the Post-Pandemic Era

To some extent, a "new type of Cold War" has actually been formed. The author believes that there are two reasons for this situation.

One was the need for Western politicians to shift blame. After January 23, 2020, the Western countries knew that the virus could be transmitted from person to person, but for about a month and a half, they did not take any measures. Even when the pandemic in Italy was very serious, other countries did not take real measures until the outbreak of the virus in mid-March. Once we took measures, we quickly kept the virus at bay, and became the first country to get out of the pandemic. Rational people in the West agree that China's control of the virus was very effective. But now some Western politicians have begun to blame China for not having told them in advance, when the virus was rampant in their countries. The blame was groundless. After January 23, all the Western countries should have taken prevention measures. The United States grounded its flights to China, but why didn't it take any prevention measures at home?

In fact, some Western officials, out of their own reasons, hesitated to adopt drastic measures to control the transmission of the virus. It was hard for them to lock down cities because the cost and social impact were extremely high.

Second, it seems that the West tries to turn the health issue into an issue of social system. I am afraid the West will reevaluate China's political system, and will fundamentally challenge China's system in unison in the post-pandemic age. This will be the biggest challenge for China. They will not discuss the important role China has played in the fight against the pandemic, and the assistance China has provided to other countries. They will attack China for its political system in one voice, and try to hold China accountable for the outbreak of the COVID-19 virus. In fact, the politicians in several major Western countries openly talked about this. The Western attack will pose a major challenge we need to deal with later.

I believe that now it is the time that Chinese scholars - especially some young scholars - should stand up and explain in theory the philosophical basis and advantages of China's political system. We should actively explain the operation logic of China's system, break through the dichotomy of authoritarian government vs. democratic government, and analyze China's political system case by case from the angle of government capability.

128 *Yao Yang*

China and the United States have competed in ideology, geopolitics, and science and technology. Therefore, it is not an overstatement that the "new Cold War" has been launched. However, the "new Cold War" between China and the United States differs from that between the United States and the Soviet Union. China and the United States still have broad space for cooperation in economy and trade, international order, counter-terrorism, and international aid. The space for cooperation differentiates the two "Cold Wars." The Sino-US relation is already a competitive one. Our attitude should be to seek cooperation in the process of competition. The United States regards China as a competitive opponent, although China did not want to acknowledge that in the past. In my opinion, China can now acknowledge that China and the United States are in a competitive situation. The competition between China and the United States in ideology, geopolitics, and science and technology has been formed. That is the fact we must face.

However, we should also tell Americans that although there is competition between China and the United States in these aspects, there is still room for cooperation between the two countries in terms of economy, trade, and international order. The author has insisted that the second round of China–US trade negotiations is a great opportunity. After the suspension of the World Trade Organization (WTO) mechanism, the United States is willing to negotiate with China. That is an opportunity for the two countries to work our rules through negotiation, which might actually become a template for the next round of reform of the WTO. In this way, China has actually participated in the formulation of international rules. Therefore, the author believes that we should not regard the Sino-US "trade war" as another tactic the United States has used to suppress us. In fact, we should take a more active attitude toward the negotiations with the United States, so that China will slowly participate in rules- making.

Seeking Wisdom from Traditional Culture to Build a Chinese Discourse System

Although the author believes that there is a great possibility of forming an ideological "new Cold War" between the two countries so far, there is still room to possibly avoid it if we adopt both short-term and long-term strategies.

We need to present the accomplishments we made during the fight against the virus in Wuhan. The greatest was that nearly 40,000 medical personnel from all over China assisted Hubei, but none was infected, not a small miracle. China showed its envious coordination and mobilization ability during the pandemic control. Recently, we are also revising the statistical data, because it was chaotic in the early stage of the pandemic, when errors were inevitable. In short, China should immediately publish a report or a White Book to clarify some points so as to prevent the formation of a "new Cold War," as there are forces that may arise against China in the midst of the virus prevention. There have appeared some very strong emotional expressions of extreme nationalism on the social media of late. They could help none, and are unacceptable.

China and the World Under the Impact of the Pandemic 129

In my opinion, we should have our own discourse system as the medium and long-term countermeasures. We must discard some in the past discourse system before we can establish a new one. The key to having a new one is to have a theoretical breakthrough as the first step, but this is an advance that is very difficult to make. All in all, we should straighten out the theory first.

We should turn to our excellent traditional culture, Confucianism, in particular, can provide the wisdom to establish a new discourse system. Strictly speaking, no national culture or thought is superior or inferior to any other's. The same is true when we compare Confucian thought with Western liberalism. China's current social system undoubtedly has profound historical and cultural origins. I think it is in line with the logic of historical development to lay the foundation of the discourse system in traditional culture, especially in Confucian culture.

11 Looking into the Financial Turmoil during the COVID-19 Pandemic

Causes, Characteristics, Impacts, and Responses

Zhang Ming[*]

The main manifestation of the global financial turmoil under the impact of the COVID-19 virus is the sharp decline in the prices of risky assets represented by stocks and crude oil, and the upward fluctuation in the prices of safe haven assets represented by US Treasury bonds, gold, and the US dollar indexes. The triggering factors of global financial turmoil are the global transmission of the virus, and the sharp decline in crude oil prices. The deep-seated reasons include the large-scale debt repurchase of stocks by American enterprises, the leveraged investment of institutional investors in passive investment products, and the trading strategy of hedge funds, which has amplified the vulnerability of the financial market. The current round of global financial turmoil may not be over, and it is currently hard to see end of the decline in the US stock market. The US corporate bond market, the southern European sovereign bond market, and some emerging market countries are points of concern for potential risk. There are similarities and differences between the current global financial turmoil, and the subprime mortgage crisis experienced in 2008. The current one is more destructive than the former in terms of governance difficulty, and the impact on the global economy. The current turmoil will cause China's economy to face the impact of intensified short-term capital outflow, shrinking external demand, and a more complex international environment, but it will also enhance China's global economic influence, and the attraction of CNY assets. The Chinese government should prudently deal with the possible short-term impact of the financial turmoil, maintain steady economic growth, and accelerate domestic structural reform.

Global Financial Turmoil

Since late February 2020, there has been a new round of volatility in the global financial market, as the prices of risky assets represented by stocks and crude oil fell sharply, while the prices of safe haven assets, represented by the treasury bonds of the developed countries, gold, and US dollar index, rose.

---

[*] Director and research fellow of the Center for International Investment, Institute of World Economics and Politics, the Chinese Academy of Social Sciences.

DOI: 10.4324/9781003433897-11

By the end of April 2020, the US Dow Jones Industrial Average, Japan's Nikkei 225 index, Germany's DAX index, Britain's FTSE 100 index, and France's CAC40 index had fallen 14.7%, 14.6%, 18.0%, 21.8% and 23.5%, respectively, from the levels recorded at the end of 2019. In particular, it is worth mentioning that the US stock market experienced circuit breakers on March 9, March 12, March 16, and March 18, 2020, four breakers in eight consecutive trading days, which historically unprecedented.

By the end of April 2020, compared with the prices at the end of 2019, Brent crude oil futures price and West Texas Intermediate (WTI) crude oil futures price had decreased by 59.9% and 69.1%, respectively. From the end of 2019 to the end of April 2020, the yield of US 10-year Treasury bonds decreased from 1.92% to 0.64%, a decrease of 128 basis points. The price of London Bullion Market Association (LBMA) gold in the UK rose from $1.515 per ounce to $1.703, up 12.4% and the US dollar index rose from 96.4 to 99.0, up by 2.7%.

It is worth noting that from March 9 to 18, 2020, both the prices of risky assets (stocks and crude oil) and safe haven assets (US Treasury bonds and gold) fell significantly at the same time in the global financial market, a phenomenon rarely seen. This means that there was a liquidity crisis in the market. In order to have liquidity, investors sold all of their assets at any cost. After the Fed adopted a series of innovative liquidity supply policies in mid-March, the liquidity crisis finally eased, the price of safe haven assets began to rise, and the price of risky assets stopped declining, moving in a volatile adjustment.

The Triggering Factors and Deep-Seated Causes of Global Financial Turmoil

In my opinion, it seems that the global financial turmoil was triggered by the spread of the COVID-19 virus, and the collapse of global crude oil prices. However, the deeper reason for the US stock market crash was the systematic risks gradually accumulated during the long-term prosperity of the US stock market.

From the end of 2019 to the end of April 2020, Brent crude oil futures price and WTI crude oil futures price decreased by 59.9% and 69.1%, respectively. On March 9 alone, Brent crude oil and WTI crude oil futures prices fell as much as 24.1% and 24.6%. The direct reason for the decline was that the OPEC countries, represented by Saudi Arabia, failed to reach an agreement with Russia on a new round of crude oil production reduction; to make the matter worse, Saudi Arabia took the lead in increasing production. Although the sharp drop in oil prices could help oil importing countries reduce their costs, it also had the following three negative impacts on the global financial market. First, the stock prices of the global energy sector fell accordingly. Second, the interest rate spread of high-yield bonds (i.e., junk bonds) issued by US shale oil and gas production enterprises increased significantly, and the market price fell sharply, which led investors to start selling such high-yield bonds, thereby causing turmoil in the US credit bond market. Third, investors in the Middle East

132 *Zhang Ming*

may have to withdraw petrodollars from the global market because of the sharp drop in oil prices, which would trigger a new round of selling pressure in the global financial market. In other words, the sharp decline in global crude oil prices since the beginning of March 2020 was the second trigger factor of global financial market turmoil.

From 2009 to 2019, the US stock market kept rising for 11 consecutive years. During this period, it experienced only one significant adjustment in 2018, but it still continued to hit new highs after the adjustment. There were a series of structural factors behind the steady rise of the US stock market, but, ironically, those factors finally became the deep-seated reasons for the current plunge of US stock prices.

One such reason for the sharp decline of US stocks was that the public companies generally repurchased their own shares on a large scale by way of issuing bonds. In the past 10 years, many companies in the United States have repurchased their shares with the purpose of improving the earnings per share of stocks by reducing the number of stocks circulating in the market. This was intended to enhance the attractiveness of stocks to investors and to further push up the stock price. The rise in the stock price will increase the market value of self-held stocks of the companies, and further improve the earnings per share. American companies buy back their shares not only through their own funds (after-tax profits), but also through the issuance of corporate bonds. According to the Bloomberg data, in 2018 and 2019 alone, the S&P 500 listed companies repurchased the stocks worth $806.7 billion and $606.5 billion, respectively. Massive repurchases will cause two problems. First, it will inflate the earnings per share of the companies. Zhongtai Securities estimated that the annual compound growth rate of the earnings per share of the US companies reached 11% in the past 15 years, while the compound growth rate of corporate profits was only 8%. The 3% gap between these two figures was created by the buybacks. This means that about 27% of the profits of the listed companies in the United States were falsely increased by the repurchase behavior.[1] Second, the public companies generally issue large-scale corporate bonds to finance stock repurchase, which will lead to the continuous rise of the corporate debt ratio. For example, by the end of 2019, US non-financial enterprises accounted for 75% of GDP, 3% higher than that before the subprime mortgage crisis in 2008.[2]

The second deep-seated reason for the sharp decline of US stocks was that a large number of long-term institutional investors with low risk appetite significantly increased the proportion of equity assets and invested heavily in passive investment products represented by Exchange Traded Funds (ETF). In the long-term low interest rate environment, the long-term institutional investors with low risk preference, represented by pension funds and insurance companies, are facing pressures of decline in the yields of traditional investment (mainly fixed income products) on the asset side and an increase in the present value of future fixed expenditure on the liability side, which significantly increases the investment in equity assets. These investments are heavily invested in the passive investment products represented by ETFs. By the end of 2019, the asset scale of the US passive investment funds had reached $4.3 trillion, counting for 51% of the asset management scale of US equity funds, which exceeded the scale of actively managed funds. Although ETF currently counts for about 10% of the market value of the stock market, due to the more frequent trading of ETF, the trading volume of ETF can reach half of the market trading volume during the peak period.[3] There are also hidden risks behind the rapid development of passive investment: the position structure of a large number of ETFs is very similar to the trading strategy. For example, many ETFs have heavy positions in such blue chip technology stocks as Apple, Microsoft, Google, Amazon, and Facebook. Moreover, many ETF managers follow the trading strategy of buying when the momentum is forming, and sell when the momentum is losing. This means that once the stock market falls below the technical key point under a specific impact, it is easy to trigger the automatic closing of the quantitative trading system, causing the market to plunge.[4] As investors sell a large number of similar blue chips at the same time, the stock market index will fall sharply.

The third deep-seated reason for the sharp decline in the value of US stocks was that the new trading strategies implemented by a large number of hedge funds exacerbated the vulnerability of the stock market. Passive investments in the US stock market are concentrated in ETFs, while active investments are concentrated in hedge funds. A series of new trading strategies implemented by well-known American hedge funds represented by Bridgewater Associates in recent years are easy to amplify market fluctuations in times of market turmoil. For example, the core of risk parity trading strategy is to increase the holdings of assets with declining volatility, and reduce the holdings of assets with rising volatility, so as to obtain income through the negative correlation of the price trend of large categories of assets. Since the US stock market and the corporate bond market have been bullish for many years, the hedge funds that implement such strategies not only hold stocks on a large scale, but also buy corporate bonds in large quantities by means of leverage to maintain the same risk exposure of stocks and bonds. Once there is a devastating impact such as the current pandemic, the plunge in oil prices, the volatility of the stock market, and bond market, the funds implementing the risk parity trading strategy are forced to sell stocks and corporate bonds on a large scale at the same time. This will naturally exacerbate the decline in the prices of stocks and corporate bonds, leading to a new round of selling of funds.[5]

By combining the above trigger factors with deep-seated reasons, we can have a systematic and clear understanding of this round of financial turmoil. First, the spread of the pandemic has led to an increase in investors' risk aversion and triggered investors' first round of selling risky assets. Second, the decline of global crude oil prices led to the rise of the default rate of US high-yield bonds, and the decline of market value. Third, the simultaneous decline of stock and bond prices leads to the simultaneous selling of stocks and bonds by hedge funds implementing risk parity trading strategy, which will further

134 *Zhang Ming*

aggravate the decline of stock and bond prices. Four, once the stock price falls below a specific point, a large-scale automatic closing and trampling of ETF funds will be triggered, which will form a vicious cycle between closing, and a decline in stock price. Finally, the rising equity risk premium in the bond market makes it difficult for the companies to carry out stock repurchase by issuing bonds. At the same time, due to the significant decline in the market stock price (even lower than the position cost of the listed companies), the motivation for the listed companies to repurchase shares no longer exists. Once the repurchase stops, the earnings per share of the listed companies will decline significantly, which will further worsen the fundamentals of the US stock market, and cause new lows.

The Global Financial Turmoil Might Linger

As the central banks of the developed countries led by the Federal Reserve adopted an extremely expansionary monetary policy to rescue the market in March 2020, the turmoil in the global financial market eased significantly in April 2020. For example, in April 2020, the US Dow Jones Industrial Average, Japan's Nikkei 225 index, Germany's DAX index, Britain's FTSE 100 index and France's CAC40 index rose by 11.1%, 6.7%, 9.3%, 4.0%, and 4.0%, respectively. But has the global financial turmoil caused by the COVID-19 virus ended? Can investors start to have peace of mind and even increase their positions in risky assets again? The author believes that the situation is not actually that optimistic.

The pandemic that caused the financial turmoil is still rampant, although the situation in China, Japan, South Korea, and Singapore has eased. In the United States, Italy, Spain, Germany, France, Russia, and other countries, the pandemic is still spreading rapidly, and has not yet peaked. What is more worrying is that the pandemic may further spread to emerging markets and developing countries with poor public health conditions, such as India, and African countries.

The negative growth of the global economy in 2020 will be a certain fact under the impact of the pandemic on economic growth. In the *World Economic Outlook* in April 2020, the International Monetary Fund (IMF) predicted that the global economic growth rate would fall −3.0% in 2020 from growth of 2.9% in 2019. In 2020, the economic growth of the United States, the Euro zone, Japan, Germany, France and the United Kingdom would lose −5.9%, −7.5%, −5.2%, −7.0%, −7.2%, and −6.5%, respectively. Economic growth in China and India would drop to 1.2% and 1.9%, respectively. The COVID-19 pandemic would not only exacerbate the global economic stagnation, but also lead to a continued recession of some economies. In addition, the pandemic would have a serious negative impact on global trade, direct investment, and the global value chain.

After a sharp decline, the valuation level of the developed countries' stock market, led by the United States, has improved significantly, and the stock market bubble is less risky of bursting. As the central banks of the developed countries have implemented an extremely loose monetary policy, the probability of further plunges in the stock market seems to be slight at this time. However, the burst of the dot-com bubble in the US in 2000 sent the stock market into a bearish state for two and a half years. After the outbreak of the US subprime mortgage crisis in 2008, the US stock market was bearish for a year and a half. The current round of decline in US stocks only lasted less than three months. Taking history as a mirror and considering factors such as the spread of the virus in the US, and the deep recession of the US economy in the second quarter of 2020, the author believes that the current round of market turmoil has not yet ended, and that the bear market may have just begun.

In addition, looking from a global perspective, there still seem to be three risk fault lines, which may become the next points of global financial turmoil in the future.

One of the potential risks is the bubble of US corporate bond market. Since the outbreak of the subprime mortgage crisis in 2008, the leverage ratio of the household sector and the financial sector has decreased significantly, while that of the government sector and the enterprise sector has increased significantly. The debt of the US corporate sector exceeded $10 trillion at the end of 2019, reaching a peak of 75% of the GDP. In recent years, the US junk bond market has developed rapidly, with a scale of about $2 trillion, of which the bond issued by the energy sector is about 15%. Among the US investable corporate bonds, the scale of BBB bonds increased from about 15% in 2008 to about 55% in 2019, which means that the average quality of investable corporate bonds has decreased significantly in the past 10 years. Once the credit rating of BBB corporate bonds is lowered by one level (i.e., to junk level), the bond yield will rise by about 3 percentage points, which means that there is a great risk of default of BBB bonds in the future. Recently, the sharp decline in crude oil prices and the impact of the pandemic have led to a significant rise in the yields of US junk bonds, and BBB bonds. It is unknown whether it will trigger a wave of bond defaults in the future. It should be pointed out that the negative impact of the sharp decline in stock prices is significantly lower than that of large-scale bond default, because investors can better accept the loss of stock investment, and credit default may spread, infect, and escalate.

The second potential risk is that the risk of sovereign debt of southern European countries is significantly underestimated. As everyone knows, Italy and Spain are the hardest hit by the COVID-19 virus. What is worse is that Italy and Spain were already fragile. By the end of 2018, the sovereign debt of Italy, Spain, and Greece accounted for 135%, 98% and 181% of their nominal GDP, respectively. By the end of April 2020, Spain's 10-year bond yield was less than 1%, Italy's 10-year bond yield was less than 2%, and Greece's 10-year bond yield was less than 2.5%. During the European debt crisis in 2012, the highest yield of 10-year Treasury bonds of Greece was close to 35%, and the yield of 10-year Treasury bonds of Italy and Spain also reached 7%–8%. In other words, investors may have underestimated the risk of sovereign bonds of

136   Zhang Ming

southern European countries. After the last European debt crisis broke out, southern European countries finally staved off the crisis with the help of such core countries as Germany and France. This time, however, the core countries has also suffered from the severe impact of the pandemic. Therefore, once the sovereign debt crisis breaks out in southern European countries, the rescue from the core countries may be more difficult to count on.

The third potential risk is that the impact of large-scale short-term capital outflows may cause a crisis for some emerging market countries with fragile economic fundamentals. Data show that the current scale of short-term capital outflows from some emerging market countries has exceeded the scale during the outbreak of the subprime mortgage crisis in 2008, and the scale during the QE withdrawal by the Federal Reserve in 2013. Continuous substantial short-term capital outflows will cause devaluation of local currency exchange rate, decline of asset prices, and rise of debt default rate in the emerging market countries, and cause a financial crisis in the countries with relatively weak economic fundamentals. At present, the risk of a financial crisis in emerging market countries such as Argentina, Turkey, Malaysia, South Africa, Russia, and Brazil is pretty high. On April 17, 2020, the Argentine government proposed a restructuring plan for the debt of $66.2 billion, which means that Argentina is about to have its ninth sovereign debt default in history.

Similarities and Differences Between the Current Global Financial Turmoil and the 2008 International Financial Crisis

The intensity of the current global financial turmoil is similar to that of the 2008 international financial crisis. The author believes that the two have both similarities and differences.

One of the similarities is that the reason for the two crises is related to the long-term asset price bubbles, and to the behaviors of the institutions that invest heavily in risky assets by increasing leverage. The reason why the US subprime mortgage crisis broke out in 2008 was that a long period of prosperity of the US real estate market lured a large number of institutions to invest in real estate financial products based on US subprime mortgage loans, such as Mortgage-Backed Securities (MBS), Collateralized Debt Obligations (CDO), etc. As the hikes of interest rate by the Federal Reserve increased the home buyers' mortgage pressure, which in turn increased the default rate of subprime mortgage in the US, the subprime mortgage crisis broke out in 2008. The reason for the current global financial turmoil is that a long-term prosperity of the US stock market attracted a large number of institutions to invest in the stock market through leverage. The outbreak of the COVID-19 pandemic, and the plunge in global oil prices led to a series of massive sell-off, which caused a few circuit breakers.

The second similarity is that after the crisis broke out, there was a liquidity shortage caused by institutional investors selling risky assets in the market, which forced the central banks to provide liquidity to the market through a number of innovative ways. After the outbreak of the US subprime mortgage

Looking into the Financial Turmoil during the COVID-19 Pandemic 137

crisis in 2008, investors' massive selling-off of risky assets led to such a serious shortage of liquidity and credit crunch that the US short-term wholesale financing market was forced to be virtually stopped. In order to avoid the worsening of the financial crisis, and the impact on the real economy, the Federal Reserve was forced to cut interest rates, and launched several rounds of asset purchases, known as QE, and a variety of innovative products to expand liquidity to financial institutions. After the current outbreak of the global financial turmoil, the liquidity shortage reappeared. The Federal Reserve cut interest rates by 150 basis points over a short period of time, restarted a $700 billion QE policy, and launched new liquidity provision models such as the Commercial Paper financing mechanism.

One of the differences is that Bear Stearns and Lehman Brothers, two institutions that ignited the 2008 US subprime mortgage crisis, were the two seller institutions, while Bridgewater Associates and the like, major players during the current global financial turmoil, were buyer institutions. In the former crisis, the collapse of Bear Stearns and Lehman Brothers became a landmark event. They were among the top investment banks on Wall Street, and suffered huge losses due to leveraged investment in toxic assets. Because they are important market movers in the US short-term wholesale financing market and derivatives market, their collapse basically shut down the US short-term wholesale financing market and derivatives market, leading to the rapid amplification of the crisis. In the current global financial turmoil, hedge funds such as Bridgewater Associates, currently at the forefront of the storm, suffered heavy losses because of their heavy bets on the US stock market and corporate bond market. However, the role of the buyer institutions is relatively simple, and its pivotal role in the financial market is much weaker than that of the seller institutions such as the investment banks. This means that even if such hedge funds as Bridgewater Associates, and others fall in the future, their impact on the whole financial market will be significantly lower than that caused by the collapse of Lehman Brothers in 2008.

The other difference between the two is that the US subprime mortgage crisis in 2008 was caused by the companies themselves, and the current global financial turmoil was the result of the pandemic's impact on the real economy. The outbreak of the US subprime mortgage crisis in 2008 was caused by the increase of interest rates by the Federal Reserve, resulting in the rise of the default rate of home buyers, which led to the default of real estate financial products. Therefore, the origin of the crisis was in the real estate market. The direct trigger of this global financial market turmoil was the global spread of the COVID-19 virus, and the plunge of global crude oil prices, namely, the impact on the real economy. As the saying goes, he who has tied a bell to the tiger must untie it himself. Before the global spread of the virus is under control, it is difficult for the financial market to stabilize itself only by the loose monetary policy of the central banks of the developed countries. In other words, it is more difficult for the global financial trouble to recover than was the case during the US subprime mortgage crisis in 2008.

138   *Zhang Ming*

The third difference is that before the outbreak of the US subprime mortgage crisis in 2008, the global economy was experiencing in a period of high growth, whereas before the outbreak of the current global financial turmoil, global economic growth had been relatively sluggish. In the five years from 2003 to 2007, the average growth rate of the global economy was as high as 5.1%, and the global economic growth rate was climbing between 2005 and 2007. In the five years from 2015 to 2019, the average global economic growth rate was only 3.4%, and the global economic growth rate was in a downward trend from 2017 to 2019. Before the subprime mortgage crisis broke out in the US in 2008, economic globalization was advancing rapidly. Before the outbreak of the current round of global financial turmoil, populism, conservatism, and unilateralism were on the rise all over the world, and global economic and trade frictions were significantly escalating. It can be said that the current international situation is very similar to that in the early stage of the Great Depression, from 1929 to 1933. This also means that the current round of global financial turmoil may have a greater weight on the global economy. The possibility is high that the global economy will fall into recession in 2020, and there is still great uncertainty about how long the recession will last.

Potential Impact of Global Financial Turmoil on China

One of the potential negative impacts of the current round of global financial turmoil on China is the intensification of short-term capital outflow, which will lead to the decline of domestic asset prices and the pressure of short-term depreciation of the CNY exchange rate. Once foreign institutional investors suffer significant losses in the US stock market, they will withdraw their funds from emerging market countries and return to their home countries to meet their liquidity needs. This means that in the short term, emerging market countries, including China, will experience large-scale short-term capital outflows. In fact, since the end of February 2020, there has been a sustained large-scale withdrawal of hot money from China. Although the proportion of hot money in the overall market value of China's stock market is limited, due to the concentrated investment of hot money in such blue chips as China Maotai, China Ping An, and Gree Electric Appliance, its continuous withdrawal led to a significant decline in the share price of these blue chips, which noticeably brought down the A-share index. In addition, the intensification of short-term capital outflow will also bring pressure on CNY devaluation. Recently, as the US dollar index once climbed to about 103, the CNY exchange rate against the US dollar fell below 7.1, reaching a new low since 2008.

The second potential negative impact of the current round of global financial turmoil on China is that the decline in global economic growth will lead to the rapid contraction of foreign demand for China's export industry, resulting in a significant adverse impact on China's export industry. In 2019, affected by the intensification of Sino-US economic and trade frictions, China's export performance was not very good, as the average monthly year-on-year growth

Looking into the Financial Turmoil during the COVID-19 Pandemic 139

rate of exports decreased from 11.2% in 2018 to 0.4% in 2019. In the first quarter of 2020, China's export industry hardly resumed its production due to the spread of the virus. From the second quarter of 2020, China's export industry is likely to face the impact of a significant decline in order growth, and this impact may last for a long time, due to the impact on global economy by the pandemic. The contribution of net exports to China's economic growth in 2020 is likely to be negative. If the export industry is seriously hit, it will not only affect economic growth, but also affect the employment of the export industry, making it more difficult for the Chinese government to maintain the stability of the employment market.

The third potential negative impact of the current round of global financial turmoil on China is that the international economic and trade frictions and geopolitical conflicts China will be faced with in the future may rise. This reflects the strategy of some governments to diverge their people's fury at their government's ineffective response to the pandemic by demonizing China. In facing the common global threat of the pandemic, the major powers should have joined hands to respond to the pandemic, and to mitigate its impact. However, with the rise of populism, isolationism, and unilateralism, we should also be prepared for the possible intensification of international economic and trade frictions, and geopolitical conflicts. There is still uncertainty about how the pandemic will affect Sino-US economic and trade relations in the short term. However, this will not change the nature of Sino-US economic and trade frictions, the nature of a "protracted trade war."

As the saying goes that misfortune may be a blessing in disguise, the potential impact of the pandemic on China's economy is not all negative. First, in the coming period of time, the relative proportion of China's economy in the global economy and the contribution of China's economic growth to global economic growth are likely to rise significantly. History is a mirror. It was after the outbreak of the international financial crisis in 2008 that China surpassed Japan in terms of total economy, and became the second-largest economy in the world. Due to the strong and appropriate measures taken by the Chinese government to deal with the pandemic, the virus in China has been preliminarily controlled. Therefore, from the second quarter of 2020, China's economy will rebound after it hits the bottom. In contrast, as the virus is still spreading in the other parts of the world, global economic growth will quicken its downward trend from the second quarter of 2020. As China increases its economic growth, and the other countries experience the opposite, China will strength its economic status in the world. Moreover, after the global financial turmoil becomes basically stable, the CNY assets will be more attractive. And China may have large-scale short-term capital inflows and promote the appreciation of the CNY exchange rate. At present, the yield of China's 10-year Treasury bonds is about 2.6%–2.7%, while that of the United States and Britain is only about 0.6%–0.7%. The yield of 10-year Treasury bonds in the euro zone and Japan is on the edge of zero interest rates. Under normal circumstances, such a large interest rate spread will attract a large number of investment funds into

140 *Zhang Ming*

China. This means that as the panic in global financial markets gradually subsides, the attraction of the CNY assets to foreign investors will rise again. Hot funds will continue to flow in again, and the CNY exchange rate against the US dollar is expected to appreciate again.

Policy Suggestions

The first policy suggestion is that the Chinese government should carefully prevent the short-term impact on China's financial market by the intensification of global financial market turmoil. Once the turmoil leads to a large-scale outflow of both domestic and foreign capital, the Chinese government should moderately tighten the management to avoid a large amount of capital outflow, because a huge outflow will aggravate the decline of domestic asset prices, and the depreciation of the CNY exchange rate. The Chinese government does not need to intervene when the CNY depreciates moderately against the US dollar under normal market conditions. However, if the intensification of global financial turmoil leads to a significant drop of the CNY exchange rate in the short term, the Chinese government should enter the market to stabilize the exchange rate.

The second policy suggestion is that the Chinese government should maintain China's steady economic growth by adopting counter-cyclical macroeconomic policies so as to avoid a rapid decline of economic growth, and avoid another "deluge of stimulus policy." The year-on-year growth rate of China's economy in the first quarter of 2020 is −6.8%. China's economic growth in 2020 may reach 2%–3%, significantly lower than the 6.1% recorded in 2019. On the one hand, we should see that under the impact of the pandemic, the downward adjustment of China's economic growth is inevitable and reasonable; on the other hand, we should also pay attention to prevent the employment pressure and systemic financial risks that may be caused by the sharp decline of economic growth. This means that the Chinese government should implement loose fiscal and monetary policies to stabilize economic growth. At the same time, however, we should try hard to avoid the impact of the macro policy of a "deluge of stimulus measures" on economic growth efficiency and financial risks in the medium and long term. It is very important to grasp the "degree" of the macro policy easing. The Political Bureau of the CPC Central Committee held a meeting on April 17, 2020, and put forward the "six guarantees" for the first time, that is, to ensure employment, people's livelihood, market order, food and energy security, industrial chain and supply chain stability, and normal grass-roots operation. The predecessor of the "six guarantees" was the "six stabilities" in six fronts, indicating the policy focus of the Chinese government in 2020, highlighting the bottom-line thinking of the Chinese government under special circumstances.[6] This also means that the probability of adopting an excessive stimulus policy has further decreased.

The third policy suggestion is that the Chinese government should speed up structural reforms to improve the efficiency of economic growth and the

Looking into the Financial Turmoil during the COVID-19 Pandemic 141

long-term confidence of investors. From 2007 to 2019, China's economic growth rate decreased from 14.2% to 6.1%. The continuous decline is due to such structural factors as population aging, and the decline of economic growth efficiency. Therefore, the Chinese government should speed up structural reforms to improve the efficiency of economic growth, and enhance the confidence of domestic and foreign investors. The structural reforms include, but are not limited to, accelerating the reform of state-owned enterprises represented by the reform of mixed ownership, accelerating the reform of land circulation, accelerating the opening of service sectors such as education, medical care and elderly care to domestic private capital, accelerating more inclusive urbanization, accelerating the construction of a new round of regional economic integration, etc. On April 9, 2020, the CPC Central Committee and the State Council issued the *Opinions on Building a More Perfect Market-oriented Allocation System and Mechanism of Factors*, which proposed to promote the market-oriented pricing, allocation and trading of land, labor, capital, science and technology, data and other factors. This means that, in future, the marketization of factor prices and the free flow of factors are expected to become an important starting point for the next round of China's economic structural reform.

Notes

1 Xu Chi, and Zhang Wenyu. "The 'Triple Collapse' of American Balance Sheet: A Comparison between the Current Crisis and the 1929 Great Depression." *Zhongtai Securities Report* 19 March, 2020.
2 Ibid.
3 Wang Han. "Causes, Current Situation and Prospects of the Current US Financial Crisis." *Industrial Securities Report* 20 March, 2020.
4 Xu Chi, and Zhang Wenyu. "The 'Triple Collapse' of American Balance Sheet: A Comparison between the Current Crisis and the 1929 Great Depression." *Zhongtai Securities Report* 19 March, 2020.
5 Zhang Ming. "Why Did the US Stock Market Plunge So Violently?" *Caijing Magazine* 13 March, 2020.
6 The "six stabilities" refer to stability in employment, finance, trade, foreign investment, domestic investment, and anticipation.

12 The COVID-19 Pandemic and the Changes in the Past Century[*]

Yuan Peng[**]

This Pandemic is Comparable to a World War, and the Existing International Order is Unsustainable

Over the past hundreds of years, changes in the international order have often been triggered by a war, such as the establishment of the Westphalia System after three decades of war in Europe around the turn of the 19th century, the Versailles–Washington System after the First World War, and the Yalta System after the Second World War. The outline of the current international order is mainly based on the system established in the wake of the Second World War. However, in the seventy-plus years since that conflict, with the end of the Cold War in 1991, the "September 11 incident" in 2001, the international financial crisis in 2008, and Trump's presidential victory in 2016, the existing international order has experienced a serious of severe shocks. Although the basic frameworks still exist, most international organizations are no longer fully functional. For instance, the role of the United Nations is limited, the World Trade Organization (WTO) is barely functional, the International Monetary Fund (IMF), and the World Bank are short of funds, the authority of the World Health Organization (WHO) is questionable, the global arms control system is close to collapse, etc. Moreover, international norms have been trampled on repeatedly, the US leadership, and its willingness to lead, have declined simultaneously, the cooperation mechanism of the major countries is chaotic, and the international order is on the verge of crumbling.

The outbreak and the spread of the COVID-19 pandemic has devastated the world: many countries have closed their borders, most economic activities have stopped or been severely disrupted, the stock markets have crashed, oil prices have plunged, and normal exchanges have ground to a halt. In addition, the exchange of evil words is common, and wild rumors abound. Previously, only a world war could have had such a great impact and influence on the existing international order. The old order is unsustainable, but the new order has not yet

---

[*] This chapter was published in *Contemporary International Relations* 5 (2020).
[**] Research Fellow, and Dean of China Institute of Contemporary International Relations.

DOI: 10.4324/9781003433897-12

emerged. This is the essential feature of the great changes in the world that have not been seen for a century. It is also the root of the current international situation.

The world during the pandemic resembles the world after the First World War. At that time, although weakening in power, the British Empire remained strong and influential, and was unwilling to relinquish its leadership. At this time the United States, a rising power with growing ambitions, lacked the military might and international influence to replace Britain, and Europe was busy with its post-war reconstruction. Furthermore, Japan and Russia took advantage of the chaotic situation to expand their influence, China was plagued with domestic and foreign troubles, and many countries in Asia, Africa, and Latin America didn't have a clue of what course to take. In a word, the world was bewildered as the major powers were confrontational. Some ten years later, the world fell into the "Great Depression," and gradually slipped into the Second World War.

Today, the United States under Trump has failed to take seriously its due responsibility of a world leader during the pandemic as it was only concerned with protecting itself. Due to the erroneous policies, the US became the world's hardest-hit area. Nearly two million people were infected, and more than 100,000 people died, a scenario far more devastating than the "September 11 Incident." In fact, more people have died of the COVID-19 virus than all the deaths combined during the Vietnam War, the Gulf War, and the Afghanistan War. It seems that the US was frustrated in terms of both its soft and hard power at the same time. As a result, its international influence fell sharply. The 2020 General Election will be a battle between Trump's policy stance of "America First," and Biden's stance of "Building Back Better." But, even if Biden wins, it will be difficult for the United States to resume its position as a world "leader," due to the internal political constraints, and the changes across the globe. However, the United States, like Great Britain after the First World War, still remains powerful enough to prevent any other country from challenging for its leading position. It will take a tougher, more provocative, and arrogant foreign policy approach and it will ramp up all its effort to contain and suppress China. It seems certain that the strategic rivalry between China and the United States will become more intense.

The pandemic has altered the existing geopolitical landscape dominated by the "one superpower with a few powerful countries." Even though its primacy currently remains intact, the United States will find it harder to dominate the world. China has rapidly emerged as a rising power, but faced the bottleneck of catching up and surpassing. Europe is declining in its overall strength, and its future direction is uncertain. Russia has become more powerful in the times of chaos. India has been thwarted in its ambition to be a major player because of its innate weaknesses and shortcomings. Japan will have a hard time after the Olympic Games has been postponed. After the pandemic, all the countries will be busy cleaning up the mess and re-drawing their blueprint. While looking forward to a period of international cooperation, they also hesitate, wait and see with a complex mentality. The "unipolar era" led by the United States will come to an end, but China is in no position to start a "bipolar era" with the United States. The prospect of having a multipolar world has become more treacherous. China, the United States, and Russia will be more influential in the area of international politics. This trilateral interaction will be crucial in reshaping the future world order. In addition, Europe, Japan, and India will each strengthen their strategic autonomy.

The momentum of collective emerging in Asia, Africa, and Latin America is halted. The pandemic with the oil situation presents the Middle East a bleak prospect, and the worst is to start a "dark era." Latin America has grasped neither the changes in the past century to accelerate reform and development, nor the time window to effectively respond to the pandemics, experiencing chaos in politics, economy and social development, and further sliding from the "middle-income trap" since the end of the 20th century to the "myth of the loss of developmental direction." Africa, long reliant on global trade and investment, has the worst public health conditions. Once the pandemic is out of control, Africa may suffer from a humanitarian disaster. India and Brazil are maneuvering around between the United States, China, Russia, and Europe, with an obvious posture of sitting on the fence. China will be challenged with its relations with the developing countries.

The Downward World Economy only One Step Away from a Great Depression

The economic foundation determines the superstructure. It follows that the economic security is the basis of national and international security. After the Cold War, thanks to the connectivity brought about by globalization and information technology, and to the overall peaceful and stable international environment, the world economy had been prosperous for some time, which enhanced China's rapid development. However, the 2008 international financial crisis exposed the deep-seated problems of the US and European economies, and revealed the imbalance of the development of globalization. The prescription for the United States to get rid of the crisis was not through painful structural reform, but through passing on contradictions, an attempt like drinking poison to quench thirst. The result was that the "chronic disease" was not cured but that it was, in fact, causing some new diseases. The emergence of non-traditional political figures such as Obama and Trump is the result of the misaligned economic and political relationship in the United States, which has led to social polarization. The European debt crisis is not over, the Ukraine crisis broke out, the refugee crisis is still serious, the impact of the "Brexit" is still grave, etc. As the saying goes, misfortunes never come singly. All these factors weigh on the world economy.

In order to "make America great again," Trump abandoned multilateralism, internationalism, and the principle of free trade, resorted to populism, unilateralism and protectionism, started the Sino-US trade war, tried to reverse the process of globalization, and obstructed free trade. Although the

US pushed its economy and stock market up by way of exerting its bullying power, they could not stay that way for long because of the fragile foundation. In general, the world economy has experienced an overall downturn, the European economy remains slow as usual, the Russian economy has not improved, even the once generally optimistic Indian economy suddenly slowed down and stalled, and China's economy began to enter the stage of a "new normal."

The outbreak of the pandemic further sank the world economy. China, the "world factory," East Asia, the most economically dynamic area, the United States, Europe, Latin America, and Africa were all hit hard. The impact spread to all sectors like finance, technology, aviation, entertainment, so on and so forth. The world's major economies contracted from between 10% and 30% of their GDP, and the unemployment rate reached about 20%. The bleak picture was seldom seen in decades. It is an international consensus that the current world economic recession far exceeded the 2008 financial crisis. Although there are different opinions on whether it will fall into the 1929–1933 type of "Great Depression" in the next stage, it is more likely that the world economy will be a little better than that of the "Great Depression," but worse than that of the 2008 financial crisis. The prolonged "Great Depression" finally led to the Second World War, and to the collapse of the world economic system. At present, it does not seem that the current recession will snowball into something like the "Great Depression" in the strict sense. However, by conventional standards (more than two years of recession plus a negative GDP growth of more than 10%), it is very likely that the world economy will fall into a general recession.

This largely depends on two factors. One is the development of the pandemic. At present, there is no certainty when we all have the vaccine available. It might take one or two years. During this interval, the pandemic may break out again in India, the Middle East, Latin America and Africa. There is a risk of secondary wave of infection in China, the United States, Europe, and Japan. At the time of writing, the recovery of the global supply chain, industrial chain and demand chain is nowhere to be seen. In a word, without the elimination of the pandemic, there is no hope for a real economic recovery. The second factor is the international cooperation. If the G20 summit is held in a timely manner, just as we did in the wake of the 2008 financial crisis, and gives rise to extensive and in-depth international cooperation, the short-term recovery of the world economy is not impossible. After all, the US financial system is still strong, China's economic resilience is extremely strong, and the fundamentals of the world's major economies are generally unimpaired. Unfortunately, during the pandemic, cooperation among the major countries was replaced by confrontation, which greatly shook people's invaluable confidence in promoting economic development. If all the countries go their own way in the post-pandemic era, especially if the United States still fights a trade war with China, and even forces enterprises to return home to produce items like ventilators, and if the United States intensifies its new economic model of "producing locally and consuming locally," or creates a new international political chaos by filing

146 *Yuan Peng*

COVID-19 lawsuits against China, global trade will continue to sink, foreign investment will continue to shrink, and the world economy will only be worse in the future. If so, another great depression is inevitable. The difference from its predecessor is only in form, magnitude, and duration.

In the era of globalization, all countries are in the same boat. Only by praying for each other to be good can we be good. Only by working together in the same boat can we overcome the difficulties of the times. The G20 summit is the beginning of a sustained effort, and more is needed and expected.

More Sino-US Confrontations while the Major Countries Seem More Divided

There are no eternal friends, only eternal interests. The division and reorganization of major country relations are the eternal theme of international politics. This round of differentiation and reorganization is led by Sino-US relations, and propels the strategic interaction between China, the US, Russia, Europe, India, and Japan. The results will have a profound impact on the evolution of the international pattern in the future.

Before the outbreak of the pandemic, Sino-US relations had already gone awry. The United States abandoned its policy of engagement with China, and adopted a policy of containment and suppression. As a result, strategic competition between the two countries overshadows strategic cooperation. Economic and trade frictions, geopolitical rivalry, and ideological confrontations have become the "new normal." The noise of a "new Cold War" can be heard all the time, and the possibility of Sino-US "decoupling" is increasing. The COVID-19 pandemic should have become a buffer, a pressure relief valve or an adhesive for Sino-US relations; instead, for all the wrong reasons, it served as a transformer, accelerator or catalyst that has intensified the Sino-US rivalry. In fact, the outbreak of the COVID-19 virus was only an accidental factor. The real reason is the fundamental change in the US strategy towards China in recent years, that is, the United States has clearly regarded China as its major strategic opponent, and ramped up "all government" power and means to contain China. In addition, the US domestic political fight aggravated the complicated situation. In order to win the general election, the Trump administration was eager to blame China for its own faults. The extremist forces took every chance to discredit and suppress China. The Biden camp of the Democratic Party had to show strength to China under all kinds of pressure. It can be predicted that Sino-US relations may further deteriorate during the pandemic, and the election. To make matters worse, the anti-China hardliners in the US could see more confrontations between the two countries, as they had always hoped.

However, the Sino-US confrontation will not evolve into a Cold War marked with a bipolar confrontation or a confrontation between two camps. First, because China and the United States are so deeply intertwined in their national interests that neither side can bear the cost of a long-term confrontation.

The COVID-19 Pandemic and the Changes in the Past Century 147

Second, because the US alliance system and the West are not what they used to be, the European and American policies towards China are not synchronized, and the rift among the Western countries became wider due to the pandemic. Actually, Sino-EU relations are at the best point in history. Third, because China–Russia relations are generally solid, it is difficult for the United States to join hands with Russia to suppress China even if it was the wish of the United States. Fourth, Japan and India generally still hope to butter their bread on both sides. In this sense, China and the United States will not move towards a "new Cold War," nor will they form bipolar camps. The more likely prospect is that the United States will accelerate the formation of a "small close-knit circle" that confronts China, and will "withdraw from some organizations" so as to establish new ones in the fields of finance, economy, trade, science, technology, industrial chain, and international organizations for the purpose of excluding China. On the contrary, China has explored a new way to survive and to compete with the US by building a "community of common destiny for mankind" through deeper cooperation with the countries along the "Belt and Road." Thus, the world may form two economic circles with the United States and China at each center. The current Sino-US rivalry fundamentally differs from the bipolar confrontations during the Cold War, because China and the United States cannot completely "decouple" from each other, and because the nature of their competition is a competitive cooperation. Since other countries cannot completely rely on either of them, they need to cooperate with both of them.

In this case, the pattern of Sino-US competition will be further solidified and will not be fundamentally changed with the results of the US election. The United States, Europe, and Japan have common interests in jointly containing China, but China, Europe, and Japan have great impetus to deepen their relations. The United States and Russia have tactical needs to get closer, but China–Russia cooperation is strategically driven. The basic pattern of the US–Europe alliance cannot be changed for the time being, but the rift between the two continents will be widened. While the tension between China and Japan is gradually eased, there are worries about the Sino-India relation, although it is stable for the time being. The United States has lost the charisma to continue leading the world as it has damaged its image. China, big but not strong, does not intend to (and indeed cannot) replace the United States for the time being. Similarly, Russia, Europe, India, and other powers do not have the ability or willingness to dominate global affairs. In the next three to five years, the pattern of international relations will be in a chaotic state like the "Warring-States period," more like a period of transition. The difficulty of the cooperation between major powers will be significantly increased. Minor countries will be forced to stay together for mutual protection.

On the whole, China is in a relatively favorable position in designing major-country relations, a position won by not only the continuous efforts to promote the kind of diplomacy with Chinese characteristics in recent years, but also as a reliable provider of public health goods for the world. However, a favorable position is not equal to a strategic advantage. There are variables in the development of the pandemic, the implementation and operation of strategies, foreign relations, and the changes of the domestic politics of various countries. Once the pandemic situation in the United States and Europe exceeds what they can psychologically tolerate, they would raise waves of accountability, lawsuits, and pressures on China that have been concocted for long. They will make a big fuss by taking advantage of the pandemic. China has already become the first country to stave off the pandemic, an envious position that might, therefore, draw a wave of collective attack. This is a new trend in China's relations with the world that has not been seen in decades.

The Global Geostrategic Pattern Continues to Evolve, and the Asia-Pacific Region Will Hold a Central Spot

Since the establishment of the modern international system and globalization, the global geostrategic center has rotated in Europe, Asia, the Atlantic region, and the Pacific region. In the period between the end of the Second World War and the end of the Cold War, the Atlantic region occupied a central spot. The United States and Europe, with their economic, military and political advantages, created new history, and vigorously expanded NATO eastward, dominating international order, and seemingly capable of doing whatever they wanted to.

However, since the beginning of the 21st century, especially after the Gulf War, the relationship between the United States and Europe has become increasingly alienated, as if the Atlantic Ocean had grown wider. China's rise has been a prelude to the eastward shift of world power, which has led to the revival of Northeast Asia, the revitalization of Southeast Asia, and the rise of India, enhancing the Asia-Pacific's position the most active region in the world economy. At the same time, the volatile security situation in the Korean Peninsula, the East China Sea, the South China Sea, and the Taiwan Strait has made the Asia-Pacific a high-risk area for potential global military conflicts. As Obama's "Asia Rebalancing Strategy" and Trump's "Indian-Pacific Strategy" show, the two parties in the US reached a consensus on a basic national policy of the eastward strategic shifting. Inspired by this, Russia began to "turn south," India began to "turn east," Australia began to "turn north," Japan began to "turn west," and even Europe began to focus on the Pacific region in spite of the distance involved. The wide Pacific Ocean suddenly became not only crowded, but also more restless. The Asia-Pacific region is incomparable in terms of its geopolitical and geo-economic significance.

Although the COVID-19 pandemic first broke out in China and East Asia on a large scale, making the Asia-Pacific region once again a global focus, China, Japan, and South Korea took the lead in controlling the transmission. China and South Korea are the first countries that have had the pandemic under control, setting an example for the world. Their success highlighted the uniqueness and comparative advantages of East Asian culture, values, collectivism, and social governance, making the rise of the Asia-Pacific region signify more than the usual economic achievement, and possibly embody the revival of Asian civilization. In this context, China, Japan, and ROK have stronger desire for more cooperation, and the "ASEAN Plus Three Mechanism" (the ASEAN countries plus China, Japan, and ROK) shows interest in closer cooperation. For a time, the Asia-Pacific region grabbed the world's attention for its comprehensive cooperative spirit.

In contrast, other regions are overshadowed. For instance, Europe, once bragging of having entered the "postmodern age," was hit hard by the debt crisis, refugee crisis, Ukrainian crisis, and "Brexit" crisis in recent years. This time, the pandemic crisis exposed all the problems of Europe. People began to wonder why the West was absent in the world health crisis. The Middle East is doing no better. Due to the strategic vacuum left by the US withdrawal and the weak influence of Russia, and Europe, the major forces in the Middle East are impatient to do something. Iran, Saudi Arabia, Israel, and Turkey all have great ambitions for more influence. However, none of them could stand out more powerful any time soon. The international oil price plunged to even negative, a sign that the Middle East would rapidly sink into a "dark age." Latin America and Africa far away from the global geographical center are also difficult to augment their overall influence in the post-pandemic era.

It can be predicted that the economic recovery after the pandemic will be more dependent on the economic situation, supply chain and industrial chain of the Asia Pacific region. International security will also be further focused on this region due to the specific implementation of the US "Indian-Pacific Strategy." The signs of the storm in the South China Sea and the Taiwan Strait are clearer. Under the background of intensified Sino-US rivalry, how to better manage the Asia-Pacific region, that is, China's surrounding areas, how to deepen and implement the "the Belt and Road" initiative first in the Asia-Pacific region, and how to deal with the risk of potential military conflict are all strategic issues that China must face after the pandemic.

Globalization Encountered a Counter Current Vortex, and Global Governance Is Facing an Unprecedented Crisis

The development of modern world history from decentralization to integration is not only the general law, but also the inevitable result of economic development and scientific and technological progress. The great geographical discovery opened the prelude from regionalization to globalization. The industrial revolution and the scientific and technological revolution accelerated the process of globalization. The bourgeois revolution with the power of capital and the market opened national borders, and connected the world into an economy with stakeholders. The socialist revolution called for "the proletarians of the world to unite" so as to make the power of thought travel far and wide. After the end of the Cold War, the advent of the information age has truly made the globe connected, increased personnel mobility, and the great economic and trade connectivity. Soon, the concept of "global village" came into being. In short, the trend of globalization, like a trickle converging into a rolling torrent, is already surging. It is an objective existence independent of human will, and no force can stop it

However, with the in-depth development of globalization, it is an indisputable fact that a series of new problems, new contradictions and new challenges come along. This is another aspect of globalization. Where will the tide of globalization flow and end? Do countries only pursue the process of globalization or care about the results? Does the integration of the global economy mean that politics should follow the same path to become integrated to symbolize the "end of history," to use Fukuyama's term? With the exposure of the chronic diseases of the Western liberal system and the capitalist system, in contrast to the efficiency, and vitality of the socialist system with Chinese characteristics at the same time, the free market economy will not necessarily help to move towards the Western-style freedom and democracy. More and more people in the West are confused about the phenomenon, which means that the economic globalization will not be synchronized with the political globalization anticipated by the Western strategic circles. In addition, if the promotion of economic globalization is not in line with a country's domestic policies, it will inevitably lead to domestic development imbalance and global development imbalance. If the internal imbalance is not corrected through structural reform, it will aggravate domestic social contradictions and boost protectionism, populism, isolationism and adventurism at the international front. The emergence of the "Trump phenomenon" is the result of the failure of the United States to carry out the national strategic transformation in response to globalization and multi-polarization in the past 20 years. The measures taken by the Trump administration were not meant to make internal and external strategic adjustments in line with the direction of globalization, but to make such anti-globalization actions as reinforcing trade protectionism, Sino-US decoupling, and enticing the US companies to shift their producing capacity back home. Ironically, the measures and the actions have not fundamentally changed the deep-seated structural problems in the United States, but led to new international tensions.

From the global level, the globalization of economy, information and resources should give birth to corresponding global governance at the same time. However, in fact, global governance is always on people's lips, but not in deeds, as short of capital, manpower, and mechanism. It seems that the economic foundation is obviously disproportionate or even disconnected from the superstructure. The International Monetary Fund and the World Bank are limited in their roles in response to the financial or economic crisis. The central banks of all countries have become the leading force in dealing with the crises. As a result, they compete to adopt more financial stimulus measures or cut taxes. The measures could work temporally, but like quelling thirst with poison. Awful consequences are sure to follow.

The outbreak and widespread transmission of the COVID-19 virus as an "invisible enemy" was a special alert to the world. It should have forced countries to rethink and straighten out the internal logic and development direction of globalization, and re-recognize the paramount importance of global governance. However, what we see is unsatisfactory or even worsens the situation. The political leaders of some countries led by the United States do not actively promote "Globalization 2.0" and strengthen the capacity-building of global governance, but blame globalization for going too far and too deep. Instead of taking the global spread of the pandemic as a mirror to strengthen leadership responsibility, and strengthen global governance, it is regarded as the defect of globalization and as an opportunity to promote anti-globalization policies. Instead of seeking cooperation between major countries or international cooperation to solve the shortage problem of medical materials, some countries narrowly believe that "localization" and "regionalization" of relevant industries are the right way, and vigorously promote the return home of some manufacturing capacity. Instead of learning from the bitter experience and strengthening the capacity of international organizations, they withdrew funds from the WHO, slandered the effectiveness and contribution of the WHO, and plunged global governance into an unprecedented difficult situation.

At present, it is too early to make an assertive judgment on the prospect of globalization. After all, globalization, which has gone through hundreds of years, is the general trend of history. Those who go with it prosper, and those who go against it die. People of insight in all countries are deeply concerned about the development of globalization. A few politicians who go against the trend are like ants trying to shake the tree. People haven't started reflecting on the post-pandemic world, yet. The so-called "decoupling" and "business-return" will eventually be easier said than done: they are empty slogans to be discarded. After the great disaster, the right way for the world is to focus, reflect and review the process of globalization, and global governance, so as to be ready to move on. China's advocacy of building a community with a shared future for mankind, the promotion of the joint construction of the "the Belt and Road," and adherence to free trade and multilateralism are the right choices, which respect history, and conform to the times. China should be unswerving and persistent in its choices. For the proposition of global governance, which was once favored by the West and is now either abandoned or too powerless to continue by the West, China can enrich and improve it from both theoretical and practical levels. Although it is like putting new wine in old bottles, it is an opportunity to enhance China's international influence.

The Core of International Political Competition: Disputes Over System, Mode of Development, and the Area of Science and Technology

One of the most prominent changes in international politics after the end of the Cold War is the rise of China, and the growing maturity and self-confidence of the socialist system with Chinese characteristics embodied behind its rise. Correspondingly, it is the decline of the West, the defects of the capitalist system, and the damage of the leading liberal international system. The Cold War confrontation between the United States and the Soviet Union over ideology and two systems has evolved into a contest between China and the United States on the current development path and development model. The fundamental change of the US strategy towards China is not only the result of its response to the changes in power relations between the two countries, but also reflects the effort to alleviate the great impact of China's development model on Western-style freedom and democracy. What are such arch anti-China figures as Pompeo, Navarro, Bannon, and Gingrich preoccupied is the so-called profound "challenge" of the Chinese system to the American system. The trade war against China launched by the United States was intended to undermine China's "made in China" plan, the state-owned enterprise subsidy policy, the structural reform, etc., it is obvious that the "war" was not really about trade itself, but rather about China's political system or politics. The signing of the first-stage trade agreement between China and the United States should have been a strategic buffer or time window for the two countries to temporarily "cease fire," and rationally view their economic situations, but unexpectedly, the outbreak of the COVID-19 virus disrupted the rhythm.

In the face of the pandemic, China quickly controlled the pandemic, and took the lead in resuming work and production, because it has centralized leadership, unified command, coordinated actions, integrated the central and local governments, assisted each other, coordinated health system and community management. All in all, China is always people-oriented, showing the unique advantages of its system, in sharp contrast to the institutional weaknesses exposed in the United States and Europe, such as party opposition, radical liberalism, political polarization, so on and so forth. As it is unwilling to admit the decline of its system or policy errors, the West is bound to increase its stigmatization of China to cover up its own defects and faults by accusing China of "concealing the pandemic," using the anti-pandemic diplomacy to "achieve geo-strategic ambitions," and preaching "ideological victory." Just as some Western media assert, the COVID-19 virus is evolving into a strategic contest between the Chinese model and the Western model. If so, it will be a great misfortune for international politics. In fact, all systems have their own advantages and disadvantages. China is firmly opposed to any attempt to impose the Western system on itself, and will never blindly promote its own system model. As a Chinese saying goes, peaches and plums never brag, but throngs of people look for them. China believes that all civilizations should learn from each other so as to enrich the world with colorful diversity.

The pandemic once again demonstrates the power of science and technology. China's rapid stabilization and control of the situation are due to the relevant scientific and technological innovation and development in recent years, including big data, health code, express delivery services, pandemic inquiry system, transmission tracking, electronic payment system, grid management, etc. China has the comparative advantage over the West in these areas. Understandably, the advantages will force the West to increase adjustment. However, subject to public opinions, election politics, and its belief in absolute freedom and human rights, the West has a treacherous road ahead in its adjustment.

Rethinking about the New Relationship Between China and the World

A permanent question for the Chinese people during the recent four decades of reform, or during the seven decades since the founding of New China, and even during the 160 years after the Opium War, has remained the same: what kind of relationship should China have with the world? China, bullied and humiliated for over a century, rose up to fight, and has finally won respect. Only the Chinese people know the taste of Sino-foreign relations. The recent four decades of reform is also the period of reshaping the relationship between China and the world. Its theme is China's "integration into the world." In fact, China's rise should be attributed to "independently build socialism with Chinese characteristics in the process of being connected with rather than separated from economic globalization."

As China's continued rapid rise has brought about economic prosperity, political confidence and strategic initiative, the relationship between China and the world is undergoing great changes. In short, the world is different from what it was, and is experiencing the great changes that have not been seen in a century. China is no longer what it used to be: it is growing from a big country to a powerful country. China and the world have been so widely linked that they act and react along with each other. From the one-way "integration" in the past to a two-way shaping and influencing each other, China is not only integrated into the world, but also creatively participates, and constructively guides in world affairs. Meanwhile, China needs to accept and embrace the world's reverse integration with China. Since the 18th National Congress of the Communist Party of China, China has taken win–win cooperation as the ideological basis, peaceful development as the strategic choice, the "Belt and Road" as the main starting point, the construction of new international relations as the goal for some time in the future, and the promotion of the construction of a community with a shared future for mankind as the ultimate pursuit, China has formed a new set of international strategic frameworks that are based on historical inheritance, and realistic consideration and innovation. In this sense, China and the world have entered a new historical stage of relations.

However, while China has increased its participation and leading role in the world, the United States has adopted the "America First" policy and chosen to "contract" strategically. It is quite ironic that China and the United States have taken opposing strategies to develop their relations with the world. As a result, the United States does not view the changing situation of China's relations with the world from the perspective of historical progress, but speculates China's intention with a strategic vigilance. That is the reason for the United States to take high-pressure actions to block and contain China. Steve Bannon and others even claimed that the "Belt and Road" initiative was China's blending of the three Western geostrategic theories to achieve its global "geostrategic ambition." Coincidentally, since the outbreak of the COVID-19 pandemic, China's reciprocating assistance to the world has also been blamed for "achieving geostrategic goals" by taking advantage of the pandemic. The pandemic and the misinterpretation of the "Belt and Road" initiative have given new connotations to China's relation with the world. A new start is expected.

In fact, COVID-19 has not altered the overall situation of the changing world, but has made the great change come faster and fiercer. It has not changed the nature of China's relationship with the world, but has made it more complicated on many fronts. Nor has the pandemic changed the basic judgment that China is still in and will be in a period of strategic opportunity for a long time. After all, China was among the first countries that had the virus under control, and began to resume work and production in a planned way. As shown by the annual convening of the National People's Congress, and the Chinese people's Political Consultative Conference, China continues to push for its strategic deployment in an orderly manner. That said, China will find it more difficult to seize opportunities, and will meet with significantly more risks and challenges. The key lies in whether China can take a good care of its own business while providing public goods for the world, and assuming the responsibility of a major country in this special period when other countries are still fighting the pandemic. This is not only the premise for the new phase of China's relations with the world, but also the foundation for the great rejuvenation of the Chinese nation.

Before setting out again, we must first look back to where we have come from so as to unswervingly promote a new round of reform and opening-up. We cannot afford giving up halfway, but can only move forward more bravely. Given that, we need to take it easy, and move on composedly. When the goal of the "first 100 years" is soon realized, we should take a break, pause a while, review our experience, draw lessons, and find general rules so as to create conditions for realizing the goals of the "second 100 years." In addition, we must liberate our minds, seek truth from facts, timely sort out, rectify, and straighten out the ideological conflicts in the era of new media on the Internet. Without a unified understanding of ideology, it will be extremely difficult to embark on the great journey of the "second 100 years." Finally, the relationship between development and security must be straightened out. The biosafety problems exposed by the pandemic, and all the other national security issues listed under the overall national security conception, indicate that development needs to be guaranteed by national security, otherwise it may face the risk of a half-way failure because of external attacks. In that case, the success of the economic development at home may return to zero overnight. Of course, development is all in all the most important, but the development after 40-year reform and opening up needs a "prefix," that is "safe development."

13 Avoiding the "Free Fall" of Sino-US Relations*

*Zheng Yongnian***

The COVID-19 pandemic not only poses a great threat to human life, but also poisons the most important bilateral relations in the world, that is, Sino-US relations. In fact, this relationship is not a simple bilateral one, but the most important pillar of the current world order. However, at a time when the world most needs these two countries to lead the world in the fight against the COVID-19 virus, people do not see any cooperation between the two countries. Instead, people watch with fear that the conflict between the two countries is becoming increasingly serious.

Although President Xi Jinping had a friendly telephone conversation with President Trump on the cooperation, and responses to the COVID-19 pandemic, and although Trump promised to personally supervise the implementation of the consensus reached by the two heads of state, realistically speaking, the Sino-US relationship that people once saw is gone forever.

Evan Osnos, a former reporter of *The New Yorker* magazine in China, published an article on January 6, 2020, wherein he quoted a senior White House official as saying that the US–China relationship is in "free fall."[1] But "free fall" is not an accurate way to describe today's Sino-US relationship, because there is nothing to resist the fall. On the contrary, there is a great push behind the fall into the "Thucydides trap" that China and the United States did not want to see in recent years.

Although COVID-19 has a strong degree of infectivity, if the anti-pandemic measures are appropriate, the virus is still controllable. However, if the Sino-US conflict gets out of control, not only will the Cold War escalate frequently, but a hot war may occur. No one can predict what kind of disaster this will bring to the two countries and the world. What is more depressing is that although people are more and more scared of the COVID-19 virus today, they seem to be willing to watch the rapid deterioration of Sino-US relations, as if it has nothing to do with them. Others even push for the deterioration, either intentionally or unintentionally.

---

* Parts of this chapter were published in *Zaobao* (Morning Paper) on 7 April and 19 May, 2020. Some revisions made here.

** Professor, and Director of East Asia Institute, National University of Singapore.

DOI: 10.4324/9781003433897-13

During the Cold War between the United States and the Soviet Union, although China and the United States could conduct nuclear deterrence against each other, the two countries still carried out effective cooperation in the fields of public health, jointly promoted smallpox vaccination, and finally eliminated smallpox, a severe infectious disease for mankind. What about Sino-US relations today?

What people see today is that politics has almost completely replaced policy. Although both countries have internal politics and their relations are bound to be affected by internal politics, if there is no effective policy to resolve the problems caused by politics, the politics of the two countries will fall into its worst form, namely, war. In the words of the Austrian strategist Clausewitz, war is simply politics by other means.

Since the establishment of diplomatic relations, the development of the Sino-US relations has not been smooth. On the contrary, it has had periods of great difficulties, and even crises, which included the US-led Western sanctions against China after the political storm in 1989, the Taiwan Strait Crisis in 1996, the bombing of the Chinese Embassy in Belgrade in 1999, and the aircraft collision in the South China Sea in 2001.

However, in the past, the leaders of the two countries had an overall understanding of the Sino-US relations, which involved at least maintaining working relations and seeking possible cooperation even in the worst times. With this deep understanding in place, although politics may interfere from time to time, there were always policies to resolve the crisis caused by politics. The two countries had significant cooperation on the international financial crisis in 2008, and during the Ebola virus epidemic in 2014.

Today, this overall situation no longer exists. Without any scientific findings, President Trump insisted that the novel coronavirus started from the Wuhan Institute of Virology, and called it the "Chinese virus." Senior officials of the US State Department also referred to it as the "Wuhan virus." American politicians and government officials blamed others for their own faults, adopting a tit-for-tat strategy, while China adopted a more aggressive style of diplomacy, known as "wolf warrior diplomacy." The way they interact makes their relationship very tense.

When Diplomats Become Politicians

When politics replaces policy, conflicts are sure to replace diplomacy. Today, with the exception of a few rational ones in the United States, who are still doing what they should do as diplomats, almost all other diplomats have become political figures, who are making diplomacy politics. It seems no one is making any policy, and foreign policy has long been a thing of the past.

This is true not only in the field of diplomacy, but also across the whole of society. In the United States, according to Max Baucus, the former US ambassador to China, "A lot of people knew what was going on was wrong. They knew it was wrong, but they didn't stand up and say anything about it.

158 *Zheng Yongnian*

They felt intimidated…And now in the United States, if anybody says anything reasonable about China, he or she feels intimidated, afraid his head is going to be chopped off."[2]

Trump can be said to be the most important example of the contemporary Western populist politicians. Over the years, the anti-China political forces in the United States were getting mobilized, and may now have been fully mobilized. This time, they grabbed the outbreak of the novel coronavirus to finally make China, rather than the virus, an enemy of the United States.

Of course, the United States does not lack rational political figures. The Democratic presidential candidate Joe Biden is one of them. However, in the political environment of rising populism, Biden has no choice but try to be hard on China. In fact, on the issue of China, Trump and Biden are only competing to outdo one another in terms of their tough stance.

During the whole process of the pandemic, Chinese leaders have never patronized other countries on how to fight the pandemic. Instead, they have tried to maintain (at least) telephone communications with the high-level officials of other countries. However, some bureaucratic officials and Netizens (trolls) in China are venting their emotions in cyber space. They should have been effectively restrained.

People have also witnessed the impact of the rise of a new generation of Chinese and American diplomats on the bilateral Sino-US relations. They firmly hold the banner of nationalism. American diplomats helped their President to shift the responsibility onto China and created various theories of shunning responsibility. Pottinger is regarded as the representative of the young and middle-aged policy makers about China in the United States. Obviously, this generation of diplomats has been very different from the generations of diplomats after Dr. Kissinger. They can't distinguish their personal feelings from the rationality required by national interests. Pottinger obviously vented his feelings from his unpleasant experience as a reporter in China when he dealt with Sino-US relations.

The tough attitude of China and the United States is not limited to the diplomatic field, but also displayed in other fields. The attitude of the United States hardliners is openly shown because of their exercise of freedom of speech. China also has a tendency to take a more aggressive attitude. On May 8, Vice Premier Liu He, the chief on the Chinese side of the China–US Comprehensive Economic Dialogue, held a telephone conversation with the US Trade Representative Robert Lighthizer, and Finance Minister Steven Mnuchin on the implementation of the trade agreement. However, *The Global Times* (English version, May 11) reported that China may abolish the phase-one of the China–US trade agreement. Although the spokesman for the Chinese Foreign Ministry immediately confirmed that China would implement the agreement, the news was explosive, not only detonating the fierce struggle between China and the United States again, but also causing the world to express doubt about the prospect of the agreement. The US side responded strongly. Trump said that he was not interested in restarting any new negotiations, and wanted to see

Avoiding the "Free Fall" of Sino-US Relations   159

if China would be abided by the agreement it signed. Trump also said that China wanted to renegotiate to reach a more favorable agreement for them.

This trend is also reflected in Hu Xijin's remarks that China should expand its nuclear arsenal. Hu is the editor-in-chief of *The Global Times*. Although what he said does not represent an official position, it raised the concerns of the United States, and the world about China's nuclear policy. Hardliners on both sides claim to be pursuing their own national interests. Although, on the surface, the goals of the hardliners on both sides run counter to each other, in fact, both sides are strengthening, helping, and supporting each other in their mutual goal of starting an open confrontation between China and the United States. It is fine with what they are doing as long as they are determined to create more conflict between the two countries. But if otherwise, what they do and say are just working against their ultimate goals.

What is more serious is that the politics of the two sides are based on an extremely deep social foundation. There is an increasingly rising nationalist mood in the United States. A public opinion survey released by the US polling agency YouGov on May 13 found that more than two-thirds of Americans surveyed (69%) believe that the Chinese government should be "partly responsible" or "very responsible" for the spread of the virus. The poll surveyed 1,382 American adults and found that about half (51%) of the respondents believed that the Chinese government should compensate the countries affected by the pandemic, and that 71% believed that China should be "punished" for the pandemic.

Specifically, 25% of the respondents want to ban Chinese officials from entering the United States, 32% think the United States should refuse to pay interest on China's US Treasury bonds, 33% want to impose additional tariffs on Chinese goods, and 41% support international sanctions. This poll is consistent with Pew's recent poll, which also shows that two-thirds of Americans have a negative attitude towards China.

Why Cannot Sino-US Relations Be What They Have Been?

So why did Sino-US relations deteriorate like this? The deteriorating political atmosphere between the two countries has sharply reduced the possibility of cooperation that could have taken place, whether it is about trade or the spread of COVID-19.

Since the outbreak of COVID-19, China and the United States are fiercely fighting each other at two fronts: the naming of the virus, and the media war. The first is the dispute over the name of the virus. There was no unified name for the new virus in the early phase of the virus outbreak. Before long, the World Health Organization (WHO) had finalized a unified name. Most countries used the standard name, with the exception of some American politicians. On March 16, 2020, Yang Jiechi, member of the Political Bureau of the CPC Central Committee, accused "some American politicians of constantly slandering China and China's prevention and control efforts and stigmatizing China" in a call with US Secretary of State Mike Pompeo.[3]

Yang Jiechi emphasized that since the start of the outbreak, the Chinese side has acted in an open, transparent and responsible manner in sharing timely information with the WHO and the global community, including the US. China is also collaborating with countries around the world and providing assistance and support to countries involved as its ability permits.[4] In the phone call, Pompeo blamed China for shifting the responsibility of the COVID-19 outbreak onto the US, stressed that this is not the time to spread false information and rumors, and said that all countries should unite to face the common threat.[5]

After some people in the United States, including politicians, unjustifiably "racialized" the novel coronavirus, China and the United States launched a dispute over the naming rights of the virus. This was not eased until President Xi Jinping and US President Trump had a phone call, which palliated the tone of the war of words over the naming of the virus.

Another one was the media war. *The Wall Street Journal* published racist articles slandering the Chinese people, and leading China to expel three of its reporters from China. The United States responded by limiting the number of journalists from five Chinese media in the United States, and registering these Chinese media as foreign government agents. China naturally countered and made the decision to expel journalists from several major US media in China and restrict Chinese personnel working for the US media. The United States responded in the same way in a tit-for-tat escalation of the conflict.

However, whether the dispute over the naming of the virus or the media war, it may only be the appearance of the conflict between China and the United States. In fact, both sides think they know the real agenda of the other behind the conflict. In the view of the United States, China wants to take advantage of this opportunity to replace the United States and dominate the world. In China's view, the United States is trying to contain China to slow down its rise. Obviously, this kind of concern on both sides is nothing new. It has been around at least since the 1990s. The COVID-19 pandemic only brought the conflict to the forefront.

Some commentators said that the United States has "racialized" the virus in order to shift the responsibility of the government's ineffective fight against the pandemic. Although the virus broke out in Wuhan, the early US government regarded it as an ordinary influenza, paid little attention to it, and wasted a lot of time. As Trump said, the United States is the most developed and largest economy in the world. It also has an advanced public health system. The virus was not even a concern, let alone fear of it.

Nevertheless, the United States has not effectively stopped the rapid spread of the virus, which has been a heavy blow to the confidence of American politicians. It is not difficult to understand that people without self-confidence are more likely to blame others for their own fault. So are countries. In fact, up to the present day, many politicians in the United States are still keen on shifting responsibilities, and not focusing on fighting the pandemic.

Avoiding the "Free Fall" of Sino-US Relations 161

However, there was no consensus in American politics to racialize the virus. Democrats in the US Congress generally criticized Trump and his administration for their responses to the pandemic. Democratic House Representative Jim McGovern said he was worried that Republicans' investigation of China would lead to racial discrimination and even racial hatred. Massachusetts Senator Elizabeth Warren also publicly challenged Trump. Many Democrats were certain that the administration was trying to shift its responsibilities.

It is worth noting that the problem is not as simple as just shifting responsibility. The novel coronavirus was a challenge to the domestic politics and foreign policy of the United States. Owing to the unusual times brought about by the pandemic, all sorts of factors worked jointly to reveal the real and profound anxiety of the United States about China, which cannot be felt in normal times.

First, the United States is worried about its high level of dependence on China's economy. Everyone knows the economic interdependence between China and the United States, but no one has ever felt so deeply about the consequences of this high dependence. According to Michael McCaul, a Republican on the House Foreign Affairs Committee, was worried that most of the pharmaceuticals came from China, and the United States was so dependent on China at this time of crisis that the United States would sink into the hell of a novel coronavirus pandemic if China banned exports. That is why he urged people to find ways to manufacture the medical material in the United States.[6]

Indeed, globalization since the 1980s has highly alienated American capitalism in the sense that the government has completely lost its economic sovereignty. Under the banner of neoliberalism, American capitalism, in order to pursue higher profits, moved most of its economic activities overseas, including medical materials that are closely related to people's lives. Of course, Trump was right that the United States has the strongest economy and the best medical and health system in the world, but what people need is simple masks, hand sanitizers, protective equipment, respirators, etc. It is these materials that can bring security to the people, but these items are no longer produced or have insufficient production capacity in the United States.

This reality is unacceptable to both the American elite and the public. It is precisely because of this reality that there are arguments in the United States that "de-globalization" is "de-Sinicization." But obviously, it is not because of China that we have globalization. It was the capital that gave rise to globalization, which completely separates economic interests from social needs. Economy is originally part of society, but when the economy is separated from a society, a crisis is inevitable.

Second, the United States is worried about the Chinese system. In the final analysis, the dispute between China and the United States is a dispute over systems. The effectiveness of China's "national system" in the process of anti-pandemic has further strengthened the concerns of American elites about China's system. As far as the US system is concerned, as American political scholar Francis Fukuyama said, the failure of the US to fight the pandemic this time has little to do with the US system: the US President should bear greater responsibility. If the American elite have no effective reflection on the American system, the fear of the Chinese system is obvious.

It is not difficult to find that in today's domestic and diplomatic discourse of the United States, the concept of "China" is becoming less and less common among members of Congress and State Department officials. There is a great tendency that the concept of China is to be replaced by the concept of "Communist China." Emphasizing "Communist China" rather than "China" reveals the deep fear of the Chinese system by the American elite.

Republican Senator Josh Hawley and Republican congressman Elise Stefanik proposed bills in the Senate and the House of Representatives, respectively, calling for an international investigation into Communist China's covering up of the spread of the COVID-19 virus at the earliest stages of the outbreak. Meanwhile, they demanded that China compensate the affected countries in the world.

At the same time, a group of House Representatives worked across party lines to propose another bill, which attributed the global transmission the pandemic to China, and urged China to publicly admit that the virus originated in China. If we are aware of the fear of the American elite about the Chinese system, it is not difficult to understand such actions. Similar actions will surely be taken more often in the future.

Finally, the US worries about being replaced by China. The rapid spreading of the virus in the United States not only threw the country in great confusion, but also revealed the nature of Trump's "Americanism": selfishness, and unilateralism. The United States unilaterally cut off shipping not only to China, but also to its European allies. The COVID-19 pandemic almost broke the arm of America's world leadership. On the contrary, after bringing the pandemic under control, China began to make use of the pandemic in its diplomacy by providing assistance not only to developing countries, but also to the European allies of the United States, and even to the United States. What made the United States more worried was that those countries accepted China's assistance unconditionally, and with gratitude in their fight with the health crisis.

This situation is unacceptable to the United States because the country is worried that the COVID-19 pandemic will deeply weaken or even eliminate the influence of US geopolitics, and create an unprecedented opportunity for China to lead world geopolitics. It should also be noted that although European countries need China's assistance, they are also highly vigilant about the geopolitical influence of China through assistance.

In today's deteriorating relationship between China and the United States, both sides have strong public opinion support. What is more worrisome is the growing nationalism in the United States. Various polls from the United States show that the number of Americans in favor of China has reached the lowest point since the establishment of diplomatic relations between China and the United States. Although there are no similar polls in China, judging from the rising dissatisfaction of hundreds of millions of Internet users, the number of Chinese who are in favor of the United States has also declined sharply.

Hope Is on the Side of China

It is undeniable that COVID-19 has escalated Sino-US friction. Now more and more people are beginning to worry about whether the conflict will turn into a hot war as the pandemic continues to spread in the United States, as American politicians are shifting the responsibility to China, as the anti-China wave is rapidly rising in the United States, and as the economic crisis, social fear and internal governance crisis are being worsened by the pandemic. Can people just watch the Sino-US relations fall into the "Thucydides trap?" Realistically speaking, there is no hope for the United States to stop the deterioration of Sino-US relations. The political environment of nationalism and populism, coupled with election politics, creates no conditions in the short term for American political figures to return to rationality.

Hope is on the Chinese side. Despite the emergence of nationalist sentiment in lower society, and the middle and lower levels of bureaucracy, China has a strong central leadership that keeps a clear head in the current situation. In terms of curbing wars, and maintaining world peace, China lacks not capability but confidence.

Although the United States is the provocative side, China must still avoid using emotional remarks by officials as usual, so as to keep diplomatic rationality and composure. China should also believe that there are forces in the world that work hard to keep peace. If China has appropriate methods, the "West" seen by the United States and the Soviet Union during the Cold War cannot be reproduced. In other words, there is no united "West" in the present-day world.

The United States hopes to prove that the virus originated in China through the "Five Eyes," an intelligence alliance composing of the United States, Britain, Canada, Australia, and New Zealand, but some intelligence agencies of the member states have expressed different opinions. On the issue of Iraq, the allies followed the United States and later realized it was a big mistake. China is not Iraq, and these countries have no reason to stand firmly on the side of the United States.

Europe is no longer what it was during the Cold War. Although some European countries have criticized some of China's practices on the issue of COVID-19, this does not mean that Europe and the United States automatically stand together. On the contrary, unlike the United States, Europe has its own interests independent of the United States. European countries want to establish at least a manageable relationship with China rather than an atmosphere of confrontation.

In fact, the relationship between the United States and its allies can be said to be at the lowest point in its history. In this crisis of the COVID-19 pandemic, none of the US allies publicly asked the US for help and support, a rare phenomenon in the 100 years since the rise of the United States. The leadership of the United States among its allies has declined rapidly.

Even for the so-called "international investigation into the origin of the virus," China has reason not to accept scientists from the countries that have the attitude of "presumption of guilt." Australia is one such country. China is not without anybody to rely on. The community of scientists from various countries is a force that China can rely on, because no society of scientists in any country claimed that the virus originated in China, and no scientists to date have said that the virus was man-made.

Since the emergence of the virus, Chinese scientists, along with their counterparts from all over the world, have been studying the origin and spread of the virus. Under the framework of the World Health Organization, China can invite a "third party" acceptable to both the United States and China to join the investigation. What China needs is a scientific conclusion, not a politicized one.

For China, the road of its continuing rise is not smooth. Despite the deterioration of Sino-US relations, this does not mean that China and the United States are destined to resolve their problems by conflict. If China has enough confidence, wisdom, and rationality to avoid direct conflict with the United States, it is still possible to finally return to cooperation between the two. In the current difficult situation, even for a great politician, it is difficult to make a choice.

Notes

1 https://www.newyorker.com/magazine/2020/01/13/the-future-of-americas-contest-with-china.
2 http://en.people.cn/n3/2020/0508/c90000-9687826.html.
3 https://news.cgtn.com/news/2020-03-16/Yang-Jiechi-has-phone-call-with-Mike-Pompeo-OUIX3LlvS8/index.html.
4 https://www.mfa.gov.cn/ce/ceie//eng/zgxw/t1756891.htm.
5 https://news.cgtn.com/news/2020-03-16/Yang-Jiechi-has-phone-call-with-Mike-Pompeo-OUIX3LlvS8/index.html.
6 https://www.dhs.gov/sites/default/files/publications/final_economic_security_sub committee_report_1.pdf.

14 Europe in the Post-COVID-19 Era and the Problems in Sino-Europe Relations

Zhou Hong[*]

COVID-19 is not only a once-in-a-century human disaster, but also a major crisis of human society. The outbreak of this pandemic was sudden, and its end is not in sight. Its impact on the global economy, society, and politics will be determined not only by the duration of the pandemic, but also by the effort and methods of controlling the virus. History has proved that the "complications" brought about by the crisis can lead to the retrogression of human society, and may also become the "catalyst" for the advancement of human society. China and the EU have experienced the challenge of this pandemic, and are fighting it in various forms. What positive and negative changes will this challenge and experience bring to the EU and China?

The Impact of the Pandemic on the General Trend of Europe as a Whole

On the Economy

The continuous development of the pandemic has put great pressure on the public health system of many European countries. This pressure will naturally affect the normal operation of the economy. Within a few weeks of the European Union (EU)'s economy being halted due to the pandemic, the economic activities of the member states dropped by more than one-third. The economic recovery momentum that the EU had been struggling to maintain for several years came to an abrupt end. It seems a recession is inevitable. In order to cope with this situation, European countries keep a sharp eye on the impact of the development and changes of the pandemic on the economic trend, and discuss the possibility of the "V" shape, or "U" shape, or "L" shape of the European economic recovery. In order to avoid the "L"-shaped economic development trend and control the spread of the virus, most EU countries have taken strong intervention measures, the magnitude of which is rarely seen since the end of the Second World War.

The pandemic is more serious in the southern Europe, a phenomenon similar to the problems exposed during the European debt crisis. In continental

---

[*] Member and research fellow of The Chinese Academy of Social Sciences, Director of the Institute for International Social Sciences of The Chinese Academy of Social Sciences.

Europe, most of the hardest-hit countries are southern European countries. Although there are a large number of confirmed cases in Germany, the mortality rate is not high. As Germany's health system is rock-solid, Germany is able to receive and treat some patients of critical conditions from Italy and France. It has hardly any impact on the German medical system. As a German professor said, "For our system, it is equivalent to dropping a few drops of water on a hot stone."[1]

The stability of the German system under the pandemic is good for the whole of Europe. Sometime ago, five famous German economic research institutes predicted on April 8, 2020, that, although the German economy would decrease by 4.2% in 2020, it would rebound by 5.8% in 2021,[2] indicating that the impact of the pandemic on the German economy is temporary. The European Commission predicted in May that the EU as a whole would enter a historic recession this year, and the economy would shrink by 7.5%. The economies of Italy, Spain, France, and other countries were affected more severely by the pandemic. However, the European Commission also believes that the EU economy as a whole will rebound in 2021, although the extent of the rebound has not been determined.

The implementation of social distancing and shutdowns to control the pandemic have not only created a risk of industrial chain disruption to many EU countries, but also had a substantial impact on the tourism, services and small business sectors. In order to ensure that enterprises will not go bankrupt after the pandemic, all countries have used financial subsidies at all costs to enable enterprises to quickly resume production after the pandemic is stabilized. As the EU countries closely follow the impact of the pandemic on economic development and adopt a series of policies to save and stimulate the economy, an economic recovery of the EU is likely to happen, which could stave off a recession.

Impact on Society

The pandemic didn't cause massive social panic in Europe. Most people paid little attention to the virus when it broke out, and soon became calm. Some people did not buy the strict social isolation measures in the beginning, but began to cooperate with the government after they knew more about the virus.

The social impact of the pandemic in Europe is mainly seen in the area of employment. The "complications" are also mainly reflected in the shutdown of businesses, layoffs, the loss of income of small business owners, and the fatal impact on the services industry. In the developed industrial society, unemployment is a serious risk for individuals and families, which may lead to the collapse of the social system. Different from the United States, European countries with the tradition of good welfare have introduced strong financial subsidies in order to help enterprises and individuals tide over the difficulties caused by the pandemic. Although there were signs of social polarization in Europe before the outbreak of the pandemic, they were not worsened after the challenge of the pandemic, which can be attributed to the subsidy and intervention policies.

Some countries subsidize owners, while others subsidize individuals, especially the poor. These practices have also been used by European welfare states in response to previous crises. For example, during the European debt crisis, Germany implemented a half-wage system. Germany has fought the pandemic in an orderly manner. Basically, it has achieved the following goals: Financial instruments are ready for use, there is no bankruptcy of enterprises, all workers have their jobs, the health system is intact, and the resumption of production is well organized. To sum up, Germany has responded to the pandemic in the following systematic manner:

A Ensuring the transfer of medical materials and reserve personnel
B Promoting the standardization of data use and intervention measures in the field of public communication
C Ensuring the adequacy of financial resources and financial market liquidity
D Being ready to provide credit, tax reduction and compensation for enterprises
E Introducing flexible working schedules for employees
F Stabilizing workers' income through direct subsidies
G Arranging online education, work from home, and other ways to effectively use isolation time to create value
H Implementing temporary nationalization measures when necessary to ensure the stability of supply chains

These policies and measures are all conducive to reducing the social impact of the pandemic.

Impact on the Government and Political Parties

The outbreak of the pandemic has tested the governance ability of the governments and ruling parties in various countries, as well as the relationship between the government and the people. For a rare disaster of this magnitude, no countries were prepared or had previous experience. Their initial responses at the early stage revealed all kinds of defects of their social systems, their differences of interests, and governance problems. But a sudden disaster is usually an opportunity to unite the people and improve governance. The governments of the EU countries initially responded differently to the pandemic; in the end, however, they all achieved effective communication with the public as the pandemic developed. Those who could not sacrifice freedom for restrictive measures at the beginning finally chose to support the government's strict control measures. They made their choice between life and freedom. Some 70 to 80% of the Italian people agreed with the government's policies to lock down cities and close borders. Spain also locked down its cities very severely. The major EU countries adopted a step-by-step "social distancing" policy and continuously adjusted their isolation policies as the pandemic developed. Their measures were understood and accepted by the majority of the people. The mainstream political parties of the EU countries showed a wartime "unity" due to the pandemic, and

168 *Zhou Hong*

their public support rates increased significantly. A poll conducted on April 2, 2020 showed that Comte's support rate was 71%, Merkel's was 79% (an increase of 11 percentage points over the figure for the beginning of March), and Macron's reached 52%, the highest in several months. The support rate of extreme populist parties declined. The national sovereign as the fundamental system of Europe, has been strengthened because of the fight against the pandemic. The mainstream ruling parties have turned the populist ideas into strong practical actions, which caused populism to have lost some popularity.

The EU Perspective

The role of the EU was widely questioned at the initial stage of the pandemic, which prompted the President of the EU, Ursula von der Leyen, to publicly apologize to all the people on behalf of the EU. Her apology on television was a roundabout way to declare the existence of the EU. In fact, the biased evaluation of the EU by the outside world is mostly made from the criteria of sovereign states, but the EU is not a sovereign state. The EU has no supranational power in the field of public health, and also has no right to centralize and allocate the resources of various countries to respond to the pandemic as a whole. At the early stage of the pandemic, the EU also emphasized the "Unity of Europe," and did not close the borders to Italy. With the development of the pandemic, closing borders and letting the member states control the virus as they found fit became the only realistic choice.

Although the EU was "limited" in its power in fighting the pandemic, it tried its best to do something. For example, after the outbreak of the pandemic in China, the EU put forward a warning to its member states to "get ready" from a professional point of view, but few member states really got "ready" as a matter of fact. Moreover, the EU opened a "green channel" for anti-pandemic materials in response to the chaos of withholding such materials by some countries, published a specific "EU road map" for lifting the ban, and coordinated "collective withdrawal," all necessary measures to protect the European unified market from the impact of the pandemic.

In addition, during the international financial crisis in 2008 and the European debt crisis in 2009, the EU carried out governance reform and created some institutional mechanisms and tools. For example, the European Stability Mechanism (ESM) has 80 billion euros in cash, and more than 600 billion euros in capital, which can be used as emergency tools, and be allocated as needed and by applications. This makes it possible for von der Leyen to mobilize 100 billion euros to ensure employment security in Europe during the pandemic. With the development of the pandemic, the EU not only approved Italy's and other countries' fiscal stimulus plans, but also established a large amount of "recovery fund" at the EU level through arduous and tortuous coordination, and issued an additional 1 trillion to 1.5 trillion euros of bonds to stabilize the EU economy and stimulate the EU's recovery as the first step of a preliminary agreement.

Europe in the Post-COVID-19 Era and the Problems 169

It can be said that without the 2008–2009 European debt crisis, the several serious crises experienced by the EU, the difficult fiscal and financial governance and the construction of new institutions and mechanisms in the euro area, and the existence and tenacious persistence of EU institutions and mechanisms, the current situation of the European countries would be even more difficult. In short, judging from the current development, the pandemic will not lead to the disintegration of the EU and the euro zone. In other words, the previous integration trend of the EU has not been reversed. The degree of integration in the field of health care may even be strengthened, and there will be new attempts in financial integration. The EU has always had internal contradictions and disputes, but they are not fierce enough to lead to the collapse of the overall system of the EU. After the pandemic, the EU will stick to its previous policies and continue to move forward.

An important principle of the pandemic control of the EU and its member states is to focus on the adaptability and stability of the existing systems. If there was a shortage of medical resources, the social management policy would be tightened; otherwise, it would be relaxed to ensure that the economic and social system would not bear too much pressure. Maintaining the system is the EU's "political correctness," which has been called "the flexibility of democracy" by the EU's senior diplomatic representative Josep Borrell, who pointed out that in the face of the criticism of the European system during the pandemic, Europe would "maintain the European model" and protect social harmony, and safeguard both the overall stability of nation states and the future of European integration. The current crisis, far more serious than that experienced in 2008, prompted Europe to plan for a post-pandemic world, focusing on the six critical areas to achieve a "strategic autonomy."[3] The gist of the plan is actually to strengthen "Euro-centrism," which includes:

A   reducing external dependence, not only in the fields of public health, but also in the fields of science and technology, and artificial intelligence in the future
B   preventing external market actors from controlling Europe's strategic actions
C   protecting critical infrastructure in Europe, and cyber-attacks
D   ensuring that the decision-making autonomy of Europe will not be weakened by offshore economic activities
E   expanding the normative power of Europe
F   demonstrating leadership in all areas

The first four priorities here all strengthen the European barriers by strengthening the internal mechanism, including transferring the industrial chain, and restricting the activities of external forces in Europe. The last two are to let the strengthened EU and its unique soft power play a leading role in the world.

Impact of the Pandemic on China–EU Relations

The reason why it is important to judge the EU's own capabilities and characteristics is that we need to know the EU's policies and changes toward China so as to make adjustment as regards China's relations with the EU. Affected by the pandemic, the EU's relations with China will be assessed in terms of three aspects: economy, politics, and society. Here is a preliminary assessment.

As the "Ballast Stone" of the China–EU Relations, Trade and Investment Call for Special Attention

Before the outbreak of the pandemic, there were some signs worthy of concern in the overall positive trend of China-EU Relations: first, the EU continuously cooperated with the United States to put forward new rules against China in the World Trade Organization (WTO); second, the EU formulated and passed new regulations restricting Chinese enterprises' investment in the EU in 2019; third, in the spring of 2019, the European Commission proposed in its communication document that China and the EU are not only "cooperation partners" and "economic competitors," but also a "systemic rival" in promoting alternative models of governance.[4] In the view of the EU, the economic and trade cooperation and competition between the EU and China is not a simple sharing of interests, but a question of which governance model is better or worse.

Long before the outbreak of the pandemic, all levels of the EU, including think-tanks and some governments, had raised the issue of "EU's overdependence" on China. Will the call for distancing from China and restricting China's market and investment be louder or submerged due to the outbreak of the pandemic? Will the industrial chain and supply chain interdependently formed by decades of close cooperation between China and Europe be strengthened or weakened? The answers to these questions depend on how China and the EU are faring during the pandemic, as well as on the cooperation and efforts between China and the EU. The spirit, mode and mechanism of cooperation may continue to develop in the post-pandemic era. At the same time, the forces of distancing and "decoupling" will also be strengthened because of the pandemic. Therefore, China and the EU will face a complex relationship of rivalry in this field.

It is undeniable that China is still a huge, growing and indispensable market for the EU. This natural attraction makes the EU not only unable to decouple from China, but also keen to further develop a win-win cooperation. This is why the EU still attaches great importance to, and seriously focuses upon, the negotiation of the investment partnership agreement with China. Although the EU hopes to maintain and expand its market in China, it is particularly vigilant and resistant to the success of Chinese products in the European market. During the pandemic, the public opinion about "overdependence on Chinese products leading to the shortage of general medical supplies and people's livelihood supplies" was loud under the pretext of "EU security." The call

Europe in the Post-COVID-19 Era and the Problems   171

for "localizing the European economy and restructuring the whole industry chain" is growing. In order to ensure the "security" of the supply chain, it is possible to forcibly transfer some industrial chains through processes of administrative and judicial intervention. Actually, there is no lack of political demand and public support in Europe in this regard. As a response, China needs to have a full understanding and get well prepared. From a macro point of view, large-scale industrial restructuring is time-consuming and not economical at all. Between China and the EU, re-emphasizing and adhering to market rules, overcoming new regulatory barriers, and achieving higher competitiveness and higher levels of cooperation are crucial to the stability of China–EU relations and the well-being of the people of China and the EU.

Raising the Level of Political Cooperation

At the end of 2019, the new leaders of the EU institutions took office. It is not only the hope of Chinese leaders, but also on the agenda of EU leaders to jointly promote China-EU relations with the EU institutions and member states. As planned, China and the EU should have a series of high-level visits in 2020, which would be an opportunity to comprehensively sort out China-EU relations and enhance the understanding and mutual trust between the two sides. However, the pandemic disrupted the high-level visits, and the summit diplomacy, which should play an important role in China-EU relations. At present, the Chinese and EU leaders frequently communicate through online video and telephone, but these cannot entirely replace the face-to-face talks between the leaders of both sides.

Although affected by the pandemic, Netizens from both sides have expressed various opinions out of different points of interest, positions, attitudes, and interpretations in the cyber space. They do not, however, represent the mainstream diplomatic position. The cyber space misinformation and biased comments, often false and exaggerated, spread rapidly, poisoning the feelings between the Chinese and European people. China–EU relations need authoritative guidance to form a strategic consensus on controlling the pandemic and mutual development.

The pandemic hit hard the existing global governance system. The United States and some of its followers provided little support to fight the pandemic, and extremely irresponsibly suppressed international organizations and China for their effort to control the pandemic. A chaos was seen on the international political stage. At this critical juncture, the general direction of international political development and grand politics should be putting aside differences in political systems and ideologies, learning from each other and acting in unity, so as to give mankind the confidence to bring the pandemic under control. China and the EU should join hands to fight the pandemic, exchange experiences, strengthen cooperation, resist harmful public opinion, reduce the global economic risks and social risks caused by the pandemic, and support the work of the World Health Organization and other international organizations.

172　*Zhou Hong*

All these efforts will be conducive to developing China–EU bilateral relations, and conducive to the cause of global management of the pandemic, and the practice of international multilateralism.

Public Opinion Needs to Be Channeled

Recently, there have been some problems in the public opinion environment between China and the EU, largely caused by misunderstanding. At the initial stage of the outbreak, the EU side and EU countries expressed sympathy and support for China's fight against the COVID-19 virus. When the epicenter of the outbreak moved to Europe, the Chinese side naturally tried its best to support the EU. Medical workers and professionals from both sides launched unprecedented cooperation. The reasonable extension and in-depth development of the cooperation should enable China-EU relations to make a fresh start. However, the China-EU relations were misled by the "cyber diplomacy," and the rapid spread of false information and rumors. Some political forces used erroneous and malicious information to put pressure on China-EU relations, launching the so-called "battle of narrative." When the EU High Representative for Foreign Affairs Josep Borrell was asked to speak to the European Parliament, he said that this invisible political virus is a "hybrid threat" not without "damage."[5] Of course, Borrell's "damage" is mainly concerned with the "European model" being shaken, but such "soft knives" will alienate state relations and are also devastating in diplomacy.

China and the EU need to reach a consensus that the pandemic is a human disaster and a common enemy of mankind, and all countries should engage in institutional cooperation, seek common ground while reserving differences, complementing each other's strengths, and tightening ties of cooperation. The institutional progress that mankind has achieved so far, whether it is European integration, China's reform and opening up, or economic globalization, has brought peace and development to mankind. There is no way out for retrogression. Therefore, we should respect each other's paths and systems chosen by the people of all countries and regions, which is conducive to international cooperation and common development.

In terms of fighting the pandemic, the world generally has a favorable feedback on China's efforts in controlling the pandemic. Although it is still experiencing a painful process of fighting the virus, the EU system will not collapse rapidly because of the pandemic. Both China and the EU will draw lessons from their fight against the pandemic. During the pandemic, China has strengthened its confidence in taking the socialist road, strengthened the link between the government and the people, found and improved the systemic weaknesses, increased the legitimacy of governance, and improved its voice in international public health governance. After the baptism of another crisis, the EU can also slowly recover from the pandemic, and readjust its economic, social and political links. As a governance mechanism, the EU is not weakening its power, but slowly strengthening through twists and turns. The EU even plans to play a more important leading role in the world after the pandemic. China-EU relations will not develop into a relationship between a "stronger China and weaker Europe" in the post-COVID-19 era. On the contrary, China needs to deal with a tougher EU in many fields in the world. This is a basic judgment on China-EU relations after the outbreak of the virus.

The EU and the World System

Although the EU will become stronger after the pandemic, it is not a sovereign state, and it cannot concentrate its power in the same way as the United States, China, and Russia. In terms of domestic and foreign policies, different departments have their own say by their functions. Even within the EU, there are not only contradictions among its member states, but also different political parties and groups within any of its member states. In a word, although the EU is trying to "speak with one voice" to declare its "strategic autonomy" and build a "sovereign Europe" that can compete with sovereign states, Europe will always be multi-leveled and diversified in reality. A diverse Europe has different views on the future world, and will strive to change the world accordingly. However, because its power composition and function distribution differ from those of sovereign states, the EU will play its role in different areas and in a different mode.

The EU's Mainstream Concept or Ideas of the Future World

In the view of the mainstream ideological circles of the European Union, the world system before the outbreak of the COVID-19 virus was riddled with holes, and the global governance system also had many defects and drawbacks. Many discussions on multilateralism and multipolarity are manifestations of the asymmetry and fragmentation of world power. At the same time, the trend of bi-polarization has emerged, which the EU does not want to see. Therefore, the EU is exploring ways to reform global governance. After the outbreak of the pandemic, having been silent for a short while, the EU made a high-profile announcement of "together first" to prevent the internalization of international politics. The EU also proposed that international politics should change from the state system of Westphalia contract to a cooperation system between sovereign states.

In the view of the EU, what should be a reasonable global governance system after the outbreak? Some EU scholars argue that the global spread of the pandemic will aggravate and accelerate the previous trend of fragmentation of the world system and global governance, which is mainly manifested in the following possibilities: widening the economic gap, increasing social division, the resurgence of nationalism, increasing noise against the international mechanism, tension in Sino-US relations, the proliferation of huge migration flows, rampant international terrorism, more poverty reduction difficulties, and the inability to kick off global governance. However, the biggest threat is the introversion and polarization of international politics. The pandemic accelerated the decline of American hegemony, and the world system established under the leadership of the United States after the Second World War fell apart. Europe must step out of the US umbrella to achieve its "strategic autonomy," and regroup with other forces in the world to form a new governance system.

The world governance system constitutes of three levels of forces. First of all, the practice of combating COVID-19 shows that emergent public health events are still principally all the responsibilities of nation states and sub-states. The pandemic has strengthened the sovereignty of states, whereas the international system built in the past 75 years has not produced an effective mechanism to deal with such crises. The legitimacy of the multilateral mechanism of global governance has been questioned, and sovereign states other than the United States have been strengthened. However, there is a lack of trust among sovereign states, resulting in "trust deficiency disorder," so it is necessary to strengthen more binding cooperation among countries.

Secondly, the regional organizations established after the Second World War did not play a governance role during the pandemic, or even showed an effective regulatory role. As the best regional organization, the EU has played a certain role in coordination and supervision, but its efficiency was low. However, regional organizations still have room to continue to strengthen in coping with future crises and mitigating the impact of the pandemic on economic and trade.

Finally, the international multilateral professional institutions (such as the WHO) have shown their indispensability, although their power, resources, and support are limited. Because all the countries concentrated their own resources for their own anti-pandemic battle after the outbreak, the global agendas, such as the 2030 Sustainable Development Goals (SDG) of the United Nations, and the emission reduction targets agreed in Paris, will be affected because of a lack of funds. The digital economy will accelerate in the post-pandemic era, but there is no international mechanism for its better development.

If global governance is considered to be constituted of three main levels, namely, the national, regional, and international, the outbreak of COVID-19 has undoubtedly strengthened the power of the nation states, or proved the "inefficiency" of the regional and international multilateral organizations constructed in recent decades. However, the establishment of the regional and international systems aims to prevent international imbalances, conflicts and even wars caused by the excessive concentration of state power and the capricious rivalry between countries. In order to prevent the world from returning to the situation before the Second World War, it is necessary to actively build a new multi-layer global governance system.

Basic Ideas on Future Global Governance

In the multi-level global governance system, although the three-level governance subjects (i.e. countries, regions, and international organizations) play the principal roles, there needs to be a clearer and more specific division of function and cooperation among the three-level governance subjects. In addition to resource mobilization by sovereign states, regional organizations should exercise democratization procedures in their own regions and act as mediators on behalf of their own regions in the world. The UN system and the World Health Organization should gain more centralized authority and legitimacy. The outbreak of the pandemic has just provided an opportunity to rebuild a clear division of labor, clear responsibilities and interrelated mechanism at the national, regional and global levels in the field of public health.

Historical experience tells us that an overly strong state system will lead to the coexistence of powerful countries, and the reappearance of the Westphalian System. Should that be the case, then shifting one's trouble to others, forming cliques for selfish gains, and following the law of the jungle will become the rule of the world again, which will surely cause global instability, and may even lead to war. To avoid historical retrogression, in addition to strengthening the peace-loving forces in the world, we also need to empower international multilateral organizations. In addition to financial support, it is necessary to establish the authority of these institutions in their professional fields, and make their decision-making processes more centralized and effective. Regional organizations should cooperate with the activities of international organizations, properly communicate the relationship between international organizations and the people in the region, and strengthen the legitimacy of international cooperation.

Could China and Europe Jointly Promote a Community of Shared Future of Mankind in the Field of Public Health?

As President Xi Jinping said at the 2020 G20 Summit, "Major infectious disease is the enemy of all."[6] The virus knows no borders and races. It challenges mankind. In this war between man and the virus, the enemy of human society is not other human beings, but the invisible, untouchable and ubiquitous virus. For the first time, the global spread of the virus has proved to the world in such a straightforward way that mankind is a community of common destiny. When the pandemic strikes, all countries or regions – whatever systems or organizational forms they have, whatever social standards they adopt, or even however hostile they are to each other – will be dragged into the battle sooner or later, since it will be impossible to stay alone and intact. To overcome the pandemic, it is far from sufficient to rely on the efforts of one country alone. China and the EU have the same understanding and have issued similar statements on this issue.

In the process of combating the pandemic, the policy and strategy choices of different countries and regions show the key guiding ideology of the country or region. The anti-pandemic campaign in the United States has not only been hijacked by various interest groups, but also exposed the laissez-faire concept of "natural selection and survival of the fittest." Most European countries have a tradition of social welfare, and there is no lack of government

176 *Zhou Hong*

intervention in the process of fighting the pandemic. China's anti-pandemic campaign embodies its guiding ideology of "people first."

Is It Possible for China and the EU to Form a Community of Common Destiny to Fight the Pandemic?

First of all, we must admit that China uses the term "community" with a different connotation from that of the EU. The EU's concept of "community" can be traced back to the European philosophers hundreds of years ago. Their concept suggests "European unification."[7] After the end of the Second World War, Europe put the concept of "community" into practice and formed such organizations as the "European Coal and Steel Community," "European Atomic Energy Community," and "European Economic Community." Although the communities have complex structures and cumbersome rules, they strive to develop in the direction of institutional convergence.

Although China and the EU have different expressions and understandings of the concept of "community," it does not hinder the two sides from having a win-win cooperation. The EU cannot expect all other countries, regions and organizations to form a community with uniform organizational and legal system such as the EU, but China would hope that equal cooperation and mutual benefit between different countries will become the shared concept of mankind. In fact, Jacques Delors, President of the European Commission from 1985 to 1995, expressed his understanding of the term "community" as referring to common responsibility and sharing. While the pandemic is still raging, China and the European Union should discuss how to mobilize and integrate anti-pandemic resources, how to popularize knowledge and achieve technological breakthroughs, how to cooperate to improve their respective public health governance, how to establish a mechanism for mutual assistance and learning, how to support and strengthen specialized international organizations, how to protect the industrial chain and supply chain from the impact of the pandemic, how to reduce the side-effects on society caused by economic stagnation, and how to deal with the spread of misinformation and rumors and achieve practical cooperation. In the process of fighting the pandemic, as the United States has lost its charisma and soft power, China and the European Union, two important forces in the world, can take the lead in implementing the human health community to empower mankind to rapidly get rid of the virus.

Notes

1 This quote is from Professor Beate Kohler's email to me on April 3, 2020.
2 https://finance.sina.com.cn/roll/2020-04-30/doc-iircuyvi0603113.shtml.
3 See Josep Borrell's "Post Coronavirus World Here." April 24, 2020. https://eeas.europa.eu/headquarters/headquarters-homepage/78098/post-coronavirus-world-here-already_en.
4 "Commission Reviews Relations with China, Proposes 10 Actions." https://ec.europa.eu/commission/presscorner/detail/en/IP_19_1605.

5 "Disinformation Around the Coronavirus Pandemic: Opening Statement by the HR/VP Josep Borrell at the European Parliament." https://eeas.europa.eu/headquarters/headquarters-homepage/78329/disinformation-around-coronavirus-pandemic-opening-statement-hrvp-josep-borrell-european_en.
6 http://www.kekenet.com/kouyi/202008/615536.shtml.
7 In 1464, the king of Bohemia, under the persuasion of Marini, a Frenchman, suggested that the kings of Poland, Hungary and Germany jointly sign an agreement to maintain peace and stability in the Christian region. With the support of other monarchs, the king of Bohemia formed a Christian Regional Congress to act according to laws and regulations, and cooperate with each other in case of foreign aggression. The executive meeting was called the "Community."

15 The US Internal Affairs, Diplomacy, and Sino-US Relations During the COVID-19 Pandemic*

*Ni Feng***

Around the end of 2019 and early 2020, a novel coronavirus (SARS-CoV-2) broke out unexpectedly and quickly became a global pandemic, unseen in a century. It spread to more than 200 countries and regions, infected tens of millions of people, and killed more than 500,000 people, making an extremely significant impact on global politics, economy, and society. The virus attacks human beings regardless of country, region, race or belief. On January 21, 2020, the United States confirmed its first COVID-19 case. In the following month, only dozens of cases were reported. But in March, the infected cases surged in the US from hundreds of infections to tens of thousands every day, quickly making the US the "epicenter" of the disease. On March 26, the number of confirmed cases in the United States reached more than 80,000, surpassing China as the country with the most confirmed cases of COVID-19, and the pandemic was still raging. On March 29, Anthony Fauci, a key member of the US Pandemic prevention team, a White House health adviser and an expert of the US National Institutes of Health (NIH), revealed in an interview with CNN that millions of people in the United States would be infected, and 100,000–200,000 would lose their lives.[1]

The United States Under the Impact of the Pandemic

The impact of this raging pandemic on the United States was shocking, comparable to those of the "9/11 attacks" and the "financial tsunami" in 2008. With the continuous development of the pandemic, a variety of crises were emerging, one upon the other. Although we need to continue to fathom the consequences of the crises, some major impacts are already obvious.

First of all, the US economy suffered a heavy blow as the "Trump Boom" ended abruptly. The recession was imminent and may get worse. The damage of the pandemic to the US economy can be described as lethal. In terms of the two economic indicators that Trump had been most concerned about since he took

---

* The article was published in *World Economics and Politics* 4 (2020).
** Research Fellow, and Director of the Institute of American Studies, the Chinese Academy of Social Science.

DOI: 10.4324/9781003433897-15

The US Internal Affairs, Diplomacy, and Sino-US Relations 179

office, the market value of the stock market and the unemployment rate. From March 9 to 18, 2020, the US stock market had four circuit breakers in ten days. On March 18, the Dow fell below the 19,000 point mark during the mid-session, once down nearly 11%, more than 2,200 points, the lowest reported at 18,917.46 points, a drop of more than 10,000 points compared with the historical high of 29,568.57 points in February. At the time of writing, the gains of the Dow since Trump took office were completely erased in the session.[2] As for unemployment data, the number of weekly initial jobless claims released by the US Department of Labor on March 26 reached 3.283 million, nearly five time the previous historical peak of 695,000 during the financial crisis in 2008.

Shortly after the release of the initial jobless claims data, Jerome Powell said that the US economy may have fallen into recession. According to the data of the US Department of Commerce at the end of April, the US real GDP growth rate in the first quarter was −4.8%, the lowest in nearly a decade; consumption decreased by 5.26%, which was the largest drag and the fourth lowest in history; the unemployment rate in April was likely to reach a record high of 14%, the historical high was 10.8% in 1982.[3] The GDP growth rate of the United States in the second quarter might hit a record low due to the lockdowns in many states taking effect in late March, the impact of which on the economy would be mainly reflected in the second quarter. Some estimated that the GDP growth rate would drop to −20%, while the historical low was −10%. Rae Rosen, former Vice Chair of the New York Fed, was even more pessimistic. She was sure that there would be two possibilities to bring the US economy into great depression. One was that if the Congress saw only trees but not forests, by being not firm enough in providing assistance and loans to individuals and companies, or attaching too many conditions. The other was that people were unable to maintain social distancing. The spread of COVID-19 led to a sharp increase in the number of deaths, resulting in social isolation and an extension of the economic stagnation period for several months more.[4]

Secondly, American social life began to stop. Different from the situation in China, the pandemic situation in the United States showed a multi-point outbreak trend. As of April 11, all states declared a state of "major disaster," the first time ever in American history. The vast majority of people were kept at home. Affected by the outbreak of the pandemic, the number of flight cancellations increased significantly. On March 25, 10,324 flights were canceled that day, 27.8 times as many as on March 13, when the state of public health emergency was declared. During the week from March 7 to 14, hotel occupancy dropped by 24%. After the outbreak began to spread in the United States in March, many film companies announced that they would postpone the release of films. In addition to the reduction in travel, the US box office revenue entered a negative growth. The growth rate in box office revenue in the week of March 19 was down by −56.2%. The catering industry was hardest hit by the COVID-19. Seattle, where the first infections were reported, saw a sharp decline in the catering seating rate since the beginning of March. The catering seating rate in New York and Boston declined only after the number of cases in the

United States exceeded 1,000. On the fourth day after the declaration of the state of emergency (March 17), the catering seating rate in New York and Boston fell to 0. Not only was social life seriously affected, but so also were the operations of the US military affected by the pandemic. On March 25, CNN reported that three defense officials disclosed that due to the spread of COVID-19, US Secretary of Defense Mark Esper had signed an order to freeze all US military operations overseas for 60 days. All these made Americans lament that many wars have taken place since 1945, but none of them was able to turn the most prosperous cities on earth into empty cities, stop all entertainment in the most developed country, put the most advanced medical system on the verge of collapse, shut down factories, and keep everyone at home. The pandemic had an all-round devastating impact on American society, politics, and economy. The most obvious include the rise of nationalism and xenophobia, the intensification of social divisions, social unrest caused by unemployment, the resurgence of big government, which became a large pharmaceutical company, the restraint of individualism, the suppression of consumerism, the return of religious influence, greater emphasis on family life, and the decline in the frequency of social activities. Also, the outbreak of the pandemic made gun possession a more common understanding, communication and consumption more dependent on digital technology, virtual reality and telemedicine more popular, professionalism more reliable, electronic voting more common, domestic supply chains more strengthened, and relations with the outside world increasingly awry.

Finally, pandemic prevention has become the focus of American politics and government action. On the Global Health Security index (GHS index), the United States scored 83.5 points, ranking first in the world. The United States should have been the best-prepared country. However, in the early stages of the outbreak, the performance of the Trump administration shattered this illusion. Although the United States received a briefing from China shortly after the virus emerged, the Trump administration's series of mistakes have repeatedly deprived the United States of its best defense opportunities. These include: when the virus swept through China, the US did not take the pandemic seriously; there were serious defects in the manufacturing of test kits, which made the whole country turn a blind eye to the crisis; there was a serious shortage of masks and PPE to protect front-line doctors and nurses, and there were not sufficient ventilators to ensure the lives of seriously ill patients. Seth Berkley, then President of GAVI Alliance, remarked that "There is no direction, unprepared, lazy and uncoordinated. The improper handling of the COVID-19 crisis in the United States is worse than what every health expert I interviewed worried about. As an American, I am scared."[5]

On February 29, 2020, the first death occurred in the United States,[6] while the number of infected people began to increase rapidly. Only after the capital market showed a strong reaction did the Trump government really pay attention to the pandemic. On March 13, the president announced that the United States entered a "state of national emergency," and would provide $50 billion

The US Internal Affairs, Diplomacy, and Sino-US Relations   181

in assistance to the states and major cities. At the same time, he announced a response plan to address the problems of funding, insufficient test kits, a lack of money for testing and treatment, unimpeded patient information and national overall planning, insufficient doctors and beds, lack of income of those who are forced to quit jobs to take care of sick family members, low-income families that were unable to cope with the pandemic, and the pressure on students to repay loans. The administration was considering adopting 100 measures to protect the economy.[7]

Only at this point did the US government and the whole society began to take COVID-19 for real. The declaration of the pandemic a national emergency greatly changed the way the US government normally operates. The declaration will grant the President of the United States by law at least 136 emergency powers, including production mode regulation, sending troops abroad, enforcing domestic martial law, controlling enterprise operations, and even using some extreme weapons. Thus, in the federal government system of the United States, the power of the executive branch has been greatly expanded, and Trump has become a super powerful President.

With the United States entering a "war time," the Democratic and Republican parties changed their inefficient decision-making situation of constant party strife. Acting together, the two parties passed the Novel Coronavirus Assistance, Relief and Economic Security Act in Congress at extremely fast speed, which was signed by Trump on March 27. The scale and strength of the bill are unprecedented, with more than $2 trillion to spend. It not only includes the basic demands of the Republican Party, but also takes into account the concerns of the Democratic Party, such as providing $350 billion in loans to small businesses, providing $250 billion in unemployment assistance and $75 billion in hospital assistance, providing up to $1,200 in cash for individuals and $2,400 in cash for married couples, providing $500 in cash for each child.

Although the Democratic and Republican parties basically reached a consensus on the measures to fight the pandemic, the pandemic caused the parties to struggle fiercely in two other aspects. One is the ongoing US general election. Before the outbreak of the pandemic, due to the "Trump Boom" in the US economy, people were generally optimistic about Trump's prospects for re-election. However, with the outbreak of the pandemic, the US economy suffered a severe setback, and this, coupled with Trump's poor response at the early stage of the outbreak, meant that the Democratic Party rekindled the hope of recapturing the White House, and launched a new round of attacks against Trump's consistent contempt for pandemic prevention, his neglect of the health of the people, and castigated him for causing such a tragedy to the United States. For example, on March 26, when the number of confirmed cases in the United States rose to be the largest in the world, Hillary Clinton tweeted satirizing Trump that "he has indeed made the United States first." The pro-Democratic *Foreign Policy* published an article with the title "The Coronavirus Is the Worst Intelligence Failure in U.S. History," claiming the outbreak of COVID-19 in the United States is "more glaring than Pearl Harbor and

182   *Ni Feng*

9/11 – and it's all the fault of Donald Trump's leadership," "Trump officials made a series of judgments (minimizing the hazards of COVID-19) and decisions (refusing to act with the urgency required) that have needlessly made Americans far less safe."[8] In short, the pandemic and its responses have become the biggest issue in the 2020 presidential election. The development trend of the pandemic and the response results of the Trump administration will ultimately determine who will be in the White House. The second is the relationship between the Federal Government and those of the states. Both the federal and the state authorities have the power to formulate public health policies. In practice, however, the management of public health is mainly the responsibility of state and local governments. It is difficult to achieve effective cooperation between the federal and the state governments, especially in the context of political polarization between the two parties. Instead, they have lots of contradictions in dealing with major public security crises. In this pandemic, most of the hardest-hit areas are democratic states, such as New York, Washington, California, Michigan, etc., so the party struggle is constantly manifested in the contradiction between the federal government and the state governments. For example, Trump and New York State Governor Andrew Cuomo had a serious dispute over the ventilator issue, and the governors of Washington and Michigan criticized the federal government for its poor response. They and Trump publicly blamed each other, creating an otherwise scene in fighting the pandemic.

The Relationship between the United States and the World in the Context of the Pandemic

Since the beginning of the 21st century, the United States has suffered several waves of huge blows, such as the "9/11" attack, and the 2020 financial tsunami, which have seriously weakened the United States in the sense that the gap between the US ambition to seek hegemony and its ability to maintain a hegemonic position has widened. In this context, populism and extreme nationalism in the US have surged, especially among the blue-collar white middle class and rural white people. They generally believe that the globalization policy pursued by the elite of Washington and Wall Street for a long time only benefits the capital and technical elite, while the vast middle and lower classes, the traditional manufacturing industry of the United States and the sovereignty of the United States have been damaged. It was driven by this turbulent tide that Trump, an atypical political figure, was elected President of the United States in 2016.

After Trump took office, the US foreign policy underwent the most significant turn since the end of the Second World War. Although "America First" was the foreign policy doctrine of the Trump administration, it reflected in essence the anxiety over the accumulated domestic problems, and over the change of international status of the United States. Its core meaning was to blame the external world, globalization, and other countries for taking advantage

The US Internal Affairs, Diplomacy, and Sino-US Relations   183

of the United States for all kinds of problems it encountered. For this reason, the United States had to "fight alone" to pursue its own interests, and view the relationship between the United States and the external world as a zero-sum game. To this end, Trump tried to mitigate the harmful impact of free trade on the loss of jobs, to reduce restrictions on the United States by global governance mechanisms such as climate cooperation, and to reduce security commitments to allies. Overall, what Trump pursued was a comprehensive exit strategy. At the same time, Trump's international outlook was "Hobbesian" in the sense that looked at the international community as a jungle where the strongest survives. He emphasized the principle of strength, and unscrupulous means to win the competition with other great powers. He advocated increasing military spending to build a stronger army. Although these policy propositions sometimes seemed contradictory, they clearly showed that Trump's foreign policy was unilateral, destructive, and adventurous. Since Trump took office, the United States took a few steps back in assuming its international responsibilities by withdrawing from such international organizations and mechanisms as the Trans-Pacific Partnership Agreement (TPP), the Paris Agreement, the Iran Nuclear Deal, UNESCO, the Universal Postal Union, the Intermediate-Range Nuclear Forces Treaty, and so on. Due to the obstruction of the United States, the Appellate Body of the World Trade Organization had to be suspended. In addition, the United States has deliberately defaulted on its dues to the United Nations and continued to reduce the total amount of foreign aid. In terms of handling relations with other major countries in the world, the Trump administration upheld the concept of great power competition, and regarded China and Russia as strategic opponents. Against China, the United States launched an unprecedented "trade war." It made simultaneous efforts to stir up trouble over the so-called Taiwan issue, the South China Sea issue. The US continued to strengthen the geo-strategic containment of China with its Indian Pacific Strategy as a starting point. The United States and Russia intensified their rivalry over the issues of NATO's eastward expansion, arms control, the Non-Proliferation of Nuclear Weapons, and the issues of Ukraine, Syria, and Venezuela. At the same time, the Trump administration tried to strengthen the US border security, and launched a comprehensive trade war against its major trading partners. The target countries include not only such competitors as China, but also NATO, and the countries of the Asia-Pacific, namely, the US allies with which the US holds its hegemonic position. In addition, the United States forced its allies to enlarge their defense budget and pay greater defense costs. For a while, the West was very puzzled with anxiety by the United States. French President Macron exclaimed that NATO is experiencing "brain death." American scholar John Joseph Mearsheimer found that the liberal international order is collapsing. The theme of Munich Security Conference held in February, 2020 was "Westlessness."

As a result of the substantial change in the external behavior of the United States, the world is currently entering an increasingly chaotic era. The optimism

184 *Ni Feng*

about globalization since the Cold War is disappearing. De-globalization, nationalism, populism, and unilateralism are making a comeback. The contradictions between countries are expanding and escalating, the gap between races is deepening and widening, and the talk of civilization conflict is rampant. The world is at a crossroads full of uncertainty. At this moment, the outbreak of COVID-19 came as the most severe global public health security crisis since the end of the Second World War. In the era of globalization, no country can be in a paradise, free from the threat and harm of this infectious diseases. As Joseph Nye points out,

> On transnational threats like COVID-19 and climate change, it is not enough to think of American power over other nations. The key to success is also learning the importance of power with others. Every country puts its national interest first; the important question is how broadly or narrowly this interest is defined. COVID-19 shows we are failing to adjust our strategy to this new world.[9]

During the outbreak, the Trump administration got stuck in the concept of "America First," and was almost absent from the coordination of crisis response, material flow, fiscal stimulus, information sharing and other aspects until it became the "epicenter" of the outbreak. Even as an epicenter, the United States failed to play a global leading role. Instead, it tried to benefit itself at the expense of others. At the beginning of the outbreak, the United States was the first country to close its borders to other countries. With the spread of the pandemic, while restricting the export of prevention materials, the United States also intercepted and robbed goods everywhere. On April 3, the Voice of Germany reported that a batch of FFP2 and FFP masks ordered by the Berlin Municipal Government from China was intercepted by the United States. Moreover, the Americans confiscated a batch of consignees' supplies for the Berlin police in Bangkok. The President of the Paris Region insisted that the Americans took away their goods because the Americans paid a higher price. Moreover, Peter Navarro, Director of the White House National Trade Council, falsely claimed that in response to COVID-19, the actions of the US allies, China, and other strategic opponents once again showed that the United States was fighting alone in the global public health emergency, and it was necessary for the United States to transfer its basic drug production and supply chain back to the US to reduce its dependence on foreign countries, so as to protect the health of citizens, and the economic and national security of the United States. Most countries blamed the Trump administration for its continuous effort to shift responsibility to the World Health Organization, suspend the payment of its WHO dues, and wrongly criticize other countries for their prevention effort. As Kurt Campbell, Assistant Secretary of State for Asia Pacific Affairs in the Obama administration, and Rush Doshi, a Yale scholar, point out in an article published on the official website of the US *Foreign Affairs* magazine in March:

> The status of the United States as a global leader over the past seven decades has been built not just on wealth and power but also, and just as important, on the legitimacy that flows from the United States' domestic governance, provision of global public goods, and ability and willingness to muster and coordinate a global response to crises. The coronavirus pandemic is testing all three elements of US leadership. So far, Washington is failing the test.[10]

They argue that "the pandemic has amplified Trump's instincts to go it alone and exposed just how unprepared Washington is to lead a global response."[11] They also remind the American leaders by evoking the Suez Issue,

> In 1956, a botched intervention in the Suez laid bare the decay in British power and marked the end of the United Kingdom's reign as a global power. Today, U.S. policymakers should recognize that if the United States does not rise to meet the moment, the coronavirus pandemic could mark another 'Suez moment'.[12]

COVID-19 and Sino-US Relations

Just as the COVID-19 virus began to rage, Sino-US relations came to a critical juncture. After a year and a half of fighting a trade war, unprecedented in scale, the two countries finally reached the first stage agreement on January 15, 2020, and the tension of Sino-US relations eased a bit. Faced with the current serious pandemic, the world generally expects that China and the United States, the two most influential countries, can put aside their prejudices and join hands, as they did during the international financial crisis in 2008, and during the Ebola pandemic in Africa in 2014, to lead the global responses to this threat, and show the world that they could work together for global development and cooperation.

However, despite the surge of the pandemic, a considerable number of politicians, strategic elites and media in the United States still viewed China from the perspective of strategic competition. Some people even saw the pandemic as an opportunity to curb China's rise. The American scholar Walter Russell Mead said in his article entitled "China is the real sick man of East Asia":

> The mighty Chinese juggernaut has been humbled this week, apparently by a species-hopping bat virus. While Chinese authorities struggle to control the pandemic and restart their economy, a world that has grown accustomed to contemplating China's inexorable rise was reminded that nothing, not even Beijing's power, can be taken for granted.[13]

186   Ni Feng

Recently, the Center for New American Security (CNAs), a think-tank, has published a research report entitled "Protracted Great-Power War," which suggested that the US strategic competition with China should evolve from "vertical escalating" to "horizontal escalating." Specifically, in the situation of mutually assured destruction by nuclear weapons and other weapons of mass destruction, when the possibility of vertical escalation of strategic competition among major powers is reduced, the scope of competition among the great powers should include not only restricting the scope of action of the competitors in space, network, and deep sea, but also curbing the development potential of the competitors in such comprehensive fields as public opinion, economy, and biology.[14] Instigated by various forces, the United States launched a new round of confrontation, which greatly interfered with the cooperation between China and the United States in combating the pandemic.

First of all, the United States made use of COVID-19 to discredit and vilify China. Some US officials and institutions have made irresponsible remarks. Secretary of State Mike Pompeo blamed China for the outbreak of COVID-19, for China's ineffective early response measures, and for China's incomplete disclose of information. He accused China for the difficult situation the United States has been in. Trump even called the virus "China virus." On March 24, some Republican Congressmen introduced a resolution calling for an international investigation into China's so-called "concealment of the spread of COVID-19" at the early stage of the outbreak, and demanding that China compensate the affected countries in the world. The US media has also set off a wave of attacks on China. The *New York Times* has repeatedly accused the Chinese government of disrupting the people's livelihood at home and abroad by failing to control the pandemic, saying that China's economy will be severely hit by the pandemic. CNBC claims that China's international image will be increasingly bleak in the future due to the COVID-19. *The Wall Street Journal* ascertains that due to the close economic relationship with China, Asian and African countries will become important "victims" of the virus. Goldman Sachs, JP Morgan Chase, Bloomberg, and other US agencies have lowered their forecasts for China's economic growth. According to the American think-tank the Enterprise Research Institute, the pandemic will worsen China's local government debt, corporate default risk is rising, CNY is rapidly depreciating, and China's economy may fall into a massive crisis. In addition, the US side also announced the expulsion and reduction of the number of Chinese journalists in the US. As a result of this political confrontation, the perceptions of the two peoples of each other have further declined. According to a poll released by Gallup in early March 2020, the Americans' favorable opinion of China reached a new low since the 1980s, at only 33%. China for the first time was perceived, along with Russia, as the leading enemy of the United States. In 2019, 32% of Americans regarded Russia their leading enemy, and 21% considered China their leading enemy. In 2020, 23% regarded Russia their enemy and 22% regarded China their enemy.[15]

Second, the United States continued to put pressure in trade to accelerate the economic "decoupling" from China. The Trump administration focused on trade as a breakthrough to make the strategic competition with China. After a year and a half of trade war of "unprecedented scale," the two countries finally reached the first stage agreement on January 15, 2020, a sign that the Sino-US relations became stable for the time being. Before long, the raging spread of the pandemic provided a new pretext for the hawkish people in the Trump administration to call for a more thorough "decoupling" from China. According to the media, the American "Hawks" headed by Navarro, a senior adviser to the White House, are formulating and implementing plans to promote the shift of some production capacity to the US as the pandemic surges, so as to reduce the dependence on China. On March 22, Trump invoked the Defense Production Act, an act enacted in 1950, which gives the President great authority to control domestic industry for the sake of national security. Within the scope of his authority, the president can require private enterprises to produce necessary materials for the country, and provide loans for the production of relevant materials and purchase them directly. The invocation provides the Trump administration with the institutional possibility to implement the forced "decoupling" regardless of the cost. On March 27, Trump appointed Navarro, who strongly advocated US economic "decoupling" from China, the policy coordinator for the Defense Production Act. On April 10, Larry Kudlow, the Director of the Economic Council, urged the American companies in China to move back to the US from China, and the US government should pay the "moving costs." At the same time, the decoupling in specific fields is also being carried out urgently: removing China from the preferential tariff treatment list as a developing country under the WTO, tightening rules for Chinese companies to go public in the United States, using various means to crack down on Huawei, strengthening rules for export control of emerging technologies, greatly expanding the export control on China's military end uses or military end users, strengthening the national security review of China's investment in the United States, intensifying the crackdown on so-called Chinese "network theft" and "economic espionage," reinforcing the crackdown on Chinese nationals who "illegally" participate in China's various talent programs or cooperate with Chinese scientific research institutions, and imposing secondary sanctions on a number of Chinese banks for violating the relevant laws of the United States on Iran and North Korea.

Finally, the United States continues to promote its Indian Pacific strategy, trying to unite with India and Taiwan Region, China, and build a major geopolitical platform for strategic competition with China. India is of paramount importance for the US Indian Pacific strategy. From February 24 to 25, Trump paid his first state visit to India since taking office. The two countries issued a joint statement on the vision and principles of the comprehensive global strategic partnership, and signed a $3 billion military procurement contract. Trump remarks in his speech, "There is all the difference in the world between a nation that seeks power through coercion, intimidation, and aggression, and a nation that rises by setting its people free and unleashing them to chase their dreams."[16] He hinted that India differs from China. In the joint statement, the

188   *Ni Feng*

two sides said that the close partnership between the United States and India is crucial to maintaining "freedom, openness, inclusiveness, peace and prosperity in the Indian Pacific region." They will strengthen consultations through mechanisms such as the "trilateral summit between the United States, India and Japan," "US–India 2+2 Ministerial Dialogue" and "US–Australia–India–Japan Consultations (the Quad)," and stressed that they would work with other partners to raise marine awareness.

The Trump administration's political manipulations have rapidly deteriorated Sino-US relations. As we all know, the transnational spread of infectious diseases is a major threat to human survival and development. Exploring disease knowledge, developing drugs to treat diseases, and formulating prevention and treatment plans are essentially areas for international cooperation. At present, the surging pandemic is rampant all over the world, becoming the world's most important public security crisis and dwarfing the traditional military and geographical issues, the usual security issues. The pandemic demands a great global effort to cope with. Looking back on the history of China–US relations, the two countries have jointly and successfully addressed major global public security threats. Whether it was dealing with terrorism, financial turmoil or global climate change, the two countries used to stand in the same trench, playing a global leadership role through cooperation, benefiting both countries and the world. In the field of public health, the two sides used to make important contributions to the well-being of the two peoples and the cause of global public health through the interaction between governments, health institutions, scientific research, and other multi-level mechanisms.

Since 2003, the Chinese and US governments have significantly strengthened bilateral cooperation in the field of global health. After the SARS pandemic was under control in China, Mr. Thompson, then US Secretary of Health, visited China and signed a cooperation document with the Chinese Ministry of Health. In 2004, after H5N1 avian influenza virus appeared in China, the National Influenza Center of China and the Centers for Disease Control and Prevention (CDC) of the United States cooperated for the first time to improve the capabilities of the two countries in pandemic monitoring and data analysis. In 2005, the two governments launched the "new and recurrent infectious diseases cooperation plan" and held the China–US Health Summit in the same year. In 2009, the new H1N1 influenza virus broke out in the United States and Mexico, and quickly swept the world. Based on the previous cooperation, China and the United States were able to share information and technology, thus rapidly promoting international pandemic monitoring and related vaccine development. In November of the same year, then US President Barack Obama visited China. In the subsequent joint statement, China and the United States promised to strengthen cooperation in preventing, monitoring and reporting of global public health issues, covering H1N1, avian influenza, AIDS, tuberculosis, and malaria. In 2013, the new avian influenza virus H7N9 appeared in China. China took the lead in developing a

The US Internal Affairs, Diplomacy, and Sino-US Relations   189

vaccine against the virus and shared it with the world, which promoted the vaccine development work of the CDC and private pharmaceutical companies. During the outbreak of H7N9 virus, the centers for disease control and prevention of China and the United States shared data, carried out joint research, and distributed virus detection reagents around the world, which was widely recognized by the world, and the scientific community. In 2014, When the Ebola virus broke out in West Africa, China and the United States quickly launched medical assistance, and conducted field cooperation in Africa.

It can be said that China–US cooperation in the medical field benefits both countries and the world, and there is huge room for development. As the pandemic continues to spread, more and more people with insight in the United States have realized the importance of this cooperation. The author of *Destined for War: Can America and China Avoid the Thucydides Trap?*, Professor Graham Allison, writes, "At the same time defeat of this pandemic underlines a vital national interest neither the US nor China can secure without the cooperation of the other."[17] On March 27, the two presidents of China and the United States made a phone call one day after the special G20 Summit. They focused on the current global pandemic prevention and control cooperation during the call, which put a brake on the continuous deterioration of the bilateral relations. As President Xi points out that the pandemic is the common enemy of mankind, regardless of national boundaries and races. The international community can only win the fight if it responds together. At present, China–US relations are at an important juncture. Cooperation between China and the United States will benefit both, while confrontation will hurt both. Cooperation is the only correct choice. It is hoped that the US side will take substantive actions to improve China–US relations, and the two sides will work together to strengthen cooperation in fight the pandemic and in other fields, and develop a relationship of no conflict, no confrontation, mutual respect, and win-win cooperation.[18] This points out the only correct direction for China–US relations in the new context. In the face of the once-in-a-century global pandemic, the world need to work together to fight it as we share the same fate.

Notes

1 "U.S. Could Face 200,000 Coronavirus Death, Millions of Cases, Fauci Warns." *The New York Time* March 29, 2020.
2 The Dow Jones Index closed at 19,872 on January 20, when Donald Trump was sworn in.
3 See https://www.bea.gov/data/gdp/gross-domestic-product.
4 See Rae Rosen's "The Impact of COVID-19 on US Economy Is More Serious than the 2008 Financial Crisis." *International Finance News* March 25, 2020.
5 See Ed Yong's "How the Pandemic Will End – The U.S. May End up with the Worst COVID-19 Outbreak in the Industrialized World. This is how It's Going to Play out." *The Atlantic* March 25, 2020.
6 See Ray Sanchez's "This Past Week Signaled a Turning Point in America's Health Emergency." CNN March 15, 2020.

7 See Tom Howell Jr., and Dave Boyer's "Trump Declares National Emergency to Deal with Coronavirus." *The Washington Times* March 13, 2020. https://www.washingtontimes.com/news/2020/mar/13/trump-declares-national-emergency-deal-coronavirus/.

8 See Micah Zenko's "The Coronavirus Is the Worst Intelligence Failure in U.S. History." *Foreign Policy* March 25, 2020.

9 Joseph S. Nye, Jr. https://www.unic.ac.cy/da/2020/05/08/how-the-world-will-look-after-the-coronavirus-pandemic-belfer-center-for-science-and-international-affairs/.

10 See Kurt M. Campbell's and Rush Doshi's "The Coronavirus Could Reshape Global Order: China Is Maneuvering for International Leadership as United States Falters." *Foreign Affairs* March 18, 2020. https://www.foreignaffairs.com/articles/china/2020-03-18/coronavirus-could-reshape-global-order.

11 Joseph S. Nye, Jr. https://www.unic.ac.cy/da/2020/05/08/how-the-world-will-look-after-the-coronavirus-pandemic-belfer-center-for-science-and-international-affairs/.

12 Ibid.

13 See Walter Russell Mead's "China Is the Real Sick Man of Asia." *The Wall Street Journal* February 2, 2020.

14 See Andrew F. Krepinevich's "Protracted Great-Power War:A Preliminary Assessment." https://www.cnas.org/publications/reports/protracted-great-power-war.

15 See Jeffrey M. Jones's "Fewer in U.S. Regard China Favorably or as Leading Economy."https://news.gallup.com/poll/287108/fewer-regard-china-favorably-leading-economy.aspx.

16 See Mao Keji, and Tong Jing's "Full Text of US President Trump's Speech in Gujarat's Ahmedabad." Trans. February 25, 2020. https://www.ndtv.com/india-news/full-text-of-us-president-donald-trumps-speech-in-india-2185045

17 See Graham Allison, and Christopher Li's "In War Against Coronavirus:Is China Foe–or Friend?"https://nationalinterest.org/feature/war-against-coronavirus-china-foe%E2%80%94or-friend-138387.

18 "President Xi's Phone Call with US President Trump." *Guangming Daily* March 28, 2020.

16 Impact of the COVID-19 Pandemic on the World and Sino-Japan Relations[*]

Yang Bojiang[**]

At present, the pandemic of novel coronavirus pneumonia (COVID-19) is rampant all over the world. While China has made major strategic achievements in battling the pandemic, the situation in Europe and the United States is grim and tragic. The COVID-19 occurred in the process of a great change that has not been seen in a century. Its complex impact and its derived variables are far greater than expected, which will significantly impinge on the international politics, world economy and global governance in the 21st century. China–Japan relations will also usher in a new phase.

COVID-19 Creates a New Turning Point in History

As a global public health crisis, compared with other non-traditional security crises, such as natural disasters and financial crises, COVID-19 is sudden, indiscriminating, and changing, knowing no borders and races. The pandemic is raging in many places, hard to harness, devastating, and long-lasting, which will cause compound consequences for the world and regional economic growth, and can destabilize a country or even the global situation. From the vertical axis of time, the outbreak is likely to become a new historical turning point. Thomas Friedman, the author of the book *The World Is Flat*, believes that mankind needs to work together to cope with common threats. In this sense, 2020 can be the first year of mankind as a community with shared future destiny.

The Direction of Globalization Will Not be Reversed, But the Rhythm Paradigm Will Be Adjusted

Globalization is the inevitable result of world economic development and scientific and technological progress, and reflects the pattern of historical development. The general trend will not change. However, the global industrial chain supply chain will be rebuilt. Some countries continue to call for the

---

[*] The chapter was published in *World Economics and Politics* 4 (2020), and *World Affairs* 9 (2020) in a slightly different form.
[**] Research fellow, and Director of the Institute of Japanese Studies, CASS.

DOI: 10.4324/9781003433897-16

shifting of key manufacturing capacity to the homeland. The scale of global trade and investment will shrink. The World Trade Organization (WTO) predicted that global trade would decline by 13–32% in 2020.[1] The general trend indicates that the world economy will ultimately be subject to the rationality of the market economy and the profit seeking nature of capital.

Generally, globalization benefits everyone. The data show that the median income of the United States and other developed countries has been increasing rather than decreasing in recent years. From the perspective of capital, the benefits of cooperation far outweigh the risks. Under COVID-19, the "supply cut-off" and "demand cut-off" just prove that globalization is an existing reality. The "isolation" for the virus prevention and control just highlights the reality of "connectedness" among countries. The pandemic can be seen as a test of globalization. It detects areas that need to be improved or abandoned. One of the findings of this test is that countries should respond to the public health crisis through cross-border cooperation in health and economic affairs. At least in theory, this will promote cooperation in the field of global non-traditional security.

However, the benefits from globalization are unevenly distributed. More importantly, this "imbalance" occurs to the world's largest economy, the United States, which leads to the complexity of the problem. In fact, since the 2008 financial crisis, the phenomenon of "de-globalization" has emerged, such as the slowdown of global trade growth and the rise of trade protectionist measures such as tariffs. However, the "de-globalization" characterized by the reduction of international flow of goods, services, capital and people is, in essence, a slowdown in the process of globalization, rather than a reversal of direction. At present, the most urgent task is to reshape the global supply chain. Some countries pay more attention to maintain "oversupply," seek to build a more diversified supply chain, increase the flexibility and stability of the supply chain, and avoid excessive dependence on the supply of remote areas. At present, China has about 30% of the global manufacturing capacity, which will inevitably become the key target of this round of adjustment.

Regional Development of International Relations Will Accelerate

The attack of the virus knows no national borders, but it has obvious regional characteristics. The farther away the production base is from the consumer market, and the more dispersed the layout is, the greater is the risk. Therefore, international trade and investment will take into account geographical factors. Many countries that have overseas enterprises are more inclined to focusing their operations closer to home, which means that geo-economic thinking will prevail.

In this case, regional cooperation and economic integration will accelerate. Some Chinese scholars have proposed that China should seize the opportunity of the shutdown of some production in Europe and the United States and the economic recession, speed up the "inflow of investment to stabilize the supply chain," by building in the Guangdong–Hong Kong–Macao Great Bay area,

Beijing–Tianjin–Hebei area, Yangtze River Delta, Chengdu-Chongqing economic circle and other regions, a number of strategic emerging industrial chain clusters with high spatial agglomeration, close coordination between upstream and downstream enterprises, efficient supply chain, and worth of hundreds of billions to trillions.[2] It is possible in China to have all the industrial chains in the local area, but it is difficult in Japan and South Korea to do so, because they are small in territory, and high in labor costs. They can only rely on the surrounding areas, especially in Northeast Asia, to make necessary adjustment. This will increase the proportion of intra-regional trade in Northeast Asia and further strengthen the economic interdependence among countries.

Different regions and countries in the world have shown great differences in the prevention and control of the pandemic. The governments and people of the EU states, East Asia (Northeast Asia, Southeast Asia) and North America are obviously different in their responses and policies. The response to the pandemic reflects the cultural commonalities within some regions. For example, compared with the so-called "instrumental rationality" thinking in Europe and the United States, the prevention and control measures of East Asian countries reflect more "humanistic" values. These cultural commonalities will become the social and cultural basis for further strengthening regional cooperation.

Great-power Strategic Rivalry Further Integrates Economy and Security

International relations in the "post-COVID era" will continue to evolve in the direction set before the pandemic. As far as the relations among the big powers are concerned, the rules and standards still remain the focus of their strategic rivalry. Developed countries generally believe that supporting the "rules-based order" is the best international structure to realize their own national interests.[3] In the "post-COVID era," with the new changes in the international situation, and the new development of regional cooperation, how to reform or establish rules and standards that best serve their own interest, and that strengthen the environment for the application of the rules, will become the focus of the strategic rivalry of big powers. At the World Economic Forum in Davos in January 2019, Japanese Prime Minister Shinzo Abe proposed the new concept of global data governance, and called for the development of digital economy regulatory rules.[4] He pushed again for the discussion of this topic at the G20 Summit in Osaka in June of the same year. Japan's digital economy started early, but its development speed and market scale are relatively lagging behind. The digital economy was on the agenda of WTO. Japan obviously wants to seize the opportunity to dominate the rule-making on this topic so as to lead the direction of WTO reform. It is not only the global data governance, but also the formulation of important rules and standards involving a series of "high-tech areas" that deserve our attention.

The United States, Europe, and Japan attach more importance to national security issues, which are integrated with economic, scientific and technological issues. As a result, the international strategic rivalry in the high-tech area

194 *Yang Bojiang*

has been greatly intensified, military and civilian technologies have converged, dual-use technologies have increased, and "military–civilian integration" in the R&D and production areas has accelerated. At the end of 2019, Japan and the United States led the revision of the "Wassenaar Agreement" to enable this group export control mechanism to put more restrictions on the export of 12 inch chips, aiming at the rapid development of China's semiconductor industry. While the United States suppressed Huawei, Japan also had talks with the heads of Chinese high-tech companies. In 2019, the EU issued new regulations on the review of foreign direct investment, strengthening the review of foreign investment in the fields involving high-tech, key infrastructure, and sensitive data industries. The United States and Japan have also strengthened similar restrictive measures. Many countries worry about losing control over their strategic sectors due to foreign acquisitions, and over-reliance on external sources for basic trade supply. This has led them to introduce new policies to strengthen their autonomy and reduce their dependence on the outside world.

The Complex and Multiple Impact of the Pandemic on China–Japan Relations

The impact of the COVID-19 on the world is intense and far-reaching, and its impact on Japan, and China–Japan relations, is multiple and complex. This is mainly caused by two basic factors. The first is the direct factor, that is, the characteristics of the pandemic impact itself. Compared with other non-traditional security crises, infectious diseases spread under the conditions of globalization, with unprecedented intensity, depth and breadth. Second, the macro background of the event is at work. Before the outbreak of the pandemic, the world was already undergoing rapid and profound changes. Japan's national strategy was in a critical period of transformation, and China–Japan relations were facing historical changes. The pandemic actually played a role of "generating change on change," and "adding change to change," making adjustments in the content, direction and strength of the existing changes.

Impact on Japanese Politics, Political Situation, and Society

The pandemic has had a great I pact on Japanese politics and then political situation. At the time of writing, Japan has confirmed more than 17,000 cases of infection, ranking it 45th in the world, with a case fatality rate of about 5.39%, 40th in the world.[5] Although the pandemic situation in Japan is far less severe than that in the United States and Europe, and although Japan has an advanced and mature medical and health system and emergency management system, the effect of the government's pandemic prevention work has not reached the national expectations. Therefore, Abe's cabinet has been under criticism, and the "end of regime syndrome" may arrive earlier than expected. Although Japan's ruling party is far more powerful than the opposition parties combined, and Abe's supreme position in the Liberal Democratic Party (LDP) remains the same, the support rate for the LDP, and for Abe's cabinet have both declined. According to a poll by Asahi News Agency from May 23 to 24, the support rate of respondents engaged in manufacturing and service industries for the LDP was 36% in March and dropped to 21% in May, reflecting the dissatisfaction of employees in the two industries most affected by the pandemic with the prevention and control measures of the LDP and Abe government.[6] The support rate of Abe's cabinet fell to 32% in the same period, the second-lowest since the "Senyou School Scandal."[7] Abe's authority in LDP has been weakened, and factional fighting has intensified around the pandemic response measures and the arrangement of the next Primary Minister in the "post-Abe" era. The criticism by the right-wing conservative forces, of the Japanese government, including that of China, has risen again, which also shows that Abe's control over his political supporters has declined. Japanese society is generally stable, and there is no upsurge of populism and xenophobia, which has once again aroused people's attention to the mystery of Japan's system.

The pandemic has dealt a heavy blow to the Japanese economy. Before the COVID-19 outbreak, the so-called "Abe boom," the longest boom cycle in Japan's post-war history, had come to an end. Japan's economy began to slide, and the growth in the fourth quarter of 2019 turned negative. As a financial response to the slowdown, the Japanese government issued a 26 trillion yen stimulus plan at the end of 2019. Against the background of the pandemic, in addition to the deterioration of the external environment faced by all countries, Japan also has two special factors that have a serious inhibitory effect on economic growth. First, the consumption tax could be raised to 10% in October 2019, which would continue to suppress domestic demand that accounts for 60% of GDP. Second, the postponement of the Tokyo Olympic Games not only wiped out its potential benefits, but also caused heavy losses in the early investment. According to the Nomura Research Institute, the delay of the Tokyo Olympic Games will reduce Japan's real GDP by one percent.[8] In the first quarter of 2020, Japan's economic growth rate was –3.4%.[9] With the superposition of internal and external factors, Japan's economy will be particularly difficult in 2020. On April 7, Abe's cabinet issued a huge stimulus plan to fight the pandemic and economic depression, the scale of which reached a record 108.2 trillion yen, about $1 trillion, accounting for about 20% of Japan's GDP. However, from the perspective of various responses, its long-term measures will take too long a time to be effective, unable to stave off the immediate difficulties in the near future. However, it remains to be seen whether the short-term effects can be released quickly. On April 14, the International Monetary Fund (IMF) predicted in the latest *World Economic Outlook* report that Japan's economic growth rate in 2020 would be –5.2%.[10] Japan's domestic forecast was roughly the same.[11]

Impact on China–Japan Relations

Although the economic cooperation between China and Japan might face structural adjustment, there will be no systematic contraction. On the contrary, the adjustment might create new areas of cooperation. Although various

196 *Yang Bojiang*

"chains" between China and Japan will be recombined, the overall scale of cooperation will continue to be maintained. Of the $1 trillion stimulus plan issued, about $2.2 billion will be used for the so-called "response measures for parts supply chain," that is, to call for shifting the production capacity of key industries from overseas, especially China, to Japan, so as to reduce the risk of supply chain disruption. However, the nature of this "call" is different from that of the "decoupling" of the United States from China. Moreover, Japanese enterprises have their own relatively independent judgment and action orientation, which may not be consistent with the government. The $2.2 billion may not be spent in the end. Some enterprises will also leave China, but in the words of Seguchi Kiyosaki, Director of Canon Global Strategy Research Institute, those who advocate "leaving China" are the people who do not understand the economy, and those who want to leave China are the enterprises of no competitive strength. The latest survey by the Japan Trade Promotion Organization (JETRO) shows that among the Japanese manufacturing enterprises in East China, 86% of the respondents said they had no industrial transfer plan, 7% of the respondents planned to return to Japan, 5% of the respondents considered staying in China, and 1%–2% of the respondents had the intention to transfer to ASEAN. Similarly, about 90% of Japanese enterprises in Southern China said they had no transfer plan.[12] In short, under the impact of the pandemic, the awareness of economic security and the thinking of "economic nationalism" of international cooperation will rise simultaneously. However, Japan has a small territory, but high labor costs, and the withdrawal of the industrial chain or even the establishment of "industrial chain clusters" within Japan is not a realistic choice. For Japan and South Korea, "localization" means regionalization to a large extent, which means opportunities for China–Japan cooperation, and China–Japan-ROK cooperation.

Politically and strategically, Japan has a stronger sense of competition with China, and has tried more diversified ways to contain China. Compared with the "four big deficits" as a global challenge, the "trust deficit" is particularly prominent among various issues between China and Japan, a remaining issue between the two for a long time. At the early stage when China fought the pandemic, the interaction between China and Japan at the civilian level, especially between local sister cities, was effective.[13] However, with the spread of the pandemic, the situation changed, and the negative comments about China by Japan's right-wing conservative forces increased. It remains to be seen whether the pandemic will ultimately play a positive role in promoting the improvement of national feelings between China and Japan, but at least the situation of high "trust deficit" will be difficult to reverse in the short term. In addition to the existing disputes between China and Japan, there are also some strategic factors that make the overnight elimination of the "trust deficit" impossible. The reasons for this are, first, the United States factor, and second, Japan's own consideration of how to be wise enough to deal with the more powerful. In 2010, the total economic output of China and Japan was reversed, and the gap between China and Japan gets wider day by day. It is impossible

Impact of the COVID-19 Pandemic 197

to change the fact of "a big China and a small Japan." In this case, Japan focuses more on the comprehensive strategic considerations to alleviate the comprehensive pressure brought about by China's rise. In the context of intensified competition between China and the United States, Japan will play the role of a key variable between China and the United States. This strategic mentality, demand, and measures will not decrease in the future, but will continue to increase.

How to Understand and Build Sino-Japanese Relations in the New Era

In June 2019, the leaders of China and Japan reached a consensus in Osaka on "working together to build China–Japan relations that meet the requirements of the new era." The so-called China–Japan relations in the new era "should not only faithfully follow the past principled positions, but also be innovative development based on reality and keeping pace with the times."[14] The new era here should first be the new era of China's development proclaimed by the 19th National Congress of the Communist Party of China, and the "great changes not seen in a century" constitutes its international connotation. Therefore, to build a "China–Japan relationship that meets the requirements of the new era" first means that it meets the needs of China's development. China needs to strengthen its subjectivity and leadership in handling China–Japan relations. "China–Japan relations in the new era" have their own characteristics of the times and new pursuits. We should make a dialectical understanding of its connotation and patterns. It does not mean that all problems have been solved, and having problems does not mean that there will no development, cooperation or progress.

In the "post-COVID-19 era," China–Japan relations will still be in the "new normal" of competition and cooperation. The two sides share common interests and hold the same position in adhering to multilateralism, advocating free trade, and promoting regional cooperation, although they have many contradictions and differences. From the perspective of Japan's domestic politics, a weak regime is more likely to emerge in the "post-Abe" period. If so, Japan's political stability and policy continuity may be affected. In the face of the complex situation, China should not only speed up the promotion of China–Japan cooperation, but also calmly respond to the challenges. Everything should be based on solid scientific research and judgment. The goal should be reasonable, and the plan feasible. We cannot replace research and judgment with expectation, and rational analysis with good wishes. Only in this way can we truly achieve the sustainable, stable and healthy development of China–Japan relations.

Opportunities for Exploring the Multilateral Path of China–Japan Cooperation

The potential highlights of China–Japan cooperation can also be explored in terms of the trilateral cooperation between China, Japan, and the ROK, and regional cooperation in Northeast Asia. This is not only the spillover effect of

198   *Yang Bojiang*

China–Japan cooperation, but also the only way for China and Japan to deepen cooperation. The prevention and control of the COVID-19 pandemic has tested the effectiveness of the long-term institutionalized cooperation between China, Japan, and the ROK. The trilateral cooperation has been given new momentum. It is an important opportunity to pursue the "spillover effects."

Trilateral Cooperation Results Passed the Pandemic Prevention and Control Test

Since the outbreak of COVID-19, China, Japan, and South Korea, especially China and Japan, China and South Korea, have maintained close communication and coordination. At the level of professional institutions, the China CDC, the National Institute of Infectious Diseases of Japan, and the South Korean CDC jointly held a technical telephone conference on the prevention and control of COVID-19, and conducted professional exchanges and consultations on the release of isolation and discharge standards of confirmed cases, measures to limit social distance, community material supply methods, the effectiveness of antiviral drugs and protective measures for special populations. At the government level, on March 20, 2020, China, Japan, and the ROK held the first ministerial meeting after the outbreak – the special video conference of foreign ministers – and reached three important consensuses: first, around joint prevention and control. The three countries agreed to explore ways to strengthen joint prevention and control, jointly curb the cross-border spread of the virus, and explore the formulation of interconnected travel pandemic prevention and control guidelines. Second, the three countries agreed to strengthen policy communication, close coordination and cooperation, reduce the impact of the pandemic on trade and personnel exchanges, and stabilize the industrial chain and supply chain of the three countries. The third is "exchange and cooperation". The three countries support their respective health, science and technology, commerce and other departments to strengthen exchanges, timely share pandemic information, carry out drug and vaccine research and development cooperation, and maintain coordination on the import and export of medical materials.[15] The three countries also agreed to hold a meeting of health ministers as soon as possible to strengthen the sharing and exchange of pandemic information and jointly safeguard regional public health security. They will seek ways acceptable to all parties and strive to maintain necessary personnel exchanges related to economic and trade cooperation. They agree to take the opportunity of jointly combating the pandemic to continuously enhance the friendly feelings among the people of the three countries.[16]

The COVID-19 pandemic is a common enemy of China, Japan, and the ROK. Cooperation in combating it has enhanced the empathy experience among the nationals of the three countries. Since the second half of 2019, Japan–ROK relations remained particularly tense. The transparent pandemic response measures taken by the Moon Jae-in administration have won the recognition of the Japanese people, and the Japanese mainstream media and Internet platforms have given praise to the Korean government, a phenomenon rarely seen in Japan. Contrastively, *Asahi Shimbun*, a famous Japanese newspaper, prefers the Korean prevention principle of testing all to have a complete picture of the pandemic to Japanese prevention principle of less testing to reduce the number of infected cases. The paper praises the Korean government for its priority of testing and treating the poor and the underprivileged. *The Tokyo News* published an editorial on March 9, calling on Japan, China, and the ROK to strengthen cooperation and jointly deal with COVID-19. Although the Korean government expressed dissatisfaction with the measures taken by the Japanese government to restrict entry and took counter-measures, the Korean people did not follow up and large-scale protests occurred. On the whole, the cooperative fight against the pandemic has played a positive role in Japan–ROK relations, especially in easing the tension between the two peoples.

Compared with other regions in the world, Northeast Asia is the region where the pandemic broke out earlier, and is the first to have the virus under control because of their effective prevention and control measures. First of all, China, Japan, and the ROK have taken a series of powerful measures in a timely manner. In addition, the three countries have their own advantages and relative strength in the field of disease control. Japan and the ROK have sound infectious disease prevention and control systems, and their construction of public health systems is among the best in the world. Japan is advanced in medical research, and equipment. Their ventilator, imaging technology, and medical robots are most advanced in the world. Moreover, Japan follows through its national policy of providing international medical aid, and received international COVID patients. South Korea, twice hit by the Middle East Respiratory Syndrome (MERS) pandemic in 2015 and 2018, has rich experience in combating viral infection. China has obvious institutional and systemic advantages, excellent mobilization ability, an increasingly sound public health system, and a significantly improved ability to prevent, control and diagnose diseases. China, Japan, and South Korea have made rapid progress in the prevention and control of the current pandemic. Their success is inseparable from the timely and effective information exchange, and mutual sharing of experience in the early stage of the outbreak. After the outbreak in Wuhan, China immediately shared relevant information and experience of fighting the virus with Japan and South Korea, which played an important role in controlling the spread of the pandemic. Japan and South Korea have adopted different and specific measures in preventing the transmission of the disease. However, based on the information and experience provided by China, they have taken common measures, such as banning large gatherings, closing large public arenas, requiring home isolation, and work from home, wearing masks, and staying away from densely populated areas, which effectively controlled the spread of the pandemic.

The track of the pandemic prevention and control shows that the China–Japan–ROK cooperation was launched in a timely manner, and carried out orderly with favorable results, due to the good cooperation foundation of the three countries in the field of public health, especially due to the institutional cooperation framework. As early as in May 2006, in order to reduce the risk of the spread of infectious diseases, the health departments of China, Japan, and the ROK signed a letter of intent on cooperation on joint response to influenza pandemic in Geneva, which identified joint response to influenza as a priority, which officially opened the three countries' cooperation in the field of public health. Since then, the prevention and control of human infection with avian influenza, Ebola virus, Middle East Respiratory Syndrome, and other infectious diseases have been listed as important areas of cooperation. In April, 2007, as suggested by the ROK, China, Japan, and ROK held their health ministerial conference in Seoul, and established an annual dialogue mechanism. China's CDC, Japan's National Institute of Infectious Diseases, and South Korea's CDC jointly held the "China–Japan–South Korea Infectious Diseases Forum" at the same time to continuously improve the level of exchanges and cooperation in the development of infectious disease research and technology among the three countries and strengthen technical cooperation in the field of medical and health research. In November 2015, in order to prevent the spread of the Middle East Respiratory Syndrome, the 8th China–Japan–ROK health ministers' meeting put forward a plan to jointly respond to public health emergencies, and reached an agreement on strengthening the three countries' information sharing, and the measures to prevent and respond to infectious diseases, etc. In December, 2019, the three countries held their 12th health ministers' meeting wherein they reached a consensus on sharing experience in the fields of infectious disease prevention and control, and population aging, renewed the action plan on jointly preventing and responding to influenza pandemic and new and recurrent infectious diseases, reaffirmed that they would work closely to deal with infectious diseases, and made recommendations on further improving the joint action plan under emergent conditions and continuing to strengthen rapid information sharing. They reached an agreement on such issues as monitoring regional public health threat, and promoting capacity-building to respond to future pandemic threats.

In a word, after more than ten years of institutionalized construction and cooperation practice, China, Japan, and the ROK have continuously enhanced their cooperation in the field of public health, accumulated their cooperation experience, gradually established relevant mechanisms, and combated many times infectious diseases. At the time of the outbreak of the current pandemic, the three countries' cooperation mechanism in the prevention and response of public health emergencies has been relatively mature. They can share the pandemic information at the first time, and take timely and effective protective measures. The effect of the long-term cooperation practice has been fully reflected in the prevention and control of the COVID-19 pandemic.

The Joint Prevention and Control Achievements to Enable Multi-field Cooperation

The achievements made by China, Japan, and the ROK in the cooperative fight against the pandemic will provide new impetus for the three countries to expand and deepen cooperation in other fields. The COVID-19 attacks were sudden, mysterious, and indiscriminating. In the face of such non-traditional security threats, no country can be exceptional and spared. That is the time when common interests appear more important. Having had the pandemic under control, all the three countries are facing the dual pressure of ensuring people's health, and restoring economic operation. The three countries should join hands to prevent the virus from surging again at home, and block the infected people from entering the countries. They should work to cope with the impact on the regional supply chain through closer industrial and deeper industrial cooperation through greater policy coordination.

First of all, the three countries should explore and optimize the cooperation mode in the field of public health security, and make a long-term cooperation plan in the field of public health, especially in crisis prevention and control. Specifically, it should include: first, establishing a special cooperation mechanism for combating the pandemic, and launching collaborative prevention and control modes such as video conference by health and pandemic prevention experts. A number of points can be outlined:

A   They should work together to strengthen border prevention and control, inspection and quarantine, explore the establishment of health travel cards to provide convenience for business travel in the three countries.[17]
B   They should strengthen the exchange and sharing of big data information network, and carry out practical cooperation in pandemic prevention and control, diagnosis of patients, clinical treatment, and nursing.
C   They should strengthen scientific and technological cooperation in medical research. On the basis of China's first identification of pathogens and the sharing of virus gene sequences with the world, we should achieve mutual exchange and complementary advantages in the field of medical science and technology as soon as possible, carry out substantive technical cooperation in the research and development of effective drugs and vaccines, and avoid repeated trials to save time and resource costs.
D   The three countries should carry out cooperation in the R & D, the production of pandemic prevention and control products, establish a joint R & D center, and reinforce the production and supply capacity in the region.

Second, the three countries should further deepen their cooperation in the economic and industrial fields. Compared with Europe, and North America, China, Japan, and South Korea are expected to get the pandemic quickly under control, and restore work and life to normal. The precious time gap has created favorable conditions for the three countries to strive for new cooperation. In the face of the severe impact of the pandemic on the manufacturing supply chain, the three countries can focus on jointly maintaining the security and stability of the manufacturing supply chain, and promoting the formation of a new mechanism of division of labor and cooperation in the manufacturing industry of the three countries.[18] Before the outbreak of the pandemic, China, the United States, Germany, Japan, and the United Kingdom accounted for 45% of the total trade volume of the global machinery and equipment, of which the first three were the regional hubs of East Asia, North America and Western Europe respectively. The continued spread of the virus will have an impact on global production, regional trade, and industrial chain. In Northeast Asia, China, Japan, and South Korea have close industrial chains and are major trading partners with each other. Their imports and exports are mainly mechanical and electrical products, automobiles and transportation equipment. In Japan and South Korea, two major semiconductor and automobile exporters, more and more enterprises will be hit by the pandemic. The existing industrial cooperation and division of labor of the three countries will be seriously affected. The three countries should accelerate the negotiation process of the trilateral Free Trade Agreement, and jointly promote the signing of the Regional Comprehensive Economic Partnership (RCEP) as scheduled. By accelerating negotiations in the fields of trade and investment, intellectual property rights, sustainable development, etc., we will reduce trade and investment barriers, and promote trade and investment liberalization and facilitation, so that the enterprises of the three countries can benefit from more relaxed market access, provide institutional guarantee for maintaining the safety and smoothness of the manufacturing supply chain of China, Japan, and South Korea, and promote the rapid recovery and stable growth of the economies of the three countries.

Third, China, Japan, and the ROK can further expand institutionalized cooperation to the level of regional affairs. In addition to public health security, they also need to further strengthen cooperation in ecological governance and other fields. By reviewing the mutual funds established in the wake of the Asian financial crisis in 1997, and the international financial crisis in 2008, the three countries should consider establishing a common response mechanism to regional public crises (including public health issues), and normalizing cooperation in crisis management and control in the non-traditional security field in the region. Such cooperation belong to the category of non-traditional security with low political significance, less sensitive, wide in range, easier to reach an agreement, and also beneficial to the ordinary people. In recent years, cross-border public security incidents, such as the outbreak of the Middle East Respiratory Syndrome in South Korea, and the Fukushima nuclear leak in Japan, increasingly require close cross-border coordination and cooperation. With a view to the future, issues of common concern to China, Japan, and the ROK, such as environmental pollution, terrorism, information security, health care, and population aging, can be included in the mechanism, so that the three countries can further expand the basis of common interests and enhance mutual political trust by expanding cooperation.

Finally, the three countries can further improve the coordination of policies in the field of social security. In May, 2018, China and Japan signed the social security agreement between the government of the people's Republic of China and the government of Japan to reduce and exempt the social security payment burden of relevant enterprises and personnel. Besides Japan, China has also signed bilateral social security agreements with 11 countries including Germany, South Korea, France, Luxembourg and Serbia. According to the standards of similar agreements signed between Japan and the United States, France and the Netherlands, China and Japan can also consider including the reduction and exemption of medical insurance premiums in the agreement, and expand the bilateral agreement to the three sides of China, Japan and the ROK, so as to further promote the economic and trade relations between the three countries and facilitate personnel exchanges. This has a targeting effect at present and in the post-pandemic era.

Promoting Regional Governance through China–Japan–ROK Cooperation

In 2019, the aggregate economic output of China (mainland), Japan, and South Korea ranked 2nd, 3rd and 12th in the world, respectively, with a total of more than \$21 trillion, surpassing that of EU and close to that of the United States, accounting for more than two-thirds of Asia and more than one-fifth of the world, and becoming the main driver of the "Asian century." China–Japan–ROK cooperation started in 1999 after the Asian Financial Crisis. At present, there are 21 summit and ministerial dialogues in operation, and more than 70 other consultation mechanisms. The countries' practical cooperation covers more than 30 fields. The annual personnel exchanges between the three countries exceed 30 million, and the trade volume exceeds \$US700 billion. The economic volume and the important position in the region determine that the cooperation between China, Japan and ROK has gone beyond the trilateral, has important regional significance, and plays a key role in promoting the regional governance of Northeast Asia.

The development of regionalization is a major trend in international relations after the Cold War. After entering the 21st century, at least 20 regional organizations in the world have been qualified as the legal persons as they have established secretariats, committees, parliaments and other basic regional organizations. Although the cooperation among China, Japan, and South Korea is wide in range, and many of them have the nature of regional governance, to date, the academic discussion on regional governance in Northeast Asia is still insufficient.[19] This reflects the overall defects of Chinese academic circles in the study of regions and countries outside Europe and the United States. The outbreak of COVID-19 and the practice of the China–Japan–ROK responses have made the issue all the more urgent. It seems that regional governance is not only a reasonable goal for their deeper cooperation, but also a must for all parties to jointly deal with more and more severe challenges in the future. From the perspective of long-term regional development, regional governance is expected to become an important fulcrum for the construction of regional order in Northeast Asia.

Based on Western historical experience and instrumental rational thinking, the construction or transformation of regional order logically leads to

204   *Yang Bojiang*

"two forms of power structures represented by the balance of power, and hegemony," which usually result in coercion, confrontation, and conflict in the process of construction or transformation.[20] Reshaping regional order guided by governance rather than by power can, on the one hand, avoid the conflicts and confrontations that often occur in the traditional model. On the other hand, we can avoid the interference factors and "high politics" that are extremely sensitive in a short time by reasonably selecting the cooperation areas. Reasonably, the three can start with the less sensitive areas and gradually move to the sensitive ones, the so-called areas of "high politics." From a practical point of view, with the increasing number of global issues, and non-traditional security challenges, no country can cope with the challenges facing mankind alone, nor can any country return to an isolated island of self-isolation. No matter in the field of economy or security, it is difficult for any region to rely solely on a powerful country within or outside a region. Instead, it is necessary to establish multilateral mechanisms to effectively respond to challenges.

The long-term accumulation of institutionalized cooperation between China, Japan, and the ROK has provided a deep foundation and broad space for regional governance cooperation. China, Japan, and the ROK live in close proximity and share a geo-ecosystem. They are closely interrelated and the need for cooperation is great. Traditionally, however, Northeast Asia is more famous for power struggles and geopolitical rivalry among the big powers, and the Korean Peninsula is known as the "living fossil of the Cold War." Fortunately, the need for cooperative governance stimulated by the COVID-19 exists between China, Japan and the ROK, as well as in Northeast Asia. Compared with key variables related to regional governance such as regional connectivity and regional institutionalization,[21] Northeast Asia already has the basic conditions to promote regional governance and start governance cooperation. Compared with the European Union and the North American Free Trade Area, the proportion of intra-regional trade in Northeast Asia is low, which is not so much due to the weak relevance of the industrial structure of China, Japan and South Korea, but rather to factors other than economic rationality. In 2019, a trade dispute broke out between Japan and South Korea, and the two countries imposed sanctions on each other, resulting in a lose–lose outcome, which illustrates the objective existence of this close relationship from the opposite side. The impact of COVID-19 has provided an opportunity for further rationalization of this close relationship.

The regional governance of Northeast Asia should follow its own characteristic path. To date, the research on regional governance in international academic circles has mainly taken the process of European integration and EU governance as the model, but "Euro-centrism" is not universal. From the characteristics of East Asia, both the historical "tributary system," and the actual state relationship structure are different from the Western historical experience and mode of thinking dominated by power. From the reality after the Cold War, East Asia has not copied the multi-polar balance of power order that once prevailed in Europe. The outstanding differences between the historical

Impact of the COVID-19 Pandemic 205

traditions and realistic needs of East Asia and the Western world makes it imperative that the idea and path of order construction and transformation in East Asia must root in its own historical process with regional characteristics.[22] China, Japan, and South Korea have shown some cultural commonalities in the process of the current pandemic prevention and control. For example, they are obviously different from "instrumental rationality" in Europe and the United States, which can also provide some reference for the path design of regional governance in Northeast Asia. According to Professor Michel Gelfand of the University of Maryland, "The difference between countries in their ability to limit cases and deaths might be linked to cultural variation in the strength of social norms," which implies that in the face of public health crisis, a "tighter culture" like China can respond more effectively than a "loose culture" like the United States.[23]

To sum up, China, Japan, and the ROK need to make good use of the "time gap" between the prevention and control of the pandemic in Europe and the United States, actively optimize the division of labor and cooperation, work together to maintain the security and stability of the manufacturing supply chain, and deepen and expand cooperation in other fields. At the same time, the three countries should go beyond cooperation in combating the pandemic, promote progress in regional governance from the non-traditional security field, and take regional governance as the starting point to promote the transformation of order in Northeast Asia. To promote regional governance through China–Japan–ROK cooperation and reshape the order of Northeast Asia from the perspective of regional governance, we can start from the following three aspects. First, the three countries should learn from the experience of ASEAN and follow the principle of "flexible multilateral coordination." Second, they need to adhere to the basic idea of "optimizing what they have."[24] The third is to explore the practical operation path step by step. While honestly facing the reality, effectively managing and controlling differences and promoting the development of issues towards proper settlement, they should make progress in the non-traditional security areas by establishing mechanisms, funds and projects from the non-traditional security field. The most practical way is to focus on one at a time.

Notes

1 See http://www.xinhuanet.com/fortune/2020-04/08/c_1125830175.htm.
2 See Huang Qifan. "Global Money Pouring into China Is Highly Probable." https://cj.sina.com.cn/articles/view/5217810437/p13701780502700qgvg?from=finance.
3 "Summary of Building a Sustainable International Order Project." Dec 19, 2019, https://www.rand.org/content/dam/rand/pubs/research_reports/RR2300/RR2397/RAND_RR2397.pdf.
4 https://www.kantei.go.jp/jp/98_abe/statement/2019/0123wef.html.
5 https://comical-piece.com/korona-virus-number/ [2020-06-10].
6 https://withnews.jp/article/f0200528007qq000000000000000W0di10101qq000021220A.

7 https://shitureisimasu.com/41401/.
8 https://www.sankei.com/economy/news/200226/ecn2002260063-n1.html.
9 https://www.msn.com/ja-jp/news/money/.
10 https://www.jetro.go.jp/biznews/2020/04/b116de1997a6cdba.html.
11 https://www.dir.co.jp/report/research/economics/outlook/20200608_021589.pdf.
12 See Oguri Michiaki's (Shanghai Representative Office, Japan Trade Promotion Agency) "Moving back Supply Chain to Japan Not from China alone. The New Report Misleads." http://www.eeo.com.cn/2020/0417/381343.shtml.
13 See Han Dongyu's "The Significance of Non-governmental Diplomacy and Cultural Sharing to the Construction of Sino-Japan Relations in the New Era: Some Thoughts on the Joint Efforts of China and Japan to Fight COVID-19." *Japanese Studies* 2 (2020).
14 See Gao Hong's "China–Japan Relations in the New Era: Core Connotations and Main Approaches." *Japanese Studies* 1 (2020).
15 See Geng Shuang's Press Conference on March 29, 2020. http://search.fmprc.gov.cn/web/fyrbt_673021/jzhsl_673025/t1758730.shtml.
16 See "China, Japan and the ROK hold a Special Foreign Ministers' Video Conference on COVID-19." http://www.xinhuanet.com/world/2020-03/20/c_1125743824.htm.
17 China Institute of Reform and Development held on April 2, 2020 an "Online Expert Forum on 'China-Japan-ROK' Industrial Cooperation under the Global Pandemic." *China Daily* 4 April, 2020. https://caijing.chinadaily.com.cn/a/202004/03/WS5e86ae0aa3107bb6b57aa96a.html.
18 ibid.
19 See Yang Bojiang's "Some Thoughts on Regional Studies." http://ijs.cass.cn/xsdt/xsjl/202001/t20200102_5069988.shtml.
20 See Liu Xuelian, and Li Xiaoxia's "Future Order in East Asia on Power or Governance." *Social Science Front* 1(2019): 208–218.
21 See Zhang Yun's "Regional Governance in International Relations: Theoretical Construction and Comparative Analysis." *Social Sciences in China* 7(2019): 186–203.
22 See Liu Xuelian and Li Xiaoxia's "Future order in East Asia on Power or Governance." *Social Science Front* 1(2019): 208–218.
23 See Michel Gelfand's "The Relationship between Cultural Tightness-Looseness and COVID-19 Cases and Deaths: A Global Analysis." https://www.thelancet.com/journals/lanplh/article/PIIS2542-5196(20)30301-6/fulltext.
24 See Yang Bojiang's "How to Stabilize China-Japan relations and Achieve Sustainable Development." In *Proceedings of the International Symposium on "China-Japan Relations under Global Changes: Practical Cooperation and Prospects."* Eds. Yang Bojiang. Beijing: World Affairs Press, 2020.

17 Africa and China–Africa Relations in the Post-COVID-19 Era

Li Xinfeng and Zhang Chunyu***

In mid-March, 2020, COVID-19 began to spread in Africa. Although the virus had a huge impact on the African economy, it has not changed the long-term trends. After the outbreak, China–Africa economic and trade cooperation is expected to create new opportunities and rise to even greater heights. The pandemic has increased the risk of social unrest in some parts of Africa, but it has not changed the trend that the overall security situation in Africa is becoming increasingly stable. After the outbreak, China–Africa security cooperation is expected to evolve and to lead to new breakthroughs. In recent years, China's international cooperation environment in Africa has become increasingly complex. Following the outbreak, this situation will continue. However, in recent years China has become Africa's most important international cooperation partner. African countries' determination for development is conducive to the deeper consolidation of China–Africa cooperation.

The African Economy under the Pandemic

The Pandemic Has Had a Serious Impact on Economic Growth in Africa

The pandemic has had a very serious impact on the growth of the African economy. As COVID-19 raged all over the world in 2020, the world economy plunged, and a global economic recession is a foregone conclusion. At the time of writing, the pandemic is still spreading in Africa. According to the data from the African Center for Disease Control and Prevention, as of June 13, 2020, the cumulative number of confirmed cases in Africa exceeded 218,000. Due to the lack of any large-scale virus detection capacity in Africa, the actual number of infections may be higher. In view of Africa's strong population mobility, weak social governance capacity and poor medical and health conditions, the prospects for bringing this pandemic under control in Africa are not good. The World Health Organization (WHO) has previously warned

* The author is executive Vice Director of the China-Africa Institute; Research Fellow and Director of the Institute of West-Asian and African Studies, the Chinese Academy of Social Sciences.
** Assistant Researcher of the China-Africa Institute.

DOI: 10.4324/9781003433897-17

that the African continent, with a population of 1.3 billion and the largest concentration of developing countries, may become the next "epicenter" of COVID-19. If we do not consider implementing public health measures, more than 10 million people in Africa will be infected in the next three to six months.[1] Evaristus Ilandou, a professor at Nairobi University in Kenya, believes that Africa's fragile health system will make it difficult to provide sufficient support for pandemic prevention and control, and subsequent treatment. Even if the virus detection capacity is significantly improved, and the scale of detection above one million is achieved, pandemic prevention and control is still an extremely arduous task for poverty-stricken and resource-poor Africa.[2]

According to predictions from the United Nations Economic Commission for Africa (ECA), the pandemic will reduce the expected economic growth rate of Africa in 2020 to 1.8% from the previous 3.2%.[3] As the pandemic continues to spread, the expectation of economic growth in Africa will be reduced still further. The impact of the pandemic on the African economy is reflected in a variety of ways. The decline in the global demand for goods and services caused by the pandemic has led to a direct reduction in the level of African exports. Africa's economy is heavily dependent on exports, and its export commodities are mainly energy, minerals, agricultural products and other raw materials, and primary products. Between 2015 and 2019, Africa's average annual trade volume was US$760 billion, accounting for 29% of its GDP. This makes Africa's economy extremely fragile to external shocks and particular policies. The pandemic has led to the temporary suspension of global trade and the reduction of import demand from Africa by its major trading partners, such as the European Union, China, and the United States. The impact of the plunge in international crude oil prices, along with geopolitical disputes, led to a sharp fall in African exports. According to ECA estimates, Africa's fuel export revenue is expected to decrease by about US$101 billion in 2020, and the income loss of African oil exporting countries is estimated to amount to about US$65 billion.[4] The pandemic has also had a serious impact on African tourism, and air transport, which are important industries in the economic activities of many African countries and an important source of foreign exchange income. According to the World Travel and Tourism Council (WTTC), Africa's tourism industry grew by 5.6% in 2018, accounting for 8.5% of its GDP.[5] Tourism revenue in 15 countries accounts for more than 10% of their GDP. The pandemic will reduce the number of international tourists by 20%–30% in 2020.[6] In 2019, the output value of African air transport industry was US$55.8 billion, accounting for 2.6% of its GDP, and providing 6.2 million jobs. After the outbreak of the pandemic, the number of tourists in the African continent decreased sharply, and many airlines grounded all their flights. According to the International Air Transport Association, the international booking volume in Africa decreased by about 20% in March and April. To take just one example, it is estimated that African Airlines will lose US$6 billion in passenger revenue in 2020.[7] Although the outbreak led to the grounding of African Airlines, the debt for aircraft purchase still needs to be repaid. Airlines in Kenya, Morocco, Rwanda and other countries are feeling pressure in this regard.

The global economic recession caused by the pandemic will reduce capital inflows to Africa. Due to the limited domestic funds available, African countries have been heavily dependent on foreign investment for a long time, including foreign direct investment, remittances, and international assistance. At the outbreak of the pandemic, the global economy slid into recession, the economic growth of the main capital source countries slowed down, and the profits of transnational corporations fell, leading to a sharp decline in global foreign direct investment. The special edition of *Investment Trend Monitor* about the impact of COVID-19, released by the United Nations Conference on Trade and Development on March 26, pointed out that the pandemic is expected to reduce global foreign direct investment by 30–40% between 2020 and 2021.[8] In this environment, the decrease of foreign capital inflows in Africa is inevitable. In addition, Fitch International, a rating agency, said that the decline in crude oil prices and the outbreak of COVID-19 may also trigger capital outflows from Africa. In fact, with the increase of market risk, international investors sold US$1.2 billion of South African government bonds in March for the sake of capital security.[9]

The increase of public health expenditure and the decrease in tax revenues caused by the pandemic will increase the financial pressure on African governments. The financial situation of African countries is generally poor, with more than half of the countries having fiscal deficits over 3% of their GDP. The outbreak of the pandemic has made it even worse. On the one hand, the decline in commodity prices and the global economic recession have led to a reduction in the fiscal revenues of African countries. On the other hand, in order to combat the pandemic, countries' medical and social security expenditures have increased, and the economy needs to be stimulated through tax relief and government subsidies, which will create a huge financial gap. Against the background of the global economic recession and the decrease of foreign capital inflows, African countries may obtain funds through international borrowing. However, African countries generally have a high debt level. In the past two years alone (2018 and 2019), African governments have raised more than US$55 billion in the debt market.[10] The continued rise of debt levels may sink some African countries into debt crisis.

The pandemic is having a serious impact on people's livelihoods and employment in Africa. African countries are heavily dependent on the import of basic food, drugs and medical facilities. Nearly two-thirds of African countries are net importers of basic food. All African countries are net importers of drugs and medical facilities, of which the external dependence on drugs is 94%. As early as the beginning of 2020, locust plague was already posing a threat to the continent's food supply. The global food crisis report predicted that more than 25 million people in East Africa would face serious food shortage in the second half of 2020.[11]

Following the outbreak of the pandemic, many countries in the world began to restrict food exports, resulting in rising food prices and supply shortages. With the pandemic spreading all across the globe, many countries in the world are short of prevention supplies, and there are no surplus products for export. The lack of medical materials has objectively accelerated the spread of the pandemic in Africa. The pandemic has also caused a large number of enterprises in Africa to suspend production. As Africans generally do not have the ability or the habit of saving, they run into substantial financial problems soon after becoming unemployed. If it lasts for a considerable period of time, it may lead to social unrest.

The impact of the pandemic on the economies of South Africa, Nigeria, and other countries offers a microcosm of the overall situation in Africa.

Although South Africa adopted some prevention measures after confirming the first infected case on March 14, 2020, the virus was still raging. On May 1, South Africa entered "Level 4" of COVID-19 risk assessment, allowing some enterprises to resume production, and personnel mobility, but the surge of new infections was very likely. Under the impact of the pandemic, South Africa's GDP was estimated to shrink by 7% in 2020, and it was also estimated that the fiscal deficit would account for some 12% of its GDP. Mining is one of the country's key industries. During the lockdown, all mining activities in all mines were stopped for maintenance, resulting in a significant reduction in both mining output and exports. Murray and Roberts of South Africa closed most of its projects. Similarly, Anglo American Platinum, Sibanye Stillwater Ltd., and Antelope Platinum Holdings, the world's three major platinum producers, announced that they would not be able to complete their 2020 supply contracts. Samanco Chrome, one of the world's largest ferrochrome producers, was shut down, and Glencore's ferrochrome joint venture in South Africa was also closed down, leading to supply disruptions in the global chrome market. The automobile industry is also an important segment of the South African economy. In April this year, South Africa's domestic automobile sales fell by 98.4% year-on-year, and new car exports fell by more than 50%.[12] The pandemic will reduce the annual output of Toyota's plant in South Africa by 15%–20%. The five-week lockdown has led to a reduction of about 13,500 vehicles.[13] According to data published by the South African Automobile Manufacturers Association, by the end of April, only 51%–60% of the automobile enterprises were able to pay their employees' wages, and 11%–20% of the small and medium-sized automobile enterprises were facing bankruptcy.[14] Even if the lockdown were to be partially lifted, the automobile companies cannot get over the plight of the severe decline in downstream market demand in the short term, and the unpredictable recovery time of offline sales. The service industry accounts for 68% of South Africa's GDP, and finance, tourism, air transport and hotel services are its pillars. Under the pandemic, South African Airways is planning to dismiss all of its 4,700 employees, and permanently close down business. The pandemic also led to the closure of a large number of travel agencies and hotels. According to the prediction of the

South African Reserve Bank, 370,000 jobs will be lost due to the pandemic in 2020, 100,000 to 200,000 enterprises will go bankrupt and the unemployment rate in South Africa will increase from 38.2% to 48%. The "lockdown" alone will cut 10% of the jobs in the South African automotive industry.[15] The impact of the pandemic on small businesses and individuals is even more serious. A large number of waiters, cashiers and factory workers have been laid off, and are now struggling for survival, a situation for possible social conflicts.

The pandemic has also had a severe impact on Nigeria's economy. According to McKinsey's forecast, Nigeria's GDP will shrink by between 2.5% and 8.8% in 2020. The International Monetary Fund (IMF) predicts that Nigeria's GDP will shrink by 3.4%.[16] Oil is a pillar industry in Nigeria. Affected by the pandemic and the decrease in international oil prices, the level of daily oil production in Nigeria will be reduced to 1.7 million barrels, and many oil wells will be forced to stop operation. However, some oil wells may not be restarted once they have remained idle for some time, because they are too old. It is estimated that the level of crude oil export revenue will decrease by US$14 billion this year.[17] Similarly, the cocoa bean is the most important non-oil export product in Africa. From February to the end of March, the price of cocoa bean fell by more than 15%. If the output remains unchanged, the annual export income of cocoa beans will lose US$100 million.[18] If the pandemic continues to spread in cocoa-producing countries, output will decline further. The Nigerian Investment Promotion Commission announces in its *Report of Investment Announcements for Q1, 2020*, that the investment in the real industry fell by 62% year-on-year.[19] According to the *National Association* of *Nigeria Travel Agencies* (NANTA), since the outbreak of the pandemic, the number of passengers on international routes has decreased by 15%.[20] The economic downturn has led to a large increase in unemployment. According to IMF estimates, the number of unemployed in Nigeria will increase from 20 million in 2018 to 25 million in 2020.[21]

Other countries in Africa have been equally affected by the pandemic. According to IMF forecasts, Ethiopia's GDP growth rate will drop from 9% in 2019 to 3.2% in 2020, while Kenya's will drop from 5.6% in 2019 to 1%.[22] In Ethiopia, the number of Ethiopian air passenger flights has been reduced by 90%, the economic loss has exceeded US$550 million, and nearly 330,000 jobs have been cut.[23] African flower exports plummeted by 80% in the first quarter, and the inflow of overseas remittances decreased by about 80%.[24] In Kenya, the average daily loss of flower exports is US$2.4 million. By the end of April 2020, tourism revenue had fallen at least 60%.[25]

Impact of the Pandemic on China–Africa Economic and Trade Cooperation

China and Africa are important economic and trade partners, and the pandemic will have a significant impact on China–Africa economic and trade cooperation. First, the pandemic will reduce the trade volume between China and Africa. Under the pandemic, China's economic activities have experienced a long-term stagnation, and the decline in demand has led to a reduction in Africa's exports of bulk commodities and raw materials to China. It is estimated that 1% drop in China's GDP growth will lead to a 0.6% drop in sub-Saharan Africa's commodity exports, with a loss of US$420 million. There are many categories of products affected. For example, affected by both the reduction of international demand (including China), and global geopolitical rivalry, the international crude oil price once fell to US$1.15 per barrel, and the oil revenue of African oil-producing countries such as Nigeria, Angola, and Congo (Brazzaville) fell sharply. Copper prices once fell by more than 8% to US$4.350 per ton, putting pressure on African mining powers such as Zambia, South Africa, and the Democratic Republic of the Congo. In addition, China's exports of some manufactured goods to Africa will decrease to some extent. The Chinese Customs data show that, in the first quarter of 2020, China–Africa trade volume decreased by about 14%, of which China's exports to Africa decreased by 10%, and China's imports from Africa decreased by 16%. From January to April, the trade volume between China and South Africa decreased by 25.9%.

Second, the pandemic will lead to a decline in China's direct investment in Africa. Affected by the pandemic, many Chinese enterprises have turned their attention inward to China, and overseas investment has not been listed as a priority for the time being. In addition to the inherent project investment, it is difficult for Africa to obtain capital inflow of Chinese enterprises in the near future. In the first quarter of 2020, China's direct investment in South Africa decreased by 40.3%, compared with the fourth quarter of 2019.

Thirdly, the pandemic has created more difficulties for Chinese enterprises in Africa, meaning that China's project contracting amount in Africa will shrink significantly. Although there is no statistical data at present, this trend is a foregone conclusion as both China and African countries are affected by the pandemic, and both adopted prevention measures. African countries have tightened border measures, which made it difficult for Chinese enterprises' employees to return to work, hindering the progress of the project, and causing a serious decline in the amount of project contracting completed. Due to the stagnation of economic activities in Africa and other reasons, the Chinese enterprises that are operating in Africa are unable to achieve the expected revenue. In addition, the pandemic has bred anti-Chinese racist sentiments in some parts of Africa, threatening the safety of Chinese enterprises and personnel there. The recent killing and burning of three Zambian Chinese, the surprise inspection of some Chinese enterprises, and the checking of overseas Chinese by Zambian officials have shown that the normal production of Chinese enterprises, and the normal life of overseas Chinese in Zambia are threatened.

Finally, the pandemic has increased the debt pressure on African countries, and China's handling of African debt has attracted much attention. In recent years, the rapid development of China–Africa relations has attracted the widespread attention of the international community. Some countries have groundlessly questioned and slandered China–Africa cooperation. In 2018, with the emergence of the debt risk of African countries, the "China debt-trap" theory emerged in the international community, accusing China of providing a large amount of funds to push some African countries into the debt quagmire. In fact, China is not the largest African creditor country. The main lenders in Africa are still Western developed countries, multilateral financial institutions and private banks. In terms of the total amount of loans to Africa, according to the China–Africa Research Initiative at Johns Hopkins University in the United States, from 2000 to 2018, China granted more than 1,000 loans to 49 African governments and state-owned enterprises, with a total amount of about US$152 billion. However, China's loan to Africa accounted for a relatively low proportion of Africa's external debt balance in that year, which did not exceed 2% before 2011, and reached a historical high of 4.78% in 2016.[26] This is mainly because at the Johannesburg Summit of the Forum on China–Africa Cooperation in 2015, China pledged to provide $60 billion in financial support to Africa. Meanwhile, in 2016, China provided Angola with a loan of $19 billion. After 2017, China's loan to Africa returned to the normal level. In terms of the use of African debt, most of the loans China provides are used for infrastructure construction. Chinese loans have played a substantial role in promoting Africa's infrastructure, self-development capacity, and economic growth.

Affected by the pandemic, African countries have generally lost some revenue, spent more on health care and social security, and thereby increased their fiscal burden. As a result, they have made repeated calls for debt relief from the international community. South African President Cyril Ramaphosa was the first to call the international community to provide debt relief, speaking at the G20 Online Video Special Summit on March 26, 2020. Later, Ugandan President Museveni called on international creditors to wipe out all African debts. Similarly, Kenyan congressman Savula proposed that the repayment of the 71.4 billion KSHS loan owed to China (in 2020) should be suspended, and be used to support the common people and revitalize the economy. The Kenyan opposition leader Mudawadi said that the Kenyan government and the ruling party should reach an agreement with China, Kenya's largest creditor, to suspend its debt. The representative of Nigeria to the Economic, Social and Cultural Council of the African Union pointed out that Nigeria's ability to repay international debts has been weakened by the pandemic, meaning that major creditors, including China, should consider debt relief or postponement as soon as possible. Mr. Kenneth Nana Yaw Ofori-Atta, Ghana's Finance Minister, urged China to take more substantial measures on the issue of effective debt relief for Africa. The Economic Community of West African States (ECOWAS) reached a resolution at the special video summit, and will fully support the relevant statements of the African Union on promoting the international community to reduce the debt of African countries, and formulate economic and social development plans in the post-pandemic era. Some Western leaders have also called for debt relief for Africa. For example, French President Emmanuel Macron called on creditors, including China, to provide debt relief for the continent. At present, the international community has no special requirements

214 *Li Xinfeng and Zhang Chunyu*

for China's debt issue in Africa. However, in view of the fierce competition among the world's major powers in Africa, some Western countries and the media have been quick to draw attention to what they term "China's debt trap." Once the African pandemic situation worsens, it cannot be ruled out that some people would urge China to provide debt relief, and slander China. Once the European and American countries are faced with worse pandemic situation, severe economic problems, and more pressure of African debt relief, some countries might make use of the debt issue to specifically target China to divert attention.

The Pandemic Has Not Changed the Long-term Healthy Trend of the African Economy

Before the outbreak of the pandemic, the international community held a favorable view of Africa's economic development. Although the pandemic has struck a huge blow to the African economy, in the long run, it has not fundamentally changed the prospects for African economic development. According to data from the African Development Bank, the economic growth rate of Africa in 2019 was 3.4%, the same as achieved in 2018. Before COVID-19, the African Development Bank had predicted, in its *Africa Economic Outlook 2020*, that the economic growth rate of Africa in 2020 would increase to 3.9%.[27] On the whole, the main driving force of Africa's economic growth has gradually shifted to investment, and the fundamentals of economic growth have continued to improve. Most African countries have gradually improved their fiscal situation, eased inflationary pressures, gradually optimized their investment environment, and strengthened their ability to withstand external shocks.

The main factors that will support Africa's economic growth in the future include: first, the positive measures taken by African countries under the conditions of the pandemic will help stabilize Africa's economy. In order to mitigate the impact of the pandemic on the economy, the African Union (AU) has established its COVID-19 Response Fund to finance the African Center for Disease Control and Prevention. AU members have committed to contributing US$12.5 million. On April 8, 2020, the African Development Bank announced that it would set up a special fund of US$10 billion to fight the pandemic: this would include US$5.5 billion for sovereign guarantee projects, US$3.1 billion for providing preferential loans, and US$1.35 billion for supporting the private sector of various countries. They also issued three-year US$3 billion special bonds to fight the pandemic. The Central Bank of West African States has taken eight measures to contain the pandemic, including: increasing the capital supply to commercial banks; expanding the range of available mechanisms for commercial banks to obtain refinancing from the Central Bank of West African States; allocating US$40.85 million to the subsidy fund of the West African Development Bank; reminding commercial banks to use the available funds in the special window of SME credit refinancing; establishing a cooperation mechanism with the banking system to provide support to enterprises with loan repayment difficulties; negotiating with e-money issuers to encourage the use of digital support; supplying sufficient banknotes to commercial banks; and, if necessary, rescheduling the issuance of government bonds in regional financial markets. At the beginning of April, African finance ministers held a special meeting, at which they called on all countries to adopt emergency economic stimulus measures totaling US$100 billion in order to protect more than 30 million private-sector jobs. They are committed to expanding the import and export of agricultural products, increasing the credit, refinancing and guarantee lines of the pharmaceutical and banking industries, and increasing liquidity. African countries have adopted a wide range of response measures, such as establishing special funds to provide financing support, tax relief, government subsidies, lowering interest rates, and extending the repayment period. For example, South Africa has made a "Social Assistance and Economic Support Plan" with a total amount of 500 billion ZAR, including an industrial fund over 3 billion ZAR, a rescue plan for small and medium-sized enterprises exceeding 1.2 billion ZAR, the tourism relief fund with a capital injection of 200 million ZAR, and the South African Unemployment Insurance Fund allocated 40 billion ZAR to establish the unemployment fund. Similarly, Nigeria has launched special public projects to create new employment opportunities. In addition, it has applied to the World Bank for special loans for the pandemic prevention, planned to seek US$6.9 billion in budget funds from international financial institutions, and set up a pandemic crisis intervention fund of 500 billion naira. Egypt announced a US$6.4 billion stimulus package, accounting for about 2% of its GDP, providing real estate tax relief for industry and tourism, increasing subsidies for exporters, and reducing policy interest rates. Kenya introduced policies to stimulate employment, including tax relief for low-income people, tax reduction for individuals and small enterprises, and allocated US$95 million to help people in need. The Zambian government has released 500 million Kwacha to the Zambian public service pension fund to pay all retirees and other beneficiaries. In addition, 170 million Kwacha was issued to the bank to repay the debts of the third party, of which 140 million was to pay the road construction contractors to relieve their financial pressure. In addition, in order to mitigate the impact of the pandemic on the economy, some African countries have begun to resume work and production conditionally. For example, South Africa has lifted the national lockdowns, and lowered the Level 5 Prevention and Control to Level 4; it has also announced that some 1.5 million people will return to work gradually. Ghana took the lead in Africa in lifting the lockdown, and reopening the market.

Second, Africa's consumption potential and demographic dividend will continue to be unlocked. In recent years, the disposable income of residents in most African countries has continued to increase steadily, as the middle classes have expanded. These people have a stronger willingness and ability to consume, an important support for Africa's economic growth. At present, whereas most developed countries have a serious population aging problem, the population growth rate in Africa has been relatively high. In 2000, the population of

Africa was only 818 million, but it had reached 1.256 billion by 2017. According to the current birth rate, Africa's population will reach 2.435 billion in 2050 [30]. Africa has a high degree of young people, and consequently a sufficient number of young workers in the labor force, and the continuous improvement of education and labor skills, which has become the key to undertake a new round of international industrial transfer. The rapid rate of population growth has brought about high urbanization demand. The combination of demographic dividend and urbanization will significantly expand the scale of consumption and form a conducive interaction with economic growth.

Third, African countries' economic diversification policies have achieved remarkable results, and the economic policy environment has been continuously optimized. Most African countries regard industrialization as the key to their economic development, and they promote the industrialization process by developing export-oriented or import-substitution industries, making efforts to promote private investment, increase the proportion of the private industrial sector, and promote industrialization through the construction of industrial parks. The improvements in Africa's industrialization have laid a foundation for undertaking a new round of international industrial transfer. The service sector is another important choice for African economic diversification. In recent years, African countries have promoted the development of both traditional and emerging service industries. In the traditional service industry, Africa has become a new frontier for the rapid development of global retail industry thanks to the enhancement of local consumption capacity. In the emerging service industry, mobile finance and e-commerce have become the new highlights of development.

The economic policy environment of African countries has been continuously optimized. Most countries adhere to the policy of opening to the outside world and have a high degree of openness. In the field of trade, they will implement a strongly free trade policy and actively encourage exports. In the field of investment, attracting foreign investment is generally regarded as the main driving force for the rapid introduction of technology, the improvement of production capacity, the adjustment of the economic structure, the expansion of employment and reductions in poverty. Most countries have formulated special preferential policies to attract foreign investment, which are mainly reflected in welfare, tariffs, other tax preferences, relaxation of foreign exchange control and property security of investors.[28]

Fourth, African regional integration has been strengthened continuously. This is reflected in many aspects: trade integration, infrastructure construction, industrial chain integration, financial cooperation, the free flow of people and so on. In 2019, the free trade zone of the African continent was officially established, with the intention of increasing the proportion of intra-African trade by gradually abolishing commodity tariffs, and promoting the liberalization of trade in services. At the same time, it will significantly reduce the cost of foreign goods entering Africa and expand the scale of international cooperation. In order to promote infrastructure construction in the African continent, the AU adopted the Program for Infrastructure Development in Africa (PIDA) in 2012.[29] The African Union pointed out, in its *Agenda 2063: The Africa We Want*, that all countries on the African continent should be connected through the construction of infrastructure such as transport, energy, and communication technologies. In recent years, several cross-region infrastructure projects have been implemented, and African countries have made remarkable progress in terms of infrastructure financing. The enhancement of regional integration is conducive to enhancing the endogenous growth capacity of the economy, and is also conducive to African countries' overall response to external risks, and their concerted push for international economic cooperation.

Fifth, the digital economy in Africa is booming. The development of the digital economy can enable African countries to use technological means to improve people's living standards, facilitate education, trade and production, and narrow the gap with developed countries. At present, the digital economy has become one of the most dynamic and potential fields in the African economy. Communication, financial technology, e-commerce retail, logistics, daily-living service, entertainment, and other industries have developed rapidly, and given rise to well-known Internet brands such as the e-commerce platform Jumia, and the mobile payment system M-Pesa. East Africa has become the world's fastest-growing region for mobile payments. At the time of writing, most African countries are actively formulating digital economy development plans.

Security in Africa after the Outbreak

The pandemic is increasing the risk of social unrest in some parts of Africa. With limited public health and medical resources, most African countries cannot conduct large-scale testing for COVID-19, nor can they ensure that all confirmed cases are properly treated. Due to the weak governance ability, the accelerated spread of the pandemic is making people panic. In order to control the pandemic, some have locked down entire countries or cities, restricting the mobility of people, partially stopping production, and bringing economic development to a standstill. As a result, lots of people lost their jobs. As Africans generally have no habit of saving, they experience difficulties soon after losing their incomes. The pandemic has also threatened the food security of some African countries. The lack of basic living conditions and security guarantees can easily lead to social unrest. In fact, the Democratic Republic of the Congo (DRC) and other countries have, to date, shown signs for social unrest. The pandemic may lead to the outbreak of existing contradictions in 2020, as the security risks in some parts of Africa got worse prior to COVID. The security situation in the Horn of Africa, also known as the Somali Peninsula, the Great Lakes Region, and the Sahel remains tense. In the Horn of Africa, Ethiopia's domestic situation is still unstable, as the ethnic, religious, and other social contradictions are acute, which gave rise to frequent intense conflicts in recent years.

The political trend of Sudan is still unclear. The controversy between Ethiopia, Sudan, and Egypt over the Grand Ethiopian Renaissance Dam is raging. The forces of Al Shabaab in Somalia have rebounded and continued their activities in Kenya and other countries, forming a terrorist atmosphere in East Africa, and becoming a major potential terrorist threat in Africa. The situation in the Great Lakes Region remains complicated, the situation in the eastern Democratic Republic of the Congo (DRC) has been turbulent for many years, and the Ugandan Democratic Alliance Army and other anti-government forces are still active and colluding with terrorist forces. The ever-lasting feud and rivalry between Uganda and Rwanda are continuing, or as they explicitly or implicitly support each other's anti-government forces to carry out activities in the eastern DRC. In the Sahel, in 2019, terrorist forces were expanding, and have developed into a cross-border flow channel for terrorists. Terrorist activities are spreading from Mali and Nigeria to Burkina Faso and other countries. In the face of attacks from the international community, although the influence of Al Shabaab in Somalia has gradually dissipated, it remains a threat as it is closely related to extremist organizations. In 2020, the trend of terrorist infiltrating into other regions of West Africa outside the Sahel is obvious. Terrorist attacks, armed conflicts, gun proliferation, smuggling, corruption and other issues are all leading to humanitarian crises in Africa. According to the United Nations, at the time of writing around 20 million people in the region are facing serious threats of persistent famine and malnutrition. In 2020, nearly 5 million children in Burkina Faso, Mali and Niger need humanitarian assistance. In addition to the above regions, the situation in those countries that would hold general elections in 2020 is also of great concern. There are uncertainties around the timing of the general elections in many countries. Anyhow, reviewing the recent general elections, we believe that there will be demonstrations and other forms of protest, but relatively little violence. In addition, there are a few African countries which are plagued with unstable domestic situations. Due to the economic recession and persistent high inflation, for example, the President of Liberia is facing strong opposition from the people, the credibility of his government is low, the opposition is active, and the domestic situation is unpredictable. As the ethnic conflicts continue, the peace agreement in South Sudan is fragile. Elsewhere President Alpha Condé of Guinea is running for a third term in office has caused domestic dissatisfaction, and the risk of political instability and international sanctions is real. Furthermore, the political and social situation in South Africa, where xenophobic riots took place in 2019, and Egypt, where anti-government demonstrations broke out, also deserve attention.

Since the 21st century, non-traditional security has become the biggest security threat to Africa. During and after the pandemic, the non-traditional security will still be a major obstacle to Africa's development, including terrorist attacks, piracy, cyber-attacks, transnational crime, infectious diseases, climate change, etc. Africa has seen the most frequent terrorist activities in the world. Terrorism has broken out of its more traditional areas and spread to the whole continent. Internet security has become a loophole as the level of governance in Africa is low. Due to the backwardness of digital information technology on the continent, African governments have no means to combat the cyber propaganda being produced by all kinds of forces. Information on the African Internet can be false and misleading, with it proving difficult to distinguish between fact and fiction. The rapid development of digital economy in Africa might bring greater challenges to African countries in terms of maintaining social stability and economic security. Climate change is causing increasingly serious damage to Africa. In 2020, Africa suffered the most serious locust disaster in 70 years, one of the consequences of climate change. Africa's marine and coastal environment is also suffering serious damage as a result of environmental pressures.

Although the pandemic has increased security risks in some parts of Africa, it has not changed the long-term positive trend of the overall security situation in Africa. Since the 21st century, the security situation on the African continent has gradually improved, traditional security threats such as war and social turmoil have decreased significantly, and the overall situation has tended to be stable. Although there are still conflicts, they are mainly local in scale, with the frequency and intensity significantly reduced. At the same time, the democratic systems of most African countries have made great progress. The multi-party electoral system has been deeply rooted in the hearts of the people. Democracy and effective governance have become the mainstream of political development. African society is becoming increasingly mature, and its influence on national decision-making has been strengthened. Generally, a democratic system with African characteristics has taken shape. The general elections in most countries are smoothly conducted, and the transfer of power is becoming untroubled. In many countries, the governance capacity has been improved and the public service capacity has been enhanced. The focus on economic development has become a consensus, macroeconomic governance capacity has been significantly improved, and fiscal conservatism and monetary policy discipline have been significantly improved. A fundamental improvement in the security situation is an important prerequisite and foundation for Africa's steady economic and social development and smooth foreign cooperation. China–Africa friendly relations will continue to be consolidated after COVID. In January 2020, Foreign Minister Wang Yi visited five African countries, the 30th consecutive year that a Chinese foreign minister has designated Africa as his first annual visit, reflecting the special feelings the peoples of China and Africa have for generations, and their commitment to standing together in times of need. 2020 marks the 20th anniversary of the China–Africa Cooperation Forum and is an important year for the implementation of the outcomes of the 2018 Beijing Summit. Africa is now facing the risk of the pandemic spread. The most urgent matter for China to do is to provide assistance within its capacity to control the pandemic, a starting point for further consolidating China–Africa relations. Both China and Africa attach great importance to African security issues. The theme of the 33rd African Union

Summit is "Silencing the Guns: Creating Conducive Conditions for Africa's Development." Discussions were focused on peace and security, conflict resolution, and development. AU Commission Chairman Moussa Faki Mahamat stated that the AU would focus on preventing the illicit flow and circulation of small weapons, disarmament, implementing peace initiatives, mediation and military intervention. African countries should unite, reject external interference and solve African problems in an African way. China has always attached great importance to African security issues, as peace and security cooperation is an important part of China–Africa cooperation. China has always believed that it should reduce the extraterritorial interference in African security, and always adhered to promoting peace through development, which is consistent with the philosophy upheld by the AU and most African countries. Africa hopes to strengthen cooperation with China in the field of security. China has an increased number of exchanges with Africa. Objectively, there is a need to promote security cooperation. In addition, the two sides hold more common conceptions. China–Africa cooperation in the field of security is expected to be further expanded.

Competition among World Powers in Africa after the Outbreak

In the 21st century, Africa, which has rich resources and huge market potential, has once again become an important stage for countries in the world to compete for resources for development, and for competitive advantage. Based on strategic interests and security considerations, Western powers have increased their attention to Africa. The United States, France, Britain, and other countries regard the development of China–Africa relations as a challenge to their vested interests in Africa, as the close economic and trade cooperation between China and Africa has sharpened their sense of crisis. The world's major emerging economies have also gradually intensified their activities in Africa. Since 2019, major countries in the world have launched a new round of "scrambling for Africa." From August 2019 to February 2020, Japan, Russia, Germany, and the United Kingdom successively held various summits related to Africa, and important leaders of France, the European Union, Germany, Canada, and the United States visited Africa one after another. Countries which neighbored the African continent, such as the United Arab Emirates, Saudi Arabia, and Turkey, are also actively carrying out cooperation with Africa.

The United States is competing with China in the fields of economy and security in Africa. One of the pillars of the Trump administration's new Africa strategy was to strengthen economic ties between the United States and Africa, an attempt to curb the development of China–Africa relations, as China was regarded as a competitor. In February, 2020, US Secretary of State Mike Pompeo visited Senegal, Angola, and Ethiopia. The purpose was to improve US–African commercial relations, deepen security cooperation, and improve the image of the United States in Africa. Pompeo openly discredited China–Africa cooperation, but his visit did not yield any major substantive results.

International people of insight generally believe that the United States' presence in Africa is not to promote African development, but to compete with China over economic interests in Africa. In addition to economic relations, the United States is also worried about Chinese and Russian military activities in Africa. In February 2020, the United States Africa Command and the Ethiopian National Defense Force jointly held the eighth African Land Forces Summit, which comprehensively demonstrated the new trend of US military security cooperation in Africa; that is, that the US military will not withdraw from Africa, but continue to maintain its military presence in Africa. The US army will have a new anti-terrorism strategy in Africa: containment instead of attack.

The EU sought to deepen the development of EU–Africa relations. In March 2020, the European Union issued *Towards a Comprehensive Strategy with Africa*, the core of which is to renew the EU–Africa partnership as Africa is no longer regarded as the recipient of "development aid" but a partner. It declares that the EU will establish five major partnerships with Africa, namely, green transition and energy access, digital transformation, sustainable growth and jobs, peace and governance, and migration and mobility. Specifically, The EU will strengthen cooperation with Africa in ten major areas, including green development, digital transformation, economic integration, business environment, scientific research, innovation training, conflict resolution, social governance, humanitarian assistance and migration management. France is continuing to strengthen its military presence in Africa. In 2019, French President Macron paid three visits to Africa. In January 2020, Macron held a summit with the leaders of the group of five Sahel countries, which stated that it would strengthen military cooperation and jointly combat terrorism. In addition, France would send more troops to the Sahel region. Germany continues to regard Africa as an important choice for seeking its global leadership. On 19 January 2020, Germany held the Berlin International Conference on Libya. In February, Merkel visited South Africa and Angola. These measures show that Germany hopes to expand its voice in African policies in Europe, strengthen Germany–Africa economic and trade relations, and play the role of a major global power by way of cooperating with Africa. Britain consolidated its economic and trade relations with Africa after Brexit. Similarly, in January 2020, the first UK–Africa Investment Summit was held in the UK. The UK hopes to consolidate and deepen its trade relations with Africa through the summit. As China advanced the "Belt and Road" initiative, Japan and India put forth an alternative model, namely the Asia Africa Growth corridor, an effort to do business with Africa, and an attempt to compete with China. Japan will continue to provide high-quality and high-standard infrastructure projects to recipient countries in the form of official development assistance.

In the post-COVID-19 era, the interest and intensity of competition among the great powers in Africa will not decline. Surely, the international environment China faces in Africa will become increasingly complex. After the 2008 international financial crisis, the balance of economic power between emerging economies and traditional Western powers has changed significantly. People of insight in Africa hope to find inspiration from the development of emerging economies and explore the path of Africa's independent development. The most typical is the "Kigali consensus" put forward by President Kagame of Rwanda. Under the guidance of this concept, Rwanda has adopted the policy of "looking east," meaning it looks not only at China, but also at East Asia, including China, Japan, and South Korea. One of the important experiences for the rapid economic development in East Asia is the establishment of a production-oriented government, or development-oriented government, which combines government guidance with market rules in developing the economy. This feature and experience are significantly different from the practice of African countries over the past few decades. Ethiopia, Zimbabwe, Botswana, Tanzania, Kenya, Angola, Namibia, and other African countries are also actively practicing the production-oriented government model. The African Union also takes the creation of development-oriented countries as the key to the realization of *Agenda 2063*. In practice, African countries have long broken through the old thinking of "looking east" or "looking west" in their choice of development path. Instead, they have generally accepted the new thinking of "looking towards development." The cooperation opportunities between countries around the world and Africa are more equal, which is beneficial to China, which pays more attention to improving the development capacity of African countries and cooperation for win–win results.

Many countries across the world continue to increase investment in Africa, which may enhance China's broader international tripartite cooperation in Africa. International trilateral cooperation is conducive to mobilizing more cooperation resources, improving cooperation efficiency and achieving win–win results for all parties. It is also becoming an important form of international economic cooperation in China. China has signed trilateral cooperation agreements with some countries. For example, China and France signed the "China–France Joint Statement on Third-Party Market Cooperation," which has had a positive effect on China–France economic cooperation in developing countries, including Africa. Africa is an important practice area for China to carry out international tripartite cooperation. There will be broad prospects for China and other countries to carry out international tripartite cooperation in Africa after the pandemic.

China and Africa Will Continue to Strengthen and Enhance Cooperation after the Pandemic

During the pandemic, China should continue to help African countries fight it within its capabilities, provide the prevention material assistance, send experts, provide technical support, and assist its medical infrastructure projects. We should also provide humanitarian assistance to those countries that suffer from humanitarian crises such as the shortage of food. China should also help African countries stabilize their economic operation as soon as possible from the aspects of trade, investment and financing, and employment. In terms of trade, we should continue to take the form of tariff relief to help Africa to export products to China, especially for those commodities that have export potential. Given the global shortage of the pandemic prevention materials, China should, to a certain extent, ensure the export of drugs and medical facilities to Africa to avoid the crisis of pandemic prevention materials in Africa. China should take many measures to provide investment and financing support for Africa. It can use the Special Loan for the Development of African Small and Medium-sized Enterprises to provide financing support such enterprises registered in Africa. According to the actual situation of various countries, China should moderately relax the financing conditions, and formulate different loan interest rates and repayment plans to meet different financing needs. As Africa will introduce various economic stimulus policies during the pandemic, China can use the China–Africa Development Fund, the China Africa Production Capacity Cooperation Fund, and other funds to provide financing for African enterprises, and obtain good investment opportunities for Chinese enterprises. As a result of the pandemic, some Chinese employees were unable to return to Africa on time, and the project construction and operation of some Chinese enterprises were affected. Chinese enterprises can appropriately increase the number of local employees, create more employment opportunities for local people, increase the proportion of local employees, and provide skills training.

After the pandemic, China and Africa should strengthen exchanges and coordination and focus on creating new highlights of China–Africa economic and trade cooperation. Africa is an important link of the "the Belt and Road", and the construction of the "the Belt and Road" has created historic opportunities for China–Africa cooperation. From the perspective of China–Africa economic development, both sides need to continue to strengthen economic and trade cooperation in the future. China's economic growth has slowed down, and the growth model has begun to transform. There is a need to open up African markets for the service and manufacturing sectors in order to strengthen China–Africa cooperation. Africa has a single economic growth model and has not yet achieved inclusive development. In addition, affected by external uncertainties such as COVID-19, its economic development is facing difficulties, and its economic dependence on China is increasing instead of decreasing. After years of rapid development, China–Africa economic and trade cooperation has come to a bottleneck. It is urgent for both sides to jointly find new directions and new growth areas to promote the quality of bilateral cooperation. China's economic structure and growth model have undergone major transformations, and emerging industries and service sectors have become the main driving force of its economic development. Africa has shown its late development advantages in some fields, such as the digital economy, modern service industries, the marine economy, etc. This requires China and Africa to strengthen the coordination of development strategies and policies, break through the bottleneck of cooperation, and boost growth. In selecting key cooperation regions and countries, China should continue to focus on Eas Africa, which has a stable political situation, obvious geographical advantages and a foundation for cooperation. Egypt, South Africa, Nigeria, Ethiopia, and Kenya, with a good foundation for economic and social development, influential in their own regions, should be good for cooperation. In addition, it is necessary to pay close attention to the construction progress of the free trade zone on the African continent, actively participate in projects related to the construction of the free trade zone, and expand the dividends that China can obtain in the free trade zone on the African continent.

Facing a more complex international situation, China and Africa need to strengthen interaction and further consolidate strategic mutual trust after the pandemic. The Chinese government should continue to strengthen high-level interaction with African countries and strengthen African countries' confidence in China. At the same time, the measures in line with the principle of long-term sustainable development will be implemented in the economic, financial, security and other fields. In terms of debt, we should effectively prevent and resolve the risks China faces in African debt. During the pandemic, China actively responded to the international community's initiative of debt relief for Africa. In the short term, in line with the practices of the Paris Club and other G20 countries, China suspended debt repayment and extended the grace period. In the medium and long term, partial debt relief for countries in serious debt crisis might be considered. Effective measures should be taken to promote the debt sustainability of African countries and improve the level of China–Africa cooperation, when the pandemic is over. We should clearly express our long-term confidence in Africa's development prospects, and our concerns about the debt issue of African countries, stabilize African countries' expectations of China's funds, and ensure the long-term sustainability of China–Africa cooperation. We should closely monitor the debt risks of African countries, and build an early warning system for debt risks. It is necessary to comprehensively understand the scale and revenue of China's loan projects in Africa, and assess the progress of future projects and the solvency of loans. We should classify China's outstanding debts in African countries, properly dispose of non-performing debts, focus on the investigation and evaluation of projects in African countries with high debt risks, and appropriately increase criteria for granting loans. It is necessary to widely connect with international multilateral organizations, so as to raise the international awareness of the fact that China is a legitimate creditor country in Africa.

China's overseas interests in Africa are growing, and the protection of these interests is imminent. Many African countries also hope to strengthen cooperation with China in the field of national security. When the pandemic is over, China should appropriately increase its participation in African security affairs with a more active, open and flexible attitude. The non-traditional security field with relatively low sensitivity can be used as a starting point so as to gradually explore feasible ways to strengthen cooperation with African security affairs. During and after the pandemic, the focus of cooperation should be in the medical and health field. In addition, climate change and ocean protection are areas where both sides have mutual needs

When the pandemic is over, major countries in the world will continue to focus on Africa, which provides an opportunity for China to promote international tripartite cooperation with other countries in Africa. The Chinese government can promote the signing of more international trilateral cooperation agreements with other countries, and expand the scope and form of trilateral cooperation agreements. Chinese enterprises can also adopt more international tripartite cooperation with other investors, and the African countries to share or reduce risks. International trilateral cooperation not only helps to expand the scope of cooperation and improve the effectiveness of cooperation, but also helps to avoid some groundless international accusations of China-Africa economic and trade cooperation.

Notes

1 See "WTO: Africa Might Be an Pandemic Center." http://www.qiaowang.org/cn/shss/wlrw/12373.html. April 18, 2020.
2 See "Special Report: SOS! The Protection War of Africa from the Attack of COVID-19 Should Start Earlier." http://www.xinhuanet.com/world/2020-04/27/c_1125911192.htm.
3 See UNECA. "Economic Effects of the COVID-19 on Africa." https://www.uneca.org/sites/default/files/uploaded-documents/stories/eca_analysis_-_COVID-19_macroeconomiceffects.pdf. 2020-03-13.
4 "The UN: The African Economic Growth Might Be Reduced to 2%." http://www.xinhuanet.com/world/2020-03/14/c_1125713487.htm.
5 WTTC. Travel & Tourism Global Economic Impact & Trend 2019. http://ambassade-ethiopie.fr/onewebmedia/Tourism-WTTC-Global-Economic-Impact-Trends-2019.pdf.
6 UNWTO. "International Tourist Arrivals could Fall by 20–30% in 2020." https://www.unwto.org/news/international-tourism-arrivals-could-fall-in-2020.
7 IATA. "Aviation Relief for African Airlines Critical as COVID-19 Impacts Deepen." https://www.iata.org/en/pressroom/pr/2020-04-23-02/.
8 UNCTAD. *Global Investment Trend Monitor*. No.35. https://unctad.org/en/PublicationsLibrary/diaeiainf2020d3_en.pdf.
9 "Fitch International Says Africa Vulnerable to Capital Flight on International Oil Price Drops." Economic and Commercial Department of the Chinese Embassy in the Republic of Equatorial Guinea. 23 March 2020. http://gq.mofcom.gov.cn/article/jmxw/202003/20200302947662.shtml.
10 Bavier, Joe, and Karin Strohecker. "Africa's web of creditors complicates coronavirusdebtrelief."March27,2020.https://www.reuters.com/article/us-health-coronavirus-africa-debt-analys-idUSKBN21E2G3.
11 "The COVID-19 and Locust Plague Will Threat Food Security in East Africa." May 12, 2020. http://www.xinhuanet.com/yingjijiuyuan/2020-05/12/c_1210614650.htm.
12 Naidoo, Prinesha. "South African Car Sales at Record Low Show Economy's LockdownPain."May5,2020.https://www.bloombergquint.com/onweb/down-98-4-south-african-car-sales-show-economy-s-lockdown-pain.
13 Reuters. "Toyota's South African Unit Sees 15-20% Hit to Production due to Virus." April 22, 2020. https://www.reuters.com/article/us-health-coronavirus-safrica-toyota/toyotas-south-african-unit-sees-15-20-hit-to-production-due-to-virus-idUSKCN2241CQ.

14 Reuters. "Exclusive: South Africa's auto industry could cut up to 10% of workforce due to lockdown-survey." April 9, 2020. https://uk.reuters.com/article/us-health-coronavirus-safrica-autos-excl/exclusive-south-africas-auto-industry-could-cut-up-to-10-of-workforce-due-to-lockdown-survey-idUKKCN21R2K5.

15 Economic and Commercial Office of the Embassy of the People's Republic of China in the Republic of South Africa. "More than 40% of formal sector enterprises in South Africa do not have enough funds to survive." 22 April, 2020. http://za.mofcom.gov.cn/article/jmxw/202004/20200402957928.shtml.

16 IMF. *World Economic Outlook*. April 2020. https://www.imf.org/en/Publications/WEO/Issues/2020/04/14/weo-april-2020.

17 Xinhuanet. "UN: Africa's economic growth may slow to 2% this year." March 14, 2020. http://www.xinhuanet.com/world/2020-03/14/c_1125713487.htm.

18 Economic and Commercial Office of the Embassy of the People's Republic of China in the Federal Republic of Nigeria. "COVID-19 to Hit hard Nigeria's Agricultural Export." April 24, 2020. http://nigeria.mofcom.gov.cn/article/jmxw/202004/20200402958821.shtml.

19 NIPC. "Report of Investment Announcements in Nigeria." March, 2020. https://nipc.gov.ng/wp-content/uploads/2020/05/Q1-2020-20200416-2.pdf.

20 Economic and Commercial Office of the Embassy of the People's Republic of China in the Federal Republic of Nigeria. "COVID-19 Shrinks the Number of Passengers on International Routes in Nigeria." 12 March, 2020. http://nigeria.mofcom.gov.cn/article/jmxw/202003/20200302944518.shtml.

21 Parviz, Salman. "Oil producers dig into savings amid fiscal deficits." https://www.tehrantimes.com/news/447315/Oil-producers-dig-into-savings-amid-fiscal-deficits.

22 IMF. *World Economic Outlook*. April, 2020. https://www.imf.org/en/Publications/WEO/Issues/2020/04/14/weo-april-2020.

23 Economic and Commercial Office of the Embassy of the People's Republic of China in the Federal Democratic Republic of Ethiopia. "COVID-19 Caused a Loss of $550 Million in Ethiopian Airlines' Revenue." April 14, 2020. http://et.mofcom.gov.cn/article/jmxw/202004/20200402954998.shtml.

24 Bhalla, Nita, and Emeline Wuilbercq. "East Africa: No Bed of Roses – East Africa's Female Flower Workers Lose Jobs as Coronavirus Hits Exports." April 11, 2020. https://news.trust.org/item/20200411032043-83609/.

25 Economic and Commercial Office of the Embassy of the People's Republic of China in the Republic of Kenya."COVID-19 Hit Hard Kenya's Tourism." April 24, 2020. http://ke.mofcom.gov.cn/article/jmxw/202004/20200402958590.shtml.

26 Brautigam, Deborah. "Chinese Debt Relief: Fact and Fiction." April 15, 2020. https://thediplomat.com/2020/04/chinese-debt-relief-fact-and-fiction/.

27 African Development Bank Group. "African Economic Outlook 2020." January, 2020.

28 Asongu, Simplice A. "How Would Population Growth Affect Investment in the Future? Asymmetric Panel Causality Evidence for Africa." *African Development Review* 25. 1 (March 2013), p. 14.

29 Yang Lihua. "Ten Years of the African Union: Leading and Promoting the Process of African Integration." *West Asia and Africa* 1 (2013), p. 78.

18 Material Interest and the Concept of Values

International Conflicts and Cooperation During the Pandemic[*]

Wang Zhengyi[**]

At the end of 2019 and the start of 2020, the COVID-19 pandemic broke out and began to spread around the world. From any perspective, this pandemic is an unprecedented challenge to human society, likely the greatest crisis of our generation. Some people have already compared the pandemic situation with the Pearl Harbor attack and the "9/11" attacks. According to Henry Kissinger, former US Secretary of State, and now political scientist, "COVID-19 will forever alter the world order."[1] Driven by the developed Internet and information technology, the debate over COVID-19 involves a wide range of topics, a large number of participants, and the widest divergence of views. Although we dare not say that the divergence has reached the widest extent, it seems not too much to say that it is unprecedented.

If we study international relations in the context of the global spread of COVID-19, there are three issues on which we need to reflect on in terms of both theoretical cognition and empirical judgment: first, who and what in international relations will be affected by the pandemic? Second, will this pandemic terminate globalization? Third, what is the trend of the world order in the wake of the pandemic?

During the Pandemic: People, Countries, and the International Community

When we study international relations, one of our primary tasks is to determine the actors of international relations. Generally speaking, there are two types of actors in international relations: one is the state, which needs to be

---

[*] This article is the revision of the three talks at the Beijing University Forum organized by the School of International Relations on "International Relations under the Pandemic" on March 29, 2020, the Tsinghua University Forum organized by the Institute of Global Development on "The World and China under the Impact of the Pandemic" on April 11, 2020, and the Renmin University of China Forum organized by the School of International Relations on "China-International Issues 2020: World Order and China's Diplomacy in the Context of COVID-19" on May 8, 2020. The article was published in *The Journal of International Studies* 3 (2020).

[**] The author is a distinguished Professor of Changjiang Scholars of the Ministry of Education, Director of the Academic Committee of the School of International Relations of Peking University, Chair of the Department of International Political Economics.

DOI: 10.4324/9781003433897-18

228　*Wang Zhengyi*

distinguished only by assuming that the state is the only actor or the main actor. The other is the non-state actors, which can be individuals (political decision-makers, professionals) or groups (interest groups). The non-state actors also need to be distinguished. Different assumptions of actors lead to different paths to study international relations, and different conclusions. If we put international relations against the backdrop of COVID-19, we will find that none of the main actors (people, countries and the international community) at the three levels of international relations can exclude themselves from it. This global disaster has triggered various indescribable debates, which are related not only to human nature, or to the political structure of countries, but also to the relevant international organizations.

Human Nature and Rationality

The "human" here has two meanings: first, it generally refers to the abstract concept of human beings, that is, human beings as a species different from animals. Although the novel coronavirus that caused this pandemic has not been fully understood, most professionals and scientists are convinced that the virus was transmitted from animals to humans, and then from humans to humans. Therefore, this is a disaster in human society. Second, it refers to specific people, that is, specific human individuals living in different regions and countries. They could be Chinese living in Wuhan, Singaporeans living in Singapore, Italians living in Rome, Frenchmen living in Paris, or Americans living in New York. Although they have different skin colors, languages, cultures, and religious beliefs, they have one thing in common. They are specific people as human beings. Therefore, this disaster is not a disaster of one nation or of one race; rather, it is a disaster for all people.

This global disaster has manifested human capability of mutual understanding, trust, care, and help, as well as accusation, curse, and even conflict due to suspicion and misunderstanding. This abrupt pandemic not only triggered a debate on human nature (such as the relationship between man and nature, the relationship between man and animals, and the good and evil to be found in human nature), but also triggered a reflection on human rationality and its limitations (such as the source of the virus, the nature of the virus, the survival time of the virus, and the vaccine against the virus). It also triggered a discussion on human rights (such as human freedom and its limits, the relationship between individuals and society).

The debates both reflect the tradition of liberal philosophy that advocates the good of human nature, but also show signs of the tradition of realistic philosophy that insists on the inherent evil of human nature. Both of these traditions have their own interpretation system, albeit with some limitations. The understanding of humans not only has a direct impact on the value orientation of each individual and his group, but also has an important impact on the domestic policy-making and foreign policy-making spheres of the relevant countries.

Material Interest and the Concept of Values   229

Governance Capability

In the face of the spread of the virus, although declaring a state of emergency, suspending traffic, keeping social distancing, and wearing masks are generally considered to be effective measures to handle the pandemic, we can still observe that different countries have adopted very different approaches. China's response measures are different from Singapore's, South Korea's are different from Japan's, Britain's approach is different from France's, and Germany's, and the United States' approach is also different from Italy's. The different ways of social mobilization currently adopted by different countries to respond to the crisis reflect the historical relationship to be found in individual countries between the state and society.

This phenomenon is familiar to researchers of international relations. In a sense, it can be said to be a repetition of history. Facing the oil crisis in 1973 and 1974, the United States, Britain, France, Italy, Federal Republic of Germany, and Japan all responded differently. Similarly, faced by the Asian financial crisis in 1997, South Korea, Thailand, and Malaysia made different responses. Finally, facing the international financial crisis in 2008, the United States, the European Union, and China also made very different responses.

If we observe the measures taken by countries to deal with the pandemic from the perspective of the relationship between the state and society, we can identify three overarching models: one is Machiavellian, such as China, South Korea and Singapore did. Such countries mainly focus on the national management capacity, and the state usually manages public affairs in a unified manner to handle public crises. One is Rousseau's and Locke's, such as adopted in the United States, Britain, France, Italy, Spain, and Sweden. Such countries mainly focus on the orderly operation of society under the framework of the rule of law. Even in the face of public crisis, they are unwilling or unable to completely place the society under the control of the state. The other is of Tocqueville and of Weber, such as Germany did, which regards the maintenance of public interests as the responsibility of the government, but leaves the maintenance of personal interests to wider society.

The above three models of state–society relations have been formed over a long period. When individuals and society are faced with sudden public crises, it is natural for different countries to adopt different measures in organizing individuals and society. It is biased in theory and undesirable in reality to exaggerate the merits of any one model or to affirm one but deny the validity of others.

Effectiveness of International Organizations

Although many international organizations and non-governmental organizations in the international community have participated in fighting the pandemic, there are two organizations that attract the most attention: one is the World Health Organization (WHO), a professional organization within the

230 *Wang Zhengyi*

framework of the United Nations. Upon receiving the initial report from China on December 31, 2019, WHO coordinated the response measures of its headquarters, and offices across the world in accordance with the international health regulations.[2] The other is the group of twenty (G20), which played an important role in coping with the international financial crisis in 2008.

How did these two international organizations perform? Let's first look at the G20. On March 26, 2020, when COVID-19 was raging around the world, the G20 special summit was held in the form of teleconference and agreed to inject US$5 trillion into the global economy to cope with the COVID-19 pandemic and its impact.[3] After the special summit, in order to implement the leaders' commitments, on March 31, 2020, G20 finance ministers and central bank governors held a video conference, issued the G20 Action Plan for COVID-19, adopted the initiative to suspend debt repayment for the poorest countries, and welcomed the International Monetary Fund, the World Bank, and other international financial institutions to provide financial support. This calls for strengthening the coordination of financial regulatory policies and improving global financial resilience.[4] However, these appeals have played a very limited role in the cooperation of relevant countries in combating the pandemic. This is mainly related to the nature of the G20, an international forum, with no incentive or punishment functions.

Unlike the G20, the WHO has a complete organizational structure, professional standards and experience in coordinating response to public health crises (such as Ebola virus and Middle East Respiratory Syndrome), but in the process of combating the current pandemic, it fell into a vortex of controversy due to its failure to coordinate the relations between major countries. First, US President Donald Trump publicly accused the WHO of centering on China in the process of pandemic prevention, and announced on April 14, 2020, that he would suspend the payment of dues to the organization. At the same time, Ron Johnson, the Chairman of the Senate Homeland Security Committee, also announced an independent investigation into the WHO and its Director-General, Mr. Tedros Adhanom Ghebreyeus, asking them to provide relevant information. Whatever the purpose of these investigations, they will have a great negative impact on the professional reputation of the WHO, and further affect the WHO in terms of its ability to combat the pandemic.

The limited effectiveness of these two international organizations reflects the reality of the international community today. Unlike the internal order of a country, which is the product of government, the international community has always been in a state of anarchy, so the establishment, maintenance and transformation of the order of the international community (also known as international order or world order) naturally become the subject of debate in international relations. One view holds that the order of the international community is determined by national interests. The logic behind this argument is that since the international community is in a state of anarchy, and each country will act rationally according to its own interests, conflicts of interests between countries are inevitable. Therefore, the most important way to avoid conflicts and even wars is the rule of power; the implication of this is that the establishment and maintenance of the international order could either rely on hegemonic power(s) or on the balance of power, or the concert of powers. Another view is that the order of the international community is determined by the common interests of nations. The logic is that, although the international community is in a state of anarchy, because each nation is rationally maximizing its own interests, conflicts or even wars can be avoided by seeking common interests, that is, the establishment and maintenance of the international order can be accomplished through international organizations or international systems.

The disorderly state of the international community after the outbreak of the pandemic, especially the performance of the WHO and the G20, reminds us once again that the world order dominated by the United States for more than half a century has indeed encountered unprecedented challenges.

Under the Global Pandemic, the "Constrained" Global Production Chain and the "Dilemma" of the State

Will the pandemic terminate the economic globalization with which we are familiar? This is an issue of concern to almost everyone after the spread of the virus, and the shortage of medical supplies in the process of fighting the pandemic brings the fate of globalization further into question.

Let's take a look at the response of several countries and regions to the shortage of medical supplies after the outbreak of the pandemic: on January 23, 2020, the authorities in Taiwan Region, China, announced that masks would be restricted for export.

On March 13, 2020, US President Trump declared a national emergency over the coronavirus pandemic. On April 2, Trump invoked the Defense Production Act to ban 3M from exporting its N95 masks so they could be used domestically. On March 25, 2020, the European Commission issued the Guidance to the Member States Concerning Foreign Direct Investment and Free Movement of Capital from Third Countries, and the Protection of Europe's Strategic Assets. Prior to the application of Regulation (EU) 2019/452 (FDI Screening Regulation) on November 11, 2020, the guidance is mainly aimed at foreign investors' acquisition of strategic assets of the EU by taking advantage of the spread of COVID-19. On March 31, 2020, when visiting Kolmi Hopen Company, a small mask manufacturer in western France, French President Emmanuel Macron suggested the production of masks in France and Europe. On April 7, 2020, Japanese Prime Minister Shinzo Abe chaired a cabinet meeting and adopted the "emergency economic response plan" with a total of 108 trillion yen, of which 243.5 billion would be allotted to Japanese enterprises to build new plants and purchase equipment subsidies to support Japanese enterprises' overseas production bases to return to Japan or transfer to Southeast Asian countries.

232 *Wang Zhengyi*

The "Fettered" Global Production Chain

Under the impact of the pandemic, did the newly issued policies for transnational investment by the relevant countries and regions of the three major regional production networks of the manufacturing industry (the EU, North America, and East Asia) really mean the end of the era of globalization characterized by investment facilitation and trade liberalization?

Global production chains and regional production networks are the concrete embodiment of the two major trends of globalization and regionalism in the field of transnational investment and production since the 1990s. The global production chain usually refers to the enterprises and workers' transformation of a product from a concept to an end use product and all related activities, including R&D, design, production, marketing, distribution, and final consumer support. The economic activities that make up the production chain can either be completed by one enterprise or dispersed among different enterprises. In the context of globalization and regionalization, if production activities are more completed by global inter-enterprise networks, we call them global production chains. If the production activities are completed by an inter-enterprise network within a certain region, we call it a regional production network.[5]

In international political economy, the formation and development of global production chains and regional production networks mainly involve two issues: one of these is the governance of global production chains or regional production networks. The other is the upgrading of the global production chain by home countries, host countries, or their enterprises.

Regarding the governance of global production chains, researchers have found that the formation and development of global production chains or regional production networks are mainly led and coordinated by transnational corporations.[6] Generally speaking, transnational corporations manage the global production chain or regional production network in one of two ways: one is internalization, that is, they mainly complete it through equity control. Specifically, transnational corporations concentrate on the international flow of goods, services, information and other assets within the enterprise through transnational direct investment, and are completely under the control of transnational corporations. The other way is externalization, which mainly adopts a non-equity mode (such as contract manufacturing, service outsourcing, order agriculture, licensing, franchising, management contract, franchise and strategic alliance) to affect the operation of enterprises in the host country.

The issue of upgrading the global production chain by a country or an enterprise is related to the status of the country in the global economy, so both emerging economies and their enterprises, and developing countries and their enterprises hope to achieve "value chain climbing" through upgrading. This is why, over the course of the past 30 years, more and more emerging economies and many developing countries have competed to promote investment facilitation and trade liberalization by formulating various preferential policies to attract transnational corporation investment.

The global production chain has changed not only the traditional division of labor among countries in the international production system, but also the structure of international trade. Trade among industries has been gradually replaced by trade within industries. According to the observation of the United Nations Conference on Trade and Development, as the global production chain is dominated and coordinated by transnational corporations, although international trade occurs between countries, it mainly occurs within transnational corporations, that is, the international flow of goods and services between parent companies and subsidiaries or between subsidiaries. In the global production chain, the two concepts of domestic value added (DVA) and foreign value added (FVA) are usually used to measure the degree of a country's integration into the global production chain. Domestic added value refers to the value created by the countries participating in the value chain through domestic production factors, so it is considered as the real value exchange in trade. Foreign added value refers to value-added transactions conducted as part of import inputs in multi-stage and multi-national production processes, so it is not considered to create new value. Therefore, the higher the foreign added value, the more dispersed the global production process, and the higher the degree of a country's integration into the global production chain.

According to statistics published by the United Nations Conference on Trade and Development, the global value chain led by transnational corporations accounts for 80% of global trade,[7] while the proportion of foreign added value in global trade rose from 24% in 1990 to 31% in 2010. Even in 2017, the proportion of foreign added value in global trade was still as high as 30%, among which the proportion of foreign added value in the export volume of developed countries was 32%, accounting for 28% of developing country exports.[8] These data show that in the past 30 years, global production chains have not only promoted the growth of trade among countries, but also strengthened the interdependence among countries

However, with the deepening of interdependence between countries in the industrial chain, those countries that master the key links of the industrial chain (such as intermediate products or key technologies) have greater power, while those countries that rely on the key links of the industrial chain and their enterprises have relatively less power. This asymmetry of power between countries in the industrial chain eventually makes countries interdependent, bound and even constrained. As Henry Farrell and Abraham Newman, two advocates of the "new interdependence," observed in the *Foreign Affairs* in early 2020:

> Globalization, in short, has proved not a force for liberation, but a new source of vulnerability, competition, and control; networks have proved less paths to freedom than new chains. Governments and societies, however, have come to understand this far too late to reverse it. In the past few years, Beijing and Washington have been just the most visible examples of

234 *Wang Zhengyi*

governments recognizing how many dangers come with interdependence and frantically trying to do something about it. But the economies of countries such as China and the United States are too deeply entwined to be separated—or "decoupled"—without causing chaos. States have little or no ability to become economically self-reliant. Hawks in Beijing and Washington may talk about a new Cold War, but there is today no way to split the world into competing blocs.[9]

Therefore, despite the dangers of interdependence, countries will still be inter-twined with each other and thus shape a new era, which we can call the era of "bound globalization." Therefore, in the face of global production chains and regional production networks led and coordinated by transnational corpora-tions, any country, whether home or host, developed, developing and emerging economies, is faced with a "dilemma": if it is to promote economic growth, it must promote investment facilitation and liberalization; If we want to ensure that our national economy is not controlled by transnational corporations, we must regulate and restrict transnational investment. It is in this sense that we believe that the policies launched by relevant countries and regions after the outbreak of the pandemic only show that these countries and regions are wor-ried about their own economic security, and do not fundamentally solve the "dilemma" they have been facing.

Global Production Chain Leads to National "Dilemma"

Since the global production chain is dominated and coordinated by transna-tional corporations, and the host countries, especially developing countries and emerging economies, hope to achieve "value escalation" of domestic enter-prises by joining the global production chain, how do countries overcome the "dilemma" of attracting transnational investment and ensuring the security of the supply chain?

For the national "dilemma" caused by the global production chain, the host country usually affects the choice of domestic enterprises in the following two ways, and then changes the spatial distribution of the production chain. One way is to directly embed national security into the transnational investment policy, and regulate or restrict the participation of transnational investment in the listed industries as "sensitive" or "strategic." In the 1960s and 1970s, this method was mainly used to control foreign enterprises' participation in the national defense industry. In the 1990s, this method was gradually expanded to protect other strategic industries and key infrastructure. It has also recently been used to protect core domestic technologies and know-hows that are con-sidered essential to national competitiveness in the era of the new industrial revolution. For example, the Report on Foreign Investment and National Security issued by the United States in 2008 applies not only to the outflow of US transnational direct investment, but also to the inflow of transnational direct investment, especially the supervision of sovereign wealth funds from developing countries. In 2008, the President of the Russian Federation also signed a decree on strategic industries, the Procedure for Making Foreign Investments in Companies of Strategic Importance for National Defense and State Security, which puts forward a detailed management framework for foreign investment in industries (strategic enterprises) that are considered to be of national security or strategic importance. In 2012, Italy established a new institution for the government to review the asset transactions of companies operating in strategic industries. In 2015, China passed the National Security Law, allowing the state to establish a national security review and supervision mechanism for foreign investment. In 2017, Germany expanded the scope of national security review, including key industries.[10]

The other way is to guide and shape the production network by signing multilateral and bilateral investment agreements. As the international community has failed to reach an international investment agreement similar to the trade field at the global level for a long time, countries are competing to sign regional investment agreements and bilateral investment agreements under the promotion of globalization and regionalism. In the European region, the Lisbon Treaty, taking effect in December 2009, transferred the negotiating power of EU Member States on FDI agreements to the EU. In the Asia-Pacific region, substantial progress has been made on the Comprehensive and Progressive Trans-Pacific Partnership Agreement (CPTPP), and the Regional Comprehensive Economic Partnership Agreement (RCEP). In North America, the United States, Canada, and Mexico completed the negotiation of the US–Mexico–Canada Agreement (USMCA). Bilateral Investment Treaty (BIT), and Free Trade Agreements (FTA), including investment, are many countries' favorite means to encourage investment. According to the statistics of the United Nations Conference on Trade and Development, 2,573 of the 5,500 international investment agreements in the world at the end of 2006 were bilateral investment agreements. By the end of 2018, with the effective termination of some international investment agreements, the number of international investment agreements worldwide had dropped to 3317, but the number of bilateral investment agreements had risen to 2,932 instead.[11]

After the outbreak of COVID-19, due to the rapid and sudden transmission, there was a global shortage or insufficient supply of medical materials such as masks, protective clothing, gloves, goggles and respirators. Some countries, taking into account aspects of national security or national competitiveness, encouraged multinational corporations to shift manufacturing capacity to their own countries, or set up multiple production lines to ensure supplies. This is understandable. But it would be premature to conclude that the era of globalization is coming to an end.

In fact, whether the EU countries and the United States, or Japan and Taiwan Region, China in Asia, if they want to influence or change the regional layout of the production chain by formulating foreign investment policies, they must face the following three challenges.

First, it is multinational corporations rather than states that dominate and coordinate global production chains or regional production networks. The development strategy of transnational corporations is market-oriented, and the interests of transnational corporations are not always consistent with the foreign strategies of their home countries. This is also the reason why the United States has had to pass the Defense Production Act in the face of the spread of the pandemic. However, the United States cannot be in a state of national emergency forever, and American multinational corporations cannot produce under the guidance of the Defense Production Act for a substantial period of time.

Second, the multinational corporations that dominate and coordinate global production chains or regional production networks are mainly private enterprises. Although the foreign investment activities of TNCs from developing countries and emerging economies have increased rapidly in recent years, the foreign investment of TNCs from developed countries plays a leading role in global foreign investment. According to the statistics of the United Nations Conference on Trade and Development, between 2005 and 2017, the developed countries' transnational corporations accounted for 60–85% of the global investment outflow. The United States, Britain, EU countries, and Japan in Asia are mainly the home countries of these transnational corporations.[12] In these countries and regions, transnational corporations are dominated by private property rights, and the state rarely participates in holding shares. The protection of private property rights and private enterprises is an important feature of the market economy in these countries. Private property rights are protected by the constitutions in these countries. Therefore, these countries can only modify their investment policies or sign multilateral investment agreements to facilitate the production and operation activities of these transnational corporations, and cannot completely dominate the operation of these transnational corporations.

Third, it is impossible for any country to include all industries in the "strategic industries" catalogue. The state may supervise the operation of foreign investors based on the competitiveness of local production enterprises, or for the consideration of foreign ownership of land and natural resources, and may also include industries involving national security or national competitiveness in the "strategic industries" list for review and restriction. However, it is impossible for any country to include the industries related to people's daily life (such as textile industry, clothing industry, agriculture, and automobile industry) in the "strategic industries" directory for control. In the wake of the 2008 Financial Crisis, although all countries strengthened the review of foreign investment, the most common sectors included in the review are public utilities, telecommunications, transportation, and media. Manufacturing is rarely included. On the contrary, in the manufacturing sector, countries are competing to introduce investment incentive policies to promote investment facilitation and liberalization.

Three Possible Trends of the World Order after the Pandemic

What is the likely trend of the world order after the pandemic? This is the most hotly debated issue when people discuss the impact of the global COVID-19 on international relations.

Material Interest and the Concept of Values 237

In the previous studies of international relations, when discussing world order, we often overemphasize the role of interests and institutions, but ignore the importance of values. In fact, values are not only reflected in the preferences formed by the interests of each country, but also in the choice of international cooperation rules and systems, but also reflected in the specific domestic and foreign policies of each country. As the famous representative of the English School, Hedley Bull, observed:

> How is order maintained in world politics? Even if states were without any conception of common interests, common rules or common institutions – even if, in other words, they formed an international system only, and not also an international society. A balance of power, for example, may arise in an international system quite fortuitously, in the absence of any belief that it serves common interests, or any attempt to regulate or institutionalize it. If it does arise, it may help to limit violence, to render undertakings credible or to safeguard governments from challenges to their local supremacy. Within international society, however, as in other societies, order is the consequence not merely of contingent facts such as this, but of a sense of common interests in the elementary goals of social life; rules prescribing behavior that sustains these goals; and institutions that help to make these rules effective.[13]

In the process of the global fight against the pandemic, we have found that, whether between individuals, groups, or even countries, there are not only fierce disputes over material interests such as goods, technology, information, but also serious differences on values such as freedom, democracy, equality, justice, faith, etc.

Here, a few examples of the specific measures taken by some countries in the process of combating the pandemic will open our eyes to the huge differences in values among these countries

On January 23, 2020, Wuhan Pandemic Prevention and Control Headquarters issued its Notice No. 1, which orders to shut down all traffic to and from Wuhan, declaring that Wuhan has officially entered the comprehensive pandemic prevention stage. The Chinese government mobilized in an all-round way to prevent and control the pandemic, and regarded the fight against the pandemic as a "people's war," and basically had the pandemic under control in some two months. While the international community marvels at China's national capacity, some Western countries consider it a manifestation of extreme politics.

On February 18, 2020, after a "Shincheonji" believer living in Daegu, South Korea, was diagnosed, the number of confirmed cases in Daegu and Kyeongbei Region increased rapidly. In the face of the spread of the pandemic, the Korean government quickly took measures to implement the real name purchase system, called the "five-part mask system," from March 9 to ensure that residents can buy masks if they need. The pandemic was quickly brought under control by vigorously promoting "social distancing," avoiding large gatherings and providing emergency living allowances.

On March 12, 2020, faced with the spread of COVID-19, the British government adopted a "risk aversion" policy. Prime Minister Boris Johnson warned at a press conference, "And it's going to spread further and I must level with you, level with the British public, many more families are going to lose loved ones before their time." He also announced that the British government "will not close schools" or "prohibit large gatherings."[14] In response to the British government's "risk aversion" policy, 229 scientists wrote an open letter to the public calling for "tougher measures," because the current ones by the government "risk" lives by the thousands," but the government responded that if tougher measures were taken, it would lead to public dissatisfaction.[15]

On January 21, 2020, the United States announced the first case of COVID-19. On March 10, the number of confirmed cases passed 1,000. On March 13, President Trump declared a National Emergency over COVID-19. More than 10,000 cases were confirmed on March 19. On April 27, the number of confirmed cases reached 1 million and the number of deaths reached 55,000, making the United States the country with the most serious pandemic. After the declaration of the National Emergency on March 13, the United States not only saw differences between the Federal Government and some state governments on the quarantine policy, but also criticisms by Democratic lawmakers on responses taken by the Trump administration. Demonstrations against maintaining "social distancing" appeared on the grounds of protecting personal freedom of action.[16]

These countries listed above carry out political and social mobilization according to their respective domestic political systems, and follow different values to implement different pandemic prevention measures. There is nothing wrong with the differences in a diversified world. However, the differences have caused extensive discussions on political systems in the international community.

Therefore, when we predict the trend of the world order in the post-pandemic era, we should not only take into account the material interests, but also consider the possible impact of values on the future trend in terms of world order. Based on the combination of material interests and values, we believe that there are three possibilities for the direction of the world order after the end of this pandemic.

The first possibility is a pluralistic multilateral world order, wherein there is not only the interaction of material interests, but also the mutual tolerance of values. The so-called interaction of material interests is to continue to promote economic globalization and govern the global economy based on the multilateral system. In the field of trade, we continue to support the World Trade Organization and various regional trade agreements, oppose protectionism, and promote trade liberalization and facilitation. In the financial sector, we will continue to support the International Monetary Fund, the World Bank and G20, strengthen cooperation in financial supervision and promote the free flow of capital. In the field of international investment and production, we will continue to promote and improve international investment agreements and strengthen the governance of global production chains and regional production networks. The so-called mutual tolerance of values means that individuals and groups (different nationalities, different races, and different beliefs) or different countries (democratic countries, authoritarian countries) can understand and tolerate each other's values. But this pluralistic world order faces two large challenges. One challenge is how to avoid the "free rider" phenomenon. In the order where there is no country that wants to take the lead, because some countries are in a state of mutual competition, some countries are unwilling to pay any price for the public goods in the world order, but also hope that other countries will pay a greater price for the public goods out of their own interests. Thus, the phenomenon of the "free ride" usually occurs. Another challenge is how to avoid "benefiting oneself at the expense of others." This phenomenon occurs when each country is rationally promoting its own interests, and is unwilling to solve the issues of common concerns in the world order (such as air pollution and the arms race), which eventually leads to a worsening situation for all countries.

The second possibility is a free world order dominated by the United States. In this world order, although there are mutual exchanges of material interests, there is exclusivity in values. The current pandemic has not only aggravated the social conflicts in some countries, such as racial discrimination, but also led to a wide division in the international community caused by populist prejudice. In fact, this trend was already apparent before the outbreak of the pandemic. After he took office in 2017, President Trump changed the US foreign and economic policies after the 2008 financial crisis. In order to restore the leadership of the United States and the free world order dominated by the United States, under the slogan of "America First," the Trump administration began to reshape not only the national interests of the United States, but also the world economic order. The principle of "America First" was reflected in US foreign policy and international economic policy. Prime examples include renegotiating the North American Free Trade Area with Canada and Mexico, conducting FTA negotiations with Japan and South Korea, conducting trade negotiations with China, withdrawing from the TPP (which it had strongly supported before), and publicly expressing dissatisfaction with the stagnation of the Doha Round of WTO negotiations. All these show that the United States is not voluntarily giving up its leadership over the free world economic order, but also trying to reshape the free world order based on the principle of "America First." The biggest challenge of this order is the confidence of relevant countries in the "leadership" of the United States.

The third possibility is that China and the United States compete with each other so fiercely that they will form a bipolar system, that is, the so-called "New Cold War" during the pandemic, with one bloc centering around the United States and the other bloc centering around China. This would mean that China and the United States are not only "decoupled" from each other in material

240   *Wang Zhengyi*

interests, but also completely opposed in values. At the same time, both sides are willing and able to establish and maintain their own systems. The possibility of such an order depends on two points: first, whether China and the United States are willing to compete with each other and are able to provide public goods that support the two different systems. Second, whether other countries can benefit from these public goods and are willing to choose between these two systems. At present, this possibility is not great.

Conclusion

Professional groups generally have three ways to respond to emergencies. The first is to provide professional knowledge for decision-makers, so that the corresponding policies are scientific and operable. The second is to provide guidance to the public with their professional knowledge so as to help the public become more rational. The third is to study the situation and become more knowledgeable. When we observe international relations under the global pandemic situation, there are many issues that need us to study. From the perspective of international relations, we have found that for all actors in international relations, there is no winner or loser in the face of a common disaster, and it is undesirable for any country to take either the policy of "benefiting oneself at the cost of others," or the opportunist policy of having a "free ride." In terms of the global production chain and national security, the pandemic has strengthened the paramount importance of supply chain security. Although it is impossible to have the global production chain completely broken, it is possible to locally re-build the supply chain. As far as the trend in terms of the world order is concerned, value orientation and material interests are equally important. A world order without the tolerance of different values cannot be sustained. Hopefully, the limited knowledge I have shared here could become common knowledge, understood by the public, and accepted by relevant policy-makers.

Notes

1 "The Coronavirus Pandemic Will Forever Alter the World Order." https://www.wsj. com/articles/the-coronavirus-pandemic-will-forever-alter-the-world-order-11585953005.
2 "WHO Timeline-COVID-19." 27 April 2020 Statement. http://www.who.int.
3 http://www.gov.cn. "Extraordinary G20 Leaders' Summit:Statement on COVID-19." http://www.g20.utoronto.ca.
4 "G20 Finance Ministers & Central Bank Governors Press Release (Virtual Meeting - March 31, 2020)." http://www.g20.org.
5 Gereffi, Gary. *Global Value Chain and International Development: Framework, Findings and Policies*. Trans. Cao Wen, and Li Ke. Shanghai: Shanghai People's Publishing House, 2018. p. 3.
6 UNCTAD. "World Investment Report 2011: Non-Equity Modes of International Production and Development." p. 124.

7 UNCTAD. "World Investment Report 2013: Global Value Chains: Investment and Trade for Development." p. xxiii.
8 UNCTAD. "World Investment Report 2018: Investment and New Industrial Policy." pp. 22–23.
9 Farrell, Henry, and Abraham L. Newman. "Chained to Globalization: Why It's too Late to Decouple." *Foreign Affairs* 99. 1(2020). pp. 70–71.
10 UNCTAD. "World Investment Report 2018: Investment and New Industrial Policy." p. 162.
11 UNCTAD. "World Investment Report 2007: Transnational Corporations, Extractive Industries and Development." p. 16. UNCTAD. "World Investment Report 2019: Special Economic Zones." p. 99.
12 UNCTAD. "World Investment Report 2018: Investment and New Industrial Policy." pp. 5–6. Figures 1.5 and 1.6.
13 Bull, Hedley. *The Anarchical Society: A Study of Order in World Politics.* New York: Palgrave, 2002. p. 63.
14 https://www.gov.uk/government/speeches/pm-statement-on-coronavirus-12-march-2020.
15 https://twitter.com/Trickyjabs/status/1238939964303454212.
16 Francis Fukuyama, "The Thing That Determines a Country's Resistance to the Coronavirus." *The Atlantic* 30 March, 2020. https://www.theatlantic.com/ideas/archive/2020/03/thing-determines-how-well-countries-respond-coronavirus/609025/.

19 COVID-19 and Global Governance Reform[*]

Sun Jisheng[**]

Since the outbreak of the pandemic, the Chinese government has always put the safety of people's life and health first, adopted strict prevention and control measures, and achieved remarkable prevention and control results. In spite of this, COVID-19 quickly broke out in many places around the world, spread rapidly in many countries, and became a typical global public health crisis. The impact of the pandemic quickly spilled over to many fields, such as the economy, society and politics, highlighting the necessity and urgency of global governance. Despite the large scope and impact of the pandemic, the global governance system seems to be dysfunctional when the pandemic spread in many countries. Neither the international organizations or international mechanisms nor the world's powers have been fast in their responses. Each country acts in its own way, and the whole world is in a state of chaos. The spread of COVID-19 has forced us to re-examine the current world order and think about the current global governance system. Why did the global governance system partially fail to respond? What are the main hindrances that prevent them from functioning? What are the problems with the concepts and rules of the global governance system? With the increasing number of global issues, countries need to reflect on how to reform and adjust the current global governance system to better respond to global challenges. In response to global issues, countries urgently need to change their ideas, abandon zero-sum thinking and outdated ideas, establish a sense of community with a shared future for mankind, and form communities of ideas, systems, policies, actions, and responsibilities. Major countries need to think about how to strengthen coordination, unite global forces, jointly participate in and promote global governance, and turn ideas into actions to better respond to global issues. For a global public health crisis such as the COVID-19 pandemic, the only way out is for the world to form a human health community and work together to cope with it.

[*] This chapter was published as a full article in *World Economics and Politics* 5 (2020).
[**] The author is Vice President, and Professor of China Foreign Affairs University, chief expert of the Research Center for Beijing International Exchange and Foreign Affairs Administration, China Foreign Affairs University.

DOI: 10.4324/9781003433897-19

Global Governance and Governance Mechanism

Global issues require global governance. Understanding global governance and its mechanism is the basis for examining the COVID-19 pandemic from the perspective of global governance. In fact, global governance is mainly to better respond to and solve global problems. The practice of global governance shows that global governance mainly depends on institutional governance. In the process of governance, major countries should play the leading role.

Global Governance Is Born to Deal with Global Problems

In the 1990s, with the end of the Cold War, the acceleration of globalization, the increasing integration of the world, and the increasing interdependence among countries, many global problems emerged, such as poverty, climate change, refugees, transnational crime and environmental pollution. Traditional security and non-traditional security threats are intertwined, high political issues and low political issues interact, and local and global issues transform into each other. It is difficult for a single country to deal with global problems, and coordination and cooperation among countries have become the only way out. The task of solving global problems at the global level has become urgent and arduous, hence the birth of the concept of global governance. In 1992, initiated by Willy Brandt, the former German Chancellor, Ingvar Carlsson, former Swedish Prime Minister, and some international celebrities, the "Committee on Global Governance" was established. In 1995, the Committee issued a report on *Our Global Neighborhood*, which gives the definition of "global governance" as "the sum of many ways individuals and institutions, public and private, manage their common affairs. It is a continuing process through which conflicting or diverse interests may be accommodated and co-operative action taken."[1] Global governance includes not only formal organizations and mechanisms, but also the informal arrangements which are recognized by the people and corresponding institutions, and are considered able to meet their interests.[2] Some Chinese scholars argue that global governance is to solve global conflicts, and international issues in ecology, human rights, immigration, drugs, smuggling, and infectious diseases through binding international regulations, so as to maintain the normal international political and economic order.[3] Others believe that global governance means a new rule, mechanism, method, and activity for the management of human public affairs, which is based on the value orientation of human holism and common interest theory, and involves multiple actors in equal dialogue, consultation and cooperation to jointly respond to global changes and global challenges.[4] Other scholars believe that global governance mainly refers to the systems, norms, mechanisms, and activities established by sovereign states, international organizations, non-governmental organizations and other international relations actors to manage public affairs in the international community in order to solve global problems and promote the common interests of all mankind.[5]

244 *Sun Jisheng*

Global Governance Mainly Depends on Institutional Governance

According to the academic definition and research on global governance and the practice of global governance, global governance so far is mainly institutional. International organizations or international institutions, and the relevant international rules and norms formulated by them, coordinate and constrain the behavior of countries, promote cooperation, and play an important role in governance. Global governance mainly involves governance objectives, governance objects, governance subjects and a governance basis. As global governance cannot rely on the authority of the government as for domestic governance, institutions are crucial to global governance and serve as a platform and basis for countries to coordinate their behaviors and cooperate. International systems mainly cover international organizations or institutions, international mechanisms, rules and norms. These are the main basis for the governance actors in the governance process, and also constitute the main content of the global governance system and the basic framework for the operation of global governance. Institutional governance under the framework of multilateralism has always been the dominant discourse of global governance. It is precisely because the international system is crucial to global governance that there have been disputes over institutions among countries, especially among major countries. Specifically, major countries compete over the creation and control of international organizations or institutions, rule-making, agenda setting, representation, voice, etc. The institutional dispute will be more obvious in terms of the transformation of the international system or in the fierce competition among major powers, such as between the United States and the Soviet Union during the Cold War, and China and the United States after 2008, which constitutes an important aspect of the politics and rivalry of great powers. The current global governance system was mainly formed after the Second World War. It is dominated by Western countries led by the United States, such as the trade governance system dominated by the World Trade Organization, the global financial governance system dominated by the World Bank, and the International Monetary Fund, and the collective security governance system dominated by the UN Security Council. In fact, the system ensures multilateral coordination and cooperation. As the world's largest and most representative international organization, the United Nations has 16 specialized agencies, such as the World Health Organization, UNESCO, the World Food and Agriculture Organization, the International Labor Organization, the World Intellectual Property Organization, the International Telecommunication Union, the International Maritime Organization, and the World Meteorological Organization. All the specialized agencies have formulated rules and norms, managing corresponding fields. All the UN member states have acceded to relevant conventions and treaties to conduct corresponding governance and maintain stability and order in various fields.

Major Countries Play a Crucial Role in Global Governance

Although the main actors of global governance include countries, intergovernmental organizations, non-governmental organizations and non-governmental forces, from the perspective of global governance practice, countries, especially the great powers, are still important forces in the process of global governance. World powers have unique advantages in terms of resources, strength, capacity, and global mobilization. At the same time, global governance is also a place where the interests of major countries are highlighted. Different countries have different priorities for threats and problems, and there are also cognitive differences in their respective responsibilities, which will directly affect the specific practice of global governance.[6] In the process of formulating global governance rules, setting a governance agenda, and creating governance institutions and mechanisms, great powers certainly have more influence. For example, in the United Nations, the G20, the G8, and the BRICs, major countries are actually playing leading roles. With regard to the world economy, the G7 led by the United States played a leading role before the 2008 financial crisis. The same is true for the solutions of some security issues. For example, with regard to the Iranian nuclear issue, the major powers participating in the negotiation of the nuclear agreement are China, the United States, Russia, Britain, France, and Germany. Therefore, the announcement of the United States' withdrawal from the agreement has had a devastating impact. At present, global governance in many fields (such as climate change, counter-terrorism, refugees, the cyberspace, the deep sea, polar regions, etc.) cannot be separated from the active participation and coordination of major countries. Great powers have greater influence when crises arise. For example, after the outbreak of the financial crisis in 2008, developed countries and emerging economies worked together so effectively that made the G20 an important platform, under which many summit meetings were held to cooperate with the International Monetary Fund to jointly respond to the crisis. Surely, the G20 played an important role in maintaining world economic stability and boosting people's confidence in the world economy at that time. Oftentimes, in the face of specific problems, major countries can effectively mobilize a large number of forces of all parties, so as to exert material influence and produce spiritual influence at the same time, such as stabilizing expectations, enhancing confidence, solidarity, and mutual assistance. Small and medium-sized countries are unable to achieve what the great powers can.

Global Governance Dilemma under COVID-19

COVID-19 broke out all over the world in just over three months. Within half a year, the pandemic continued to spread in Europe, North America, and other places. Many countries and cities had to implement lockdowns, and declared a state of emergency or war. The shortage of public health resources was the serious problem many countries had. What is worse is that situation will continue.

246 *Sun Jisheng*

The world economy has been hit hard, and the spillover effect has become increasingly serious. It is hard to imagine that in an era when science, technology and information are so developed, and resources are so abundant, mankind has fallen into such a difficult situation. As UN Secretary General António Manuel de Oliveira Guterres said, "We are facing a global health crisis unlike any in the 75-year history of the United Nations – one that is spreading human suffering, infecting the global economy and upending people's lives."[7] In the face of such a serious global crisis, the global governance system is in a state of partial failure, as shown by the slow response and action of international organizations. The international mechanisms partly failed as well. The great powers could not coordinate or cooperate as there was a lack of leadership. All this makes us reflect on the current global governance system and the future of global governance.

International Organizations Fell into a State of Partial Failure

International organizations are important actors in global governance. In terms of the current global governance system, the United Nations and its specialized agencies should play an important coordinating and guiding role. However, since this outbreak, the role of the United Nations has been minimal. Although Secretary General Guterres has made several speeches on COVID-19, asking all countries to unite, declare war on the virus and jointly respond to the crisis, in fact, the United Nations has failed to play an important role in unity and coordination. WHO has played a role in tracking and informing the world of the pandemic situation, but it cannot regulate and constrain the behavior of countries by its recommendations and guidelines. For example, after receiving the relevant notification from China on January 3, 2020, WHO began its first phase of work, mainly on conducting relevant research on how the virus spread, how serious it was, and what measures should be taken to prevent infection, and determining the extent of the pandemic. On January 30, the pandemic was declared a public health emergency of international concern (PHEIC). At the end of February, the global risk assessment of the pandemic was raised to "very high," indicating that every country needs to be prepared for possible large-scale community transmission. The "global pandemic" was announced on March 11. After declaring PHEIC, the anti-pandemic action was upgraded to a global effort coordinated and supported by the WHO headquarters, such as determining scientific research priorities, mobilizing resources to deliver testing reagents and personal protective equipment to all countries, sharing China's anti-pandemic experience, etc., so that other countries can at least understand and get useful tips from it, and understand how China did it and what methods were effective.[8] However, in terms of coordinating national actions, WHO is obviously unable to regulate the behavior of the countries, and change their response to the pandemic and prevention and control measures. WHO asked all countries to submit relevant information, but some countries did not cooperate. WHO emphasizes that the

COVID-19 and Global Governance Reform   247

travel ban is not an effective preventive and control measure, but many countries issued the travel ban as their initial response. More importantly, the WHO's recommendations on the severity and route of transmission of the COVID-19 virus have been overlooked by many countries. Unfortunately, the overlooking resulted in the loss of valuable time in many countries in effective prevention and control at the initial stage of the pandemic. Although other specialized agencies of the United Nations have carried out some relevant work in response to the pandemic, such as the World Bank's US$12 billion fund to assist countries in coping with the impact of the pandemic, and the International Monetary Fund's recommendations on fiscal policies to protect people during the pandemic, no substantive effect on curbing the spread of the pandemic was observed.[9]

In addition to the international level, international organizations have also failed at the regional level, the most typical of which is the European Union (EU). The EU is a regional organization with strong institutions and clear rules, orderly, and highly integrated, but it failed to play the role of leadership, coordination, and solidarity as it should have as a supranational regional organization. France and Germany, the backbone of the EU, failed to play their leading roles, showing that the organization is far from forming a community of common destiny. Facing the severe pandemic situation, many EU countries did not take joint actions with other countries, but first took protectionist measures to safeguard their own interests. On March 10, 2020, although the European Council held a video conference to discuss with the leaders of EU member states to jointly combat the pandemic, it determined the top tasks of the EU at that time, namely, limiting the spread of the virus, ensuring an adequate supply of medical equipment, promoting the research and development of vaccines and other medicines, and coping with the socio-economic impact of the pandemic, and pointed out that the EU needs to develop a set of unified anti-pandemic norms, but none of these has not been translated into specific actions.[10] Italy turned to the EU for help after the outbreak, but the EU and its member states did not provide timely help to curb the spread of the pandemic. The EU member states intercepted pandemic prevention materials from other states. Following the worsening of the pandemic in Italy, the virus quickly spread to Spain, France, Germany, and other countries. The EU has also implemented export restrictions on other European countries. Ursula von der Leyen, President of the European Commission, announced on March 15, 2020, that the EU would completely ban the export of some protective medical equipment, and the export to non-EU countries must be authorized by member states to ensure adequate supply within the EU. This policy has undoubtedly widened the rift between the EU and other European countries and weakened the EU's attraction and centripetal force. President Aleksandar Vučić of Serbia made it clear that European solidarity didn't exist at all.[11] With the aggravation of the pandemic in Germany, France, Spain, and other countries, the EU member states only skinned their own skunks, as the proverb goes. It was not until the EU finance ministers' meeting on April 9, 2020 that

248   *Sun Jisheng*

an agreement was reached on the implementation of a large-scale rescue plan with a total amount of 540 billion euros to deal with COVID-19 in Europe.[12]

Various International Mechanisms Failed to Respond Quickly

Compared with international organizations, and international institutions, international mechanisms are relatively stable institutional arrangements, which have been formed on the basis of certain rules and procedures, but have not become real institutional organizations. Compared with international organizations or international institutions, their membership relations and operating procedures are relatively loose and flexible, their institutionalization level is relatively low, and their creation cost and process are relatively simple. Nevertheless, international mechanisms are still an important part of global institutional governance, such as the G20 and BRICs countries. In recent years, China has also launched many new mechanisms, such as the dialogue of Asian Civilizations, and the South–South Human Rights Forum. In the past, international mechanisms played an important role in the process of global governance. For example, after the outbreak of the international financial crisis in 2008, the G20 became an effective mechanism to deal with the crisis. At the critical moment, the G20 united the developed economies and developing countries to curb the spread of the crisis. The G20 held consecutive meetings and replaced the G8 as an important platform for global economic governance at the Pittsburgh Summit in 2009.[13] For another example, in the field of climate change, the United Nations Climate Change Conference has played an important role in the global response to climate change. It has not only formulated relevant rules, but also brought together all forces in the world to jointly address the issue of climate change. However, after the outbreak of the pandemic, various international mechanisms generally responded slowly, failed to act effectively, and failed to exert a substantive influence. On March 12, 2020, the second meeting of the coordinators of the G20 Riyadh Summit was held in Huber, Saudi Arabia. After the meeting, the statement of the G20 coordinators on COVID-19 was issued, calling on the international community to actively respond, strengthen coordination and cooperation, control the pandemic, protect people, mitigate its impact on the economy, maintain economic stability, and avoid stigmatization. It also expressed support for the work of WHO.[14] It was not until March 26, 2020 that the G20 Special Summit on COVID-19 was held in the form of a video conference to discuss the pandemic prevention and control, and the maintenance of global stability. On March 31, G20 finance ministers and central bank governors held a special video conference to discuss the implementation of the G20 leaders' statement on coping with COVID-19. At this time, the COVID-19 pandemic broke out on a massive scale in the world, and the impact on the world economy and other fields was extremely serious. In addition, the newly formed BRICs mechanism in the 21st century did little in curbing this pandemic. In contrast, only ASEAN and China, Japan, and

COVID-19 and Global Governance Reform   249

South Korea ("10 + 3") are pragmatic in the fight against the pandemic, proposing a series of pragmatic measures against the pandemic after the Special Leaders' Meeting on April 14, such as strengthening the construction of an early warning mechanism, considering the establishment of "10 + 3" important medical material reserves, strengthening epidemiological scientific research cooperation, and establishing a special fund to deal with public health emergencies.[15]

Absence of Leadership Makes Coordination and Cooperation More Difficult

As mentioned earlier, great powers play a key role in global governance. In addition to strength and resources, great powers should also be able to guide in concept, policy coordination, unity, cooperation, and responsibility at the international level. At present, major countries play a key role in maintaining confidence, coordinating cooperation, and mobilizing global forces in dealing with global issues in various fields. It is even more necessary for major countries to play a role in times of crisis. In response to emergencies such as COVID-19, the reporter of the *New York Times* wrote an article stressing that major countries need to successfully manage and control domestic crises, unite allies, lead alliances, provide global public goods, and organize a global common response.[16] After the outbreak of the pandemic, the United States, as the world's most powerful country, did not do much in these areas, but got stuck to the principle of "America First." Stephen Walt, an American scholar, wrote the article "The Death of American Competence," specifically evaluating the impact of the US withdrawal in responding to the pandemic, and undertaking its international responsibility.[17] After the outbreak of the pandemic in China, the negative voices of the United States against China continued to rise. In an interview on January 30, 2020, US Secretary of Commerce Wilbur Ross said that the new pandemic in China would help accelerate the return of manufacturing to the United States, a clear sign of his zero-sum thinking. Since February 2, the United States closed its borders to all Chinese citizens, and foreigners who had been to China 14 days before, and imposed a strict travel ban on China. In the most difficult period of the pandemic in China, Russia, Belarus, Japan, and South Korea quickly sent medical supplies to Wuhan. Leaders of more than 160 countries and international organizations expressed support to China in different ways. All sectors of American civil society donated medical supplies to China, but the US government did not provide substantive help to China. Not only that, but some American media and officials stigmatized China from time to time. On February 3, *The Wall Street Journal* published an article entitled "China is the Real Sick Man of East Asia" and refused to apologize, which triggered a strong protest in China. In response, China revoked the press credentials of three *Wall Street Journal* reporters in Beijing. On March 2, the US State Department announced that it would impose restrictions on the number of personnel of five Chinese media in the United States, requiring them to reduce the total number of employees from 160 to 100. After that, the Chinese side requested *Voice of America*, *The New York Times*, *The Wall Street Journal*, *The Washington Post*, and *TIME* to report to the Chinese side in writing all their staff, finance, business, and real estate information. Trump ignored the relevant naming regulations of the WHO on the virus and frequently used the word "Chinese virus" in his speeches and tweets, trying to blame China for the pandemic. There were many head-on clashes between China and the United States on social media such as Twitter.

During the pandemic, President Xi Jinping spoke twice with President Trump by telephone, hoping that the United States would calmly assess the pandemic situation, and reasonably formulate and adjust response measures. He also said that China and the United States could maintain communication, strengthen coordination, and jointly prevent and control the pandemic, unite in the fight against the pandemic, strengthen international cooperation in the fight, and stabilize the global economy. Trump also said that the United States would fully support China in combating COVID-19 and would be willing to send experts to China, and provide assistance to China in various other ways.[18] However, the conflicts between China and the United States following the outbreak of the pandemic, coupled with the impact of previous trade frictions, weakened the atmosphere of cooperation and strengthened the atmosphere of confrontation on the whole. As some scholars pointed out, the United States has been responsible for establishing and maintaining the world cooperation order in the past 75 years, but during this pandemic, the United States did not actively advocate cooperation.[19]

At the same time, as an ally of Europe, the United States did not provide necessary help to its allies under the increasingly serious pandemic in Europe, and neither did it give any notice before issuing the travel ban on Europe. At the same time, the United States did not take active response measures at home until the pandemic situation worsened badly. Emmanuel Macron even made it clear that the United States was no longer able to lead the West, and that it should select a new leader. In the face of the pandemic, European powers such as France, Germany, and Britain lacked action in the global fight against the pandemic, and showed little leadership to speak of, even within Europe, making the prevention and control situation in Europe increasingly difficult. Their non-action worsened the pandemic situation in many countries. The policy based on the "herd immunity" theory initially announced by Britain was in sharp contrast to the prevention and control policies of other European countries. On March 10, 2020, Angela Merkel told the lawmakers from her bloc that "60%–70% of people in Germany might be infected with Novel Coronavirus," showing as sign of helplessness and frustration. While focusing on the control of the virus domestically, China also took the responsibility as a major country by sharing relevant information with the international community, donating medical materials to many countries, and sending expert to help other countries. However, it was difficult for China to cope with this global crisis on its own, especially

COVID-19 and Global Governance Reform 251

when the willingness of the United States to cooperate was weakened and cooperative actions were limited.

Global Governance Reform from the Perspective of a Community with a Shared Future for Mankind

The process from the outbreak of COVID-19 to the adoption of measures to prevent and control it once again reminds all countries that the world is an interconnected global village in the face of the pandemic, mankind is an interdependent community of destiny, and no country can succeed in isolation. Global issues need common responses from all countries. At a time when the world order and international pattern are constantly changing and adjusting, how to better conduct global governance is a major challenge? The original governance system has failed, and the new governance system has not been established. In the face of COVID-19, the global governance system in transition is in chaos and disorder. The global governance system urgently needs to be reformed, new ideas need to be established, and the original system and operation mode need to be reformed and updated. This pandemic has exposed many flaws and weaknesses in the current global public health governance, and further highlights the urgency of strengthening the construction of the global public health governance system. President Xi Jinping clearly put forward the goal of building a human health community when talking with President Macron on March 23, 2020, by the phone, which is the concrete embodiment of the concept of a community with a shared future for mankind in the field of public health. He stressed that all countries should cooperate sincerely, promote joint research projects, strengthen health and quarantine cooperation at the borders, support the work of WHO, and jointly help African countries prevent and control the virus.[20] To achieve the goal of a health community, all countries should uphold the thinking of a community with a shared future for mankind, and build a community of ideas, systems, policies, actions, and responsibilities to ensure the long-term stability of human society. This can be done from the following five aspects.

Maintaining the Existing World Order, Promoting the Reform of the Global Governance System, and Forming a Community of Shared Future

The partial failure of the global governance system is closely related to the evolution of the world order and international pattern in recent years. The United States continued to "retreat" from the international organizations and affairs as its willingness to provide global common products and international cooperation decreased. The retreat has an impact on the cooperation of major countries. In addition, the trade disputes with many countries, and a series of twists and turns in Sino-US relations have actually damaged the image of the United States as the most powerful country on earth, caused instability to the current world order, and damaged the global governance system. In the past,

252   *Sun Jisheng*

the United States regarded itself as a global leader, able to coordinate its Western allies to respond to various emergencies around the world. For example, in his 2003 State of the Union Address, President Bush announced the President's Emergency Plan for AIDS Relief (PEPFAR) to combat global HIV/AIDS, which provided up to US$90 billion in funds to fight AIDS, and was regarded as the best effort made against a single disease. The plan saved thousands of lives in Africa alone. During the fight against the Ebola virus, US President Barack Obama made it clear that "we must lead the global fight against Ebola."[21] During the current anti-pandemic period, the United States actually gave up its traditional role of leading the Western allies. In fact, the United States and China used to have good cooperation in the field of public health. During the severe acute respiratory syndrome (SARS) pandemic in 2003, for example, the United States sent a 40-person medical team to China to help fight SARS. Finally, the SARS pandemic was basically controlled in Asia, and both China and the United States benefited from it. After the SARS pandemic, the United States and China had good cooperation in dealing with the new type A H1N1 influenza, H7N9 avian influenza, and Ebola virus, as they shared information, technology, and conducted joint research. However, during this pandemic, the United States chose to "decouple" from China in this field.[22] For Europe, the "Brexit" of Britain and the differences among EU member states weakened the leadership and cohesion of the EU. Due to the lack of European unity in the early stage of the pandemic, it was difficult for other countries to do much to help others when their pandemic situation got worse day by day. Together, these changes shook the stability of the world order formed after the Second World War, weakened people's confidence in it, the action capability, authority and credibility of the global governance system. This was also the reason, from a global perspective, for the chaotic responses when the pandemic broke out. Therefore, countries urgently need to maintain the stability of the world order and promote the reform of the global governance system on the premise of stability.

Updating Concepts, Enhancing Community Awareness, and Forming a Community of Same Ideas

Building a community with a shared future for mankind means that people of all countries work together to build a clean and beautiful world of lasting peace, universal security, common prosperity, openness, and inclusiveness. In recent years, China has always emphasized the concept of a community with a shared future for mankind, which was included into the Constitution of the People's Republic of China, and the Constitution of the Communist Party of China. China actively participates in, and provides guidance for, global governance. The concept of a community with a shared future for mankind has been written several times into relevant resolutions and documents of the United Nations. COVID-19 once again calls our attention to the importance of the concept of a community of shared future for mankind. The virus knows

COVID-19 and Global Governance Reform   253

no borders, and no country can stay away from it. Henry Kissinger stressed during the pandemic that no country, even the United States, can defeat the virus using only its own resources. To deal with the current situation, we must have a global vision and a coordinated global action.[23] The world must establish a sense of a community with a shared future for mankind, unify understanding, and form a community of same ideas.

First, we should have a sense of the whole. With the deepening of globalization and scientific and technological progress, mankind has long been a whole, especially in the face of global problems. Only by establishing a sense of unity can all countries have a sense of cooperation and a spirit of solidarity, and can they share responsibilities, jointly respond to problems, and form a joint force. The process of global pandemic prevention and control proves that any country without this sense of community will encounter more problems in dealing with the pandemic. As Dr. Bruce Aylward, a senior advisor to the Director General of WHO, described after inspecting the anti-pandemic situation in China: "Everywhere you went, anyone you spoke to, there was a sense of responsibility and collective action, and there's war footing to get things done."[24] It is precisely because the whole country has a unified understanding that everyone actively protects and regards their efforts as part of the fight against the pandemic that the pandemic has been effectively contained in China. The same will be true for the world. Without this awareness, the negligence of any country may produce a butterfly effect in the world.

The second is to have a sense of unity. The pandemic fully shows that all countries must provide assistance to each other, showing a cooperative spirit that is needed to address such global issues as climate change, natural disasters, and environmental pollution. During China's active prevention and control of the pandemic, some countries just watched from the sidelines, believing that it was none of their business, and did not take effective response measures in their own countries, resulting in the outbreak of the pandemic in many countries. When talking with leaders of many countries on the phone, President Xi Jinping stressed the need for unity and cooperation in the fight against the disease.

Third, we should abandon the biased old thinking and eliminate the tendency of pan-politicization. The outbreak of the pandemic in many countries was closely related to people's understanding and consciousness. China has basically contained the pandemic in two months, and accumulated valuable experience and lessons, but the arrogance of some Western governments failed to make effective use of the time China has won for them. Ian Johnson, an American journalist, published an article entitled "China Bought the West Time, but the West Squandered It," where he points out that the attitude of the United States and most European countries towards the outbreak of COVID-19 is very passive, if not completely negative, thus missing the best time to curb the spread of the virus. Some foreigners seem to regard China's experience as unique or think that China is far away from where they live. The most important is that these people, especially those in the Western countries, have prejudices against China, which makes them underestimate the potential value and significance that China's preventive measures can bring to their countries.[25] Some countries regard China as the "other" in the international community, often unconsciously holding double standards. For example, *The New York Times* commented on the "lockdown" of Wuhan as coming "at the great cost of people's livelihood and personal liberties," but that, by contrast, the "lockdowns" in Italy were "risking its economy to contain Europe's worst coronavirus outbreak."[26] Some Western countries politicized public health issues. They not only despised and lacked confidence in China's anti-pandemic measures, but often had prejudice against China, which actually implied their doubts about China's systems and actions. This was clearly reflected in their habitual stigmatization and vilification of China in the early stage of the pandemic, the "responsibility-shifting" on China in the medium term, and fabrication of "China responsibility," and then the questioning of China's prevention and control data, the defamation of China's anti-pandemic medical expert group, and the quality of China's medical material after China achieved good prevention and control results. According to *Neue Zürcher Zeitung*, a Swiss newspaper, if it is not distracted by the idea of institutional competition, the world can use Chinese knowledge to make better preparations for containing the pandemic.[27] In dealing with global challenges, all the countries need to abandon the zero-sum thinking and the Cold War mentality, transcend the differences in ideology and political systems, put down arrogance and prejudice, and truly treat the world as a whole. Only in this way can countries become partners in global governance, achieve unity and cooperation, treat each other equally, share wisdom, learn from each other, and overcome difficulties together.

Reforming the Existing International System, Increasing Its Authority and Action Capability, and Forming a Community of Institutions

After the Cold War, the trend of multi-polarization has become increasingly obvious. In addition to the United States, the EU, Japan, and other developed economies, the collective rise of developing countries is also an important driving force for multi-polarization. The change in the balance of power between countries has become an important driving force for the reform of the overall governance system. This pandemic has exposed the vulnerability of the global governance system and many systemic and institutional problems, which is also an important reason why the global governance system failed to respond effectively to global challenges such as the spread of COVID-19. Therefore, it is necessary to reform, replace and supplement the existing international system, and strengthen the governance capacity, which can be achieved from three aspects.

First, we should strengthen the leadership and appeal of existing international organizations and mechanisms. The United Nations needs to shoulder the responsibility of uniting the world, increase its action capability, and take more substantive actions. The importance mission of the United Nations is to maintain world peace, stability and security. Due to the rights conferred by the

COVID-19 and Global Governance Reform   255

Charter of the United Nations and its unique international nature, the United Nations can take action on a series of issues facing mankind in the 21st century, including maintaining international peace and security, protecting human rights, providing humanitarian assistance, promoting sustainable development and defending international law.[28] All countries should strive to safeguard the authority of the United Nations, because there is no international organization that can replace it at present. In his phone calls with other heads of state, President Xi Jinping repeatedly stressed his support for the leading role of the United Nations and the WHO in improving global public health governance.[29] In response to global issues such as the spread of COVID-19, the United Nations itself also needs to carry out corresponding reforms and adjustments, enhance its operational capability, and establish corresponding early warning systems for crisis and response mechanisms. For example, the UN can convene relevant meetings at the first time, convey confidence to the world, unify the understanding and objectives of all parties, and formulate a global action road map and various global plans. At present, the world is in an era when the traditional security and non-traditional security issues are increasingly intertwined, and the impact of non-traditional security issues is increasingly far-reaching. The United Nations Security Council should also include them in its agenda and establish corresponding working mechanisms. At the same time, the specialized agencies of the United Nations need to take action around their respective tasks and themes, update their own rules and norms in a timely manner, and strengthen their respective response measures.

Second, we should continue to promote the reform of the G20 from a short-term crisis response mechanism to a long-term governance mechanism by strengthening its institutions. The pandemic once again shows the important role of the G20 in today's world politics. The first video conference of the G20 Special Summit held on March 26, 2020 was an important event during the fight against the pandemic, whose significance appeared more prominent when the world is facing the risk of economic recession and even economic crisis. The Special Summit statement adopted after the meeting focused on fighting the COVID-19 pandemic, safeguarding the world economy, responding to the disruption of the pandemic on international trade, and strengthening global cooperation, sending clear governance signals and goals to the world.[30] In view of the influence and representativeness of the G20 states, the G20 should not be limited to the economic and financial fields, and its functions can be extended to other areas of governance to better play its role in global governance. In the future, we can consider adding some new mechanisms under the framework of the G20, such as the core member mechanism, that is, the mechanism immediately launched by several key powers in the event of global challenges. In addition, it can promote the transformation of the G20 into a formal international organization, and consider setting up a secretariat or a special committee to refine the work under the G20 into different areas (such as public health, climate change, economic, finance, etc.), so as to better transform it into a long-term governance mechanism.

256   *Sun Jisheng*

Third, some new institutional arrangements should be added if needed. At present, the world is undergoing complex and profound changes, and the institutional arrangements of global governance should also keep pace with the times. In terms of public health, we can refer to some institutional arrangements for peacekeeping, such as military observer missions, peacekeeping forces, multinational forces, humanitarian intervention forces, standby mechanisms, and standing peacekeeping police mechanisms set up by the United Nations. For another example, in recent years, China has also promoted and participated in the construction of some new institutions and mechanisms in the financial field, such as the Asian Infrastructure Investment Bank, the Silk Road Fund, the BRICs New Development Bank, etc., which have made a necessary supplement to the existing international financial governance system. In the field of public health, we can also refer to such practices to strengthen system updating and system supplementation, and better improve the public health governance system. In addition, at the regional level, because the population and commodity circulation are more concentrated, the commonality of public security is more obvious, and the governance needs are relatively concentrated compared with the global level.[31] It is easier to reach a consensus of interests. Therefore, at the regional level, we can rely on the regional organizations and mechanisms, promote the institutional construction and transformation of regional organizations such as the European Union, the African Union, and ASEAN, improve the effectiveness of global governance at the regional level,[32] establish a multi-regional joint prevention and control mechanism, and reduce the pressure at the global level to respond to public health events, such as establishing a regional public health emergency contact mechanism in the field of public health and improving the emergency response speed of public health emergencies at the regional level.

Empowering WHO, Expanding Its Functions, Strengthen Its Institutional Power, and Upgrading the Global Public Health Governance System

In recent years, the impact of public health on world politics has become increasingly prominent. From SARS, Ebola virus, Middle East respiratory syndrome (MERS), and the new type H1N1 influenza to the current COVID-19, the global impact of public health problems has been escalating and may even become normal in the future. Some scholars have made the judgment that "we are living in the era of pandemic."[33] The pandemic has exposed many deficiencies in global health governance, highlighting the urgency of reform. We should improve the overall status of public health governance in global governance, raise the international status of WHO, and empower it and expand its functions, so that it has an international status similar to the International Monetary Fund and the World Bank. In view of the professionalism, scientific nature, complexity, and long-term nature of public health, countries should strengthen financial and human support for WHO, such as establishing a public health fund under WHO, so that it can organize global public health experts to concentrate on scientific research, vaccine research and development, data sharing, etc. At the same time, it can help those developing countries with weak health infrastructure to improve their public health response capability, and manage the global public health issue as a whole.

The international financial support for WHO is insufficient in the recent years. As of February 29, 2020, the United States still owes more than half of its 2019 dues, and has not paid its 2020 dues of US$120 million. Moreover, the United States only plans to provide the WHO US$58 million in 2021.[34] President Trump announced on April 14, 2020 that the United States would suspend its contributions to WHO. After the outbreak of the pandemic, the 2019 COVID-19 Solidarity Response Fund, jointly established by the United Nations Foundation, the Swiss Charity Foundation, and the WHO, has been launched to raise funds from individuals, the private sectors, and foundations to support the WHO to better respond to the pandemic. Similar efforts should be more institutionalized in the future. At the same time, the WHO should strengthen its own mechanism construction, such as the establishment of a global infectious disease monitoring system, an early warning mechanism and an emergency starting mechanism, further clarify the rules and norms of public governance, formulate international rules and guiding principles that all countries must abide by, unify standards, and improve the control and binding force on relevant behaviors of all countries, rather than just reporting information, conducting temporary investigations, and evaluating the situation.

Only in this way can all the countries establish effective pandemic prevention and control systems, and strengthen global public health governance under the overall coordination of the WHO. Only in this way can the world be prepared for the next possible pandemic. In fact, the international community has made some efforts. For example, after the SARS pandemic in 2003, the WHO strengthened the International Health Regulations. During the World Economic Forum in Davos in 2017, the Coalition for Pandemic Preparedness Innovations (CEPI) was established with the support of the Wellcome Trust Foundation, and the Bill and Melinda Gates Foundation to accelerate the research and development of new pandemic vaccines. In addition, there are some new initiatives to raise funds for the fight against pandemics, such as the WHO Emergency Response Fund and the World Bank Pandemic Emergency Financing Facility. On the whole, there is still a long way to go in this regard. All the countries and regions need to increase their support for the WHO.

Adopting Common Policies, and Build a Policy Community and an Action Community

The response to, and solution of, global problems need strong policy support, and the world needs to form a policy community. On the one hand, countries should formulate policies with the same goals and act in the same direction. Although the domestic basic conditions and social and cultural environment of each country are different, we should have a unified understanding and

258 *Sun Jisheng*

adopt similar policies in policy-making. After the outbreak of the pandemic, China has accumulated prevention and control experience for the world, and won time for prevention and control. Singapore, South Korea, Japan, and other Asian countries have also achieved good prevention and control results. However, the pandemic worsened in some Western countries due to inadequate response measures. Therefore, in dealing with such problems, countries should not differ too much in some important aspects. It is necessary to increase communication and coordination, establish mutual cooperation networks, and regard health as a global public product, so as to strengthen cooperation, deepen mutual trust, and establish a scientific data platform, avoid stigmatization or discriminatory practices, and avoid pan-politicization. On the other hand, we should build a community of action. The solution of any problem should ultimately be from the implementation of ideas and policies to specific actions. In the face of global problems, all countries should transcend the differences in values, political systems, individual interests, but act together and help each other. Only in this way can the cluster effect of action be produced. Even though the local infected cases were basically cleared in China owing to its effective responses, the situation was still serious in other countries. China has to focus on the inflow of affected cases from abroad, and on avoiding a rebound of COVID-19. In the face of the pandemic, the final success is the success of all countries. Therefore, all countries must work together and act together.

After the outbreak of the pandemic, China actively shared all kinds of information with WHO, and the international community, did its utmost to provide assistance, and shared diagnosis and treatment plans to other countries and regions. After the virus was effectively controlled within China, China began to increase its international assistance, and information exchange. As of April 10, 2020, the Chinese government had provided, or was providing, material assistance, including medical masks, protective clothing and testing reagents, to 127 countries, and 4 international organizations. On top of the previous cash donation of US$20 million to the WHO, China donated another US$30 million for the prevention and control of COVID-19 and support for the construction of health systems in developing countries. China has sent 13 batches of medical expert teams to 11 countries, and held more than 70 expert video conferences with more than 150 countries and international organizations.[35] Facts show that, in the face of the pandemic, it is difficult for countries to win the final victory alone in the fight against the pandemic. The world must form a community of action, and a strict network of joint prevention and control. Other choices are inconceivable.

Forming a Community of Responsibility Among Great Powers

Major countries are the key to the success of global governance, because they can effectively govern their countries at a critical moment, provide global public goods, and lead other countries to respond to the crisis. In the current situation of the transformation of the world order and the frequent difficulties and failures of the global governance system, the cooperation of major countries is more critical, otherwise it may make the global governance system from being dysfunctional to failure. In terms of current global governance, the crucial China–US cooperation is also the responsibility of the two countries to the world. On the one hand, since he became President of the United States, Trump showed little willingness to cooperate on those global governance issues he believes are too expensive or unimportant. As a result, the United States withdrew from the Paris Agreement on climate change, and UNESCO. On the other hand, at least for now, China cannot completely replace the United States in regard to many global issues, and become the leader of global governance. In this period of transition, both China and the United States need to adopt a more inclusive and pragmatic attitude towards global governance, and China and the United States may need to participate in many areas.[36] The two countries can complement each other and maintain cooperation in competition, which is very necessary for the stability of the global order and the global governance system, and is also of great benefit to the two countries. When talking about the pandemic, the former president of the World Bank specially emphasized the importance of the United States' immediate sharing of information. At the same time, he remarked that believed that the United States could also learn lessons from other countries in pandemic prevention and control, early warning systems, preparation, testing, key material reserves, containment, and mitigation methods, and transition to the recovery stage.[37] Kurt Campbell, former Assistant Secretary of State of the United States, also stressed that China and the United States could cooperate in vaccine research and development, clinical trials, financial incentives, information sharing, production of prevention and control facilities, and jointly provide assistance to other countries to benefit the world.[38] When speaking with Trump, President Xi Jinping also stressed that China and the United States should unite to fight the pandemic. China is willing to work with all parties, including the United States, to continue to support the WHO to play an important role, strengthen the exchange and sharing of prevention and control information and experience, speed up scientific research cooperation, and promote the improvement of global health governance. The two countries should strengthen the coordination of macroeconomic policies, stabilize the markets, ensure growth and people's livelihoods, and secure the openness, stability, and security of the global supply chain.[39] On March 29, 2020, the first batch of 80 tons of anti-pandemic materials from China arrived in the United States, including 130,000 N95 masks, 1.7 million surgical masks, and 50,000 sets of protective clothing, reflecting China's willingness to cooperate and the demeanor of a great power. However, it is difficult to achieve international cooperation through relying on the efforts of only one side. In the face of global issues, the leaders of major countries need a high degree of self-discipline, abandon narrow concept of interests, narrow nationalism, and properly control differences. The media and academia should also play their respective roles and strive to

260 Sun Jisheng

create a cooperative atmosphere. As Cui Tiankai, Chinese Ambassador to the United States, emphasized in an interview with Ian Bremmer, President of the Eurasian Group of the United States, that both sides should ensure to have an atmosphere of public opinion, which is helpful for Sino-US cooperation.[40] Only with the joint efforts of all parties can we ensure the realization of cooperation.

Conclusion

With tens of thousands of newly confirmed cases and rising death numbers every day, COVID-19 has exposed the challenges and governance difficulties in the field of global public health, highlighted the urgency and importance of building a human health community, and also highlighted the profound connotation and significance of the concept of a human community of shared future. In addition to threatening human life and health, the pandemic had devastating impacts on the economy, finance, trade and employment, and brought all-round chain impact and destruction to the world. Historically, massive outbreaks of pandemics usually threaten lives, cause panic, destroy the economy, threaten social stability, and even lead to war. Biosafety, therefore, has become an important part of national security. As the pandemic still rages, it cannot be ruled out that it will have a deeper impact on politics, society, values, ideology, culture, and other fields in the future. Even if the pandemic is contained globally in the next few months, how to eliminate its impact, how to repair its damage in various fields around the world, and how to further promote a new round of globalization or the transformation of globalization will also be issues that the global governance system needs to deal with in the "post-pandemic era." The repairs will stretch from the field of public health, to finance, debt, economy and social governance, involving both the domestic and global governance.

The pandemic once again warns us that global issues are increasingly affecting human beings in terms of both scope and depth, and strengthening global governance has become a top priority. The prevention and control process of the pandemic also shows that no country can become a self-enclosed island, and mankind may experience similar tests in the future. In the era of globalization, such a major emergency will not be the last. Various traditional and non-traditional security issues will continue to bring new global challenges. The impact of climate change, natural disasters, cybersecurity, and ecological environment degradation may appear at any time. The international community must establish a sense of a community with a shared future for mankind, and form a community of ideas, systems, policies, actions and responsibilities. Only in this way can countries abandon zero-sum thinking, abandon stereotypes, eliminate narrow nationalist and racist ideas, strengthen coordination and cooperation, stand by each other, form a real community with a shared future for mankind, and jointly protect human life security, development, and prosperity.

COVID-19 and Global Governance Reform   261

Notes

1 Commission on Global Governance. *Our Global Neighborhood: The Report of the Commission on Global Governance*. New York: Oxford UP, 1995. p. 4. https://en.wikipedia.org/wiki/Commission_on_Global_Governance

2 Commission on Global Governance. *Our Global Neighborhood: The Report of the Commission on Global Governance*. New York: Oxford UP, 1995. p. 2.

3 See Yu Keping's "Introduction to Global Governance." *Marxism & Reality* 1 (2002). p. 25.

4 Cai Tuo. "Chinese Perspective and Practice of Global Governance." *Social Sciences in China* 1 (2004): 95-96.

5 Chen Yue, and Pu Ping. *Building a Community with a Shared Future for Mankind*. Beijing: Renmin University of China Press, 2017. p. 83.

6 Qin Yaqing. *Global Governance: Order Reconstruction in a Pluralistic World*. Beijing: World Affairs Press, 2019. p. 83.

7 See "Secretary-General's opening remarks at virtual press encounter on COVID-19 Crisis."https://www.un.org/sg/zh/content/sg/speeches/2020-03-19/remarks-virtual-press-encounter-COVID-19-crisis.

8 See "China has demonstrated COVID-19 course can be altered – WHO." Interview with Dr. Gauden Galea, the World Health Organization (WHO) Representative in China. https://news.un.org/zh/story/2020/03/1052882.

9 See https://www.un.org/zh/.

10 "EU Holds Video Conference to Determine Four Urgent Tasks." *Beijing Daily* 12 March, 2020.

11 Campbell, Kurt M., and Rush Doshi. "Coronavirus Could Reshape Global Order." *Foreign Affairs* 18 March, 2020. https://www.foreignaffairs.com/articles/china/2020-03-18/coronavirus-could-reshape-global-order.

12 "The EU Finance Ministers Reached a 540 Billion Euro Rescue Plan." *People*'s *Daily* 12 April, 2020.

13 He Yafei. *Choice: China's Participation and the Global Governance*. Beijing: Renmin University of China Press, 2016. p. 4.

14 "G20 Coordinators' Meeting Issued a Statement on Coping with COVID-19." 13 March, 2020. https://www.fmprc.gov.cn/web/ziliao_674904/1179_674909/t1755427.shtml.

15 "Joint Statement of the ASEAN Special Summit, and China, Japan, and South Korea to Combat COVID-19." 15 April, 2020. https://www.fmprc.gov.cn/web/zyxw/t1769820.shtml.

16 Erlanger, Steven. "Another Virus Victim: The U.S. as a Global Leader in a Time of Crisis." *The New York Times*. March 22. 2020.

17 Walt, Stephen. "The Death of American Competence." *Foreign Policy*. 23 March, 2020. https://foreignpolicy.com/2020/03/23/death-american-competence-reputation-coronavirus/.

18 "President Xi's Call with President Trump." 8 Feb., 2020. https://www.fmprc.gov.cn/web/zyxw/t1741788.shtml; "President Xi's Call with President Trump." 27 March, 2020. https://www.fmprc.gov.cn/web/zyxw/t1762304.shtml.

19 Neumann, Iver B. "Will the Corona Virus Be the Deathblow of the World Order?" *Aftenposten* (Norwegian Daily) 23 March, 2020.

20 "President Xi's Call with President Macron." 18 Feb., 2020. https://www.fmprc.gov.cn/web/zyxw/t1760147.shtml.

21 Erlanger, Steven. "Another Virus Victim: The U.S.as a Global Leader in a Time of Crisis." *The New York Times* 22 March, 2020.

22 Beinart, Peter. "Trump's Break with China Has Deadly Consequences." *The Atlantic* 28 March, 2020. https://www.theatlantic.com/ideas/archive/2020/03/breaking-china-exactly-wrong-answer/608911/.

23 Kissinger, Henry A. "The Coronavirus Pandemic Will Forever Alter the World Order." *The Wall Street Journal* (Eastern Edition)3 April 3, 2020.

24 See https://www.science.org/content/article/china-s-aggressive-measures-have-slowed-coronavirus-they-may-not-work-other-countries?cookieSet=1.

25 Johnson, Ian. "China Bought the West Time. The West Squandered It." *The New York Times* 13 March, 2020. https://www.nytimes.com/2020/03/13/opinion/china-response-china.html?searchResultPosition=1.

26 "Lockdowns Mean so Differently for an American Media: An Example of Double-Standard Practice." 12 March, 2020. https://m.haiwainet.cn/middle/353596/2020/0312/content_31740359_1.html.

27 Guo Jiping. "A community with a Shared Future Can Overcome Difficulties through Unity and Cooperation." *People*'s *Daily* 28 March, 2020.

28 See https://www.un.org/zh/.

29 "President Xi's Call with President Macron." 18 Feb., 2020. https://www.fmprc.gov.cn/web/zyxw/t1760147.shtml.

30 "G20 Special Summit Statement on Coping with COVID-19." 13 March, 2020. https://www.fmprc.gov.cn/web/zyxw/t1762165.shtml.

31 Zhang Yunling. "What Does COVID-19 Tell Us about the Governance of International Public Security?" *World Affairs* 7 (2020). P. 16.

32 Chen Yue, and Pu Ping. Building a Community with a Shared Future for Mankind. Beijing: Renmin University of China Press, 2017. P. 89.

33 Whipple, Tom. "Coronavirus: We're Already Living in the Age of the Pandemic." *The Times* 28 February, 2020.

34 "Under the Pandemic, America's Dues to WHO Is Also a Moral Due." 17 March, 2020. http://www.myzaker.com/article/5e6f70678e9f094d4b6b26a5/.

35 "Regular Foreign Ministry Press Conference by Spokesperson Zhao Lijian on April 10, 2020." https://www.fmprc.gov.cn/web/fyrbt_673021/jzhsl_673025/t1768268.shtml.

36 Pu Xiaoyu. "Is China a New Global Leader? Rethinking China and Global Governance." in Huiyun Feng and Kai He. Eds. *China*'s *Challenge and International Order Transition*. Ann Arbor: University of Michigan Press, 2020. p. 292.

37 Zoellick, Robert B. "The World Is Watching How America Handles COVID-19." *Wall Street Journal* (Eastern Edition)8 April, 2020.

38 Campbell, Kurt M., and Rush Doshi. "Coronavirus Could Reshape Global Order." *Foreign Affairs* 18 March, 2020. https://www.foreignaffairs.com/articles/china/2020-03-18/coronavirus-could-reshape-global-order.

39 "President Xi's Call with President Trump." 27 March, 2020. https://www.fmprc.gov.cn/web/zyxw/t1762304.shtml.

40 Cui Tiankai (Chinese Ambassador to the US). "Focus on Positive Issues and Work together to Cope with the Global Crisis." 12 April, 2020. http://world.people.com.cn/n1/2020/0412/c1002-31670157.html.

20 The Outbreak of the COVID-19 Virus

Nowhere to Avoid it and an Interrogation of Misery

Zhao Tingyang[*]

Suddenly, Nowhere to Be Spared

The 2020 COVID-19 pandemic rapidly turned the virus moment into a political moment, a social moment, an economic moment, and a historical moment, and even was considered watershed in history. According to Thomas Friedman, there is a "New Historical Divide: B. C. and A. C," namely before COVID (B.C.) and after COVID (A.D.).[1] Henry Kissinger, a man who has seen so much of historical rise and fall, argues, as the title of his *Wall Street Journal* article suggests, "The Coronavirus Pandemic Will Forever Alter the World Order," and its political and economic impacts will be felt by generations to come. Such predictions reveal a real premonition that the world will change. Robert Schiller from the perspective of Historical Sociology looks at the COVID-19 pandemic as "a story," and "a narrative," and argues that COVID-19 can spread like a story because narratives can be as contagious as a virus. He believes that if a story dominates public opinion for several years, it will change many things like an "pandemic."[2]

However, the virus moment has not yet been finalized, and it is still evolving in uncertainty, because whether or not the virus moment really becomes an epoch-making moment depends on the subsequent actions and attitudes of the world. Part of the answer is in the hands of the virus, and the other half is in the hands of humans. Both the virus behavior and human actions are "irrational" that are difficult to predict. Here, for the time being, we don't look for the answer, nor can we predict what the answer might be. Let's first analyze the problems raised by the virus. It is believed that the virus moment is an "epic-like" event or "historical watershed." These literary descriptions need a clear frame of reference to be clarified. If we use the epoch-making events with the least controversy as the reference scale, comparison in magnitude may be a good starting point. The most important events in history are the inventions that have changed the mode of life, production or thinking, such as the written form of language, wheels, agriculture, industry, logic, calculus, relativity, quantum mechanics,

---

[*] Member of the Chinese Academy of Social Sciences, Research Fellow of the Institute of Philosophy, the Chinese Academy of Social Sciences.

DOI: 10.4324/9781003433897-20

vaccines, antibiotics, the Internet, genetic technology, artificial intelligence, etc. Or spiritual inventions, such as the major religions, the Greek philosophy, Pre-Qin thought, etc., or political revolutions, such as the French Revolution, and the October Revolution, or massive wars, such as the Second World War, or economic upheavals, such as geographic discoveries, capitalism, global markets, and the dollar system. According to these rough frames of reference, unless there is an unexpected political or spiritual upheaval imminent to happen, the COVID-19 event itself does not have the magnitude of power for fundamental change. However, according to economists' estimates, it may be devastating enough to cause an economic depression similar to that of 1929–1933.

We can also change the analytical framework or historical standard to view the virus moment by using Fernand Braudel's famous three-tiered view of historical time. The "event" is temporary, which is equivalent to the short span of the flow of historical time. Then, what kind of wave can spread to the medium span of time that is long enough to form a "general trend" in historical time, and even through the long-span deep-water layer of stable "structure"? It is almost certain that the impact of the COVID-19 pandemic exceeds that of short-term events, or it may form a general trend in a medium span. But, it would be terrifying if it could really determine the general trend for decades. If the COVID-19 pandemic will cause a consequence similar to that of the Great Depression in magnitude, it still seems to belong to the category of events. Although it is a major event, it is not enough to form a general trend. If it leads to a change in the political pattern, it is the general trend. Although the possibility of this general trend is faintly felt, it has not yet formed a sufficient and inevitable certainty. We also need to take into account the resistance from the long-term established "structure." The deep structure of civilization, society, and thought is stable, inert against change.

From the perspective of historical experience, there is often a rebound after the impact of abrupt events, and, oftentimes, things will return normal by going back along the path to where they were disrupted. As the saying goes, it is "forgetting the pain when the wounds are healed." This rebound is not only psychological, but also rational, especially in cost calculation. The "structure" formed over a long period of time concentrates a large number of costs, e.g., time cost, economic cost, technical cost, and cultural, ideological, and psychological costs. The superposition of these costs forms a stability that is not worth changing. Destroying the "structure" is tantamount to taking drastic measures, which is an adventure that endangers the conditions of existence. Therefore, revolution is a change with extremely high costs. Successful revolutions always occur when the old structure has completely failed, that is, the old structure has lost its spiritual vitality, unable to guarantee social security and order, and unable to maintain the economic level. It can be noted that a large number of continuous "deconstruction" movements have taken place in the world since 1968, but they mainly disassemble some surface structures of civilization, such as the concept of art, the concept of gender, social identity and self-identity, which have not shaken the deep structures of economy, the political system, and mode of thought. The most radical "deconstruction" almost exists only in the text, difficult to turn into reality. The historical impact of the deconstruction movement is equivalent to the "renovation" of the structure. Since we are unable to build a new house, we can only decorate it in a variety of ways. If there is no idea of the ability to form a new structure in the new dimension, and there is no idea, principle and social energy with "constructive power," the "deconstruction" will not turn into a revolution after all. Instead, the actions of deconstruction will be absorbed into the old system in a short time, which helps the old system in the way that an old tree blooms again.

According to Fernand Braudel, geographic structure, economic structure, social structure, ideological structure or spiritual structure belong to the long-span deep structure, which has super stability, and is difficult to alter. For this reason, once a great event happens, such as the formation of modernity or capitalism, it has become a major issue that has been constantly reflected for 200 years. In a sense, the great mystic modernity is waiting for the "deep-structural alteration" to start a new era. However, whether the COVID-19 pandemic can trigger a new structural change is still an open question. As for the result of the pandemic, one of the most popular and serious predictions is the end of globalization. If it turns out so, the COVID-19 pandemic will undoubtedly reach the general situation of the medium-span change, and even touch on the long-span structure.

Globalization is an outcome of capitalism. As long as capitalism exists, it is difficult for capital to resist the temptation of the global market. The current mode of globalization is only the initial or primary stage of globalization, which is "the globalization of division of labor" as far as the economy is concerned. In the chain of the division of labor, all the countries involved in the primary globalization have benefited, though differently. Even if the "globalization of the division of labor" may be ended, all regions still need the global market to ensure economic growth, and the technology-based and information-based economy needs to expand to the greatest extent. Therefore, in terms of economy, the end of globalization is not a very positive rational incentive for the development of economy, technology, and information. Of course, this does not rule out the political ending of globalization. Politics has its own unique power. In any case, pursuing the maximization of independent security and exclusive interests will indeed become a prominent problem in the future. Therefore, there may be a transformation of globalization, from the "globalization of the division of labor" to the "globalization of competition." In this case, it will at least form a major trend of in a medium-span of historical time.

The "globalization of competition" means that the global market continues to exist, and the globalization of economy, technology, and information continues, but the nature of the globalization has changed. The proportion of "cooperative rivalry" in primary globalization has been greatly reduced, while the proportion of "non-cooperative rivalry" has been greatly increased, and may even form a situation wherein "non-cooperative rivalry" obviously overwhelms "cooperative rivalry." The danger is that the globalization of competition may intensify and lead to the dissipation of the rent value of globalization, so that globalization itself evolves into a dilemma. It is not profitable to exit, and it is not profitable not to exit. Of course, this is an extreme possibility, and the greater probability is that when the non-cooperative rivalry is unprofitable at all, the cooperative rivalry will become attractive again as Axelrod's model of the dissemination of culture would suggest. Historical experience also shows that human beings are always in trouble, but they can always find ways to get out of trouble.

How far and how deep the "problem chain" of the COVID-19 pandemic will be, and whether it will touch and shake the deep concept of human thought, that is, the concept at the philosophical level, will determine whether this novel coronavirus has long-span impact. We cannot jump to the future to see the results of the pandemic in advance, but some "reminders" can be discerned at present. The reminders may not indicate the outcome, but they hint at the problems.

Among the reminders, the first we see is the "state of nowhere to be spared" as the result of a long period of joy. Many parts of the world have forgotten the state of nowhere to be spared from disasters in the regular and ubiquitous "carnival state." Whether it is holiday tourism, concerts, sports competitions, product launches, premieres, TV programs, company annual meetings, employee appreciation day, sales activities, shopping malls, art exhibitions, etc., can be transformed into carnivals, so that carnivals not only occupy time, but also become space itself. When temporal existence occupies the space long enough, it can change the nature of space. Even if the temporal activities are over, space has been infected with the carnival spirit that is difficult to fade. Finally, both living space (outer space) and psychological space (inner space) are infected with the nature of carnival.

The novel coronavirus speaks with facts. Its high infectivity makes the whole world vulnerable, as nowhere can escape its rage, overwhelming the infectivity of the carnival. Originally, the "state of nowhere to be spared" as an extreme possibility, was never absent from theoretical discussion, but the theory itself was absent. Happiness does not need theory, so theory was forgotten. "Nowhere to be spared" is not an abstract possibility. It conjures many specific images such as a nuclear war, an asteroid collision with the earth, unfriendly alien civilization invasion, etc. The probability of such a possibility is said to be very low. Once it happens, it is the end of mankind, and the end of any thinking. Therefore, "nowhere to be spared" is not considered a problem, but a conclusion, or the end of the problem. "Nowhere to be spared" disappeared from the list of issues, but was psychologically identified as a legend of horror or science fiction story, which has a safe distance from reality, so it could be masochistic at a safe distance. The story of mass destruction is entertaining and surreal. However, the "state of nowhere to be spared" is not without historical precedent. Although the extinction of dinosaurs is a disaster for dinosaurs, the possibility contained in it is also significant for human beings. The story of the diluvia, the Black Death in the Middle Age, the 1918 pandemic, the nuclear war that almost occurred during the Cold War: all these histories have been obscured by old stories so separated by time that they are no longer problematic. Novel coronavirus may not be as deadly as the above historical events, but it has formed a thunderbolt effect due to modern transportation and globalization, which directly turns the "state of nowhere to be spared" into a reality, thus exposing the relevant problems that need to be faced, and turning what was not a problem back into a problem. This "problematization" is creative, which means that the originally trusted social systems, institutions, and concepts can suddenly become problematic under unexpected conditions. The human social system can withstand slow and dramatic changes, but it cannot withstand sudden changes. What is serious is not only the virus, but the moment of the virus – a contemporary moment when the circulation energy of globalization exceeds the ability of every place to bear risks.

Infectious pandemics are not a unique phenomenon of globalization, but an ancient problem. Before globalization, the virus spread "slowly," and eventually spread all over the world, if not terminated somewhere mystically. Although there is nothing new under the sun, novel coronavirus has pushed the old problems to new conditions and turned them into new problems. The high-speed transmission of novel coronavirus under contemporary communication and traffic conditions has formed an effect similar to the "blitz," which has caught off-guard the medical system, the social management system, economic operation and related material resource systems in various places, and plunged them into trouble, and turned infectious diseases from a simple disease problem into a complex problem of social, political, and economic implications, directly causing two outcomes: one single problem becomes a problem for all, which is the most difficult situation in politics, and one place is for all places, which is the most difficult situation for society to deal with. If this chain reaction pops up, like a dyke failure, it will penetrate the fragile social system and erode the basic structure and concepts of human life. If the basic concepts of civilization are partially changed, the novel coronavirus event may have the long-span historical significance.

A Practical Problem Becomes Metaphysical

The outrageous COVID-19 pandemic directly raises a practical question, that is, the vulnerability of modern social systems. In other words, or according to the rivalry-based theory, modern systems lack "robustness." Almost all aspects of the modern social structure have been systematized. And interlocking systematization means both efficiency and vulnerability. Modern systems constantly pursue the minimum cost and maximum benefit, so the lack of buffer margin usually aggravates the vulnerability of the system. In order to maximize benefits, the capital, materials, equipment, production, transportation, and supply systems in modern society are all linked and operated at full capacity, jeopardizing the future safety as they are operated at the critical point of capacity overdraft. In fact, many systems are in deficit, so it is difficult to deal with sudden changes. Long before, Nassim Taleb explained the vulnerability of

268 *Zhao Tingyang*

modern systems with his "black swan" theory. The only system with a huge surplus in modern society is probably armaments, such as nuclear weapons that can destroy the world several times, and the financial system is probably the one that has prepaid for the future to the greatest extent. Finance is the basis for the operation of modern society. Therefore, "pre-payment for the future advance" has become a major feature of modernity. Although the basic contemporary systems hate uncertainty, uncertainty cannot be avoided. In terms of factual state or ontology, uncertainty is the real state of affairs, and "certainty" is actually a concept, an invention of logic and mathematics, which does not exist in reality.

The pandemic of novel coronavirus is a precise blow to the modern system, because it destroys humans or life. The vulnerability of the modern system itself is only a hidden danger. In most cases, even in the face of uncertainty and serious challenges, the system is often able to finally hold out. The reason is that the key factor of the system is people, who can solve the problems. Humans are flexible, whose thinking and action ability have natural "robustness." The system with humans in it is dynamic. However, the target of novel coronavirus is people. When people's lives are generally threatened, what force can the modern system expect to pull people through?

A fatal blow that can paralyze modern systems, or directly threaten human life, or threaten the basic needs of human survival and endanger human life is the shortage of basic human needs. Technology can help people live in virtual reality like in science fiction, but no matter how advanced modern technology is, the basic human needs are the most crucial as long as human beings are still carbon-based life forms. In terms of the order of survival, basic human needs precede their political needs, economic needs, value needs, pleasure needs, and cultural needs. More precisely, the basic needs are the biggest political, economic, and social questions. Although it is not sure whether novel coronavirus is an "epic-like" challenge, it must be an exemplary challenge, because it accurately tramples on the nerve of the modern system: the question of life. This is the Achilles' heel of the modern system.

For a long time, discussions on the world crisis have focused more on topics such as the financial bubble, climate warming, threat of big data and artificial intelligence to freedom, animal protection or glacier melting. Serious issues as they are, they are incomparable to the imminent threat of the novel coronavirus. Some of the above issues, such as climate warming, are even controversial in the scientific circle. But this is not the point. The problem is that after making those issues chiefly the concerns of the middle class, the discussions covered up a more deadly crisis, forgetting that farmers, workers, and doctors are the only people we can rely on for survival. The reason why the pandemic so touches people's nerves is that it is a sudden reminder of the collective security of mankind, which makes the fundamental question all the more realistic, that is: "to be or not to be."

Crises always break out from where there is practical vulnerability. For many economists, the COVID-19 pandemic means an economic disaster that only happens once in a century, the depression of the real economy, and the collapse of the financial system. This is much more serious than the financial crisis caused by the financial bubble, because the depression of the real economy must aggravate the financial crisis, which in turn will hit the recovery of the real economy, thereby forming a circular recession. Related to this, political scientists are more concerned with the possible political consequences of COVID-19. Whether out of worry or rejoice, some political scientists believe that globalization will terminate due to the COVID-19 pandemic. Ending a certain movement (including globalization) may start a new beginning, or may mean a dilemma, depending on whether there is a better way out. Dissatisfaction with something does not automatically produce better options. Globalization has never been a happy cooperative movement. Any cooperation will encounter the problem of how to share profits. Perfect cooperation only exists in philosophical theory, just as "complete free market" has always existed in economic textbooks. As Xun Tze, a Chinese philosopher, discovered more than 2000 years ago, where there is cooperation, there is injustice, dissatisfaction, conflict, and struggle. We can even say that cooperation always sows the seeds of conflict, and always creates the destroyers of cooperation itself.

However, globalization has changed the concept of the world in terms of survival. In the traditional concept of the world, the cooperation between any entities cannot reach the limit of possible interests, because there are always better cooperation opportunities in theory. Globalization pushes the spatial dimension of interest maximization to the whole world, and establishes the limit standard for interest maximization. Therefore, occupying world market becomes the way to maximize interest, because there is no other world. The world is the ontological boundary of rivalry strategy. Here we can see how ontology limits logic: logic is infinite. There are infinite possibilities in "logical time," but those infinite possibilities do not really exist. Once they are put in real situations, the infinite possibilities are subject to a specific state of conditions, hardly leaving any other options. This means that if you want infinity, you cannot exist. If you want to exist, you can only yield to finiteness. The consequence of globalization in the past 200 years is that globalization has become a "dominant strategy" to maximize benefits. From this point of view, the rivalry of globalization will have conflicts or experience strategic regressions. As the possibilities analyzed above, change from the "globalization of division of labor" to the "globalization of competition" may cause a dilemma that is unprofitable, once the competition intensifies. Therefore, in the medium term to the long span of historical time, the world may upgrade globalization for stable interests. The current globalization is a low-level one, which is a coarse movement in an anarchic world. It has energy, but has no order and system. That is to say, low-level globalization has not yet had a stable globality. According to the ancient Greeks, the chaos has not become a cosmos, an ordered whole. It can be said that the COVID-19 pandemic is not necessarily a full stop to the end of globalization. Perhaps it is an exclamation mark that suggests that there is still the question of global construction.

270   *Zhao Tingyang*

Any change of the existing order needs to be done at the conceptual level; otherwise it is only a superficial makeup. Therefore, the serious practical problems will lead to metaphysical problems. The novel coronavirus reminds us that if we want to correct the fragility of the metaphysical system of contemporary society, we may need to correct its metaphysical conceptual assumptions, and ways of thinking. Philosophy is not a pure idea, but a hidden virus. Philosopher Markus Gabriel believes that after the COVID-19 pandemic, mankind needs "a metaphysical pandemic."[3] Although this is an imaginative suggestion, we do need a metaphysical reflection as powerful as a pandemic so as to have the herd immunity of human thought. The realization of this requires that we find a breakthrough in the "dimension" of human thinking, that is, finding or creating an ideological space one dimension higher than the modern thinking space, so as to get rid of the limitations of the modern thinking space. If there is no breakthrough in the dimension of thought, the reflection on modern thought will be still confined to the existing space and runs in the hermeneutic cycle. Even if its interpretation angle is getting richer and deeper, it is not powerful enough to get out of the centripetal force of modern thought, because it is confined in an internal cycle, hence impossible to transcend the status quo.

Gabriel is right to criticize modern science for suppressing morality, but the humanistic morality he calls for still belongs to the internal concepts of modernity, such as equality and compassion. There is a difficult dilemma here: if modern science suppresses morality, it proves that the current moral concept, obviously weaker than modern science, is unable to define life, society, and rules. It can be found that the object that really needs to be reflected is nothing but "our" moral concept system. What we need more is a Wittgenstein "ruthless" reflection, reflecting on ethics from the outside, otherwise the result is nothing more than self-affirmation, that is, affirming the values we want to affirm in advance.

The modern mainstream thinking mode emphasizes and pursues universal inevitability, which symbolizes perfection and power. Although postmodernism critiques modern thought, it does not touch on the ontological structure of modernity. As long as a problem goes beyond discourse, and is imminent, there is still only a modern scheme, and no postmodern scheme. Modernity is too deep-rooted to collapse, because it has shaped the most popular myth of mankind. Human beings try to control their own destiny and establish universal necessity according to human values – the glory of universal necessity originally belongs to God or the universe, which is a metaphysical myth created by modern people for themselves. When postmodernism criticizes modernity, it especially criticizes the myth of science. In fact, modern myth is not science, but the humanistic concept of human beings. The myth of man assumes the perfect concept of man, which surely plagiarizes many qualities belonging to God, including that man should become the master of nature, the master who creates rules according to his own will, and everyone should have absolute freedom, so that the concept of "man" almost becomes the epitome of God. However, human mythology lacks the basis of ontology, and human beings have no ability to define universal inevitability with subjectivity, and have no ability to inevitably turn "probability" into "reality." Modern people do try to establish universal inevitability for the human world with the help of science, but this is a humanistic belief, not the intention of science itself. In fact, science always recognizes contingency and complexity, and always thinks about dynamic variables (from function to calculus to relativity and quantum mechanics). On the contrary, humanistic beliefs are imagining universal values, unchanging norms or sacred rights. What cannot be ignored is that this is not an epistemological belief, but a political belief. Leibniz has long proved that the ability to define universal inevitability requires the ability to "see" all possible worlds in logic, which is equivalent to the ability of infinity. Obviously, human beings do not have such ability.

No matter which values are selected as the basic principles of a society, if they are set to be "unconditional" or generally effective in any case, they will lack flexibility and elasticity, which will easily lead to paradoxes in the actual situation. Immutability is not a feature of any possible form of life. If the rules are dead, people are dead. If it is allowed to give a "mathematical" description, I would like to say that life forms have the property of "topology," and their essence can remain unchanged, similar to the continuity of topology, while their concrete performance is like the plasticity of topology, which is shaped according to specific circumstances and needs.

Although Georg Wilhelm Friedrich Hegel's proposition "what is realistic is reasonable" is easy to be misunderstood, the problem is that if an idea is not feasible in reality, it can only show that the idea is suspicious, but cannot prove that the reality should not exist. Hume believes that it is impossible to infer value from facts (inference from "to be" to "ought to be"), which is correct in most cases. However, it seems that it is more difficult to infer facts from values (inference from "ought to be" to "to be"). The universal inevitability sought by philosophy is difficult to witness in real life. It only exists in the mathematical world, because the mathematical world is defined and constructed by the mathematical system, not the mirror image of the real world. The existence in the mathematical system exists either by definition or by "the quality to be shaped." According to intuitionistic mathematics, existence is constructed, and the existence in mathematics is an internal fact of the mathematical system, so it can establish universal inevitability according to logic. In contrast, the problems and things to be explained by the humanistic concept have externalities, contingent on uncontrollable factors, practices and changes. The humanistic concept can only find a suitable foothold in the changing world. Just like substances that are evaporative, soluble or oxidized due to environmental influence, the concept used to explain life lacks stability. During the uneventful period, the humanistic concept is also calm, but in the troubled times, it becomes problematic itself.

Most humanistic concepts can be self-justified, so few humanistic concepts or "doctrines" (unless prohibited from expression) can be refuted in the debate. However, humanistic concepts are easily refuted by reality, so concepts are most afraid of concretization or contextualization. Once made concrete, they become problematic, and, once problematic, they are deconstructed by reality, especially such grand concepts as happiness, freedom, equality, win–win, people, community, and so on. Jacques Derrida made great efforts to deconstruct the grand concepts, authority, and center. In fact, those grand concepts have never existed perfectly in the unpredictable and contradictory practice.

Human beings lack infinite multi-dimensional intelligence that can match nature. Although human beings can understand the multi-dimensional world abstractly and despise the one-dimensional or linear way of thinking, the limitations of practical ability force people to do things only in one dimension, so the "sorting" problem required by practice is difficult for people – although it seems to be only equivalent to the arithmetic difficulty of the first grade of primary school. On the one hand, things are complex and dynamic, so life needs a variety of juxtaposed important and irreducible values to be explained. On the other hand, practice forces us to rank values, that is, to prioritize. As long as there is a sorting problem, it is difficult to maintain a balance between a variety of things or values needed in life. Losing the balance means that each thing or value loses its own stability, and the system of mutual support and mutual assurance. As long as there is a serious crisis, values and systems will fall into a dilemma. This is a problem that order or system has never been able to solve. This shows that not only the artificial social system is fragile, but also the thought or value system that directs behavior is also fragile, which is the deep crisis of civilization.

If the practical crisis is caused by a real "severe problem," then a "deeprooted problem" caused by the practical crisis becomes a metaphysical crisis. Novel coronavirus is a "severe problem" that causes some "deep problems." One of them is that the modern understanding of the concept of politics itself is a hidden suicidal virus, which destroys the concept of politics. Whether government, media or a new form of power, if a political force has the power to designate values, it is autocracy. Values can only be the collective choice naturally formed by people in long-term practice. Obviously, people have many groups, so there are many collective choices, hence differences and conflicts. Politics that is capable of protecting civilization is not a struggle, but a structural art that establishes a balance between the richness and complexity of the conflict of civilizations. If politics is just a struggle, it is nothing more than repeating and strengthening the conflicts that already exist in reality. Adding struggle to struggle is both redundant and doubly harmful. Struggle is instinct, not politics. Politics is the art of creating cooperation – what is the use of politics if it cannot create cooperation?

Therefore, the metaphysical question that needs to be reflected is not which values should be approved and supported – this is just a practical struggle, but whether the ideological system as a shared resource of mankind is reasonable and sufficient to deal with the possibilities encountered in life. In other words, what is the basis of the effectiveness and rationality of ideas? For what can man have the final say? For what can't man have the final say? For what things do we need to follow the ideal? For what things must we respect the facts? In the COVID-19 scenario, the question is even more specific. For what must we listen to science? For what must we listen to man? For what can we leave it for the virus to do?

Crisis: The Way of Survival and the Rules of the Game

A theory can justify itself in its own space, but it is likely to collapse when it is applied in practical cases. This happens because theory and reality stay in two spaces. The law of theoretical space is logic, while the law of real space is norms and rules. The two cannot be restored to each other, so reality does not follow theory. Although theory can partially "reflect" reality – the usual reflection theory is an inaccurate mirror metaphor, its way of construction is completely different. Only when reality is in a stable, calm, and certain state, the theoretical reflection of reality is partially certain. As long as reality enters a turbulent and "uncertain" state, theoretical concepts conflict, and interfere with each other, failing in function. Theory is not afraid of argument, only afraid of the crisis of reality. Since reality will not approach theory by itself, theory needs to approach reality.

If the extreme anxiety for the future is a major feature of contemporary thought, another relevant feature is the state of crisis. In fact, a large number of crises are caused by the extreme anxiety for the future. Almost all contemporary systems are in a state of over-operation, and crises form the critical condition of ideological dilemma. A typical situation is that crises often lead to ethical paradoxes. The most common ethical paradox is the dilemma of whomever to rescue first (such as the "trolley dilemma" implies). The novel coronavirus pandemic provides an example of the problem of treatment priority. Countries with sufficient medical capacity, of course, do not have this dilemma, and everyone can have access to treatment. However, in some countries, the lack of ventilators makes it difficult to give priority to treatment. Realistic conditions exclude the ideal choice, and delaying the choice is also a crime. Here, imagination is challenged. In fact, there are only the following five possible options in making the treatment priorities of the COVID-19 patients: One is to follow the principle of "first-come-first served," a principle that emphasizes equality. The second is to be determined by the patients' conditions, a medical standard. The third is affordability, a commercial standard. The fourth is to give priority to women and children, an ethical standard. The last one is to give priority to young people, both men and women, also an ethical standard. All the standards, except the third, have their own reasons for rational argument. If we consider the reasons of epistemology, then the second is the most reasonable. If ethical reasons are considered, then the fourth and the fifth are more reasonable. Assuming that some places give priority to the treatment of young people who have a better chance of survival (purely hypothetical), this choice will be questioned, but this choice is already one of the relatively optimal choices, which is juxtaposed with the second, and relatively optimal. No choice is strictly optimal, and they all have flaws. Perhaps the second has the lowest "sense of guilt." Although people all hope for optimal ethics that can save everyone, the optimal idea beyond practical ability only exists in books. Kant has long found that "should" cannot exceed "can."

This kind of analysis must not be misunderstood as opposing the optimal ethical assumption. The key is that the optimal ethical assumption is not necessarily an optimal theory. An optimal theory must have sufficient theoretical ability to cover all possible worlds. On the one hand, it takes into account the "best possible world" – otherwise, there is no ideal scale to check the defective reality. On the other hand, it takes into account the "worst possible world" – otherwise, there is no ability to prevent or cope with serious crises. If ethics or political philosophy does not consider the "worst possible world," but assumes superior social conditions, it is a fragile theory that lacks sufficient adaptability to withstand the crisis. The mandatory quarantine policies adopted by many countries to contain Novel Coronavirus are highly controversial. In fact, compared with war, floods, famine or social riots, isolation is not the worst.

It was owing to the Italian philosopher Giorgio Agamben that "isolation" became the focus of philosophical debate. Agamben believes that isolation under the pretext of "unwarranted emergency" is an abuse of power, and the temptation of the abuse of power is likely to lead to the "state of exception" wherein the authority could deprive people of their freedom.[4] He believes that power tends to be autocratic in nature, which is not obvious because it sees no opportunities or excuses in normal times. This is an important issue. But whether the purpose of isolation is really political, or whether there is no more critical consideration than politics, this is also a question. The various needs of human life have a practical order according to their severity. Surely, survival usually ranks the first. But Agamben seems to question what society it is that only believes in survival but nothing else. This is a deeper question. If living is being merely alive, it is no better than death. However, these questions seem to escalate the context of COVID-19 without restraint, leading to the dislocation of the question. Has the novel coronavirus isolation reached the extreme situation for people to choose between "death or freedom" or "dragging on a wretched existence or dying a noble death?" Agamben's response to the isolation policy might be, as Nietzsche would say, too humanistic. Defending freedom by opposing isolation suggests that its negative opinion seems to support the abuse of power – but this is a trap. The real opposite of Agamben's view is that people can only admit that life has unavoidable paradoxes. The freedom, equality, and material life enjoyed by mankind are the achievements of civilization, which are the result of tens of thousands of years of arduous experience. These achievements of civilization are not to be enjoyed once and for all. To defend civilization means that we have to suffer the hardships sometimes. Just as economics can never eliminate the concept of "cost," any achievement of civilization can never exclude the concept of "payment," because "payment" is an existential concept and a condition for existence.

The Outbreak of the COVID-19 Virus   275

There is a related question that needs to be clarified: the current isolation differs from the long-gone isolation. It is an ancient experience to implement quarantine law for infectious diseases. During the Qin and Han Dynasties, there was a local isolation method, which was called "pandemic place," that is, leprosy isolation place. Ancient Rome also invented leprosy isolation during the reign of Justinian the Great (527–565). The modern concept of "quarantine" comes from the isolation of the Black Death in the middle ages, which means a 40-day isolation. Medical quarantine is different from "social isolation." Social isolation is usually political and discriminatory, such as the historical segregation of the Jews in Europe or the segregation of blacks in the United States. Mixing quarantine and social isolation will mislead the judgment of the nature of the problem. The isolation policy during the COVID-19 pandemic is obviously preventive quarantine, not a social one. Although the possibility of turning the preventive by the authority into a social isolation cannot be completely ruled out, the preventive isolation is not political in nature. Assuming that Agamben still insists on the political interpretation of the quarantine policy by calling it the "state of exception" for the authority to use special power, then we would ask a question as a detective could when solving a crime: who have benefited from the medical quarantine? It is not difficult to see that it is the people that have benefited from the quarantine in times of crisis. If it is for all the people, then, it is not creating a state of exception. Quarantine is one of the responses to the emergency. In addition to the safety of all the people, quarantine also effectively protects the medical system from collapsing. If the medical system collapses, there will be no medical security for the people. If social order, the medical system, and the economy all break down, individual rights will be embodied by a bundle of useless bills that have nominal value, but use value. In that scenario, individual rights will become unprotected bare rights, and bare rights will certainly not be able to save the "bare life" that Agamben cares about.[5] That will be really a political time.

The political question is: what is it that protects individual rights? The answer is certainly the Constitution and the legal system. However, nothing can take effect before it is put into practice. Similarly, rights must also be implemented into practice to be meaningful and real. Practice involves almost all aspects in life, exceeding the analytical ability of any academic discipline. It follows that practice can only be understood in a super-disciplinary concept. Practice is equivalent to Wittgenstein's language game concept. According to Wittgenstein, a game needs mutual recognition to take effect. At the same time, game participants also recognize the rules of the game, which has tacitly accepted a meta-rule of the game, that is, no game participant has the privilege to break the rules, or no participant has the privilege to be exceptional in the sense that they cannot cheat, disobey the rule or be treated differently. The concept of game helps to explain that if society is a game, individual rights are not a private right, that is, individual rights are equal rights determined by the game, not a privilege defined by private will. Thus, in the game, there are only legal (equivalent to rule-based) personal behaviors, but no legal private behaviors. Private behavior by one's own will is only valid in private space and time. If private behavior invades the public space and time of the game or the private space and time of others, it is no longer legal. This is exactly the basis of the law. For example, it is a private act if a person shoots him dead in his own room, but if he kills himself by detonating a bomb in a public space and injures others, it is no longer a private act, but a personal act that breaks the rules of the "game," that is, an illegal act. Similarly, in the "game" of the quarantine, if a person insists that he has the right to do whatever he wants, which might harm others, he mistakenly understands human rights as personal privileges. Just as nobody has his own effective private language (Wittgenstein theorem), nobody has his own private politics. Politics, like language, is a public and effective system. If individual rights are defined as absolute and unconditional, there is a hidden danger of privatization. It will not only fall into self-contradiction in theory, but also fall into self-contradiction in reality when encountering the same absolute and unconditional rights of others.

But a contemporary ideological landscape is that ideas are no longer afraid of logical contradictions or science, but gains power by virtue of politics. Foucault's archaeology of knowledge found that this is the phenomenon with us since humanity. The interactive relationship between knowledge and power has produced a "knowledge-power" structure. As a result, in the field of social knowledge, the basis of knowledge is no longer the reason of knowledge itself, but that of a political reason. This can explain how ideas become ideologies. When ideas try to dominate reality as a political identity, they become ideologies, or dominant "discourse." Ideology is one of the foundations of the contemporary "post-truth era," and the other is the technical platform where anyone can speak. The combination of the two produces the effect as the "Cultural Revolution" did. It can be said that the post-truth era is the contemporary "Cultural Revolution" on a global scale. In social sciences, theoretical discussion, rational analysis, and dialogue have been marginalized or even disappeared, almost completely giving way to the grand criticism guided by politics. It is not that the truth has disappeared, but that our "eyes" and "ears" have no ability to move out of the post-truth discourse. The consciousness barrier formed by post-truth discourse in turn strengthens ideology. In the post-truth era, not all discourse is ideological, but every popular discourse is ideological. Ideology is the condition of the discourse to be present, otherwise there is no opportunity to be present on the discourse platform. The narrative assistance of post-truth discourse may turn the sudden temporary crisis into a long-term one. The virus is only a natural crisis, but the narrative about the virus may become a collateral disaster.

The Origin of Suffering

The pandemic of novel coronavirus has awakened the philosophical question of "suffering," a long-forgotten question in deed, although suffering is forever there. The myth of man and the great achievements of modernization have contributed to the arrogance of contemporary ideas. Although radical thinkers have been criticizing modernity, they still have no ability to change the dominant "episteme" of contemporary times. Contemporary societies tend to replace the concept of "fate" with the concept of "fortune," anxious about "failure" but unwilling to face the "tragic" discovered by ancient Greece. The progressive theory that highlights "positivity" and refuses to recognize "negativity" leads to ideological imbalance. In fact, balance or symmetry is not only a mathematical phenomenon, but also an existential condition for survival. Contemporary thinking has invented an unbalanced logic, focusing only on the stories of success and happiness, fantasizing that benefits can be unconditionally provided, rights can be unconditionally enjoyed, nature can be indefinitely exploited, so on and so forth. This fantasy is based on an ethically idealized requirement of "should be": the cost or pay should be infinitely small and the benefit should be infinitely handsome. This challenges the logic we have learned from Aristotle, Frege, and Russell, as well as from physics, such as the conservation of energy or the second theorem of thermodynamics.

Following Foucault's method of knowledge archaeology, we might find that the target philosophical topics, though various as shown in the acceptance tendency of the media, the education system, and the large-flow network platforms, focus on a common "knowledge," that is, "wellbeing." Maximizing everyone's wellbeing and welfare is the common ground of the discussion in this regard. Wellbeing theory tends to claim that everyone's subjectivity has absolute "sovereignty," so as to maximize personal freedom and legalize personal preferences. Individuals can independently and legally define their identity, gender, value and lifestyle, and even in the context of extremism, "personal" may be equivalent to "private," and to being right. I humbly admit that in my *On Possible Life* (1994) is also a discussion of wellbeing.

Wellbeing is a human ideal, but it is far from enough to explain life, because it cannot explain the possible suffering, and even covers up the question of suffering. If we use the simplistic coordinate system to explain life, wellbeing is only one coordinate, and at least suffering is needed as another coordinate to determine the position of the elements in life. In the binary coordinate system of wellbeing and suffering, wellbeing is a rare luck, an exceptional state of life. Contemporary wellbeing theory does not talk about wellbeing as the supreme good; rather, it focuses on happiness, a substitute for wellbeing. The modern system can provide material or physical happiness, but it cannot produce wellbeing as the supreme good, and it lacks the ability to resist suffering. The reason why the question of suffering cannot be omitted or avoided is that suffering falls outside the ability of subjectivity and has absolute externality like the thing itself, so suffering is an absolute metaphysical question.

The COVID-19 pandemic reminds us of the question of suffering and brings our thought back to the adversity at the beginning of life. If the initial state of human beings is wellbeing without suffering, it is impossible to produce civilization. The Eden is a metaphor for "non-civilization," and man's exile is an ontological event, which means that suffering is the founding condition of civilization. The question of suffering not only explains the origin of

278   *Zhao Tingyang*

human civilization, but is also likely to be a permanent question of mankind, because only suffering can maintain the vitality or "aggressive force" of the origin. It can be noted that almost all religions are based on the question of suffering, which also proves the commonality of suffering. If you avoid the question of suffering, you can hardly understand life. Religion gives theological answers to suffering, but the answers given by various religions are inconsistent. And none of the answers can be proved, which means that the real answer is no answer. Therefore, in terms of thought, suffering can only be a metaphysical question, always open. No answer to suffering is the answer, which keeps the vitality of thought.

The metaphysical significance of the question of suffering lies in bringing thought back to the original state of existence. The "origin" and "persistence" of suffering are integrated, which shows that the origin has never disappeared. Once the origin is always present, suffering runs through the whole historical time. Anything that runs through time and is always present is a fundamental question. In this sense, the question of suffering is infinitely close to the initial conditions of civilization, and there must be a core secret about existence or origin. Neither philosophy nor religion can demystify it. They only constantly remind us of the existence of the secret. Only in the context of un-knowability can we understand what we can know. It can be said that the reflection on the question of suffering means the reconfiguration or "restart" of philosophy and thinking. I believe that the question of suffering may be a better choice for the "metaphysical pandemic." In the words of the contemporary Sci-fi writer Liu Cixin: if you lose the ability to enjoy, you lose a lot, but if you lose the ability to overcome suffering, you lose everything.

Notes

1 See Thomas Friedman's "Our New Historical Divide: B. C. and A. C.: the World Before Corona and the World After." *The New York Times* March 17, 2020. https://www.nytimes.com/2020/03/17/opinion/coronavirus-trends.html.
2 https://bcf.princeton.edu/wp-content/uploads/2020/11/Combined-Slides-4.pdf.
3 Markus Gabriel's "Signs of Life: We Need a Metaphysical Pandemic." https://www.uni-bonn.de/en/news/we-need-a-metaphysical-pandemic.
4 See Giorgio Agamben's "State of Exception." Trans. Kevil Attell. https://press.uchicago.edu/ucp/books/book/chicago/S/bo3534874.html.
5 See "Bare Life." Oxford Reference. https://www.oxfordreference.com/view/10.1093/oi/authority.20110803095446660.

Index

Abe boom 195
Abe, Shinzo 193, 231
accurate regulation 52
action capability, increasing 254–256
action community 257–258
Africa: China–Africa economic and trade cooperation 211–214; competition among world powers in 220–222; demographic dividend of 215–216; digital economy in 217; economic diversification policies 216; economic growth in 207–211; economic policy environment of 216; economy under pandemic 207–217; enhancing cooperation 222–225; Kigali consensus 222; long-term trend of economy of 214–217; pandemic security in 217–220; regional integration 216–217
Africa Economic Outlook 2020 214
African Airlines 208–209
African Center for Disease Control and Prevention 207
African Development Bank 214
African Land Forces Summit 221
African Union (AU) 214, 217
Agamben, Giorgio 274
Agenda 2063: The Africa We Want 217
Alibaba 34, 38, 42
Allison, Graham 189
America First, concept 184
Anglo American Platinum 210
Antelope Platinum Holdings 210
anti-globalization ix, 23, 74–75, 79, 85–86, 88, 105, 114–117, 150–151
Appellate Body, WTO 183
Apple Company 113–114
Argentina 136
artificial intelligence (AI) 35

Asahi News Agency 195
Asahi Shimbun 199
ASEAN 149
Asia-Pacific economic integration 95–96
Asia-Pacific Free Trade Area 95–96
asset-backed commercial paper (ABCP) 58–59
Asset-backed Commercial Paper Money Market Mutual Fund Liquidity Facility 69
Association of South East Nations (ASEAN) 77
Australia 25
Aylward, Bruce 253

balance of financial terror 71
balanced globalization 79
Baucus, Max 157
Bear Stearns 137
Belt and Road Initiative 84, 154, 223
Berkley, Seth 180
Bernanke, Ben Shalom 69
Biden, Joe 143, 158
Bilateral Investment Treaty (BIT) 235
Bill and Melinda Gates Foundation 257
bipolar era 144
blue-collar voters 75
Bull, Hedley 237
Borrell, Josep 169, 172
bound globalization 234
Brandt, Willy 75, 243
Braudel, Fernard 264–265
Brazil 136
breakthroughs, China-Japan-ROK cooperation 91–94
Bremmer, Ian 260
Brent crude oil 131
BRICs 245, 248, 256
Bridgewater Associates LP 66, 133, 137

280 *Index*

Britain 29, 134, 143, 238, 245, 252
Bush, George W. 252
business environment, creating 98–99
business-return 151
business, supporting 47–48
ByteDance 34

Camp Funston, Kansas 21
Campbell, Kurt 184, 259
Canada 25, 106, 220
Carlsson, Ingvar 243
Center for New American Security
    (CNA) 186
Centers for Disease Control and
    Prevention (CDC) 188
Central Bank of Brazil 68
Central Bank of Denmark 68
Central Bank of Korea 68
Central Bank of Mexico 68
Central Bank of Norway 68
Central Bank of Sweden 68
Central Economic Work Conference 35
Central Government Document 48
China 106; China-Africa economic and
    trade cooperation 211–214; China-
    Africa relations 207–226; China-EU
    Relations 170–173; digital age
    economic growth 31–35; economic
    nationalism and 125–127; global
    supply chain 103–114; globalization
    and 84–86; under impact of
    COVID-19 120–129; impact of
    financial turmoil on 138–140;
    industrial chain of 121–123;
    international political competition
    and 151–153; long-term favorable
    conditions 35–41; and new type of
    Cold War 127–128; responses to
    de-globalization 26–29; rethinking
    China-world relationship 153–155;
    seeking wisdom in traditional culture
    128–129; trend of economy
    of 123–124
China Association of Hotels 39
China Association of Scenic Spots 39
China debt-trap 213
China National Offshore Oil Corp 42
China-Africa relations *see* Africa
China-centered global supply chain
    system 106–107
China-EU Relations 170–173;
    community formation 175–176;
    investment 170–171; political

cooperation 171–172; public opinion
    172–173; trade 170–171
China-Japan cooperation: joint
    prevention and control achievements
    200–203; promoting regional
    governance 203–205; trilateral
    cooperation 198–200
China–Africa Research Initiative 213
China–EU Free Trade Agreement 89
China–EU integrated market 94–95
China–EU Investment Agreement 89
China–France Joint Statement on Third-
    Party Market Cooperation 222
China–Japan cooperation 197–198
China–Japan–ROK Free Trade
    Agreement 89, 93
China–Japan–South Korea Infectious
    Diseases Forum 200
Chinese currency (CNY) 56, 138–140
Chinese discourse system 128–129
Chinese Spring Festival 105, 107–108
*Civil Code of the People's Republic of
    China* 99
Cixin, Liu 278
Clinton, Hillary 181
Coalition for Pandemic Preparedness
    Innovations (CEPI) 257
Coase, Ronald 37–38
Cold War 243, 254
Cold War, post-pandemic era 127–128
Collateralized Debt Obligations (CDO)
    58–59, 136
commercial paper financing facility
    (CPFF) 68–70
Commercial Paper Fund Facility 69
Communist Party of China (CPC) 1
community, forming 175–176
competition, Sino-US relations 11–17
competitive cooperation 13–14
Comprehensive and Progressive Trans-
    Pacific Partnership Agreement
    (CPTPP) 90, 235
Conde, Alpha 218
consumption, boosting 126–127
cooperation, political 171–172
cooperative rivalry 265–266
coordination 53–54
corporate bond market, bubble of 135
counter-current vortex 149–151
COVID-19: avoiding free fall in Sino-US
    relations 156–164; changes in past
    century 142–155; China-Africa
    relations 207–226; China-EU

Index   281

Relations and 170–173; current world economy and 115–119; de-globalization and 19–30; digital economy and 31–43; economic globalization 88–102; Federal Reserve and 58–72; financial turmoil caused by 130–141; global governance reform 242–262; globalization and 73–87; impact on global supply chain 103–114; international community 227–241; long-term recession and 44–57; outbreak of 263–278; Sino-Europe relations 165–177; Sino-Japan relations 191–206; Sino-US relations in context of 1–18; US internal affairs/diplomacy 178–190; US macroeconomic response to 68–70; world under impact of 120–129
COVID-19 Solidarity Response Fund 257
CPC Central Committee 50–51
Cuomo, Andrew 182
cyber diplomacy 172

Dario, Ray 66
de-globalization 19–20, 161; Chinese responses to 26–29; populism and 20–22; in post-COVID-19 age 22–26
de-Sinicization 7, 16, 118; guarding against 55–57
debt crisis 54–55
Decision of the CPC Central Committee on Some Major Issues of Comprehensively Promoting the Rule of Law 99
decoupling 15
Defense Production Act 187, 231, 236
Delors, Jacques 176
Democratic Republic of the Congo (DRC) 212, 217–218
Derrida, Jacques 272
development aid 221
digital economy: Chinese development of 35–41; economic growth in 31–35; enhancing 38–41; market as leading role in 41–43
digital silk road 111–112
digital technology 32–35
dilemma, countries caught in 120–121
DingTalk 38
Discount Window 69
disputes, Sino-US relations 5–8
Doha Round 76

dollar shortage 56
domestic value added (DVA) 233
Doshi, Rush 184–185
Dow Jones 131
downsizing 54–55

Early Harvest Plan 94
East Asia 145, 193
East China Sea 8, 148
Economic Commission for Africa (ECA) 208
Economic Community of West African States (ECOWAS) 213
economic globalization: challenges for 88–91; changing existing pattern of 90–91; establishing new high-level open economic system 96–102; responding to pandemic impact on 91–96
economic nationalism 125–127
Economic Partnership Agreement (EPA) 90
economic/financial security, disputes 7–8
employment, promoting 48–49
enterprises 41–43
Esper, James 1
Esper, Mark 180
Euro-centrism 169, 204
Europe, effect of pandemic on: China–EU Relations 170–173; community formation 175–176; economy 165–166; EU perspective 168–169; government 167–168; political parties 167–168; society 166–167; world system 73–75
European Stability Mechanism (ESM) 168
European Union (EU) 24, 90, 165, 220, 247; China–EU Relations 170–173; community formation with China 175–176; global governance 174–175; impact of pandemic on general trend 165–169; mainstream concept of future world 173–175; world system and 173–174
Exchange Traded Funds (ETF) 68, 131–134

Fannie and Freddie bonds 71–72
Farrell, Henry 233–234
Federal Reserve 7, 46; avoiding new financial crsis 64–68; economic recovery 70–72; quantitative easing

282   *Index*

(QE) 61–68; responding to subprime mortgage crisis 61–63; subprime mortgage crisis 58–63; US macroeconomic response to COVID-19 68–70

Federal Reserve Bank of New York 70

Fighting COVID-19: China in Action 4

financial barrier, dismantling 70–72

financial field, de-Sinicization in 56–57

financial turmoil: causes of 131–134; global 130–131; lingering nature of 134–136; policy suggestions and 140–141; potential impact of 138–140; similarities/differences 136–138

First World War 1, 11, 21, 142–144

fiscal policies 50–55

Food and Agriculture Organization (FAO) 82

Foreign Affairs 185

Foreign Policy 23, 181

foreign value added (FVA) 233

France 11, 25, 105, 106, 134, 220, 229, 245

free fall, avoiding 156–157; diplomats becoming politicians 157–159; hope on side of China 163–164; tracking deteriorating political atmosphere 159–162

free rides 239

Free Trade Agreements (FTA) 235

Friedman, Thomas 23–24, 191, 263

future, anxiety for 273–276

G20 82–83, 146, 175, 189, 193, 213, 230–231, 245, 248, 255

G20 Special Summit 255

G7 82–83

Gabriel, Markus 270

GAVI Alliance 180

Gelfand, Michel 205

General Agreement on Tariffs and Trade (GATT) 73–74

geostrategic patterns 148–149

Germany 11, 25, 105, 106, 134, 165–167, 220, 229, 245

Ghebreyeus, Tedros Adhanom 230

glass doors 47

global governance reform 242; absence of leadership 249–251; dilemma under COVID-19 245–251; governance mechanism 243–245; international mechanisms 248–249; major countries playing a role in 245; partial failure 246–248; from perspective of community with shared future 251–260

global governance, basic ideas on 174–175

Global Health Security (GHS) 180

global problems, dealing with 243

global production 231–236

global production chain: and national dilemma 234–236; upgrading 232–234

global recession 89–90

global supply chain 112; challenges to 106–107; distribution of 103–105; improving security 107–112; risk of pandemic impact on 105–106; summation of impact on 112–114

Global Times, The 158–159

globalization: characteristics of challenging 88–89; China and 84–86; counter-current vortex and 149–151; development of 73–75; direction of 191–192; global supply chain and 103–105; impact of pandemic on 78–81; international economic governance under adjustment 82–83; reflections on 75–78; thoughts on 115–119

Globalization 3.0 104

globalization of competition 265–266

globalization, challenging 9–10

Goldman Sachs 113

governance capability 229

government 41–43

Great Depression 138, 143, 144–146

Great Lockdown 55

great-power strategic rivalry 193–194

Greenspan, Alan 52

Guangdong–Hong Kong–Macao Great Bay 192–193

Guterres, António Manuel de Oliveira 246

H1N1 influenza 188

H7N9 virus 189

Harris Poll 4

Haskell County, Texas 21

Hawley, Josh 162

He, Liu 158

Hegel, Georg Wilhelm Friedrich 271

high politics 204

high threshold 47

high-level open economic system, establishing 96–102

historical divide 263–267

Index 283

hollowing out 74–75
Hong Kong Monetary Authority 61
Huawei 34, 38
human nature 228

Ilandou, Evaristus 208
India 25
Indian Pacific strategy, US 187–188
industrial Internet 36
industrial transfer 73–75
Influenza Pandemic 21
institutional governance,
    depending on 244
instrumental rationality 193, 205
interaction of material interests 238
Intermediate-Range Nuclear Forces
    Treaty 183
international community: constrained
    global production 231–236;
    governance capability 229; human
    nature 228; national dilemma
    234–236; organization effectiveness
    229–231; during pandemic 227–231;
    possible trends after pandemic
    236–240; rationality 228; upgrading
    global production chain 232–234
International Customs Organization 112
International Health Regulations 257
International Labor Organization 244
International Maritime Organization
    112, 244
International Monetary Fund (IMF) 10,
    19, 55, 82, 134, 142, 195, 211,
    238, 244–245
international organizations: effectiveness
    of 229–231; partial failure of 245–251
international political
    competition 151–153
international relations, regional
    development of 192–193
International Telecommunication
    Union 244
Internet plus 36
investment 170–171
Investment Trend Monitor 209
Iran Nuclear Deal 183
isolationism 116
Italy 25, 105, 229

Jack Ma Foundation 41
Japan 105, 106, 108, 134, 143, 229, 258
Japan Trade Promotion Organization
    (JETRO) 196

Japan, impact of pandemic on: China-
    Japan relations 195–197; political
    situations 194–195; politics 194–195;
    society 194–195; understanding/
    building Sino-Japanese relations 197
Jiechi, Yang 159–160
Jinping, Xi 3, 13–14, 156, 160, 175, 250,
    255, 259
Johannesburg Summit of the Forum on
    China–Africa Cooperation 213
Johnson, Boris 238
Justinian the Great 275

Kant, Immanuel 274
Kerry, John 1
Kissinger, Henry 253
Kiyosaki, Seguchi 196
knowledge-power structure 276
Kraft, Mark 1
Kudlow, Larry 80, 187

large-scale, short-term capital
    outflow 136
Latin America 144
leadership, absence of 249–251
Lehman Brothers 137
Lenovo 34
leverage ratio 60
leverage ratio commonly 59–60
Leyen, Ursula von der 168
Liberal Democratic Party (LDP) 194–195
limited globalization 79
Limits of Growth, The (Brandt) 75
lockdown 120–121
London Bullion Market Association
    (LBMA) 131
long tail effect 33

Macron, Emmanuel 183, 213, 221
Malaysia 136
managed globalization 79
maritime/strategic security, disputes 8
market 41–43
market failure 43
market opening, expanding 97–98
market, rescuing 61–63
massive online open classes (MOOCs) 32
maximum employment, promoting *see*
    employment, promoting
McCaul, Michael 161
Mearsheimer, John Joseph 183
medium-sized business 47–48
Meituan 39

284 *Index*

Merkel, Angela 221, 250
metaphysical system 267–273
Mexico 106
micro-business 47–48
Middle East 149
Middle East Respiratory Syndrome
(MERS) 199, 202, 230, 256
Mnuchin, Stephen 69, 158
modern monetary theory (MMT) 54
modern system 267–268, 277
Monetary Authority of Singapore 68
monetary policies 50–55
money market mutual fund liquidity
facility (MMLF) 68–70
Mortgage-Backed Securities (MBS)
58–59, 136
Multilateralism Alliance 11
multinational corporations 104
Munich Security Conference (MSC) 1–3
mutual tolerance of values 239

Nagoya Earthquake 80
National Association of *Nigeria Travel
Agencies* (NANTA) 211
National Bureau of Statistics 26
national conservatism 79
*National Defense Authorization Act for
Fiscal Year 2019* 5
National Emergency 238
National Institutes of Health (NIH) 178
National Security Law 235
nationalism, economic 125–127
NATO 148, 183
Navarro, Peter 184, 187
Netherlands 106
Neue Zürcher Zeitung 254
New Cold War 239–240
new infrastructure 40–41, 48
New York Times 23–24, 186, 249–250
New Yorker, The 156
Newman, Abraham 233–234
Nigerian Investment Promotion
Commission 211
19th Politburo of the CPC Central
Committee 35
Nissan Motor Company 108
Nomura Research Institute 195
North America 105
North American Free Trade Agreement
(NAFTA) 76
North American Free Trade Area 106
Northern Rock 61

novel coronavirus 22, 157–158, 160–161,
178, 181, 191, 228, 250, 266–268,
270, 272
Novel Coronavirus Assistance, Relief
and Economic Security Act 181
Novel Coronavirus Pneumonia 22

Obama, Barack 148, 188, 252
Ofori-Atta, Kenneth Nana Yaw 213
old infrastructure 48
One China, policy 4
*Opinions on Building a More Perfect
Market-oriented Allocation System
and Mechanism of Factors* 141
Organization for Economic Cooperation
and Development (OECD) 104
Our Global Neighborhood 243
outbreak, COVID-19: anxiety for future
273–276; metaphysical system
267–273; new historical divide
263–267; origin of suffering 276–278
overcapacity materials 49
overnight index swap interest rate
(OIS) 66

pandemic *see* COVID-19
Paris Agreement 183
past century, changes in: comparing
pandemic to world war 142–144;
counter-current vortex 149–151;
geostrategic patterns 148–149;
international political competition
151–153; nearing Great Depression
144–146; rethinking China-world
relationship 153–155; Sino-US
confrontations 146–148
Paulson, Henry M., Jr. 71
Pearl River Delta 110
Pelosi, Nancy 1
personal hygiene protection
equipment (PPE) 9
personal protective equipment (PPE) 27
PetroChina 42
Pew Research Center 4
Phase-one Sino-US Trade Deal 6
policy community 257–258
political systems and values, disputes 6
politicians, diplomats becoming 157–159
Pompeo, Mike 1, 159, 186, 220
populism 20–22, 116
post-COVID-19 era: de-globalization in
22–26; digital economy 31–43

post-liberalism 80
postmodern age 149
Powell, Jerome H. 46, 179
President's Emergency Plan for AIDS
    Relief (PEPFAR) 252
Primary Market Corporate Credit
    Facility (PMCCF) 68
printed circuit boards (PCB) 37
problem chain *see* historical divide
Procedure for Making Foreign
    Investments in Companies of
    Strategic Importance for National
    Defense and State Security 235
protection plans 46
public construction projects 49–50
public health emergency of international
    concern (PHEIC) 246
public opinion, channeling 172–173
public opinion, disputes 6–7
Purchasing Managers' Index
    (PMI) 26, 121

quantitative easing (QE) 61–68

R & D 42, 201
Ramaphosa, Cyril 213
rationality 228
Reagan Doctrine 5
Reagan, Ronald 5
real economy 36
real-time supply chain 79
recession 44–45; economic situation
    under pandemic 45–47; fiscal policies
    50–55; guarding against de-
    Sinicization 55–57; monetary policies
    50–55; policy orientations 47–50
reform, deepening 99–102
Regional Comprehensive Economic
    Partnership (RCEP) 77, 89, 93, 95–96,
    202, 235
Report of Investment Announcements for
    Q1, 2020 211
rescue measures, economic
    nationalism 125–127
Reserve Bank of Australia 68
Reserve Bank of New Zealand 68
response measures for parts supply
    chain 196
risk aversion, policy 238
risk off 57
Rosen, Rae 179
Ross, Wilbur 249
rump, Donald 148

Russell, Walter 185
Russia 15, 136, 143, 220, 245
rust zone 74–75

safe haven currency 57
Schiller, Robert 263
Second World War 3, 23, 73–75, 142–144,
    174, 244, 252, 264
Secondary Market Corporate Credit
    Facility (SMCCF) 68
service industry, focusing on 97–98
severe acute respiratory syndrome
    (SARS) 252
shared future, community for: adopting
    policies 257–258; community
    awareness 252–254; empowering
    WHO 256–257; forming 251–252;
    forming community of responsibility
    258–260; reforming existing
    international system 254–256;
    updating concepts 252–254
Shengyibang 37
Shincheonji 237
Sibanye Stillwater Ltd. 210
Singapore 258
Sino-Europe relations: impact of
    pandemic 165–169; US internal
    affairs/diplomacy 178–190
Sino-Japan relations: COVID-19 as
    turning point 191–194; exploring
    multilateral path of 197–205; impact
    of pandemic on 194–197
Sino-US relations: avoiding free fall of
    156–164; challenging globalization
    9–10; competition 11–17; de-
    Sinicization 55–57; fighting pandemic
    3–4; foreshadowing decline of 1–2;
    four great disputes 5–8; future
    direction of 12–17; post-Cold War
    evolution of 1–2; public opinion and
    4–5; reverse trajectory 2–3; strength
    gap 10; third parties 10–11
Sino-US Relations: COVID-19
    and 185–189
Sinopec 42
six guarantees 140
small business 47–48
smart bike 40
Social Assistance and Economic Support
    Plan 215
social distancing 167
social isolation 275
South Africa 136, 209–215, 218, 221, 224

286 *Index*

South African Automobile Manufacturers Association 210
South African Reserve Bank 211
South China Sea 8, 148–149, 157, 183
South Korea 105, 106, 108, 148, 198–205, 229, 237–238, 258
sovereign debt 8, 148–149, 157, 183
Spain 25, 229
Spanish Influenza 21
Special Loan for the Development of African Small and Medium-sized Enterprises 223
Special Purpose Vehicles (SPVs) 68
Spring Festival of 2020 26
State-owned Assets Supervision and Administration Commission (SASAC) 101
Stefanik, Elise 162
stimulus plans 46
stock market bubble 64–68
stocks 61, 63, 65–66, 69, 130–135
Strategic Approach, policy 6
subprime mortgage crisis 58–63, 120, 137–138
suffering, origin of 276–278
Supply Chain Counter-terrorism Partnership Plan 111
Supply Chain Natural Disaster Response Plan 111
supply chain relationship 107
survival 273–276
Sustainable Development Goals (SDG) 174
Sweden 229
synthetic reasoning 60

Taipei Act of 2019 4
Taiwan Region 187, 231, 235
Taleb, Nassim 267–268
Tencent 38, 42
Term Asset-backed Securities Loan Facility (TALF) 68
Term Auction Facility 69
third party 10–11
Third Plenary Session 44
33rd African Union Summit 219–220
Tiankai, Cui 260
tiegongji 48–49
TIME 250
TNCs 236
Tokyo Olympic Games 195
Towards a Comprehensive Strategy with Africa 221

trade 170–171
trade war 1, 6, 84, 112–113, 128, 139, 144–145, 152, 183, 185, 187
Tradeshift 105
traditional culture, seeking wisdom from 128–129
Trans-Pacific Partnership Agreement (TPP) 183
Trans-Pacific Partnership Relationship Agreement (TPP) 76
tribalism 79
trigger factors 131
Trump Boom 178–181
Trump phenomenon, emergence of 150
Trump, Donald 22, 76–77, 121, 143, 160–161, 230, 238–239
trust deficit 196
Tsinghua University Strategy and Security Research Center 10
Turkey 136

UNESCO 183, 244
United Nations (UN) 39, 82–83, 218, 252, 255; Climate Change Conference 248; Conference on Trade and Development 233, 235; Development Programme (UNDP) 82; Industrial Development Organization (UNIDO) 82
United States 21, 52, 53, 106, 108, 229, 245; under impact of pandemic 178–182; relationship between US and world 182–185; Sino-US Relations 185–189
United States Strategic Approach to the People's Republic of China 5
Universal Postal Union 112, 183
US Federal Reserve 52
US–Mexico–Canada Agreement (USMCA) 235

Versailles–Washington System 142
Vietnam War 3
virus moment *see* historical divide
Voice of America 250
Voice of Germany 184
Volcker Rule 66
VooV Meeting 39
Vučić, Aleksandar 247

Wall Street Journal, The 4, 160, 186, 249–250, 263
Walt, Stephen 249

Washington Post 250
Wassenaar Agreement 194
wellbeing 277
Wellcome Trust Foundation 257
West Texas Intermediate (WTI) 115, 131
Western Pacific 15
Westphalia System 142
Wittgenstein, stocks 275
Wolf, Martin 71
World Bank 19, 82, 244, 247, 256, 259
World Development Report 2019 50
World Economic Forum 193
World Economic Outlook 55, 134
world economy 123–124; thoughts
 on 115–119
World Food and Agriculture
 Organization 244
World Health Organization (WHO) 3,
 22, 105, 142, 159, 171, 207, 229–230,
 244, 256–257
World Intellectual Property
 Organization 10, 244
World Meteorological
 Organization 244

World Trade Organization (WTO) 19, 74,
 82, 128, 142, 170, 192, 244
World Travel and Tourism Council
 (WTTC) 208
world war, comparing pandemic
 to 142–144
WTO World Trade Statistic Review 89
Wuhan Pandemic Prevention and
 Control Headquarters 237
www.zbj.com 36

Xiaomi 34
Xijin, Hu 159

Yalta System 142
Yangtze River Delta 110
Yi, Wang 219
YouGov 159
Yunnan 50

zero inventory 79
zero-sum competition 15–16
zero-sum game 112
Zhejiang 50

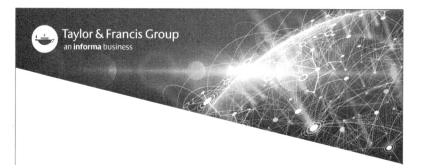